A CELEBRATION OF POETS
NEW JERSEY
GRADES 4-12
FALL 2009

AN ANTHOLOGY COMPILED BY CREATIVE COMMUNICATION, INC.

Published by:

1488 NORTH 200 WEST · LOGAN, UTAH 84341
TEL. 435-713-4411 · WWW.POETICPOWER.COM

Authors are responsible for the originality of the writing submitted.

Copyright © 2010 by Creative Communication, Inc.
Printed in the United States of America

ISBN: 978-1-60050-315-3

A CELEBRATION
OF POETS

NEW JERSEY
GRADES 4-12
FALL 2009

creativeCOMMUNICATION
A CELEBRATION OF TODAY'S WRITERS

FOREWORD

In today's world there are many things that compete for our attention. From the far reaching influence of the media, to the voices we hear from those around us, it is often difficult to decide where to commit our energies and focus. The poets in this book listened to an inner voice; a voice that can be the loudest of the many voices in our world, but to pay attention to this voice takes self-control. The effect of these words may not be far reaching, but to even make a small difference in the world is a positive thing.

Each year I receive hundreds of letters, calls, and emails from parents, teachers, and students who share stories of success; stories, where being a published writer provided the catalyst to a different attitude toward school, education and life. We are pleased to provide you with this book and hope that what these writers have shared makes a small but meaningful difference in your world.

Thomas Worthen, Ph.D.
Editor
Creative Communication

WRITING CONTESTS!

Enter our next POETRY contest!
Enter our next ESSAY contest!

Why should I enter?
Win prizes and get published! Each year thousands of dollars in prizes are awarded throughout North America. The top writers in each division receive a monetary award and a free book that includes their published poem or essay. Entries of merit are also selected to be published in our anthology.

Who may enter?
There are four divisions in the poetry contest. The poetry divisions are grades K-3, 4-6, 7-9, and 10-12. There are three divisions in the essay contest. The essay divisions are grades 3-6, 7-9, and 10-12.

What is needed to enter the contest?
To enter the poetry contest send in one original poem, 21 lines or less. To enter the essay contest send in one original non-fiction essay, 250 words or less, on any topic. Please submit each poem and essay with a title, and the following information clearly printed: the writer's name, current grade, home address (optional), school name, school address, teacher's name and teacher's email address (optional). Contact information will only be used to provide information about the contest. For complete contest information go to www.poeticpower.com.

How do I enter?
Enter a poem online at:
www.poeticpower.com
or
Mail your poem to:
  Poetry Contest
  1488 North 200 West
  Logan, UT 84341

Enter an essay online at:
www.studentessaycontest.com
or
Mail your essay to:
  Essay Contest
  1488 North 200 West
  Logan, UT 84341

When is the deadline?
Poetry contest deadlines are August 18th, December 2nd and April 5th. Essay contest deadlines are July 15th, October 19th, and February 17th. Students can enter one poem and one essay for each spring, summer, and fall contest deadline.

Are there benefits for my school?
Yes. We award $15,000 each year in grants to help with Language Arts programs. Schools qualify to apply for a grant by having 15 or more accepted entries.

Are there benefits for my teacher?
Yes. Teachers with five or more students published receive a free anthology that includes their students' writing.

For more information please go to our website at **www.poeticpower.com**, email us at editor@poeticpower.com or call 435-713-4411.

TABLE OF CONTENTS

Fall 2009 Poetic Achievement Honor Schools

* Teachers who had fifteen or more poets accepted to be published

The following schools are recognized as receiving a "Poetic Achievement Award." This award is given to schools who have a large number of entries of which over fifty percent are accepted for publication. With hundreds of schools entering our contest, only a small percent of these schools are honored with this award. The purpose of this award is to recognize schools with excellent Language Arts programs. This award qualifies these schools to receive a complimentary copy of this anthology. In addition, these schools are eligible to apply for a Creative Communication Language Arts Grant. Grants of two hundred and fifty dollars each are awarded to further develop writing in our schools.

Bartle Elementary School
    Highland Park
        Jaclyn Couzzi
        Janet Garnett*
        Lenore Hall*
        Rachel R. Pasichow
        Nicole Stahl

Battin School #4
    Elizabeth
        Lynn Rubin*

Bayonne High School
    Bayonne
        Donna Zervoulis*

Catherine A Dwyer Elementary School
    Wharton
        Sue Fuchs
        Vanessa Greenwald
        Nancy Reeves
        Sandra Struble

Christa McAuliffe Middle School
    Jackson
        Nancy Dell'Osso*

Christopher Columbus Middle School
    Clifton
        Roslyn Herwitt
        Johanna Palestini*

Cinnaminson Middle School
    Cinnaminson
        Garwood Bacon
        Andrea Guinan

Clinton Public School
    Clinton
        Barbara J. Shaffer*

Durban Avenue Elementary School
    Hopatcong
        Carol Procter*

Frankford Township School
    Branchville
        Jennifer Thompson*

Galloway Township Middle School
    Galloway
        Cynthia Fedo
        Michelle Fishman*
        Marie King

Garfield Middle School
   Garfield
      Mrs. Fiduccia*
      Joanne Lo Iacono
      Diane Nunno*
      Anna Psarianos

Good Shepherd Regional Catholic School
   Collingswood
      Sr. Bianca Camilleri
      Karen Regan

Greenwood Elementary School
   Hamilton
      Sherry Burger*

Hammarskjold Middle School
   East Brunswick
      Michele Green*

Herbert Hoover Middle School
   Edison
      Judy Medina*

Hillside Elementary School
   Montclair
      Carryanne Eckardt
      Lisa Frankle*
      Dr. Saundra Woody*

Holy Cross High School
   Delran
      Thomas Gowan*

Keyport High School
   Keyport
      Karen Strickland
      Judith Zdanewicz*

Lakeside Middle School
   Millville
      Mrs. Fithian
      Jennifer Scaringello*

Little Falls School #1
   Little Falls
      Jean Ermenville*

Marie Durand Elementary School
   Vineland
      Joan Bergamo*

New Egypt Middle School
   New Egypt
      Shana Crinnian*
      Renée Hogan*
      Donna Westlby-Gibson

New Providence Middle School
   New Providence
      Christine MacBurney*
      Lynn Mitchell

Old Turnpike School
   Califon
      Amy Allen*
      Kim Hill
      Jeanette McCall

Olson Middle School
   Tabernacle
      Pamela Adamczyk*
      Jean Drozd

Perth Amboy Catholic Upper Grades School
   Perth Amboy
      Marilyn Gibney
      Georgia Stromick

Richard E Byrd Elementary School
   Glen Rock
      Cindy Lota
      Viola Stanley*

Riverside Middle School
   Riverside
      Regina Villecco
      Lori Wareham*

Roosevelt Elementary School
   Rahway
      Natalie Polanin*
      Deborah Prakapas*

South Hunterdon Regional High School
    Lambertville
        Heather Damron*

St James School
    Basking Ridge
        Katherine Morra*

St Mary School
    Gloucester City
        Helen Guittar*

St Mary's School
    Pompton Lakes
        Patricia Andrews*
        Elizabeth Green*
        Edie Kimak*
        Carol Porada*

St Peter Elementary School
    Merchantville
        Sr. Veronica*

Texas Avenue Elementary School
    Atlantic City
        Mayra Cruz-Connerton*

Township of Ocean Intermediate School
    Ocean
        Joanne DeVito*
        Christine Fogler

Village School
    Princeton Junction
        Fran McDonough*

Westampton Middle School
    Westampton
        Nancy Tuliszewski*

William Davies Middle School
    Mays Landing
        Daniel P. Weber*

Zane North Elementary School
    Collingswood
        Kimberly Nguyen*

Language Arts Grant Recipients 2009-2010

After receiving a "Poetic Achievement Award" schools are encouraged to apply for a Creative Communication Language Arts Grant. The following is a list of schools who received a two hundred and fifty dollar grant for the 2009-2010 school year.

Arrowhead Union High School, Hartland, WI
Blessed Sacrament School, Seminole, FL
Booneville Jr High School, Booneville, AR
Buckhannon-Upshur Middle School, Buckhannon, WV
Campbell High School, Ewa Beach, HI
Chickahominy Middle School, Mechanicsville, VA
Clarkston Jr High School, Clarkston, MI
Covenant Life School, Gaithersburg, MD
CW Rice Middle School, Northumberland, PA
Eason Elementary School, Waukee, IA
East Elementary School, Kodiak, AK
Florence M Gaudineer Middle School, Springfield, NJ
Foxborough Regional Charter School, Foxborough, MA
Gideon High School, Gideon, MO
Holy Child Academy, Drexel Hill, PA
Home Choice Academy, Vancouver, WA
Jeff Davis Elementary School, Biloxi, MS
Lower Alloways Creek Elementary School, Salem, NJ
Maple Wood Elementary School, Somersworth, NH
Mary Walter Elementary School, Bealeton, VA
Mater Dei High School, Evansville, IN
Mercy High School, Farmington Hills, MI
Monroeville Elementary School, Monroeville, OH
Nautilus Middle School, Miami Beach, FL
Our Lady Star of the Sea School, Grosse Pointe Woods, MI
Overton High School, Memphis, TN
Pond Road Middle School, Robbinsville, NJ
Providence Hall Charter School, Herriman, UT
Reuben Johnson Elementary School, McKinney, TX
Rivelon Elementary School, Orangeburg, SC
Rose Hill Elementary School, Omaha, NE

Language Arts Grant Winners cont.

Runnels School, Baton Rouge, LA
Santa Fe Springs Christian School, Santa Fe Springs, CA
Serra Catholic High School, Mckeesport, PA
Shadowlawn Elementary School, Green Cove Springs, FL
Spectrum Elementary School, Gilbert, AZ
St Edmund Parish School, Oak Park, IL
St Joseph Institute for the Deaf, Chesterfield, MO
St Joseph Regional Jr High School, Manchester, NH
St Mary of Czestochowa School, Middletown, CT
St Monica Elementary School, Garfield Heights, OH
St Vincent De Paul Elementary School, Cape Girardeau, MO
Stevensville Middle School, Stevensville, MD
Tashua School, Trumbull, CT
The New York Institute for Special Education, Bronx, NY
The Selwyn School, Denton, TX
Tonganoxie Middle School, Tonganoxie, KS
Westside Academy, Prince George, BC
Willa Cather Elementary School, Omaha, NE
Willow Hill Elementary School, Traverse City, MI

Grades 10-11-12 Top Ten Winners

List of Top Ten Winners for Grades 10-12; listed alphabetically

Aaron Combs, Grade 12
Carroll High School, Corpus Christi, TX

Kellie Lenamond, Grade 12
Home School, Wills Point, TX

Jordyn Rhorer, Grade 12
Lafayette High School, Lexington, KY

Miranda Rogovein, Grade 12
Greenwood College School, Toronto, ON

Sydney Rubin, Grade 11
Cab Calloway School of the Arts, Wilmington, DE

Kyle Rutherford, Grade 12
Rosebud School, Rosebud, MT

Sara RuthAnn Weaver, Grade 12
Grace Baptist High School, Delaware, OH

Jessica Webster, Grade 11
Boyne City High School, Boyne City, MI

Abigail Yeskatalas, Grade 10
Avonworth High School, Pittsburgh, PA

Mariam Younan, Grade 12
Bayonne High School, Bayonne, NJ

All Top Ten Poems can be read at www.poeticpower.com

Note: The Top Ten poems were finalized through an online voting system. Creative Communication's judges first picked out the top poems. These poems were then posted online. The final step involved thousands of students and teachers who registered as the online judges and voted for the Top Ten poems. We hope you enjoy these selections.

Pop-Pop

"Hallelujah! I'm a bum!"
was the simple tune you would hum
with a fedora on your balding head
and drinking a beer before bed.

Bringing me a donut when I was sick
always was your special trick.
You would stay with me for the day
making sure I'd get better right away

"Hallelujah! I'm a bum!"
was the simple tune you would hum
with a fedora on your balding head
and drinking a beer before bed.

In your coat pocket is where you kept seeds,
you'd throw it out for the birds you'd feed
Exclaiming, "Hallelujah! I'm a bum!"
Oh, that simple tune you would hum.

Yet, it's still every time I go upstairs
that I feel your presence everywhere
the squeaky rocking of your chair
can still be heard from here to there.
Chloe DeFilippis, Grade 12
Bayonne High School

Have You Read Orex?

Their love cannot be foul
Would gallows transition this
And manipulate their past to their doom
Add to their dead end

Would gallows transition this
A peace they found in themselves
add to their dead end
What! In their foul bedding

A peace they found in themselves
What brush with stars meant higher hills
What! In their foul bedding
Well their days are marked

What brush with stars meant higher hills
Horrid tales, a curse to any man
well their days were marked
Abominable love they never saw

Horrid tales, a curse to any man
Abominable love they never saw
Would gallows transition this
Their love cannot be foul
Maxine Amadi, Grade 10
Teaneck High School

Wish

Each and every single night as I wait to wish on the first star that I see,
I think of what I will wish for even though I know what my wish should be.

I should wish for world peace or at least some harmony.
I know I should wish for a normal life or that my family should be healthy.

I should wish for money, just enough so my family won't ever be poor.
I know I should wish for me to do well in school even though it is such a bore.

Although I know I should wish for these things when I see that first nighttime star,
The thing I always end up wishing for is in regards to my friends — the best by far.

I wish that no matter what happens, it's them that I don't ever lose
Because they are the very best friends that a girl could ever choose.

The day that I lose them will be the day that I die
Because they are the ones who keep me sane and comfort me when I cry.

So each and every single night, when I wish upon the first star I see,
I wish that I won't lose my Best Friends because with them is where my heart will always be.
Estee Kahn, Grade 12
Bat Torah Girls Academy

Grandma

Happy and laughing was your fancy; you're the one who made smiles occur
You left before I had the chance, the chance to know you — who you were

Mother to your children, so loving and kind
You left before I had the chance, the chance to know you — who you were

Wife to your husband faithful and kind, even though you received the worst of it all
You left before I had the chance, the chance to know — who you were

Grandmother to your grandchildren: opening your arms like wings of love
You left before I had the chance, the chance to know you — who you were

Smoking caught up; in the hospital you lay with a dying personality
You left before I had the chance, the chance to know you — who you were

In memory of you — the quarters you left me; I hope I remember the truth of who you were
You left before I had the chance, the chance to know you — who you were
Tyler Darvalics, Grade 12
Bayonne High School

In Your Dreams

You start, I stop.
You rush, I run faster
Across the rainbow striped heart of your senseless mind.
You can feel my feet stepping and splashing in the puddles of tears on your heart.
My piercing brown eyes meet your dull green ones, at sight it's love
You've mistaken my identity, the identity that sneaks through your dreams
Your misty green eyes turn black,
And your pupils resemble broken hearts,
As you glance at what you'll never have.
Cassandra Malvone, Grade 10
Keyport High School

Dried Beauty

You were gone.
You were cold.
But not as cold as I was.
My heart,
No, I had no heart,
For not a tear I could shed for you
You were dead.
but not as dead as I was.
You were perfect.
You looked the way I remembered you.
Like dried roses hanging from a window,
You looked better then,
Better than being caged by a needle.
You are the beauty of eternity.
You are the queen of majesty.
That's your true identity.
Now, years later,
I sit with my cup of tea.
Then a drop,
Into my cup,
A tear I could shed for you.
Brielle Cameron, Grade 10
South Hunterdon Regional High School

Fantasy

As I ponder the unknown,
I know that I am not alone.
For there are others just like me,
The blinded, who attempt to see,
To see the world they have forgot,
Left in darkness, there to rot.
But you and I have seen this place,
And stared into the Devil's face.
And let him know we're not afraid;
We paid the price that must be paid.
And here we stand atop the mountain,
Drinking youth from a golden fountain.
I rule the world and it rules me,
When all that's real will cease to be.
Julia O'Connell, Grade 11
Bridgewater Raritan High School

Breast Cancer the Color of Pink

October is the month of pink
A month of hope
The time to come together
And become one
A time to not forget
What women are fighting against
A sense of pride lingers in the October air
Giving support for those who need it
This is October
The month of pink
Brigit LaRose, Grade 12
Holy Cross High School

Dear God

Dear God, I only call Your name,
When the devil plays a hard game;
And to be honest I feel quite ashamed,
Because I have only myself to blame.

Dear God, I'm Your number one fan,
Please listen to this chunky tanned man;
I have only one thing to say,
About what went on yesterday;
I had a dream and it reminded me of Your word,
In the dream I was a sheep that went astray from the shepherd's herd.

Dear God, help me find the right way,
I know I need to change and that is today;
I'm not going to be doing the wrong things anymore,
I'm tired of being scared and running away that will be no more.

Dear God, I hope You change me,
So the devil can leave me alone and I can be free;
I know You're there and will always be,
I need You like a little girl needs her father when she falls from a tree.

Dear God, it looks like I've found You, You completely drowned me with all of Your love,
Although You have no beginning nor end; like You, I'm a stone I have my mind set,
You remained in my heart since the first day we met.
Gabriel Tineo, Grade 10
Kearny Christian Academy

Who Are You?

Who are You? — I thought I knew me, but You confuse me, judge me.
How did You become so cruel?
You make me question what in that mirror I do see.
I used to be happy, but somehow this is no more,
Because You've broken me down, changed my mind, my size.
Without You, I understood my core!

Who are You? — Who causes me grief as You judge me from above?
As to how You got so high up I have no clue.
But now, I have no confidence left to speak of!
Your stare makes me sweat, makes me cry.
On Your high horse You trample me down.
You have broken me into my lowliest form, but why?
Why do You wear my confidence's crown.

Who are You? — But now, who am I?
I feel alone while battling You.
Yet as I look in the mirror, We see eye to eye.
Quit hiding behind the glass!
I need to know who makes My thoughts scream such torturous things!
So much confusion, yet all I know is a broken pile of glass at My feet, and
You Are berating Me.
Rachel Slovak, Grade 10
South Hunterdon Regional High School

I Guess That's Why They Call It Fall

As the leaves fall from the sky
You can't help but try
To rake them as they fall
From every tree so tall
The leaves they never stop
Even if they all drop
You can never get them all
I guess that's why they call it fall
Autumn is a cooled time
So warm but sublime
It's not as cold as winter
But it always makes me wonder
How the leaves come back
Put that question on the rack
I guess that's why they call it fall
Trees that start as green as grass
Turn as red as cherries
Then bare
Desolate roads
On an autumn day
Bring peace and pleasure

Bobby Brown, Grade 12
Holy Cross High School

Memories of Bells

Jingling…Jingling…
Jingling in my head
Are those bells I hear?
Jingling of the Christmas season
Can't be quite clear
They are always oh so near
Memories of bells are so far away
In my bed I must wait
As Yuletide approaches
On an eight reindeer sleigh
Jingling…Jingling…
Jingling in my head
Could it really be?
Are those bells jingling only for me?

Nicole Bowers, Grade 11
Hopewell Valley Central High School

Pause

To fade from existence
for but a moment,
To pause life
for but a breath,
To be able to retain my sanity
without having to fight it constantly,
would bring a respite
only achievable by death.
But I'd come back.

Alexandra Boden, Grade 10
West Morris Mendham High School

Grandma

She carelessly clutches her colorless sheets
As her beautiful memories rest against a soft, white pillow.
Her weightless body just lying there.
Her paper skin   Thin   Delicate.
Her straw hair   Dry   Withered.
Her bones like toothpicks   Skinny   Weak.
As her expiration date soon approaches, she gazes out the window,
For 15 minutes she watches a single, autumn leaf dance in the courtyard.
It is at this moment that she realizes that there is
An entire life behind things. An entire world of hidden meanings.
A benevolent force that wants her to know that there is no reason to be afraid.
There is sometimes so much beauty in the world
That she feels like she can't take it anymore, but when she looks out that window
She knows that the
Rain
Like the blood trickling through her lifeless veins, and the
Wind
Like the oxygen barely breezing through her brittle body, and the
Sunshine
Like her last bit of gratitude for her forgetful life,

Are soon approaching.

Miles Young, Grade 11
West Essex High School

Civilizations Abstract Locker

Academically speaking what makes a civilization?
Is it ego, the likes of which erected lavish lounges for passed living gods in Egypt?
Nope. It's paperwork.
So academically speaking we don't have one…
Thank you white-out, copy machines, forgers, frauders, politicians and cut and paste!
I'll speak abstractly to give a specific example:
Earth's the room from which we must release ourselves
Because language hinders our comprehension of fascination
With life where parts may be equal
But is the whole larger? The Devil lends me his fork to retrieve
My damaged retina that squinted too hard
And long trying to blur out the context of soul.
Can you immediately know the candlelight is fire
Or must you first feel the burn of ice? Being a star screwer
was a noble pursuit for knights clad in beret armor long before
Chief said, "What we are, we're going to wail with on the whole trip."
And we should, and we should as lava lamps bubble
Brightly beneath desert storming laughter at Humpty Dumpty
Because so it goes with love.
Will this my paperwork create a civilization?
Or will it fade in the dawn?

Michelle Bayman, Grade 12
West Morris Central High School

The Fear in My Life

My life is perceived by others
As if it were the cover of a book,
Judged before it is even known.
No one takes time to
Discover who the person is
Hiding behind the mask.
The mask that covers my real identity
And conceals who the real me truly is.
I hide behind this mask, afraid that the real me
Might just be reveled at a time I prefer not to be.
When the time comes to finally revel myself
I hope honesty will start to take over.
I'll be terrified to try, but I do it anyway.
This moment goes like every other.
I don't know what I'm saying
But I do know I'm not making
A very good first impression.

Adam Alyan, Grade 12
Williamstown High School

Lie

I'll lie and say you knew me best.
A tight smile forms as I listen to you
preach about right and wrong.

Who could have known,
that you'd use my mistakes against me.
Who are you?
Did I even know you?

The light has been switched on,
exposing the naked truth.
I'm not sure who you are,
worse is I don't know who I put my faith into.

Gabrielle Winant, Grade 11
Jackson Liberty High School

The Love of Siblings

Atoms are always there
Even when we can't see them.
They are still holding things together,
Giving us what we need.
You and I don't always show it.
We don't always say it.
But we know it's there.
It holds us together so that we can live our lives.
This one thing keeps two people together forever.
Just the thought of it gives us comfort and hope.
I don't need to hear it to know it.
I love you.
You love me.

Beth St. John, Grade 11
Freehold Borough High School

Nivis

Below the great moon,
its shadow casts a dark spell.
The night's breath stops,
the stars begin to dance,
darkness swallows the city.

Where the sky is crimson,
the land is black.
The wind and air, creating harmony,
whispering secrets in my ear.
Brightening the night.

A gentle wavering spirit comes down from the clouds,
walks on top, gently rolling its feet
and rocks till it falls asleep.
A translucent cold touch of the shoulder.
Glass stained over soft lush green
lay softly on the ground.
Forget nothing.
Just lay comfortable knowing.
Till the night falls restless
and the fingers of light reach me.

Yura Jang, Grade 10
Indian Hills High School

Frosty Woods

Little boy
Lost his dog through the dense fog
In the dark forest, around the bend.
Little hearts can't easily mend.
Searching all night and into the day,
The little boy lost his way.
So he — now lost — feels the frost.
As he cries, it freezes tears.
This most, he fears.

Little dog
Alone in the wood, running as fast as he could —
Seeing shadows, hearing deep wails.
Here he stops, feeling frail,
Turning around to try to find his master,
Running ever faster.
Frost comes near and, as he lies,
He slowly dies.

Boy and dog now joyous,
For they meet
Near Father's feet.

Morgan Bailey, Grade 10
Kearny Christian Academy

Anguish

You tug my heart, you yank my soul,
the hatred grows, my life you stole.

I trust no more, for this you've done,
I've lost all love and now I run.

From open arms I've never seen,
from your disease with no vaccine.

There is no hope for us inside,
there's no one else to be my guide.

I am detached, my path unknown,
your mind games which I have outgrown.

For I have given all my strength,
and I have reached past life's length.

I walk alone, never followed,
with no trust, my heart is hollowed.
Kristi Froisland, Grade 12
Hanover Park High School

Look at Me

When you look at me
what do you see?
Do you see me for who I am
or do you see me for my weight?
When you look at me
what do you see?
Do you see me for my heart
that is kind, warm and gentle
or do you see me for my weakness?
When you look at me
what do you see?
Do you see me for my soul
that holds years of pain
or do you see me for my heart.
When you look at me
see me as a person
who doesn't care what people say!
Emily Hayes, Grade 12
Mercer Jr/Sr High School

The Other Side

Beyond the forest
Beneath the shining moon
Where the ocean ends
And flowers bloom
Lies endless imagination
Non-opinionated minds
Holding countless possibilities
For future time
Paige Cornell, Grade 10
South Hunterdon Regional High School

One Kingship

A kingdom of majesty, adorned with fields of glory,
Satisfying those who hunger for righteousness, those who thirst for justice,
Those who long for mercy, those who pray for life;

A fiery heart of passion, burning eternally for the world,
For the elderly, the sick,
The suffering, the defenseless;

Arms of forgiveness,
Granting mercy on the merciful, shelter to the meek,
Care to the humble, grace to the peaceful;

Eyes graced with love,
Comforting to the mourning, sight to the blind,
Power to the lame, voice to the weak;

A bloodstream of passion, tears of sorrow,
Streams of mercy, shed for the world,
For the weak, for the merciful,
For the kindhearted, for all.
Nicholas Sertich, Grade 11
Paramus Catholic High School

Who I Am

I have a height as a small child, short and petite.
I have long fingers like spider legs, long and skinny.
I have hair like hay, golden and brown.
I am like a kitten because I am warm and cuddly.
I am like summer because I am relaxed and sunny.
I am like a cupcake, I am short and sweet.
I am like a bubble, delicate and light.
I am like the color pink because I am happy and loving.
I am like a lamp brightly glowing.
I like my height because I like being short.
I like my weight because I like being light as a feather.
My hair is long and straight.
My personality is bubbly and I am fun to be around.
Gymnastics and cheerleading are my talents.
For me waking up is a little difficult, I need to get better at it.
I am an outgoing person once you get to know me I just might burst.
For my future I hope I will be graduating in June.
I hope to be going to college and a bar tending school.
I hope to transfer to a university in Florida.
Then one day own my own business.
Katie Dwyer, Grade 12
Williamstown High School

Stand-Up Philosopher

He stands upon the central stage
And the people all applaud
A brief pause, and he exclaims
"What am I doing here!?"

They laugh, of course,
They've heard his entertainment
But most are unaware of the maze
Of gears and banana peels
Arranged within his head

He strings together fire and ice
Deep thoughts, wild nonsense, and scientific fact
Drags them into the world of consciousness
This is that, that is this, but what is anything?

Grabbing vague, faded thoughts
Like wisps of hair in the shifting breeze
Alas, that voice has now been stilled
When thousands were unaware
Of his rants and ramblings on the stage

Geoffrey Stoddart, Grade 11
Holy Cross High School

The Wandering Mutt

Sunlight hits the mirror and it bounces back again
Bending as particles of dust fall onto my hair
I shake my head like the scruffy mutt I am
(The puppy that runs in circles chasing its tail)

But if things come around
Hope will come around again
Save me from this animal shelter
So I can find home

Although the reflected rays shine colors I can't ignore
I would rather be outside where the air is fresh and warm
Where the soles of my feet can grow worn out
Proof that I have lived and how

I have seen every street, every house, and every tree
Answered as many questions as the world allows me
Met every who and lived every when
(I shake my head like the scruffy mutt I am)
And if things turn out well
I'll never turn around again

Amina Cami, Grade 10
Fort Lee High School

mining mine.

with tears forming behind my eyes
and a wicked grin on my lips,
i alone hold the shovel's point to my soul
i alone have, quite viciously,
carved my initials into the wooden shaft
over and over again, screaming to myself:
"it's me. it's mine. i did it."
i dig this hole, i create this void
for a reason i know not of
my tongue is as sharp as the shovel's tip
used only to deceive myself
i am a worker whose weekly hours are not definite
whose salary is determined by effort
who is paid in unpopular currency
and i use my paycheck
if, and only if,
i need a new shovel.

Mirian Wosu, Grade 11
McNair Academic High School

Precious Memories

As you walk down memory lane,
you might remember all the anguish and pain.
Take the journey, follow through;
these were the things that helped you become you.
Contemplate on the heartache you bared,
you recovered, you are stronger, yet unaware.
Times may have gotten tough,
the storm might have been blinding;
yet your strength and endurance kept you striving.
Look back at the road you've walked,
filled with cracks, twists, and turns;
this is your mold, what has helped you grow.
Take life one step at a time,
you have what it takes;
you've gone through the worst,
just take a glance down memory lane.

Marilyn Pichardo, Grade 11
McNair Academic High School

Inspiration

I need inspiration,
Not more frustration.
The cool air blowing through my soul…
Without my problems taking its toll.
A new day, the rising dawn, the radiant flower,
The shining stars, the graceful trees, and the refreshing rain shower.
No more the usual and swim against the annoying tide,
And watching all my hopelessness and problems subside.

Nicole Meily, Grade 11
Monsignor Donovan High School

Nana

Every day I get to see you.
And every day I miss you more and more.
Wishing I could just relive
That moment just one more time.
Seeing the both of us smile.
Changes my life.
Every day I wish God will give me one more day with you.
I miss you, Nana.
Forever I will keep this picture.

Michael Miller, Grade 12
Holy Cross High School

User

If only I did not get so soaked in,
Then, others would not use me as a path.
He tossed me away, as an old has-been.

But, I do not possess the strength within
To unleash, on my former love, a wrath.
If only I did not get so soaked in.

His devotion had suddenly worn thin,
But I am in the bitter aftermath
He tossed me away, as an old has-been.

Taking lies like water in pruned-up skin,
Or like a sponge in a cold sudsy bath.
If only I did not get so soaked in.

How could he have provoked so much chagrin?
This hurt results from a true psychopath.
He tossed me away, as an old has-been.

No longer will I remain his trash bin.
Unwillingly, I have my own by-path.
If only I did not get so soaked in,
He tossed me away, as an old has-been.

Corinne Siberine, Grade 11
New Providence High School

Trapped in a Myriad of Fear

What seems but a dream
Of running helter-skelter
Through endless avenues
Filled with the enigmatic night
Fearful illusions of another presence with me
In this strange world of black and white

Hesitant glances over my shoulder
Reveal that it was no more than paranoia
But the feeling does not subside
I come to a dead end
Bones aching with the feeling of this invisible force drawing near

Just as the fear,
Becomes too much to bear
I'm falling through a nightmare of red
Into meadows of green and gold
The open air a stark contrast to the claustrophobia of the alley
Running through the fields yearning for a glimpse of escape

Another flash
And I'm blanketed with the verdant darkness
Of a thicket of trees
Again the fear takes over.

Sarah Wrigley, Grade 12
Randolph High School

Mommy

Whether breakfast in bed, or a ride to my friends,
you're always the one on whom I depend.

You're the best mom, there's no question in that,
sorry when I yell or act like a brat.

Even though I don't always show it, I appreciate you much,
without you I'd be very messed up.

You keep me in line, but give me my space,
what more could a daughter ask for, not much in my case.

I love you a bunch, we get along great,
it's fun to go on a mother-daughter movie date.

We spend your money,
if you ask me it's quite funny.

But not today,
I'll pay your way!

Happy Mother's Day!

Kelsey Robb, Grade 12
Holy Cross High School

The Farmer's Summer

Tall grass sways, in a friendly wind
Grasshoppers jump, from limb to limb

A single tractor, strives to bail more
Sunlight and Timothy, dance on the floor

Sweat rolls down, her back and her face
She puts every bail, into its place

Not a cloud passes, in the open blue sky
The green stalks grow, as each day goes by

Her family surrounds her, with pride and joys
The long hours spent, bailing at Stoy's

She will never forget, how her love grew stronger
During that happy calm of the farmer's summer.

Kelly Albanir, Grade 10
South Hunterdon Regional High School

What Does the Amp Say?

Boom boom says the amp as I play it loud
it's a bass amp of course, are you wowed?
The swiftness of my fingers, oh so smooth
boom boom says the amp as it's meant to soothe.

Kevin Briede, Grade 10
Delaware Valley Regional High School

My Daddy's Girl

I have short brown hair
To match my short body
Eyes like spring grass
Hands soft as silk
I'm my Daddy's girl
Who always finds something to be happy about
Like a rubix cube I'm detailed and complex
My complexion could be better
And my hair a little longer
I may not always be happy
But I'll always be my Daddy's little girl.
I'm just like Spring, colorful and warm.
Like a puppy, loud but small.
I want to travel to Europe; I want to attend art school
I want to open my own bakery
And be my Daddy's little girl
Like the color yellow, I'm loud and bright
I can play the drums; I can play the piano
And I can learn from my mistakes
I may not go to Europe and I may not open a bakery
But I'll always be my Daddy's girl.

Christine Eastburn, Grade 12
Williamstown High School

Holding You in My Heart

In my heart, we still have not broken our last embrace.
In my heart, I can still look down at your smile.
In my heart, I can still hear your laughter,
and feel the warmth of your cheek against mine.

In my heart, we dance to a song that has no end.
In my heart, time stands still as we sway.
In my heart, your hands still hold mine,
and nothing can pry them apart.

In my heart, I can hear your wisdom.
In my heart, I can see the love in your eyes.
In my heart, God smiles down on us,
as we smile at each other.

These treasured feelings
These memories of you
They keep me strong
'til next we meet.
'til I hold you in my arms again,
I shall hold you in my heart.

John-Paul Helk, Grade 12
Holy Cross High School

Firemen

They dash to the fire
And put it out
That's what firemen
Are all about

Steven Fox, Grade 11
Keyport High School

Anger Building Inside

She sits at home day and night, the days pass by
She sits at home day and night, the weeks pass by
She sits at home day and night. Months pass by…I pass by
Anger enrages me
She sits at home, it's been a year now
No motivation, just there I've tried to motivate
I get locked away, drugged away
You say I should always come to you,
But when I do I want to cry
A picture in my mind of me, drowning during struggles
Can't get it out of my mind
Punch my feelings to the world outside
I'm supposed to look up to you, but I look down
Please find your way, please find yourself
Help, I've tried
I need you to stand up in the morning
I need you to stand day after day
Week after week
Month after month
If not for me for you
I love you, Mom I truly do…

Sarah Walker, Grade 12
Holy Cross High School

I Forgive You

One year ago.
Remembering the argument
that always kept repeating itself.
The madness that never stopped
showing its broken face.
Remembering the heartless truth,
that you've been hiding for so long.
Your calm and gentle eyes,
which always kept me at ease.
Now all I see is rage and fire,
hurting my brightened soul.
I still remember all the good times we had,
talking and playing like we always do
but yet I know you are still there,
only chained to doubt and pain.
I don't hate you, I don't dislike you.
I still remember all the good things you've done for me
and you know I always will.
So put down that book,
and look into my eyes so I can say.
"Mother, I forgive you and I will love you always."

Vanessa Snead, Grade 12
Mercer Jr/Sr High School

I Feel Like I'm in Detention

Just a simple expression
Trying to catch your attention
But instead it stays unmentioned,
I feel like I am in detention.

Lina Restrepo, Grade 10
South Hunterdon Regional High School

Total Desolation

Seeing the destruction all over the place
Wishing that everything will come back
Hugging yourself waiting for that warm embrace

Looking over all the empty space
The surprise of everything will not lack,
Seeing the destruction all over the place.

Everything is gone except for the base
You don't even have anything to pack,
Hugging yourself waiting for that warm embrace.

All the memorabilia that you cannot replace
You're so mad that you need something to attack
Seeing the destruction all over the place

In your mind, this sight will never erase
The time is very black
Hugging yourself, waiting for that warm embrace

Seeing everyone's face
You're ready to crack
Seeing the destruction all over the place
Hugging yourself, waiting for that warm embrace.

Amanda Williamson, Grade 11
Pascack Valley High School

The Pearl Ring

Each granddaughter gets one.
One has a diamond.
The other has her birthstone.
But I have the greatest of them all.
I have the Pearl Ring.
The beautiful under the sea treasure.
The oyster's precious baby.
The lovely gift a boy gives a girl. The Pearl Ring.

They say every girl needs a diamond.
They're wrong.
Every girl needs a pearl.
True beauty of the Earth.
The gracious gift God gave us. The Pearl Ring.

It may cost. But I would never trade my pearl ring.
For all the money in the world.
More than a ring to me.
Lifts my spirits when I am down.
Makes me feel like everything will be okay. The Pearl Ring.

From the one person who was there for me.
Always was and always will be. My grandmother.
Her Pearl Ring.

Alyssa Walsh, Grade 10
Holy Cross High School

If Only You Could Tell Me

If only you could tell me where I have to go,
what to do, when to plan, why it is and what to say.
If only you could tell me what I need to know.

The present sprints by, never daring to be slow
and I question what will happen the next day!
If only you could tell me where I have to go.

Will I meet a friend or will I meet a foe?
Will I survive? Will I be okay?
If only you could tell me what I need to know.

Anticipation sits, like a day before it snows.
I have to ask: "What will come along the way?"
If only you could tell me where I have to go.

Should I dread the next day like Edgar Allen Poe?
Or should I scream to fate "Come what may!"
If only you could tell me what I need to know.

But as my life opens — the beginning of the show —
I feel the need to ask, to wish, to pray.
If only you could tell me where I have to go.
If only you could tell me what I need to know.

Alexia Polachek, Grade 12
Jackson Liberty High School

Without You

Every night I see your face
It's a thought I can't replace
Every day I hear your voice
I hate this feeling, it's not my choice

The more you push the harder I fall
Just promise me this, please don't call
I'm moving on so let me be
I'm taking those steps, one, two, three

You made it hard, he makes it easy
My stomach stopped turning, I'm not so queasy
I see you standing at my door
I thought I cleaned up this mess before

Now just leave me in the dark
A life without you can't be so hard
I erase your memories on by one
Just leave me here, go have some fun

One day soon we'll try again
These feelings can't be hard to mend
But for now just run and never look back
I'm giving you the chance to forgive and forget

Gianna Sabidussi, Grade 10
South Hunterdon Regional High School

Intrinsic Bellicose

Simon wasn't there to carry his cross.
We all walk our path of shame,
even when the faults not ours.
It's our own flaws that shower thoughts.
Built for the oppressed.
May a smile lighten the way.
The sunshine, blinded by clouds of despair.
The fire of endurance,
the fire of hope,
the conflagration in your eyes.
Tears from heaven are cast into the twilight,
absorbing into pillow cases.
Surrendering to the battle in your mind,
you dance with yourself,
to your own melody,
as the crowd scoffs and laughs, ignorantly.
A sword in both pockets,
for each left and right hand.
A duel with no armor
but the bulwark to encumber you.

Heather Intelicato, Grade 12
Holy Cross High School

Winter Night

It's quiet, a peaceful quiet
It's dark, but it's a pretty dark
It's the quiet and darkness of a winter's night
The snow falls lightly, lightly like a feather

The snow begins to fall a little faster and harder now
I sit inside by the fireplace staying nice and warm
As I drink my hot chocolate with tiny marshmallows
The snow is finally deciding to stick

It's getting later and later at night now
And I'm starting to feel very tired
I make my way upstairs to get ready for bed
Then I get to turn off the lights and go to sleep
I dream many dreams, hoping for another peaceful winter night

Ashley Johnson, Grade 12
North Arlington High School

Out to Sea

As the waves crash and split the midnight air
I sit on a rock with the wind blowing through my hair.

Now I walk along the sandy beach,
And the water comes to cover my feet.

Walking along and gazing out to sea
A ship sets anchor at the pier beside me.

I wonder where it has been, to lands I will never walk or be
And as it sets sail again, I see my heart sailing out to sea.

Shivonne Hancock, Grade 11
Wayne Hills High School

Always and Forever

Giggles, laughs, and cute photographs.
Secrets, play dates, and making "arts and crafts."
Our time together has been the best,
As I look back at the years, I cannot detest.

Through the smiles, the tears;
The days, the minutes, the months, the years;
You brought me joy, gave me hopes, and together
our life was endeared.

My friend, you can take a day and turn it around,
Take my frowns, and turn them upside down.
Being hurt, anxious, or even scared,
You feared nothing, and always cared.

Now that we are much more mature,
I hope we do not grow demure.
My friend, I know that we will be together,
As we said;
Always and Forever.

Lindsay Hussey, Grade 12
Jackson Liberty High School

Living for Tomorrow

Placed your heart in a little glass box,
Hid the keys to the seven different locks,
Buried it six feet deep in the yard,
Behind the house with your little dog to guard.

If strangers come by,
They'll stay clear,
When they see the sign,
"No trespassing here."

So worry not,
Your heart will be okay,
Don't be afraid,
Love, friendship, and happiness can wait another day.

Laura Chen, Grade 11
Governor Livingston High School

The Angel

Tattered wings and broken bones,
Bruised by words and bruised by stones
Flying to wherever she can escape,
Held together by hope and tape
Hiding in fear and hiding in shame,
Carrying their judgment and carrying the blame
Pulled from her freedom and pulled from her sky,
Pushed over the edge to see if she could fly
Ripped from her happiness and ripped of her wings,
Loved by nothing and afraid of everything
Pushed further without knowing how to fly,
Down falls the wingless angel rejected from her sky.

Joanna Zbozien, Grade 10
Union High School

My Room

The place where I like to be
Where I find peace
Where I relax
Where I do my homework
Where I sleep
Where I go to take my mind off of things
Where I go when things get rough
Where I keep my personal things
Where my trophies are
My room

I have a special place
Where I go to when things are bad
Where no one can disturb me
Where I daydream
Where everything gets better
Where I have the best times with my friends
Where I express myself
Where I wrote this poem
My room
Caitlin Chase, Grade 11
Holy Cross High School

The Bird That Couldn't Fly

A little bird singing
It is all locked up

She wants to run out to freedom
But she can't lift her wings up

She hears her momma's cries
She thinks she wants to die

She flaps and cries
Hoping that one day she flies

She wants the wind to take her wings
But all she can do is sing
Hank Meade, Grade 11
Keyport High School

alone

like someone pulled the cord on me
and turned off the electricity
i turn around and put on my face
my hardened exterior to get me through life
ha, barely.
but without you i feel
alone in a different kind of way
like my world is over
but i am still alive
crawling now, cannot walk without you
fingernails in the muck
alone with the worms.
Isabelle Petersen, Grade 12
Montclair High School

Reading Between the Lines

If the words were hard to reach, then how do I say them now?
Every time I attempt to begin, I always back down.
I'm a fighter and a leader
Much like yourself.
Yet lately it seems, I've been put away and left.
I feel unwanted and lonely
Like a box of old books.
Please tell me you miss me, and take a second look.
Turn the pages of my novel
And question each and every word
Some of the things I have to say, I know you've never heard.
Wipe the dust off of my cover and hold me in your arms
Tell me how you always knew this; it's no subject for alarm.
Put me next to your old sitting chair, and choose me when I'm needed
Don't forget me in your life
Though I know you have proceeded.
Talk about me when you're lonely
If you need a couple words
Even though no one is listening, you know you can be heard.
Kiss me goodnight, like you always used to do.
I have now found the words; I have conveyed them to you.
Katie Martucci, Grade 12
Pinelands Regional High School

War of Attrition

There are strong red apples hanging with
solidity, weighing down the sad, crimson leaves of fall.
She sits beneath the seasoned grenades, ponders romance:
buying lipstick to camouflage liquid red evidence
and rouge to disguise the apples of her cheeks,
hidden under a geography of branched blood vessels.
Such a relief to be still after long nights of twitching
under blistering comforters, which didn't bring much comfort
after all. Ice pack awaiting a crooked nose, swollen red
with a purple heart at its epicenter; his "I love you."
He slowly saunters back to where she is,
the look of a soldier caught in his eye.
She longs to be a bird, a winged angel. Springing from her own Medusa,
she would be the perfect emissary between Earth and Olympus.
Between worlds, perhaps she would stumble upon Persephone,
the goddess she does not want to be anymore:
beautiful but ephemeral, forever stuck with a pomegranate
cupped in her fleshy palm, binding her to a world without light.
Somewhere far away, a red-bellied robin
perches in an apple tree,
looking for something worth having.
Randie Adler, Grade 11
Tenafly High School

There Will Come a Day

There will come a day
When I'll have to say
Goodbye to you and move on
I just can't stay
And deal with what you put me through
It's been enough
Although I'm tough enough to be yours
You were too rough to the one you loved
I'm leaving you behind
I'll never forget the time I've spent with you
Laughing, learning, loving in your arms
Those memories will be all you have so keep them close
I need something more out of life
Something you simply can't supply
I'm leaving you behind because I deserve better
someday you'll understand that I'm destined for greatness
You're on a one way street in Nowhereville
I'm leaving you because I need to
I need someone who will treat me like gold
But I'll never forget the old you

Katie Smith, Grade 11
Keyport High School

From a Star

If I could write a sonnet on a star
Then bottle it and send it out to sea
Where would it travel on the great big Earth?
Would it go where I wanted, or too far?
My message would travel past house and tree
And hopefully find you to warm your heart
You could finally know the love I feel
In your eyes, in your smile, they are perfect
This love has been here since the very start
No one could ever find a better deal
Every time with you is like a new trip
I pray this message can find your great ship
If somehow this bottle cannot find thee
At least it will travel eternally

Joseph Randazzo, Grade 10
Holy Cross High School

The Appearance of Winter

Come, little child and see the soft snow,
Its beauty you will soon come to know.
Nature's own white confetti for you to enjoy,
Plentiful enough for every lucky girl and boy.
A lovely scene it is to behold.
Enjoyed by all — both young and old.
Although it brings a rather dreaded chill,
Winter can be harsh or quiet and still.
Snow drifts in the air until captured within the trees,
Changing its direction with every winter breeze.
What? You want to keep it forever, this wonderful thing?
Sorry, little child, but it disappears in the presence of spring!

Justine Fairman, Grade 10
Morris Catholic High School

I Am the New World

I am greeted by golden light
Kissing my eyelids
I am swaddled in it
Bathed in it
I am melting into the world
Soon, I am a part of everything
I am the heart at the core
I am beating, beating
I am tearing down the boundaries
We live our lives by
I reach out,
To pull everybody in
I let them live in me
Because I am the new world,
I am the heart thumping in every single chest
The downfalls of humanity are dead
Jealousy and anger have been defeated
And loneliness is finally loved
Together we all share the beauty that makes us burst
And every night we all smile at each other
Close our eyes and dream

Marcy Hannemann, Grade 12
Holy Cross High School

The Pen

The pen with which I am writing this poem is black.
black like the night sky
black like the stickiest tar
black like the darkest chocolate
black like a murderer's soul

The pen with which I am writing this poem is light.
light like the whitest cloud
light like the morning air
light like a dove's feather
light like a loveless affair

The pen with which I am writing this poem is plain.
plain like open fields of grass
plain like an ugly pet
plain like toasted bread
plain like me

Megan Trinidad, Grade 12
North Arlington High School

A Dark, Cold Morning

It was a dark cold morning like the bottom of the sea.
My legs were shaking like rain sticks,
heart pounding like a base drum,
ears popping like Chris Brown.
I was alone like an inmate on death row.
The wind was yelling while blowing
and my body was shaking like a belly dancer.
My bus taking too long.

Ja'Quis Smith, Grade 10
Somerset County Alternative Academic High School

Love Is Blind

When you used to hug me I got the chills,
That made me never want to let go.
It's amazing how we were always,
laughing together and put on a great show.
Now our days are over,
And there's no time to come back to them.
There's no way on earth,
I'd forget about us back then.
Because my love for you is,
Like an eternal love story.
A story that ten years from now
Would never be forgotten, there's no worry.
Every passionate kiss we had come true
Was a sign to me,
A sign that made me believe
That we've got something special for everyone to see.
The last time I saw you I knew it would be the very last time.
Because you're off to a long journey like an endless line.
Now I know why love is blind,
Because I can't seem to get you off my mind.

Melitza M. Ortiz, Grade 10
Somerset County Alternative Academic High School

Aaliyah Haughton

You are more than a million
Your songs speak beautiful words to people's ears
When played from time to time

You still shine bright
We did not forget you
because if we did
we would all be sad and blue

The day you went away
many of us found
It wasn't the same without you
It was so unbelievable hearing on the news
That you have gone to a better place — it was true.

You are an angel now up high
With a beautiful soul in the sky
You are truly one in a million
Because we love your music
it will play on in our hearts and minds forever.

Jazmeen Murray, Grade 12
Bayonne High School

You Understand Me

A dream seems so far away —
It comes closer with every word you say.
When hope seems so far out of reach —
You're there to take my hand and guide me.
When I'm holding onto life by a string,
When doubt is pulling me in,
You know how to help me —
You make the world clearer to see.
Everything you do —
You make it seem so simple.
A word, a nod, a smile…
I'd do anything to keep you around for awhile.
You're making me into everything I wanted to be —
You know me, you love me, and you just understand me.

Emily Hart, Grade 10
South Hunterdon Regional High School

Untamed Wind

Wild.
The breeze whipping through his mane,
As if it was caressing,
Stroking.
His hooves like thunder, tearing up the ground under him.
Sweat beading on his neck,
The corded muscles rippling under his skin.
Above him, an eagle soars, letting out his song.
The huge stallion looked up at the eagle,
Feeling his own sense of freedom.
The stallion stopped at a ledge, the eagle continuing on.
Even if he had to stop there, he still knew he was free.
He knew what he was.
An untamed wind.

Gina Fantacone, Grade 12
North Arlington High School

Killing Black

Killing black means death and silence.
I don't mean to be violent.
But you must understand that we are all one man.
Image the world like a ball in your hand.
We look up to the sky and sing asking why?
And he will look down upon us with a tear in his eye.
Then he will ask why?
And we look at the ground with no reply.
No love no hope just
Killing Black.

Kaila Walton, Grade 11
Burlington County Institute of Technology

River

A river of blood
Runs through my family
Connecting us all together.
As our family gets bigger,
The river becomes longer.
The current will always be stronger,
Like the bond my family shares.
A river overflows because of a storm
My family has it's problems but the rain will end
And our differences will fade away.

Jenna Kane, Grade 10
Holy Cross High School

Inching Closer

Convulsions reverberating in the mind
Unknown voices sing
The fall of all mankind
Piercing bells ring
The time has come, the time has come
Demise by our own hands
The man above begins to strum
Playing on the thinnest strands
Tick tock, tick tock
The end inches closer
Final warnings from the clock
Fire rains from the sky
Water overflows from the sea
Constantly asking why
Scream transforms to plea
What once was is no more
Reality slips to the past
The heavens even the score
All ends at last

Miranda Persaud, Grade 12
Lodi High School

My Neverland

Follow me to the edge of time
Where all things cease to be
And the wind is a chime
Which beats to the waves of the sea
Come with me and hide
From the cruelness which is life
Dance around to another side
Where there is no more strife
Run away into the night
And seek what must be sought
Leave behind that ancient fight
You know you won't be caught
Follow this map to the brim
And wait for the light in the sky to dim

Jaimee Nadzan, Grade 12
Monsignor Donovan High School

Forever Unknown

Being real is too hard so act like a clone.
Do what they tell you and be a good drone.
Become like the others, fear of being alone
But who you are is forever unknown.

Your soul, unloved, slowly
Turns stone
Inside you yearn to scream
And moan
Surrounded by companions
But always alone
For your true self is
Forever unknown.

Thomas Sollazzo, Grade 11
Keyport High School

Pain of the Mortal Life

There was a full moon up in the skies
It was far from the time when sun was going to arise
There was a girl on her knees holding a skull
Her delicate heart from this pain turned awfully dull
No one knew where she was from and what was her name
For her tears she didn't know whom she must blame
She wore a white dress and had a couple of wings
She had to deal with everything that the mortal life brings
Above her raised a dead tree with blossomed roses on it
With only the moon light was that gloomy night lit
Wolves howled somewhere and she just sat with the skull in her hand
She didn't have enough power in her legs to stand
Some say she's a devil; some say she's an angel from above
She sought for sympathy and love
She stared at the moon with eyes full of tears
She was lonely and miserable for all these years
The doors of her heart were opened to sincerity and love
But her heart turned into a dried-out grove
Because she learned that there was no sincerity, and clearly, no one to love

Adrine Lalabekova, Grade 11
Fair Lawn High School

Seen and Unseen

When one is unseen can they see clearly where they want to go?
Obscurity begins to blind minds, until they no longer show
Fallen behind yet forgotten and forsaken, no one notices their absence
They don't seem to care, do they? No, they don't even wince
Concealed by their own thoughts, are they absent from their own physical being too?
Bodies disconnected from brains, each operating on its own cue
Society can't see them, but they still have a reflection
At least they can see it they themselves, an impossible resurrection
Watching the seen, they envy them — or not?
Never having to worry about being caught
They slither behind their nonexistent walls, sneakiness undiscovered
Amongst the seen, they are somehow hidden while clearly uncovered
Those who are seen remain ignorant, clueless to the rights of others they've denied
The seen don't seem to care, do they? No, they don't even hide
Unconscious of their own discrimination and blindness
Can their hearts still contain kindness?
Regardless, the seen and the unseen each take their own street
Separate yet still the same, will they ever meet?

Emma Budiansky, Grade 10
Scotch Plains-Fanwood High School

The Isolated Mind
Swallowed up whole
In a sea of pitch black,
Surrounded in silence
In a room all alone.
Sitting and rocking;
Back and forth.
Sitting waiting;
Tick and tock.
Waiting for a few minutes.
Waiting for a few hours.
Days turning into nights,
And nights into days.
Sense of time is lost,
But the madness is found.
A gateway is opened.
The fragile mind is set free.
Playing games on itself,
When left to its own devices,
Your mind finds its own escape:
Where the unreal becomes real.
Jenn Kastner, Grade 12
Jackson Liberty High School

It'll Be Over Soon
Solitude is a calm word,
It can mean many different things
Isolated, alone
And sometimes at home
Or even quiet and depressed
Can seem like a mess
Don't let it bother you
For you know things will change
It might take long it might be quick
Solitude is never permanent
The worst thing in the world
For you think it's forever
It will end, I swear
Just be aware
That there are people who love and care
Just be brave
And get ready to be saved.
Devin Conlon, Grade 10
South Hunterdon Regional High School

Losing What's Left of Her Hope
The ache in her heart is great today;
I can tell with a single glance.
She's starting to drift farther away,
Losing what's left of her hope.

Why does she try so hard to win your heart?
She knows you do not care.
She's slowly starting to come apart,
Starting to rip. Starting to tear.
Alex Tucker, Grade 10
South Hunterdon Regional High School

I Am
I am a hyena I'm always laughing and running
I am a TV always active
I am like the color green always bright and joyful
I am like the season of summer bright and happy
I am like a steak can be tough but can also be soft
I am like a window you can see right through me
I am always hyper like a group of freshmen
I am always happy like my dog when she sees food
I am really cheerful like my personality
I am a fan of the color blue like my eyes
I am always making friends laugh it's just the way I act
I am not caring about what people say to me or think about me it's just how I feel
I am me because I do a lot of stupid things, I wish I thought before I acted
I am me because I say things at the wrong time I need to learn to stay quiet
I am hoping to be a construction worker
I am a real hard worker when it comes to projects
I could be a chef if the other fails, I am a pretty good cook
I am hoping to be married some day
I am hoping to have kids some day
I am in love with my girlfriend and she's my everything
I am happy with who I am
Sean Sullivan, Grade 12
Williamstown High School

Monster
Among the cluttered closet
The only thing un halcyon was the monster.
Twin sanguine paper lanterns jabbed into a hook.
Masquerading in between the penumbras of my room.
The ghouls and fiends are perpetual.
The ghouls and fiends and body snatchers are perpetual.
Salient foot —
Hand —
Face —
The mundane effulgence on its guise.
Bubbling, abominable claw grapples onto the sill,
Rotting and corrupting it —
Erosion gurgles on the carpet. Uncouth. Its back hunch,
Breathing and oozing its gunk in abeyance — Harbinger of Bereavement.
Watery, gooey arm reaches and flails with a concrete impact — Oblivion —
Delving in a labyrinthine of lethargic doses of lullabies —
Thirsting for a hole in the bulwark of time.
The floor falls asleep and loses its strength.
Falling down a chasm of celestial depth, you panic and wake up
Face to face with yourself — a reflection in the eyes
Of the gluttonous Boogeyman.
Jordan Dubinsky, Grade 12
Barnegat High School

Central Park

I sit on the bench and look up at the crystal blue sky.
I see the skyscrapers as high as clouds.
To my left are peaceful people resting in the green grass,
To my right are giggling children gallivanting on the rocks.

There is no other place, I'd rather be than sitting here watching a
slew of characters traipse by.
Dull businessmen in gray suits chattering away on cell phones,
Colorful artists lugging supplies,
Nannies pushing strollers and comforting babies that are not theirs.

A warm breeze comes and lifts me up
And I float above the lush green forest.
The foliage is changing colors in the autumn air
And the people on the ground look like multicolored ants.

As I land back on that bench I shiver
And wrap myself in the sun's warmth
This pocket of green is an oasis,
Where anyone can escape for an hour or two.

Rebecca Shack, Grade 12
Jackson Liberty High School

Now That You're Gone

I'm okay
That's what I try to convince myself of every day
Your words hurt more than they should
I would put you in the back of my thoughts if I could
It's weird to think about how we used to be
It seems that you are the only person who truly knows me
I never wanted to let you down
I miss you and the way you used to act like such a clown
To me you were always so sweet
Seeing you always quickens my heart beat
Do you notice that I'm not there
This feeling that you give me is rare
The tears fall silently down my face
If only you knew I yearned for your embrace
The end of us had been so abrupt
As our relationship became so corrupt
So here I am with my heart on my sleeve
Do you want to figure this out or just leave
I only wish that you would stay
I'm not okay

Melissa Aversa, Grade 10
South Hunterdon Regional High School

The Lonely Boy

I walk alone through the weary night,
I look around, but no one's in sight
I try to convince myself that someone's there
But sadly there is nobody.

I wonder if someone will ever come,
Will I live my life alone
I hope not,
But slowly the truth is starting to sink in
I am starting to get lonely, but what is this!

Is it my imagination,
I start to see something or someone get closer
Is it my mind playing tricks on me or is it reality,
The person got closer and I could not believe my eyes
It was Jesus Christ, my Lord and Savior
Coming to me in a human form.

That's when I realized that I was never really alone
It was just my state of mind.

Barry Wilson, Grade 10
Kearny Christian Academy

One Heart Could Touch Millions

Given in by anger,
Defeated by the pain,
With thoughts running rampant,
There's no room for any gain.

Given in by temptation,
Things you know you shouldn't do,
Helplessness cried out,
I know you didn't want to.

Given in by association,
People tell you yes,
Vigorously shake your head,
But they sell you and make you say "I guess."

Given in by hate,
How you wish to make them end,
When all you ever wished,
Was simply just one friend.

Kerri O'Brick, Grade 12
Camden Catholic High School

Americans Dreaming
See the Americans under their covers,
the dream never ceases,
thoughts of money and materialistic pleasures,
not crossed between these classes,
the hopeless dream of success,
those things they'll never acquire,
sitting down so low,
but always pleading to be higher,
those who don't need hope,
don't have much on their mind,
simply thoughts of corruption and greed,
while generosity and compassion subside,
everyone is sleeping,
except those who are dead,
and those who are dreaming,
lay with smiles, in their bed,
concentrating on a new hope,
or a new way to cope,
while forever reveling in surreality,
but still ignoring reality.

Tristan Duff, Grade 11
Hillsborough High School

discover me
it's like an explosion of words
waiting to come out
and when it finally did I can't believe what I said
it was too soon but now
it's too late
to think I'd want to wait
this is what it is to speak words of love
but words turn into a mess
and made my story a treasure chest
filled with unknown secrets
I'm lost and afraid
what happened yesterday has disappeared
and everything is clear
there's nothing left now
so discover me
because I'm gone
without a trace.

Nicolly Moura, Grade 11
David Brearley Middle/High School

Years of Friendship
Years of friendship turned to something so great
Like you asking me out on our very first date.
You were ten and I was eight
When I first saw you I knew it was fate.
Even back then I knew we were meant to be soulmates.
Screaming and fighting can't tear us apart,
Because you're the boy that stole my heart.
Six months later, and still together,
I don't know about you, but I want this forever.

Alexa Guirk, Grade 11
Keyport High School

Unattainable
Unattainable, you are, as the clouds that dress the Earth.
My arms are outstretched. You appear, to me, so close.

Your look is deceiving; it incites my vain hopes.
Yet, while you float along, I feel a hint of your caress.

Your touch, still distant, raises and commands me.
Your fragile frame reveals its breast, booming, with such power.

Without pity, you trap me in your ivory wisps.
You devour me slowly, knowing I have no one else.

Then you speak to me in a language I wish to know.
Your words are faint, but their syllables surround me.

You leave me, and I watch you.
The grass consoles my body, and I am timid and defeated.
My forsaken eyes look to the sky. You leave a trail that I will follow.

Jessica Gonzalez, Grade 12
South Brunswick High School

My River
My river is my blood,
My heritage,
My race,
My upbringing,
That's me.
My ancestors,
That's me.
R-H-O-A-D-E-S
That's me.
Through the mountains and deserts of Africa,
Italy, and Ireland
That's me.
Through Georgia, New Jersey, and Pennsylvania
That's me.
Muse's, Houston's, Herbert's, and Lee's
That's me.
The river of many directions
We will all become ONE…

Jalen Rhoades, Grade 12
Holy Cross High School

Never Be
Never have I hated you, as much as I've tried.
All the hurt and tears that I've cried.
Seeing you makes me smile
And the butterflies begin to fly, tickling me inside.
You give me this warm feeling that I can't live without;
You're the best without a doubt.
Seeing your face brightens my day,
Kissing your lips makes me fly away.
Fly away from the dreams
And into the reality that you and me can never be.

Kaitlynn Astringer, Grade 11
Keyport High School

Waiting
I sat there waiting for your call
When you never called at all
You left me here without a word
Something about that is so absurd
Especially since you started it all
You couldn't give me a last call?
To say you want to end it all
Now my brain's mangled around your name
I sat here waiting but you never came
I felt like crying but I never did
Something like that feels like a sin
I will never give you my tears
I sat here waiting fighting my fears
The lights were off
But so was my brain
I think I may be going insane
The more I wait, the less I care
I don't think I still want to sit waiting there.

Courtney Russell, Grade 11
Keyport High School

New Again
Four years pass me by while nothing changes,
Emotions run a cycle every time.
The kids bother with bitter exchanges.
As this fourth year moves, the emotions climb.
Drama is the new focal point in life.
Nobody wants to be held down like this.
The hallways are ringing with constant strife.
This last year was supposed to just have bliss.
There's no difference from the three years before.
The rumors of the last year are just myth.
There's still time for this year to become more.
For improvement, action must be forthwith.
Otherwise, next year will have to be when,
College starts, and I can be new again.

Pierce Hacking, Grade 12
Holy Cross High School

Purses
Purses make me happy
they come in different colors, shapes, and sizes.
You can color coordinate them with your outfit
and look fabulous!

Name brands are the best —
Channel, Juicy, Coach
although they are super expensive
believe me they are worth it.

They hold all your belongings,
keeping them safe in their own special compartments.
Purses are the best!
They simply make me happy.

Alissa Frederick, Grade 12
North Arlington High School

Half-Wet
September 11th started it all; watching the news,
Seeing that it was people of Arab descent
Who caused the fall, I knew I was in trouble.
Being Egyptian, people looked at me differently
Because of that day. About a week after,
I was at the laundromat with my mother and brother.
I was a child, a carefree, innocent child. Neither color nor race
Nor religion nor face
Mattered to me; I never knew a difference,
I thought we were all the same.
Outside the laundromat,
Me and my brother were playing a game.
A white middle-aged lady came out, looking mad.
Eyes bloodshot, blond hair flying. I knew I had done
nothing bad or wrong; I wondered why she looked like that.
Her blue eyes glared right at me.
She hissed, "Go back to your own country!"
My heart dropped and so did my face; I cried and cried and ran
into my mother's arms; we took our laundry out of the dryer,
Half-wet, and went home. Not home as in Egypt,
but home as in here, where I belong.

Mariam Younan, Grade 12
Bayonne High School

Corporate America*
They work everyday from nine to five.
Like drones, they're barely alive.
Typing endlessly in front of a bright screen,
Computer drive.

They are Mindless Workers.
They only know labor,
But they keep following orders
And living in the same routine.

And working,
Working, with superficial intentions.
They sit at their desks in cramped little cubicles
That are full of pens and papers and pictures of family,
A schedule that never ends.

Julie Howell, Grade 10
Colonia High School
Based on "The Bean Eaters" by Gwendolyn Brooks.

When All You Seem to Have Is Gone
When all you seem to have is gone
What will you have to give?
When you're all alone and have nowhere to go,
What will you have to give?
While your dreams are slowly turning dark,
What will you have to give?
To yourself you gave nothing but
Your own intentions,
But to the world you gave nothing but actions.

Rebecca Froncek, Grade 11
Keyport High School

The Open Eyed Crouch

A pack of wolves descend on my isolation but they don't want me
They glance and water at the mouth
Their eyes water from impurity and mockery
I used to run in this pack
My fur was as black as silence and so was theirs.

I see them now running and playing and attacking
That was me I could have attacked twice as hard
I rammed and pushed and fought and screamed
I was the center of the corner of the pyramid the very top
It was tiresome to climb

One day I fell it was slow and a couple reached
It did nothing
Nothing, and it hurts like hell. The pain numbs my empty soul and mind and thighs and stomach
The forest is a battle field now my eyes are constantly open, aware, ready to defend but never attack
Attacking is for the wolves composed of midnight

But I am composed of dusty sun a bright future with no present
Floating across the river in the forest with a shield
After all, a dusty sun can't see midnight
Midnight disappears for the dusty, murky sun
Why did the river turn? Why did the winds change?

Was it me, or midnight? Was it want or need? Was it…no use. Float crouched down until the brightness.

Lacey Kaplan, Grade 10
Pascack Valley High School

Uncle Earl

Uncle Earl was a man who was happy and free
He was never angry or with fear I never saw him have an enemy or ever shed a tear
He lived by a motto I continue to say

"Live life day by day and everything will be okay"

Uncle Earl took care of me when I was young he made me laugh when he told me to look at my nana when she sung
He made me feel better when I had the chicken pox he stayed up with me and read me stories such as Goldie Locks
But then he looked at me and would to say

"Live life day by day and everything will be okay"

As I got older I did not see Uncle Earl as much but when we did see each other we would catch up on life and such
His nickname for me was "Otis" he said he called me this because he loved me the mostest
Still to this day I can hear him say

"Live life day by day and everything will be okay"

October 2008 was when my whole life changed
My uncle's kidney failure took his life and I will never be the same tears roll down my face when I think of the pain
Yet I look up at the sky with a smile and say

"Live life day by day and everything will be okay"

Erica Hayes, Grade 12
Bayonne High School

The Great Memory: Henry Nawrocki

I wish he never passed away.
I wish I could go back to that day,
He gave me everything including love
I wish I can say that it was enough.
He is such a great memory,
I hope he is still looking after me.

He knew how to do everything, literally.
He was manly and such,
Yet had a gentle touch.
He was a hard worker,
Yet a strong lover.
He is such a great memory,
I hope he is still looking after me.

I am desperate to see him.
There is so much I want him to know,
There is so much I can't let go.
I can still remember how he'd look at me,
And what he would tell me.
He is such a great memory,
I hope he is still looking after me.

Izabella Kluczyk, Grade 12
Bayonne High School

A Tribute to the Holocaust

Woke up in a different place today,
There are many missing parts of me,
My mom and sisters were taken away,
They left before I had last words to say.

Now I'm lonely,
Only left with my daddy,
I can't bear the smell of human flesh,
It's very scary,
People eat rarely.
I even had to use a fake age and job,

My name was taken away,
I am now a7713,
A lot has changed since yesterday,
I wonder how it feels to be a Nazi

It's cold out.
I got thinner no doubt
I'm stuck in Auschwitz with no shoes,
Shaved heads, no pillows for our beds.
How many days of torture can we get?

Taylor Perrucci, Grade 10
Paramus Catholic High School

The Act of Giving Up

Oak eyed,
She rains
In line for a cup of coffee.
Her thumbs move like the legs of a runner:
Muscle fibers tearing with every over-cut stride,
The impact causing a once straight, stripe frame
To oscillate, quiver, and melt her hair
    Then her skin
        Then her blood
    Then her muscle
Until she (barely) stood before me —
Bare-boned.
Stop light lenses caressing my disgusted pupils.
Then, like a prey to a predator,
She crawled through the deepest and thickest layers of my integument
And took shelter in my heart,
My brain begging it to beat faster
And keep her warm.
So that the next day,
When she returned to the boy who stole my name,
She looked like I didn't want her anymore.

P.J. Verhoest, Grade 12
Wayne Valley High School

Consequences of Love

I feel like there's a permanent imprint on my lips, where yours should always be.
And I'm afraid that if you leave, no one will ever be able to fill that space.
And I won't ever be able to kiss again.

I feel like there's a shape cut out of my heart that only you can fill.
And I'm afraid that if you leave, I won't ever be whole again.
And I'll slowly and painfully drift away.

I feel like there are burn marks on my hands and fingers from your touch.
And I'm afraid that if you leave, they'll heal up and I won't be reminded of you.
And I'll lose the feeling of your skin on mine.

I feel like there's only one set of arms that can hold me just right.
And I'm afraid that if you leave, I'll never be held again.
And I'll live without warmth forever.

I feel like I'm upside down, with my head swinging under my feet.
And I'm afraid that if you leave, the blood will rush to my head too quickly.
And I won't ever be able to feel these things again.

Kaitlyn Allen, Grade 12
Pascack Valley High School

Reach of Hand

May you be greeted at the pearly gates with welcome from above
When you feel sadness overwhelm you 'cause you've lost touch with the ones you love.
May the sun shine its light but, more importantly, its hope.
May the likeness in your children give your family the strength to cope.
And for your children, may God grant you opportunities to touch land,
So they may feel your Guarding presence within their Reach of Hand.

Stephanie Pasternak, Grade 11
Cranford Sr High School

My Ocean

Love, you are my ocean.
I walk beside you always.
In warmth and in winter,
I will forever return to you.
I breathe to the beat of your tumbling waves,
while my heart thumps in sync.
You're the only thing that makes me feel beautiful,
on the cloudiest of days.
The only thing that keeps my soul laughing,
and my heart warm at night.

Love, you are my ocean.
My sea of faith.
I run along your shores,
while your tide kisses my feet.
Your horizon stretches for miles,
but that is a journey I am willing to make.
Love, you are my ocean.
Your endless body of water represents all that we share.
May our bond last forever.
May we never drift apart.

Love, you are my ocean. Love, the possessor of my heart.
Sofie Kohler, Grade 12
Morris Knolls High School

Exquisite Wonders

Nature's great beauty is always my cure
Comparing you to dazzling flowers
Enchanted by your looks that are just so pure
Nature and your beauty are mine for hours

Running my fingers through the lush green grass
Its texture feels like your satiny skin
Dreaming about these smooth textures in class
But I woke up due to some senseless din

My eyes crave nature's vibrant and bright hues
They match your beautiful and brilliant eyes
Your eye color is emerald bamboos
Loving you and nature is my prime prize

This exquisite guy is just a sweet dream
Nature's existence is highly supreme
Tracy Ng, Grade 11
Colonia High School

To Give Up

When I see everyone go to the second floor ahead of me
I feel so small
But even when I feel like giving up and walking away
The clouds that cover the stars still shine through
So I don't even have a good enough reason
To give up
Gillian Carr, Grade 10
South Hunterdon Regional High School

This Masquerade

The mask is on,

I hide my shame;
But who's to blame
If not myself,
Here, in this audience of one?

Start the music,

The soundtrack of my affliction begins to play;
Notes of darkness that drive out the day,
Like a black wind.

The ball begins,

And so I dance with my regrets;
No structure, no form, just an eerie silhouette.
But it's all I know,
It's all I've ever known,

The mask is off…

This is me,
And I'm afraid,
To live this life, this masquerade.
Vincent Cuccolo, Grade 12
Columbia Sr High School

What I Am

I have eyes like mud pies.
I have lips that are like chips, tasty.
I have a snail-like steady pace.
I have supported people like a chair.
I have been cheerful like the color green but never dull.

I am the summer that everyone loves.
I have my own car, I have a lot of friends.
I have been sweet and sour like sour patch kids.
I am very funny.

I am as loving as a pet.
I have been called a care bear because I'm caring.
I am not a hater.
I have been outstanding.

I would like to listen, I would like to talk less.
It would be cool to read more.
I have to be more caring.
I want to be less prejudiced.

I am hoping for the stars.
I have planned to hit Jupiter.
I have planned for a steady job to help my family.
I hope for the best…every time.
Matthew Moderski, Grade 12
Williamstown High School

Insignificant?

Today was the day that Miss Perfect lost it,
The day she wouldn't return.
Today was the day that she reached the point,
She curled up, caved in, no crash, just a burn.

Looking back, her life wasn't pressing
Not privileged, yet so far from deprived.
That incessant, modest, middle placement,
On creativity she formerly relied.

Her disposition was once scarlet red,
Yet as a flamingo in a pigeon cage,
The pigment began to fade,
Society made her pale as dead.

She calls these mirrors "liars,"
Reflections haunt her to the core.
Seeking out, she can't see the surface,
I don't know this girl anymore.

And then, one morning, her flowers bloomed,
Divine threads stitched up her soul.
One trivial morning, He smiled upon her,
And began to fill the hole.

Gina Lione-Napoli, Grade 10
Paramus Catholic High School

Best Friends

Nothing can break a bond between two,
It's a friendship that will always last,
Remember the times we had together,
Those times we look to the past

I go to you with the secrets I hold,
And the heart to bare it all,
You're never to judge the words I speak,
And catch me whenever I fall

There for each other through thick and thin,
No walls can block us now,
'Cause you're like family to me,
That I can't picture my life without

Best friends then, sisters now,
No one can ever see,
What a bond we both share,
What a change you've had on me

Friends forever, nevertheless,
These words I speak are true,
My life would be so difficult,
If not for a friend like you.

Molly Carroll, Grade 11
Keyport High School

Happiness at Last

There were no signs, no way to know
How lonely the days of life would grow
Look into my eyes and see my soul
Empty, lonely and out of control

I want to return to what I've left behind
Childhood serenity and peace of mind
Now stress is overwhelming, pain intense
I can't find happiness, there's no defense

Against the cruelty I witness wherever I go
the emptiness in the faces of everyone I know
There is no love, no joy, no happiness at all
Just relentless selfishness and an emotional wall

Keeping out all we accepted in our youth
Making us unable to ever see the truth
That we hold the key to our own chain
We are able to free ourselves from this pain

We're not rendered helpless in the face of insanity
We don't have to accept what we're taught must be
We'll follow not in the footsteps of those from the past
We'll replace the terror with happiness at last!

Maureen Busund, Grade 12
Williamstown High School

Samuel Salters

He gave me life
He gave me air
Gave me pride
He's the reason why I'm here

You offered plenty
And gave to many
You're the reason why I have
Respect instilled in me

You showed me the way
The way to succeed
You gave me a way
A way to believe

I'm mad you're not here
But glad you are there
I thought I'd never see the day we were gone
Just your name alone can be the lyrics to my favorite song

You're the wind beneath my wings
The reason why the caged bird sings
You don't know the joy you bring
And one day I hope to see you again

Malcolm Salters, Grade 12
Bayonne High School

Grendel

We are all drifters in this spinning world,
Spinning. Spinning. Spin around in circles.
Never planting firmly but shifting always shifting.
Floating. Float around through s p a c e
No where to go to. To be [wanted].
Wanted, wants, wanting to be loved. Loathed.
Balance on our scale both good and bad.
Balance was. is everything. Anything. Life.
Life is not meaning, need a meaning,
Find a means by which to live. What purpose?
Found purpose, find life, get wealth.
Get infamy, immor[t]ality. Live or exist?
We exist to live or live to exist? Remembrance,
Want to be remembered. Point being?
What point is there? Nothing matters, mattered, will.
Presently, actions matter, good or bad.
Past stays past. Immediate past. D I S T a n t past.

Alexis Morales, Grade 11
Paramus Catholic High School

Broken

Too sad to sleep
Too tired to cry

My heart feels full
It beats so fast
Can't resist the pull
Can't remember the past

Burning happy
Sickening sad
Tragic angry
No sign it will pass

Past inspirations so empty
When will it end?
Support beams falling down
Can it even end?
Thunder clouds the flash
Will I make it end?
Dense fog covers reason
Does it matter if it ends?

Suffering on and on and on
Just waiting so long so long so long
So long.

Kayla White, Grade 12
Montclair High School

What I Love

Playing music is my passion
It's what I love to do
I do it all of the time now
Even in front of you

Always driving, driving, driving
Always a brand new place
Some are very small, some are large
Never with a sad face

"Life is nothing without passion"
"Something you cannot grasp"
While you have nothing that gives hope
Music's a thing to clasp

So go now and get an instrument
Go now and hold a note
Oh all the feelings you will have
When songs come from your throat

And when I hear the music start
I feel like screaming, "yay!"
I feel like this is my calling
To do for all my days.

Jon Dolan, Grade 12
Boonton High School

Trouble

I try to search
But I do not find
Peace from this Trouble
It's in my mind

I try to grasp
But do not attain
Escape from this Trouble
It's in my brain

I try to run
But do not reach
"Finish Line" for Trouble
It's faster than me

I try to be hidden
But no place, there is
Trouble is smart
It hid where I did

I try to stay out
But it brings me back in
Trouble gets lonely
Guess it wants friends

Davynte Pannell, Grade 11
Immaculate Conception High School

Alone

I am caught between two infinites,
For what seems to be an eternity,
Abandoned, stuck in what I can only call, the unknown.
I have been here before, and vaguely remember this agony.
Passionate feelings of mine untamed,
Confusion messing with my conscience,
Independent, depending on the undiscovered,
My state of mind is no state of reality.
I am lost, vulnerable to anything and everything I fear.
I am confused, disoriented by this solitude and isolation.
Helpless, for I am left mystified, in my own deep thoughts.
I genuinely need to find my heart somewhere in your soul,
To know it still exists there, to know I am not alone.
Reassure me I have not been forgotten.
Let your words assuage my uncertainties.
Bring me to your warmth again.
Save me, remind me to breathe, tell me I will live,
Blinded by the darkness,
Deafened by the stillness,
Silenced by the voices in my head,
Take me from this place.

Christina Findakly, Grade 10
West Morris Central High School

The Game

Perfect. Just Perfect.
To come this far and fail.
To be blinded by what you thought you knew.
Piece by piece, the lies blinded you.
There were so many signs,
Signs to make you see this would happen.
That's the worst part.
Until, the twist of truth.
So unexpected and surprising it impairs you.
Some truths, may not be heard the way we hope they would be.
But, they linger long after they've been said.
In the end, it's all an untidy heap inside of you,
To care about something you were so oblivious to.
You open your eyes to this new light
Because now you know exactly how to play the game,
Don't play at all.
Simply perfect.

Danielle Choinski, Grade 12
North Arlington High School

Within Me

Sharp as a blade, malleable as molten steel
As sudden as death, but cold to the feel
Twisting my mind to a spring that will snap
Waving at me in my head, even while I nap
It's always there, no matter where,
Under steady lock and key
It's always there, no matter where.
Alone, inside of me

Mike DeRose, Grade 12
Somerset County Alternative Academic High School

Safe Trip Home

I've resolved to love you silently.
Through the stained-glass dome of space
I will occupy myself with your pilgrimage,
perched atop tall buildings, telescope in hand,
to watch you, lost, among the stars,
the sharp beacon of your smile naught but a spark
immersed in fog…your voice crushed to fine fragments
beneath anchor-weight hemispheres.
It is with longing that I will monitor
the proceedings of your journey, with care
that I will mark your progress as you drift
across horizons…and when at last you are absorbed
by cosmic vapors, the faint glow of moonlight
no longer lending itself to familiarity,
I will neatly withdraw my affections and part.
Be still, Youssef!
Across distances impenetrable I love you
and I hope you have a safe trip home.

Nestor Collazo, Grade 12
Pioneer Academy of Science

The One That Got Away

To me you are as beautiful as a gem.
Your smile would light the kids at the orphanage with joy.
But, what I loved the most about you was your kindness.
I loved this thing called "us."
Why can't things go back to the way they were?
I miss you so much, that I can still feel your warm touch.
I wish that we could smile and laugh together once more.
I miss you so much that my heart won't stop mourning you.
I wish and wish upon a star just to be with you.
I want you back, my love.
Because you are the dove
That is forever perched on my shoulders.
You're the only one that can soothe my troubled world.

Guy-Adler Dorelien, Grade 12
Belleville Sr High School

Just His Pride

A long time ago
I walked into a store
With my father — his hands dirty from work
Up and down they looked
Trying to find what he took.
He took nothing
Except his pride with him
When he left
I held my breath
God took care of the rest
We left together hand in hand
Knowing the truth
At peace with ourselves

Katie Soler, Grade 12
Bayonne High School

Ricky

Hot Puerto Rican December sun blaring down, gruffly bearded teens strapped and strolling town
Causing havoc while tragedy permeates the sky, clothed with things they did not buy
Pregnant and young already with son, standing while her belly weighs a ton
Family together, talking to their favorite brother, he stood prominent hugging his loving mother
Young and strong, handsome as a god should be, there he stood alive for all the world to see
His pregnant sister and her very young son, almost two-tenths of a decade had I won
This hubris man had taken to flight, he went out alone into the night
Fiendishly he searched for someone to rob, to support his habit he fervently trod
No thought of his wife or his kids, only on a thief's mind he had bid
Searching for a victim to gain monetary prize, he had no understanding of his demise
Young and strong, handsome as a god should be, there he stood alive for the world to see
These young men whom I had earlier described, they were the men he had then prescribed
He chose of them to reap his prize, unaware of what they had kept disguise
They then revealed their weapons to open eyes, these young foolish teens cared not for lives
Their bullets they unloaded in this loving brother, they certainly cared not about his loving mother
The police had came later the next night, to tell of my dear uncle's flight
I could not grasp any of the happenings, but I understand all of the horrible sad things
Young and strong, handsome as a god should be, no more he stood for the world to see
I felt all their pain although I had barely known, of my dear uncle or the tragedy shown
I really do wish that Pandora's Box had a closed lid, one thing to learn from this, don't play with guns kids

Christopher Cabreja, Grade 12
Bayonne High School

Last Words

Seeing the soldier sitting in his chair where he left the world filled with despair.
The world keeps moving, spinning, carrying on.
But the thoughts of the older soldier in the chair still proceed.
Searched for a breath, but it was not there.
I hope he fell into a peaceful slumber, put it that way so my mind is at ease.
I miss the way he used to teach and tease.
I delivered the last meal he ate, filled his milk to make him strong, but his life just moved along.
The last words will forever run through my head, the exact words that helped the soldier get through the life he lead.
Jolly, rough, but kind, which made your nickname, Grumpy, completely out of line.
But you loved it and made Disney another memory of you in my mind.
Reality hit me hard, patriot in his flag covered fate.
Everyone there in his honor can relate.
When your battle cry was sound, the tears fell all around, for the soldier who fought to see his granddaughters turn sweet sixteen.
Time is against us, the world's faults against us.
Push through it, but don't run!
Watch over me as I live your last words, "have fun."

Lauren Thomson, Grade 11
Raritan High School

Reality

I wish clocks didn't exist, so I could lose track of time, and wander forever. Follow the waves of the ocean, and the light of the constellations above me. The perfect map to take me where I always wanted to be. Where shattered glass and broken hearts pulled its bits and pieces back together, with gravity and miracles. When mistakes and mishaps erased themselves, and allowed you to take back yesterday. When waking up isn't so hard to do, because the pain you fell asleep with, disappeared into thin air. And the memories of laughter greeted you on the drips of morning dew. It's unfortunate and irrelevant that it doesn't quite turn out this way. With going through each and every day, I came to realize that if you walk through the worn pages of a fairy tale, you'll see what dreams are made of, and what they never will be.

Dolores Mohamad, Grade 10
Matawan Regional High School

Grandma Neama

O where did you go, O Teata my dear, O where did you go, I miss you so much here
Seeing you after school every single day, it feels like a nightmare not seeing you today
You led a great life that no one can parallel, that's only one part, in a nutshell

The way you took care of your kids showed us your true love, sent from the sky, a heavenly dove
Seven great kids were led from you, Janet, Fadia, and Ramzy are just to name a few
The pain you went through was not easy, it affected you so much, it drove you crazy
Every day after school, to you I would come, doing my homework, staying with you was my fun

So many memories, throughout the years, the ones I remember bring my eyes' tears
Hospitals, nursing homes, were where you stayed, O poor Neama, in those beds you laid
Visiting you for so many hours, your smile would blossom, just like flowers

The day you left, stabbed my heart, it was hard letting you go, since we were one part
Looking down at us from above, please don't forget you are our one true love

Kyrolos Zaki, Grade 12
Bayonne High School

Aaron Stallworth

Like a brother to me with you I felt free
Closer to me than others were without you my life's been a blur
Not fair at all I thought you'd never fall

Such a great person, did everything right then all of a sudden became a fright
Medicine gone and no one home diabetes took over and God took you home
Not fair at all I thought you'd never fall

Hanging out with you the weekend before never thought you'd soon enter God's door
I want you back and here so bad I never thought I could feel so sad
Not fair at all I thought you'd never fall

You were the happiest person I ever knew I could imagine you're mad seeing everyone so blue
So I'm going to suck it up and smile. I know I'll see you again, even if it's not for a while
Shouldn't have happened at all but for you I'll stand tall

Kaitlin Valencia, Grade 12
Bayonne High School

Winter

As I look out my window, I see the bare trees without the leaves.
When I look up in the sky I see it cloudy and dark and sometimes windy.
I keep looking in the sky, always hoping I'll see a snowflake fall from the big white cloud as fluffy as a sheep.
As I walk through the woods, all I hear is the leaves crunching under my shoes.
As soon as I get home, about to open the door, I feel the wind pick up and I look up
and I see a snowflake fall from the sky and onto my foot.
I stay outside longer, just to see how much snow there is going to be on the ground.

Lisha Hoff, Grade 10
South Hunterdon Regional High School

Recognition

I cannot justify between the lies or the truth. Sometimes the recognition, of your voice, disguises how negatively you are, towards, me, my word, and my heart you cross the line of ignorance, crossed over to deceitful. That the truth is too difficult for me to handle or stress when I fall I do not have time to peel open my eyes to realize, I hit my head on the useless thing you call your word.

Audriana Smith-Hinson, Grade 10
Garfield High School

Carry On

Though the pain seems unbearable,
And the trials incomparable.
Carry on my friend,
Carry on.

Though they laugh at your pain,
They will have no gain.
So carry on my friend,
Carry on.

You will fall there is no doubt,
And stumble all throughout.
But carry on my friend,
Carry on.

In the end your joy will be great,
And your pride show in your gait.
Because you carried on my friend,
You carried on.

Mark Apuzzo, Grade 10
Koinonia Academy

Wind

The wind blows into our town
Where the leaves scurry around
Children want to run and play
Teachers gather them to stay.
The air carries its cold song
Father winter will be right along
Cold air travels up my back
And reminds me it's on track.
Soon snow will be on the ground
Winter will be all around
Schools may have to close
To let children have a repose.
Until it comes I will know
Wind will be free to blow

Brian R. Goldfarb, Grade 11
Marlboro High School

Disdain

I have never known it
Nor ever felt its sting
My lips will never touch
Such a horrid thing

But my eyes have seen it
And its many colors.
The colors of disdain
Have filled me with pain.

Others have used looks
And these words against me
So dripping with disdain.

Shannon O'Connor, Grade 12
Bayonne High School

The Face of Freedom

Like an eagle above the sky, I don't want to hear the word
goodbye. Alone and independent, my worst feature
you could say, at least I'm going to live another day.
Like the color white, so neutral still so cold like the winter snow,
one good feature, my face, still glows. I glow red like a tomato.
Just waiting to go home and lay in my cozy bed, like shackles
chained across my feet, I try running but don't get far, I can never tell
my best features, my lips, my looks, or maybe my style, my smile,
my eyes or maybe my thighs. Whose to judge what's outside, when words
can never describe the tears that I cried inside. Yes I lied, and I'm conceited,
yes even then I have cheated, but does that mean I should be mistreated?
Yes I cursed, and even stole but I'm only human, my heart is still whole,
Like an eagle above the sky. A woman whose past was so shy
will now be married to the greatest guy. Now it's time to say goodbye,
And let this eagle fly.

Jeannie Rein, Grade 12
Williamstown High School

A Haunting Past

The breeze rushed around my feet,
As the leaves blew over head.
I caught you staring back at me,
On the way we took to school.

But what about our past?
These thoughts, they filled my head.
I couldn't push them back at all,
I only wished them dead.

Try and try with all my might,
Our memories like a ghost.
And then the light came clear through trees
The truth was oh so clear.

I still have feelings for you darling
Though it scares me so,
I can only hope that how I feel
Is mutual.

Madeline Wodeshick, Grade 11
Raritan High School

Dreamland

Trust me
Come and take my hand
Lets go someplace
A dreamland
Somewhere far away
Where others have
Not a thing to say
It belongs to us
It's our place
And we decide
Our fate
Oh I can't wait
For the time when there exists
Such a place
Such a beautiful place
A land of dreams
For you and me
Could it be
Oh could it be?

Shayla Lawz, Grade 11
McNair Academic High School

Juana

Querida come inside and eat come inside and eat
I've got your favorites for coming today it's time to come and eat

I came today dear grandma of mine I came today for you
So you need not make dinner and things of the sort just come her and rest your feet

Querida so won't you eat so won't you eat dinner with me
I've made all your favorites for coming today and although you've come for only me for me
Come and sit just have dinner with me

I cam today dear grandma of mine I came today for you
And since you want me to have dinner with you this is what I'll do

Querida it's time for me to rest it's time for me to sleep
I'll lay here and close my eyes and sleep…and sleep…and sleep…

Goodnight dear grandma of mine

D. Liz Polanco, Grade 11
Bayonne High School

Are You Cold or Is It Just Me

I swear since I was birthed in this Earth I became the problem
Depression, tribulation, violence it seems we cannot solve them

My mother struggles with four I am the youngest
But in mental circumstances I swear I am the eldest

Are you cold??? Or is it just me
Are you the problem??? Or is it just me
Do you strive for excellence??? Or is it just me

Do you have faith in things that seem to never come through for you???
I'm sure the Jews can relate through their sufferance in the Holocaust
But why suffer if their is a God??? So why live if we have to die???

Are you cold??? Or is it just me
Do you dream??? Or is it just me
Do you have faith and Believe??? Or is it just me

Joseph Littlejohn, Grade 12
East Orange Campus High School

Grades 7-8-9
Top Ten Winners

List of Top Ten Winners for Grades 7-9; listed alphabetically

Gemma Bush, Grade 8
Dominion Middle School, Columbus, OH

Heather Kinkade, Grade 7
East Marshall Middle School, Gilman, IA

Sasha Kogan, Grade 7
Public School 334 Anderson, New York, NY

Hayley Lange, Grade 7
Mater Dei School-Nativity Center, Sioux City, IA

Colleen Maher, Grade 8
Our Lady Star of the Sea School, Grosse Pointe Woods, MI

Coralynn Nydokus, Grade 9
ES Laird School, Lloydminster, SK

Addie Pazzynski, Grade 9
Waynesburg Central High School, Waynesburg, PA

Taylor Thornton, Grade 9
Shepherd Jr High School, Mesa, AZ

TJ Wells, Grade 9
Cardinal Spellman High School, Brockton, MA

Joanna Zou, Grade 8
West Jr High School, Columbia, MO

All Top Ten Poems can be read at www.poeticpower.com

Note: The Top Ten poems were finalized through an online voting system. Creative Communication's judges first picked out the top poems. These poems were then posted online. The final step involved thousands of students and teachers who registered as the online judges and voted for the Top Ten poems. We hope you enjoy these selections.

A Best Friend's Betrayal

You act crazy and mean
Which drives me off the wall
You "two faced back stabber"
Time after time you turned on me
You created hurtful rumors about me
You talked about me behind my back
You exposed my deepest, darkest secrets
You pretend like you didn't know me
But through all the pain and frustration
A "Best Friend Betrayal" is how it ends

Nedjee Corriolan, Grade 7
Battin School #4

Music

Music is everywhere I go.
Can you hear those beautiful notes?
Its tone could be sad.
Or maybe mad.
You can hear it on the streets.
And start getting the beat.
It's also in town.
Just listen it's all around.
You can hear it everywhere.
In anywhere.

Christian Trujillo, Grade 7
Garfield Middle School

Missing You

Even though you've passed on,
you'll never really be gone.
Every day I miss you,
and thinking of you makes me blue.
Someday I'll see you again,
but I don't know when.
Your heart always smiled,
even when you worried about your child.
My heart aches,
from the pain the grief makes.

Hollie David, Grade 8
Wall Intermediate Middle School

Snowflakes

Twirling down to the ground,
snowflakes drop like a ballerina.
A blanket on the city,
gracefully descending to the earth,
there is not a care in the world.
Watching another one fall,
creating space,
adjusting for impact
and waiting, they fall.
What a tremendous sight!

Craig Scharf, Grade 8
New Providence Middle School

Disappear

You were once here with me, then you disappeared
You gave me hugs and shared your love with me
Every day you were with me and now you're gone
You only left the memories we shared

You're in the ground for good
I can dig all I want and still won't be able to find you
I just stare at the stone that you are under
The stone writes the years you were here on earth

Once you were with me and now you're gone
It seems you just left me here in this place alone
I had you with me all the time until this day you just disappeared
You are just the ashes of the fire that float up and disappear into the sky

You're not coming back to this earth
I try to remember all the good times we had
There's so much love that we shared
You will always be here in my heart though now you're gone

Brianna Jacobs, Grade 8
Township of Ocean Intermediate School

Winter to Spring to Summer

As the snow comes down without a care,
As rain pours like no one's there,
All is well in the world as the sun shines bright right on you,
All of a sudden you realize that winter is no longer here.

A lovely fragrance fills my mind,
Then I walk into a field full of thousands of flowers in all different colors,
Some red, some white, and even some yellow,
As the day draws near all you see is a sea of beautiful colors right before your eyes.

The lovely sun shines on you,
Bringing a tan you've never seen,
As you are taking a walk into the forest,
All you see is life succoring around or stretching their limbs.

As the rain pours without a care,
As the weather starts to change like no one's there,
And the sun shines bright right on you,
All of a sudden you realize that spring is no longer here.

Taylor Overton, Grade 8
Westampton Middle School

Snow Days

Spreading throughout the streets,
and settling in the trees,
the snow comes falling down.
Holding me inside,
the snow helps me avoid stress from school.
Descending the temperature, forcing us to stay home, and permitting me to relax,
The weather is great at this time of year
Snow days are the best surprise of the year!

Don Gomber, Grade 8
New Providence Middle School

Cookies
A tasteful treat,
Creamy white,
Soothing blue,
Brilliant brown.
The aroma
fills the air,
Your taste buds dance
With joy.
As I eat the cookie,
My hunger is
No longer there.
Cookies.
The cookie is the snack
For when you are cold,
Your new best friend.
You can feel the warmth
As it passes
Through your throat.
From the first
Drop of milk to
The final ding of the oven.
Ian Galamay, Grade 7
Herbert Hoover Middle School

Winter
Windy, cold, snowy fun,
School's out for everyone!
Snowmen here
Snowmen there.
Houses at every corner
Dressed with bright lights.
Look outside,
What do you see?
Kids with snowballs
Ready to aim.
Look inside,
What do you see?
Fireplace, a Christmas
Tree, hot cocoa,
And the TV showing
Charlie Brown's Christmas.
Winter, bring on the smiles,
Bring on the smiles,
Bring on the fun.
Days that thrill everyone.
Winter!
Jurgena Fejzullah, Grade 8
Christopher Columbus Middle School

Scary Night
Haunting scary noise
Who makes this night so scary
I know who wants to
Krista McGuire, Grade 7
New Egypt Middle School

I Am
I am an artistic girl that loves dolphins
I wonder if I could ever own my own dolphin
I hear the splash of dolphins jumping through the waves
I see people for who they really are
I want world peace
I am an artistic girl that loves dolphins

I pretend that I don't care when I really do
I feel the smooth back of the dolphin, as I ride the waves
I touch the rippling water, circling my dolphin
I worry about my family and friends
I cry when someone dies or gets hurt
I am artistic girl that loves dolphins

I understand how hard it is for some people
I say we should work to make the world a better place
I dream that someday I will be able to come home to my own dolphin
I try to do well in school and be nice
I hope that in 2 years from now, there won't be any war
I am an artistic girl that loves dolphins
Sonika Kohli, Grade 7
Hammarskjold Middle School

Dance!
I am a fun girl who loves to dance.
I wonder if there ever was a dancer who did 50 leaps across a stage.
I hear the clacking of the tap shoes.
I see dancers twirling around in the sky.
I want to dance gracefully across a stage.
I am a fun girl who loves to dance.

I pretend I am a NY Rockette.
I feel the bright lights shining on me as I kick my leg up high in the air.
I touch the clouds as I jump up high.
I worry that I will fall and hurt my leg.
I cry when a dancer gets very injured.
I am a fun girl who loves to dance.

I understand I won't be able to dance forever.
I say, always succeed your dreams.
I dream about the day I am a famous dancer.
I try to be the best dancer in the world.
I hope to dance all my life.
I am a fun girl who loves to dance.
Angelea Villalona, Grade 7
Hammarskjold Middle School

The Delight of Monica
I am the icicle that slowly melts in the warm sun
I am the smooth glassy ice in a skating arena
I am the oxer jump of a midnight black thoroughbred
I am the hot-pink hibiscus that grows in the green lush of the tropical islands
I am the pink sand that lays underneath the refreshing aqua water
I am the quiet mouse that creeps during the night
Monica Paterno, Grade 7
Old Turnpike School

Basketball Is My Life

Basketball is the best
Never a time to give it a rest
The court is my home like a nest
I pass the rock like a test

The NBA is my quest
I am blessed with skill
On the court I kill
I am Ezra Hill

I give the assist
I never miss
Teamwork is on my list
I play the game

Take the pain
Your skill will gain
When you play me
I'm insane
Ezra Hill, Grade 8
Keyport High School

Rainy Days

When the sky cries,
It makes me cry too,
I don't know why
But it makes me feel blue

Though it is sunny, it's all a joke,
The wind is blowing and I feel a slight poke,
Nipping at my side, instead it is a stroke,

Instead of it awakening,
The sun decides not to,
So let be, please,
I will stand here as I feel blue,

I will awaken as soon as it's morning,
For without the rain, I am so boring,
I need it, I want it, I thirst it right now,
If it does not rain,
I will remain feeling down
Joelynn Hill, Grade 8
Westampton Middle School

The Rain

I feel the coldness
on my skin, as I
heard the wind
I know it's coming

It's clear as air
But cold as ice.
It is the rain.
Shannon O'Brien, Grade 7
Buckshutem Road Elementary School

Vicious Vampires

I am a spooky vampire.
I wonder if people will get scared of me.
I hear people already screaming.
I see other spooky vampires.
I want to have long fangs.
I want to be a spooky vampire.

I pretend to scare tons of people.
I feel that I am very scary.
I touch my rough black coat.
I worry that someone won't be scared of me.
I cry that tonight is the night.
I am a spooky vampire.

I understand that I try too hard to be scary.
I say that it's frightening time.
I dream that it will definitely happen.
I try to scare some people by jumping out at them when it's really dark out.
I hope it works out fine.
I am a spooky vampire.
Conor Schaible, Grade 7
New Egypt Middle School

The Desperate Sea

The salty, silken, satin surf washes against the shore.
It breaks open like an eggshell
only to be slurped back by the vast flood of sea.
The cycle repeats.
The wetness reaches further, further.
Reaching for an unknown object that could very well not exist.
Reaching…reaching…never achieving.
The cries of the desperate sea fill my ears and senses.
Salty spray stings my face and envelopes me in a cloud of mist.
I can taste…only what can be described as pure joy
And it dances in my mouth.
It tickles my tongue
The wetness under my feet turns the once sturdy shore into quicksand.
Slowly, slowly my feet slip under the sand: my heels then my ankles.
Arms outstretched, I feel as if the ocean responds to my joy
becoming a little happier, more alive.
Suddenly its quest for the unknown object
does not seem so impossible,
and the salty wetness seeps forward
Once more…Once more…Once more…
Sara Stark, Grade 8
William R Satz Middle School

Artistic Artinburack

This is an Artinburack.
It lives in attics, apartments, animals, and Arkansas.
An Artinburack eats artichokes, apples, ankles, and automobiles.
It likes arguing, attacking, analyzing, and answering.
It acts like an acrobat, asks annoying questions, and has attitude.
Yesterday an Artinburack ambled into my room, annoyed me, and ate this awesome poem.
Shira Blain, Grade 7
Kellman Brown Academy

The Poor Little Scarecrow
Poor little scarecrow,
Waiting in the field,
Protecting all the corn stalks
Like a big oversized shield.

Poor little scarecrow,
Arms full of hay,
Not even the slightest fright
Could scare the crows away.

Poor little scarecrow,
Watching the hay rides go about,
Wishing you could be there,
Instead of your insides being pecked out.
Robert Dunphy, Grade 7
Herbert Hoover Middle School

The Only Snow I Know
The palest snow falls to Earth
The sky a steel-like gray
The sun eclipsed by endless clouds
The shadows dance and sway.

Amber flames pop against the wood
Smoke rises through the cracks
Into the heavens they go
From the chimney black.

So out into the sheet of frost
Yes, out into the snow I go
Oh, how I love a Jersey storm
The only snow I know.
Emily Scialabba, Grade 8
Linwood Middle School

Welcome to the Future
Welcome to the future
It isn't like the past.
Thanks to new technology
Today will be a blast.
But we should be more careful,
More energy be saved
We can't renew all resources
The road will soon be paved.
Although we love technology
It might harm Mother Earth
We need to take a look around
And decide what life's worth.
So glance around and take a stand
Make what's right your first command.
Laura Lin, Grade 7
St James School

Victory
My palms slams into elastic skin,
sending shots of pain back at the
opponent.

My eyes dart across,
ready for a counterattack.
I hear the screech
from across the court,
and my body shifts,
bringing my hands up.

My legs sprint across,
following the flying ball.
Readying myself,
I slap my hand through
the air, sending my
energy back towards them.

I watch as the ball
plops down.
The smack heard loudly.
I smirk proudly.

Victory.
Helen Caicedo, Grade 7
Schuyler Elementary School

Beauty Is a Starry Night
Beauty is a starry night
sitting all alone
spending hours watching
your mind straying far from home.

Beauty is forgetting
all that's going on
staring at a shooting star
from sunset until dawn.

Beauty is the feeling of
peace and conciliation
listening to the crickets
lost in relaxation.

Beauty is the tingling
from your head down to your toes
the feeling of serenity
as you try to recompose.

Beauty is a starry night
sitting all alone
spending hours watching
your mind straying far from home.
Cory Skloff, Grade 8
Township of Ocean Intermediate School

Apart
I was so scared about the future,
about what would happen.
I thought you would suffer,
and cry every night,
just like me.

I'd go back to you and apologize,
but you don't want me,
you don't even need me.

Eight years ago we promised forever,
through everything thick and thin.
But I changed,
you changed,
and we eventually grew apart.

I love you,
and if what you need is time,
take as long as you need.

I miss our forever,
I miss our stories,
I miss our laughs,
I miss us.
Allison Bowler, Grade 8
Markham Place Elementary School

Permanent Heartbreak
I've got those love sick blues.
I feel them more than ever.
How could you do this to me?
Looks like your guitar
wasn't the only thing being played.

You used to be the harmony in my heart.
Now you're just a sad jazz song.

I loved when you played
guitar for me.
"My Beautiful Rescue."
You were mine.
I wasn't yours.

I listened to music to quiet
my broken heart.
It screamed to me,
from all the pain
you put it through.
Sometimes I miss the way
you made my heart sing.
I finally found the nerve to say,
I never loved you anyway.
Ashley Moraski, Grade 7
Schuyler Elementary School

Thanksgiving

Entering the house
I smell wonderful turkey
The football game is on TV
My father is baking
Five pies
I set the table
Silverware clanks
The food is out
I'm excited
I feel hungry
I put food on my plate
And dig in
The turkey was good
I feel stuffed
I help clear the table
Time for dessert
Pies, cake and ice cream
That was good
Very tired
Going to sleep now

Taylor Sheridan, Grade 8
Keyport High School

Summer

Summer days are clear and warm
I hear kids splashing in the pool
Seagulls flying in the sky
Smell of the crisp cut grass
Listening to the birds chirping
Smell of summer air
Yumm! Ice cold lemonade
Are you ready to swim?
The beaches are full of people
Clear blue skies
Going to the beach with friends
The nights are cool and full of stars
Summer has just begun
Going to the beach
Sand between my toes
The sound of the waves crashing
Now it's time for school
Summer's over
Getting out of school
It's still too hot

Brianna Hicks, Grade 8
Keyport High School

iPods

iPods are musical instruments.
They are little musical friends.
iPods are a vacation to a music video.
They are relaxation to a teenager.
iPods are relaxing and loud.
They are a little peace of heaven.

Joshua John, Grade 7
Galloway Township Middle School

My Inner Thoughts

Every single day, I cannot wait to see your charming face.
Whenever I hear your melodic voice, tiny butterflies escape throughout my body.
I really hate the way you make me feel, I wish it would soon end.
I never thought I could imagine these things about you, I thought we would only be friends.
I'm trying really hard to express my emotions to you, but I just don't know how.
You have no clue how much I feel for you,
I feel as if I'm shouting your name as loud as I can
So you can hear my desperate pleading.
Every night I always ask myself the same question, thinking of a way to answer them.
Can't you see how much I care for you?
Do you have the same feelings towards me?
Are we even meant to be?
I know there will never be any hope for you and me,
No matter how much I try to believe I can no longer hold back these salty tears,
This strong pain just hurts me very much. Maybe someday…
I will tell you how much you mean to me and I'll promise you it'll be face to face
For now the only way I can express this feeling deep, down inside of me is in three words
I…
Love…
You…

Lourdes Mendez, Grade 7
Battin School #4

I Am

I am a teen, waiting for the world to change.
I wonder if people will see the world like I do.
I hear people fighting for world peace.
I see an amazing world, but can reach it.
I want help from others, but no one speaks.
I am a teen waiting for the world to change.

I pretend that I can be anything. Do anything.
I feel the weight of the world on my shoulders when life gets tough.
I touch God's tears when the rain comes down.
I cry when I've had enough.
I am a teen waiting for the world to change.

I understand that perfection can't happen.
I say we should at least try and give.
I dream about my life the way it should be,
I try to take life day by day and live.
I hope that things get better, maybe to not be so strange but no matter what
I am a teen waiting for the world to change.

Michelle McCarthy, Grade 8
St Mary School

For What Cause?

Squirming quickly,
the worm searches for a place to rest.
Toiling hard every day,
not to notice that in a second he could be squished.
Slithering fast, wiggling rapidly, and meandering,
he finds a way to live with the little guidance he has.
On this planet, these creatures make a difference in life, but the question is, for what cause?

Ryan Malone, Grade 8
New Providence Middle School

Leaves

Once green, gently hanging on the trees
Shading me while the summer breeze blows by
Its canopy sheltering the birds from rain drops

Then the days begin to get shorter
While the birds are flocking together
The colors start to change from green
To bright red, yellow and rusty orange

A colder breeze begins blows stronger
And what was once a colorful show
Are now brown and burnt gold
Holding onto the same limb that now tries to shake them free

Now lying crumbled on the ground
Crunching under my feet
Making a bed all around the tree
Are the leaves.

Andrea Sammons, Grade 7
Woodland Country Day School

The Restless Sea

I am water.
My mouth is salty as I drink betrayal
And drown out the taste.

My body is battered
As I am hit with blows
From resentful words
Spoken to me.
My waves barreling
Over all my enemies
As they try to swim on my body.

Their feet digging into me —
Their hands — scythes slashing through me.
Their slovenly execrable and baleful bodies contaminated my soul.
I am no longer benevolent. They have turned me pernicious.
I will now plunge them into the depths of my soul
Where they will never be found.

Stephon Thompson, Grade 7
Galloway Township Middle School

About Me

Cody
Intelligent, creative, artistic and friendly
Brother of Dylan
Loves animals, water parks and movies
Who feels nervous on the first day of school, tired in the morning,
Annoyed when doing homework
Who needs less homework more sleep, less school
Who gives advice to others, money to family and food to animals
Who would like to have no homework or tests
A resident of East Brunswick

Cody Haws, Grade 7
Hammarskjold Middle School

Ghosts

Ghosts and ghouls roaming around
While we trick or treat.
Coming along beside you
Nothing to help and hide you they will find you
Ghosts cats and dogs, ghost people creeping around
Around for people to scare
Ghosts Ghosts Ghoooooosssssttttttttttttssssssss
Ghosts rising from their graves on Halloween night
Chilly winds everywhere moans and groans coming
Out of every corner every creepy house
Kids screaming out of every house
Ghosts and ghouls every where trick or treating
Kids go to houses ringing door bells "trick or treat" kids will say,
"Trick or treat" a ghost will say when the kids arrive
Screaming kids will run away!
Mwahahahahahahahahahahaahhh
All the ghosts will laugh at the screaming kids,
Moans and groans everywhere you hear
Who can it be?
GHOSTS!!!

Collin Kowalski, Grade 7
Hammarskjold Middle School

Halloween Night

Greedy kids with 20 huge bags run around
fill them with candy over and over again.

It's raining candy,
a long hail shower.

Everyone's running, shoving,
to gather the candy,
as if it was Armageddon.

Kids run home with full bags of candy
to dump it all in their candy vault.

Then some come back out to see
if they can find their next victim.

The kids start dreaming about Hershey, Reese's, 3 Musketeers —
all of their favorite candies.

The Halloween countdown starts again.

Urvish Patel, Grade 7
Galloway Township Middle School

True Beauty

She always told me, "No need to run away."
She stood by me and told me, "Everything's okay."
She helped me to find who I really was
And she did it just "Because"
I am her daughter and she is my mom;
True Beauty that will never be gone!

Antonia Mercado, Grade 8
Garfield Middle School

Opposing Moods of Chincoteague
The roundup has come!
The ice-cold ocean makes me numb
A spotted colt neighs loudly
And his mother nuzzles him proudly
A herd bolts past my eyes
But their speed is no surprise
You can smell the horsey smell
And taste humidity as well!

The commotion is gone!
Warmth comes with the peaceful dawn
Silence is the only sound
A pony walks by, homeward bound
You can feel the gentle breeze
And taste the salty seas
This is where I feel free
The only place I want to be
Rachel Horn, Grade 8
New Egypt Middle School

I Love Winter!
Snowflakes are flying in the air,
Little children go out to stare.
They run out in the cold and cheer,
"Yay! No school!"
They're running as if they have a
Toy store all to themselves.
Plop! To the ground one by one.
Flying through the snow
Flapping their arms and legs.
Pop back up and see their little angels.
As they run back inside
They look back to find
Their little angels flying away.
Now sitting by a cozy fire,
Drinking hot chocolate.
The children look out the window,
Thinking, I love winter!
Gabriela Morfin, Grade 8
New Egypt Middle School

Colorful Winged Friend
Look up
What do you see?
It's special to me
Floating above the tree
It's graceful
It's peaceful
It's blue, red and green
It has eyes
It has wings
What a beautiful thing
What a special friend
My friend the butterfly
Kalee Neal, Grade 8
Township of Ocean Intermediate School

Around the World
You see both almost every day
Flying through the air
Stop to eat the little nuts
Or some black gold

All across a country
Or maybe around the world
A small stop here and there
To go almost anywhere

Loud like thunder
Soft like a whisper
The smell of oil in the air
And the soft, soft feathers
Neal Vinaixa, Grade 7
New Providence Middle School

Urge of Comprehension
It hunts my mind
Day and night
What I find
Is a dreadful sight

I need to know
What it desires
Might not ever show
Show me what it admires

My dreams are filled with terror
I might be getting paranoid
When I look in the mirror
I feel horror I can't avoid
Gabriela Jedryczka, Grade 7
Garfield Middle School

The Singer
As she takes the stage
She softly turns each page

Happiness fills her up inside
Those nervous feelings are set aside

As she sings, her voice is so pure
For any disease this is a cure

Each audience member is truly amazed
How can they help looking so dazed

Her last notes of this beautiful night
Show her in a surprising light.
Carolyn Field, Grade 7
St Mary's School

Is It Love?
Is it you I think about
Every night and every day
That I go crazy
Just by your sight
The word
"LOVE"
Keeps running in my mind
Is It Love?
Every time I hear your
Name I go wild
So just to say
Is It Love?
I think it's you I love
Is It Love?
Taniyah Wiseman, Grade 7
Battin School #4

Winter
Winter is coming
The snow is falling
The icicles are getting bigger
And it is getting colder

The kids make snow angels
And throw snowballs at each other
Adults plow the drive
So they don't have to miss a day of work

The fires are getting warmer
Houses are warmer
The sun comes up
Like always the snow melts away
Ryan Hagen, Grade 8
New Egypt Middle School

Winter
Winter is arriving
Snow covers the ground
The leaves have fallen
Houses heated by fire

Hot chocolate is made
The drinks were as hot as the sun
Everyone trapped in their homes
Houses covered in snow

Everyone trying to stay warm
You can only hear the wind blowing
It is freezing outside
Christmas is near
Trevor Cardone, Grade 8
New Egypt Middle School

Fall

I eat apple pie
Jumping in leaves at my house
I'm helping cook meals

My mom making pie
Picking apples and pumpkins
Raking leaves for friends

Going to parades
I'm playing soccer with friends
I'm doing school work

Jesse Liguori, Grade 7
New Egypt Middle School

Falling Fun Fall

Flickering candles
Cold air is hitting your face
Leaves are falling fast

Bags full of candy
Kids are running house to house
Trick-or-treating fun

Carmel, chocolate, mint
There are so many other kinds
All tasty candy

Michael Cardella, Grade 7
New Egypt Middle School

Writing

With endless possibilities,
At every comma, period, and paragraph,
Each idea pulls you further in.

It twists and turns,
Taking you on a wild adventure,
Not knowing where you will end up.

Writing is a marvelous thing,
That has no limitations,
And endless possibilities.

James Marriott, Grade 7
New Providence Middle School

Winter

The winter season is very cold.
Ice and snow cover the streets,
causing people to have frostbitten feet.
Though winter stories never get old,
every year the same stories are told.
In the winter you have certain treats,
and because of the hot chocolate,
you are always ready to eat.
The winter season is very cold.

Steven Masino, Grade 8
St Mary School

Midnight Delight

Dark shadows loomed through the empty streets of night
The moonless starry-sky was the only witness to this sight.
Far below on the streets were small feet that scurried away, for he was the bait!
And out from the shadows was the butcher's hungry cat who soon filled his plate.
The others hurried past the cat into the kitchen's storage
That poor tiny soul would never be forgotten for his courage.
The divine smell of cheese, fruit, and meat
With spices, vegetables, pastries, and wheat,
All lay ahead just waiting to be found,
All creatures were quite careful not to make a sound,
Their whiskers trickled and brushed against the food,
Just to tease their palate and get them in the mood.
But once they were so very full,
They knew they had more weight to pull.
Now up the slippery pipes they struggled all that night
Finally to fall into thatched nests of delight.
Then all the tiny, delicate feet suddenly stopped to sleep
As each mouse huddled for warmth in the family heap.

Veronica Kelly, Grade 7
Oxford Street School

School

School is coming, it's almost here.
Finally seeing all your old friends, and making new ones.
Visiting your past teachers, and getting to know your new teachers.
Playing sports with your closest friends, or doing a project with a group.
How proud you get when you ace a really hard test!
Thinking you can't wait for the weekend,
and when it comes you're lying on the bed thinking what to do.
Having so much fun at school,
and then you hear the last bell ring on the last day of school.
Just crying to yourself trying to suck it up.
Reminiscing the memories, and looking through your yearbook.
These are the things you would normally do.
School is my closest friend.
I always rely on it to boost my self-esteem.
I love school because it's everything I've ever wanted.
I met new people easily because of it; so many things happened here.
I'll never forget why I love school.

Haris Muric, Grade 7
Garfield Middle School

Coal

Underneath blankets, on a bed, he sleeps the day away.
On the bed he stretches and rolls while dreaming of treats, scratching posts and catnip.
After he awakes, he slowly decides if he'll play with his sister Lucy, explore or eat.
Between your legs he twists and turns, attempting to get your attention.
Within seconds, he impatiently wails for his food like a siren.
Upon devouring his meal he seeks out Lucy and me.
From me he wants to cuddle before he hunts down Lucy for a rough play session.
In a short while he is exhausted and finds refuge behind the bed or couch.
Across the room, my parents and I can see his little gray head peering out.
Amid my papers and books he often sits while I do my homework.
Against my side he sleeps at night, purring and dreaming once again.

Tracy Homann, Grade 8
Clinton Public School

The Black Sky
The sky was crying
While jets killed it
And the sky was falling.

The jets roared at the people
Like a lion.
The sky was under the jets' feet
While the jets started shooting.

The sky called for help
As the jets giggled.
The sky took intervenous
While the jets punched and kicked.

The sky started collapsing
As the jets took it apart.
The sky was drowning.

The sky doomed as
The jets enjoy the horror.
Abdullah Panah, Grade 7
Galloway Township Middle School

Happy Hopping Halloween
I am creepy and cool
I wonder what's around the corner
I hear nails on a chalkboard
I see a goblin
I want to be the scariest costume
I am creepy and cool

I pretend I creeped everyone away
I feel that my candy bag is heavy
I touch the underworld
I worry that something is going to get me
I cry that I don't have enough candy
I am creepy and cool

I understand that I am really spooky
I say try to be scarier than me
I dream about all the sweets
I try to be the biggest treat collector
I hope for tons of sugar coated delights
I am creepy and cool
Eric Katz, Grade 7
New Egypt Middle School

Summer
S unny more often
U nder the water I go
M ad is not what you're feeling
M eeting new friends every day
E ager to play
R ising up with a smile every day
Courtney McCarthy, Grade 7
Lakeside Middle School

My Best Friend
I walked into kindergarten class as nervous as can be
You took my hand and smiled ever so sweetly at me.

You told me your favorite things to do and they were the same as mine
We clicked instantly and began to hang out all the time.

Barbies and playing dress up were our favorite things to do
Together we even learned how to tie our own shoe.

As we said good bye to the young years and welcomed the new
I threw out all our Barbies and our fancy clothes, too.

Friday night sleep overs after shopping at the mall
We painted our nails, fixed our hair, and ended the night with a hilarious prank call.

You were there when I got my first ear piercing and held my hand tight
You made me feel good by complimenting it all that night.

I've told you all my secrets and can trust you very well
You applauded me for being brave and coming out of my shell.

When times got rough and I sometimes was ready to give up the fight
You always told me that at the end of the tunnel there would be light.

We know everything about each other so there's no need to pretend
I love you with all my heart and am honored to call you my best friend.
Jillian Higbee, Grade 7
William Davies Middle School

Golf with a Pro
"Tee up, Mooch!" he declares.
BAM!!! Into the woods.
"It's ok, hit another one."
"Close the club face. It makes a tremendous difference," he informs me.
I nod in amazement.
How can he pick that up in my split second of a swing?

The pro steps up to the tee, Shhh!
The quiet signs are up.
SWOOSH!
Right down the middle
straight as an arrow.

I clap, but he says he could do better.
I think no way you can do better than that.
I guess that's his way of showing off.
After that hole it is a long day,
I don't play so well but he does.
It keeps my spirits up to see him so happy.

As we finish hole number 18 I'm upset,
but I don't show it because I play with a pro.
It's a once in a lifetime opportunity.
On the way home, I realize that pro is my Grandpa.
Adam French, Grade 7
Schuyler Elementary School

Sense of Fall

As I walk downstairs,
My feet are bare.
I put on my mittens,
So I wouldn't get frostbitten.

As I skipped outside,
I realize all the leaves had died.
The leaves hit the ground,
Without a sound.

As acorns bounce down the street,
I think to myself what a great beat.
All of the leaves in shades of red,
Paint a picture in my head.

The sky is crystal blue,
And the clouds are white as glue.
The cold wind in my face,
Made me walk at a fast pace.

Ashlyn Borik, Grade 7
New Egypt Middle School

Art

Art;
It is a beautiful thing,
It makes my heart sing.
You can splatter it, Paint it;
Do what you want.
Whatever you do,
It comes from the heart.
From stick figures, to detailed drawings;
Creativity is made.
From Black and white, to color;
Do it quick before it fades.
From singing, to dancing;
Art comes in many forms.
From instruments, to fashion;
Creativity is born.
From acting, to drawing;
They have gotten great pride.
From reading, to writing;
Pictures come alive.

Heather Olson, Grade 8
Cedar Drive Middle School

Gone

You were here
But now your gone
Wouldn't think this day would come
We weren't very close
I will miss you
And I want you to know
I love you

Michella Wayne, Grade 7
Robert Morris Public School

The Delight Song of Anna

I am a vibrant sunset in the coral and blue sky above
I am a radiant rainbow right after a rain storm
I am a mystical creature from a far away land
I am a fierce lion in a herd of zebras
I am one of the many unique snowflakes that drifts from the arctic sky
I am a lost pet all alone in the threatening wilderness
I am the loyal friend that cheers people up when they are sad
I am a role model for a group of classmates who look up to me
I am one of the many who strives to accomplish goals
I am an honest and good person; I am Anna

Anna Babiuk-Murray, Grade 7
Old Turnpike School

Wonderful Washington

Without a worry or a care, we went to the airport.
Between my sister and the bags, I am excited for the trip.
Through the window I look and see the planes ready for takeoff.
Inside the plane, the pilot tells us to get ready to go.
Above the clouds we soar, heading for our final destination.
Beside a stranger who snores, I look at my sister and try not to laugh.
Until now everything is fine; we hit turbulence and have to take cover.
Beyond the window is the darkening sky.
Near the ground we head and get our bags from under the seats.
Behind the cars and trucks, my family and I head to my aunt's house in Spokane.

Meghan Gregory, Grade 8
Clinton Public School

The Delight Song of Ava

I am the only pebble in a sea of pearls
I am the sunrise in a time of darkness
I am the hard working soldier trying to win a war
I am the untapped potential of Michael Jordan in high school
I am the seven year old wanting to make a change
I am the last leaf to fall off the trees in November
I am the Ferrari crossing the finish line first
I am the sword of a fighter conquering all of its battles
I am one of the only owls still up at midnight preparing for the next day
I am the last one shooting the basketball when practice has ended

Ava Solina, Grade 7
Old Turnpike School

The Delight Song of Robert Berman

I am the glowing and luminous sunshine of my family
I am a beach ball on a hot summer's day
I am the bumpy rock on a high and steep mountain
I am the extraordinary baseball player that made his dream come true
I am the brightest star in the big and dark galaxy
I am the angel that makes everyone happy all the time
I am the one that wants peace, happiness, and love in this world
I am the three in pi out of all the numbers
I am the one that wants it for others instead of him
I am Robert

Robert Berman, Grade 7
Old Turnpike School

I Am a Goalie

I am a wall
A guard at my posts
I keep intruders out
'Till they're down for the count
For I am a wall

I am a soldier
A warrior standing strong
I play hard 'till the end
And never give in
For I am a soldier

I am a hero
A keeper of my net
I'm a soldier standing tall
I'm as tough as a wall
For I am a Goalie
Bailey Herr, Grade 8
Township of Ocean Intermediate School

Steak

A juicy meat,
Golden brown,
Scrumptious black,
Shiny yellow,
I hear it cook.
I smell the aroma.
I see the amazing meat.
The awesome steak,
The wondrous scent,
The delicious taste,
When it reaches your mouth,
You swallow and get the taste.
I am no longer famished.
The taste overpowers the mind.
Just like,
A dog
When it receives a bone.
Eugene Selby, Grade 7
Herbert Hoover Middle School

Grandparents

Warm, loving, and happy
I call them mama and pappy
She taught me to cook
He taught me to fish
I always get a hug and a kiss
I'm always welcome no matter what
Whenever I go I get a buckeye nut
They are my world
When I'm with them I'm never bored
Their hugs are like prodigious teddy bears
They're always fun
What can I say they're my number one
Kayla Bancroft, Grade 8
New Egypt Middle School

Progression of Life

A seed is planted in the ground
Soft, warm hands cover it
While pressing dirt down
Patiently waiting
Week by week
Slowly
A green sprout rises
The gardener smiles
Moment by moment
The flower grows
Until there is a small bud
Petal by petal
It begins to bloom
Until
Flower by flower
The plant is grown
Paola Batarseh, Grade 8
Little Falls School #1

God's Love

God's love is always with me
He never leaves me alone
Because every time I'm in trouble
He treats my problems like His own
His power is like sunshine
Which lightens up my fears
He's watching over upon me
So, my eyes are not filled with tears
In presence of the Almighty God
It's impossible to frown
Because you feel high spirited
He won't let you feel let down
He always makes me realize
There's nothing I have to face alone
His presence is like magic
And my love for Him has grown
Herleen Kaur, Grade 8
Township of Ocean Intermediate School

Zakiya Douglas

Z eal
A dorable
K een
I ntelligent
Y earning
A rtistic

D ecent
O utragous
U nselfish
G lamorous
L ovable
A wesome
S uccessful
Zakiya Douglas, Grade 7
Lakeside Middle School

Color

There are many colors in the world

Red is the color of evil power
Pink is the color of a lovely flower

Green is the color of a big wild dragon
Orange is the color of a bright wagon

Blue is the color of the bright blue sky
Purple is the color of a nice tie

Gray is the color that makes you snore
Brown is the color that gives you bore

How do colors make you feel?
Kulsum Khan, Grade 8
Linwood Middle School

Away

We try to run away

Away from what is undesirable
Away from what is frightening
Away from what is upsetting
Away…

We try to hide away

Away from what can hurt
Away from what can hate
Away from what can love
Away…

We try only to fall short
Caroline Weiner, Grade 8
Township of Ocean Intermediate School

Autumn

There's a time of the year
that everyone recognizes.
It's the time of the year when
colorful leaves fall to the ground.
This season is called autumn.
Autumn is when it is a bit chilly,
And later on it's cold.
It's the time of the year where
Families rake leaves together.
It's the time of the year when
squirrels gather nuts for the winter.
It's the time of the year when
some birds fly away to hotter countries.
It's the time of the year when
We get ready for winter.
Marta Zak, Grade 7
Garfield Middle School

The Soundtrack to Our Friendship

The sound of the ball
hitting the floor
The sound of the whistle
echoing through the crowd
The sound of the sneakers
squeaking across the court
We all thought that this was
the soundtrack to our friendship.

We heard no more
of the ball hitting the floor
no more of the whistle
echoing through the crowd
no more sneakers
squeaking across the court
the song had ended
but our friendship did not.

Danielle Rachubinski, Grade 8
St Mary School

Still Scarecrow

All day I wait
For someone to scare
I can't move
I'm stuck on a pole
Oh look!
Someone is near
Time to scare them
Booooo!
Look at him run
My life is boring
My life is dull
I find enjoyment
In children's fear
I wait all day
I wait all night
To give someone a fright
Look here comes someone else

Nicholas Bergen, Grade 8
Keyport High School

What If

What if the world was to end today
What if we could just run away
What if the grass refused to grow
What if you caught the tiger by the toe
What if we were able to fly
What if we never had to say good-bye
What if the earth stopped turning 'round
What if all people lived underground
What if all food we ate was rotten
What if the clouds were made of cotton
What if the world was finally free
What if you be you and I be me

Rosa Franzé, Grade 8
Township of Ocean Intermediate School

You Think?

Time is a valuable thing
You wake up to alarm clock's ring
You think
Where did the day go?
People are missing
You realize that you weren't dreaming
You think
where did they go?
You see people laughing
Is at you or with you?
You think
What do they know?
You can barely talk
You don't know if you can walk
You think
Where can I go?
You lie there wondering
Is your time up?
You think

Where did the time go?

Jake Hansen, Grade 9
Holy Cross High School

Nighttime New York City

Sun setting, night is coming
Bright night lights light up the dark
Busy New York night a-humming
Walking in caliginous Central Park.
Broadway marquees, restaurants aglow
Coming home from work you will see
All building lights through the window
Everyone as busy as a bee.
City musicians are still playing
While feeling the coldness of the night
Constant scent of food still staying
Some people are afright.
Taste the smoke in the air
It's not the nicest feeling
A whiff of smog fumes isn't rare
Games of Chance, 5 Card Monty dealing.
On Broadway many plays are showing
Little Mermaid and *Lion King* only a few
In *Wicked*, the tornado still is blowing
Who knows what else is new?
Another amazing night in New York City.

Devin North, Grade 7
New Egypt Middle School

Raindrop

mist, wetness
falling, nourishing, cleansing
It drips from the fog
dewdrop, sprinkle

Veronica Bonano, Grade 7
Lakeside Middle School

Growing Up too Fast

We have all been there.
But some have forgotten
What it is like being a kid.
Too many things to do.
Not enough time for fun.
They make us grow up too fast.

More homework and chores
Than ever before.
Not our choice;
It was theirs.

There is more expected of us,
A little too much.
Can't you see?
We just want to be kids.

No one understands.
Even though they say they do.
We can tell when you're lying

Just let us be kids.
We will grow up,
But let us take our time.
We'll all get there when we're ready.

Brianna Sandorse, Grade 9
Red Bank Regional High School

Angel of Darkness

In the Garden of Delight
Love and Beauty reign
The skies are bright
The waters warm
The Angels of Light play games and laugh

But at night
Tonight!
The Angel of Darkness
Will change everything
To make paradise for itself

When Darkness falls
Pain is all
The Angel of Darkness
Will leave behind
One Angel will fight

A one-on-one battle
Dark vs. Light
Love vs. Hate
The Light has lost
Darkness consumes

The Darkness is our new kingdom

Jeanine Hila, Grade 8
Keyport High School

The Delight Song of Harley

I am the crowd pleaser at a prime time comedy central show in NYC
I am the sun shining down on the planet Earth
I am a Mr. T blowing up a Ferrari in an action movie
I am a car going down the freeway at 80 miles per hour
I am a skydiver pulling his parachute at the last second
I am a loud boom of thunder roaring across the sky
I am the last leaf falling off the tree to make it winter

Harley Sacks, Grade 7
Old Turnpike School

The Delight Song of Nancy

I am the middle string on a Fender Firebird guitar
I am a bright yellow leaf on a fall tree
I am the golden retriever that is always by your side
I am the leather that makes up a softball glove
I am the stars that give people light during the night
I am the goldfish in a world of ravenous sharks
I am a bright light that shines during the darkest night

Nancy Donoghue, Grade 7
Old Turnpike School

A Tiny Teek

This is a Tiny Teek.
It lives in teeth, tongues, tables, totes, and teabags.
A Tiny Teek eats tator tots, tomatoes, tangerines, and tables.
It likes tumbling, teasing toddlers, tasting, thumping, and tripping.
It tattles, taps, tidies, and traps.
One day a Tiny Teek tiptoed into my room
and took tissues to make a tree as tall as the Tiny Teek.

Sophia Reznik, Grade 7
Kellman Brown Academy

Delight Song of Marc

I am the middle tooth in my cool friend's mouth.
I am a papa bear watching over my little cubs.
I am an equation in a really hard math class.
I am a cloud in a sky of bright stars.
I am a dolphin in a school of slimy stingrays.
I am a blue feather on a toucan in the rain forest.
I am a period in a 70,000,000 long page book.

Marc Pineiro, Grade 7
Old Turnpike School

Dangling Dlaughterluck

This is a Dlaughterluck
It lives in dumps, dens, ditches, and Detroit.
A Dlaughterluck eats ducks, donuts, dandelions, and deer.
It likes dancing, drilling, drawing, and dangling.
It doodles, digs, and devours.
One day a Dlaughterluck dangled into my room from a rope,
doodled on my desk, and downed my donuts.

Lior Algrably, Grade 7
Kellman Brown Academy

The Christmas Tree

Trekking through the sweet smelling pines,
I searched to find that perfect tree.
Inspecting and finding that special tree
Could take hours for us to do.
Scanning through, sweetly scented, swaying pines,
I'm determined to find that perfect tree.
I finally found that perfect tree.

Nicole Carolan, Grade 8
New Providence Middle School

The Delight Song of Kristian Tonnesen

I am the tree that holds up my family from danger
I am the last leaf to fall off the tree of life
I am the shining ornament on the dull, boring tree
I am the crunchiest apple in the award winning pie
I am the cloud that cries when there is a crummy day
I am the funniest commercial that played during the Super Bowl
I am the music disc being reached for right before the driver crashes

Kristian Tonnesen, Grade 7
Old Turnpike School

Tiger Lily

Flourishing among a terrace of tulips,
the Tiger Lily stands out with its tangerine color.
Towering above the rest,
it soaks up the rays of the rose-colored sun as it rises into the sky.
As winter rolls in and the air turns cold,
the Tiger Lily begins to fade away and is swept along with the wind
What a lovely flower it was!

Sarah Clowes-Walker, Grade 8
New Providence Middle School

Evergreen Ecstasy

Tiptoeing through the fields,
An icy wind bites my nose, but I steadily venture forward.
Lining my path
Are fraisers and firs.
Then, singing, glowing, and illuminating to my eyes
Stands the tree, our tree.
Oh, how lovely, crisp, and green.

Lena Miskulin, Grade 8
New Providence Middle School

The Life of the Beach Awakens

Relaxing in the sun,
I allow the heat to hit my face.
Cushioning at my feet,
the sand feels so great.
Squawking above, squishing between my toes, tumbling besides me,
the spirit of the beach embraces me.
Peaceful and entertaining, the life of the beach awakens.

Natalie Barrett, Grade 8
New Providence Middle School

The Changing of Holiday

Hearts, flowers, chocolates galore,
Red roses, caramels and so much more.
"I love you" and "Be Mine" are on those candy hearts,
Be sure to give them to somebody with smarts.
I love the taste of cookies and hot cocoa,
They always make me go loco.
Although I love this wonderful holiday,
It is almost over to my dismay.
Halloween is almost here,
It is the scariest time of the year.
Pumpkins, candy, ghouls, and ghosts,
The blinking light of the street lampposts.
As you ring the doorbell,
Be sure not to yell!!!
The monsters might get you, and scream "BOO!!!"
Staying out late is so much fun,
It's ten o'clock,
Too bad we are done!!!

Danielle Exner, Grade 7
New Egypt Middle School

Winter

Winter comes and winter goes
but when it snows it always shows.
Without a fight it comes in a delight.
Kids play outside until they are
as cold to touch as a snowman.
Then they come back inside to have some
mouthwatering hot chocolate
and then they're back outside again
Building big towering slippery, snowmen.
When winter finally ends it's off to summer we go.
No more icicles but now there's popsicles.
No more frigid freezing days,
but now warm welcoming warmth
exceeding from the gleaming sun.
Flowers are blooming,
showers make the day start glooming
but then and again comes winter.

Jon Scutellaro, Grade 8
New Egypt Middle School

Hunt in the River

Running up and down the river,
I see a frog
I try to catch it in my green net,
fish trapped in pools,
They leave and the river pulls
fear strikes
If they leave the pool at the trunk of the tree,
moss glimmers in the light,
Spots of light shine on the tree,
I catch one,
It is over.

Lil Sloginski, Grade 7
Garfield Middle School

Summer

In the summer there are vibrant, beautiful colors everywhere to see
Others are nice and cold inside but not me
The scaly, slimy fish swerve and spin
The water is moving there might be a wind
As the branches "whoosh" and shake in the breeze
I'm covered in sweat down to my knees
The orange, bright sun burns on our faces
I need something cold, I check all places
I am on fire, I am burning red hot
I need something cold, I need a lot
We hurried fast, and sprinted into the store
I was looking for ice cream but they don't have anymore
"What do I do on this hot, bright day?"
"I have an idea I'll give the hose a spray"
I'm drenched in water out on the lawn
Now the heat and my problem, both are all gone.

Jacob Taylor, Grade 7
New Egypt Middle School

School

Chalk marks on teacher's pants.
Coffee stains on graded tests,
Red pens marking F's and corrections,
Broken pencils stuck in the heater,
Ripped off erasers in the air,
Squeaky chairs,
Eraser shavings all over the floor,
Gum under the desks,
Teachers yelling at kids running in the hallway,
Papers stuck in between lockers,
Cell phones ringing in the middle of class,
Broken glasses,
Worn out textbooks,
Bragging when getting a test,
Getting yelled at for chewing gum,
Notes being passed in class.

David Ramirez, Grade 7
William Davies Middle School

Through the Eyes of a Child

Watching stars twinkle at midnight
Loving someone with all your might

Laughing until tears stream down your face
Growing up, at your very own pace

Twirling around until your sight is unclear
Singing at the top of your lungs for all to hear

Finally accepting that sometimes you are wrong
Dancing to nature's rhythmic song

Letting your inside out, and spreading your wings
Discovering the gifts that childhood brings

Maggie Madamba, Grade 7
William Davies Middle School

Miss New Jersey Pre-Teen

I was standing there in top 30
My feet swelling in my high-heeled shoes
My heart thumping as if someone was beating a drum in my chest
Then I heard the emcee say "and your new Miss New Jersey Pre-Teen is…Caitlin Detreville!"

I was stunned and could not believe the judges chose me out of 181 girls
Shocked, stunned, shined, surprised
I walked to the 2007 queen to get crowned Miss New Jersey Pre-Teen 2008
As the crown was placed on my head, I knew I had a duty and my hands clasp over my mouth

I had a whole year in front of me that I was going to fulfill
I was going to stay gold for I did not want to go green
After the crowning they took lots of pictures
I was still crying hysterically and this went on for about an hour I felt like I wasn't going to stop

Even though I won a trip to California to compete in the national event and won $1,000
I still wanted to make a difference in my community, state, and the WORLD
After my pageant finale was over and I was the official queen there was another event right after
I had a first wave of being Miss New Jersey; the crowd went wild like I was the president

Caitlin Detreville, Grade 8
Westampton Middle School

New Student

This school, school, school!
Not fun, not nice, nor cool.
Lots of gum chewing and writings on the walls,
Kids stuffed in lockers, and loose papers in the halls.
Snobby old teachers, big noses and big glasses,
The big mean principal along with long, boring classes.
Paper airplanes flying through the room,
A horrible odor, much worse than terrible perfume.
The nerds sit in the front, and bullies in the back, (The typical order)
The "Gossip Girls" are in the center, and "Lonely Lisa" sits alone in the corner.
No one respects the teachers; no one even pays attention,
No one does what they say; no one goes to detention.
Bathrooms are in the first floor, detention is in the basement, and the main office is in the center of it all.
This school is so bad; it needs a sign in the front which says, "Do not enter these haunted halls."
I wished there was nothing to be scared of. I hoped and I prayed
However, there was no hiding the fact that I was extremely afraid.
I was in pain as if in war with need of the first aid
The blonde teacher opened the door and said, "Welcome new student, this is the 7th grade!"

Billy Torres, Grade 7
Garfield Middle School

Longhorn-Luke

I am the seams of a baseball that spins toward the catcher's mitt.
I am the gold paint wiped on the jerseys of the Hunterdon Lions.
I am the sound of the buzzer signaling the end of a winning season.
I am the crunch under the Burton Custom board as it rides over the ice crusted newly groomed snow.
I am the tallest redwood in the western forest reaching to the heavens.
I am the speedboat cruising over the waves across the sea.
I am the owl in the tree hooting all night and sleeping all day.
I am the acoustic guitar in a country singer's hands.
I am the battery overheating from a nonstop day of texting.

Luke Beveridge, Grade 7
Old Turnpike School

Candies

Softness in my hands,
Rectangle bars of chocolate,
Creamy brown,
Tasty white,
Midnight black,
Rainbow colors,
Dark caramel,
Seeing the tempting bar,
Makes me go crazy,
Hearing crunchy noises in my dry mouth,
Chewy peanut butter fillings,
Tastes like homemade brownies,
The wonders of candies are…
Delicious, heavenly, and luscious,
Crunch, Three Musketeers, Reese's, and Hershey,
Top four best candies on my ultimate list.
My favorite of all time is the Three Musketeers,
Feeling a light bird's feather in my hands.
From touching the fragile chocolate bar,
It goes in my mouth and the next thing you know it is all gone.
Candy's the greatest feeling that fills me with joy.

Caroline Nguyen, Grade 7
Herbert Hoover Middle School

Christmas

Waking up on the cold winter day
Zoom down the stairs
Tear open my presents
Then go to the stocking
Grandparents arrive early
Tearing their presents apart too
My mother cooks a nice Christmas breakfast
Gulp it down, asking for more.
More family comes with presents in their hands
It feels good to get, but now it's time to give.
I give family presents, and they love them
Smelling the crispy turkey in the oven
Boy! I love Christmas!

Daniel O'Steen, Grade 8
Keyport High School

Wintertime

Laughter fills the cold, crisp air
The amount of snow was quite fair
The sun makes the snow glimmer like gold
Every time it snows, it never gets too old
The adults shoveled the snow off of the driveway
"Let's have a snowball fight!" the children say
They make the snowballs
Soon, from the sky they fall
The snow shimmers like silver in the moonlight
A beautiful image on a perfect night
The snow turns into ice on the lawn
Snowflakes dance in the sky, dusk 'til dawn

Olivia Hauge, Grade 8
New Egypt Middle School

Thanksgiving Mystery Meal

I am the only one that people run away from.
I wonder when I will be eaten.
I hear the "ching" of the cutting knifes.
I see the rest of the food being eaten.
I want to be eaten.
I am getting colder now.
Warm at first, up until the dinner bell.

I pretend to look good.
I feel left out from the squad.
I touch the other green foods around me.
I worry I will never be eaten.
I cry to foods, other than me.
I am long, and I am green.

I understand that I am of the leftovers now.
I say that I am leftover right now.
I dream that I will be eaten someday.
I try to roll onto somebody's plate.
I hope that they will not notice my green.
I am…

Bailey Villipart, Grade 7
New Egypt Middle School

What Brings Happiness

Opening a present on Christmas day
The sweet smell of a flower bouquet
When someone compliments your new clothes
Getting a pedicure on your toes
The sound of the bell ending school
Jumping into a nice, cold pool
When someone simply smiles at you
Going to the mall and buying something new
Getting an 'A' on a very hard test
Just being able to relax and rest
Being able to give and not take
The taste of a big, juicy steak
Going to the beach on a hot summer day
Painting, drawing, and playing with clay
Sleeping in late on a weekend
Hanging out with a good friend
Winning a sports game or contest
Reading a book when you are stressed
These things are alike in one way
They bring people happiness from day to day

Cara Kobylarz, Grade 8
Little Falls School #1

Brothers

Annoying and a pain in your neck.
They never do what people tell them to do!
They're lazy like a sloth.
But you love them like a mommy and a child…
Only because you HAVE to love them.

Maressa Worbetz, Grade 7
Galloway Township Middle School

When Winter Comes

When winter comes,
A hush falls upon the ground.
Leaves from trees start twirling around.
Yet, there is a very peaceful sound.
Summer warmth starts to fade away,
And blistering cold winter starts to stay.
When winter comes,
Fireplaces stay on,
With warmth and coziness surrounded all around.
You don't hear the birds chirping,
And that tends to get me down.
When winter comes,
Schools are closed,
And children wake up late to go ride their sleigh.
Snowmen are built,
And then get knocked down.
Christmas trees are displayed
With glittery lights,
Like a rainbow in the sky.
When winter comes…

Dorota Bodyziak, Grade 8
Christopher Columbus Middle School

Gym

The unpleasant smell of the smelly mucky feet,
The smell of the lunch ladies cooking our meat.

Piercing sounds of screaming, yelling, and running,
The score of the kick ball game is not changing.

Hurry pass me the blue and purple ball,
Come on keep going catch them all!

Four outs is what the team will need,
Mr. Dempsey the best gym teacher ever will lead.

Drops of sweat dripping down our faces,
Everybody needs to tie their shoe laces.

Stepping out of the blue baseline is breaking the rules,
Mr. Dempsey looks at us like we're such fools.

The bell has rung its time for class,
Off to take a test I hope I pass!

Delaney Hoffman, Grade 7
Oxford Street School

A Limerick

A limerick is very hard to write,
And it is harder than flying a kite
One day when you do it
You'll find there's nothing to it
And you'll tell me that I wasn't right.

Gabriella Locantore, Grade 8
Good Shepherd Regional Catholic School

Summer and Winter Spent at the Lake

As summer arrives,
the children await,
the long summer spent at the lake.
The birds will fly,
and the fish will swim,
as the people dive quickly right in.
The smell and taste of food on the grill,
and the hard beating of the sun,
is what makes this day so much fun.

As the chilly snow comes down,
the lake will eventually freeze,
right along with the frigid winter breeze,
children will skate and happily play around,
all around the icy winter ground.

Jessica Glab, Grade 7
New Egypt Middle School

Winter Wonder

A sprinkle here a sprinkle there,
They fall so softly from the sky.
The snowflakes cover everywhere.

The anxious children go out to play.
They make lots of snowmen and beautiful snow angels.
The snow is bitterly cold, utterly white, and here to stay.

As I stick my tongue out, I feel a wondrous chill.
I see my breath and my nose get frigidly cold.
The first snowfall of winter gives me such a thrill.

Dusk emerges and the sun goes down.
All the snowmen and snow angels glisten in the moonlight,
As the snow still falls upon the ground.

Elena Brown, Grade 8
New Egypt Middle School

I Love You

The one I'm in love with,
from the first time our eyes met,
'til the moment he left,
he who made me smile, blush, and stumble
he's not here with me, but to me he'll always be
my baby, my love, my hubby whom I love
June fifth our date that I will never forget
tears running down my cheeks like rushing streams
memories and emotions filled my heart with glee
his aroma is like a smelling rose sent down from heaven
I dream about every second we spent together
every time I stared at him my feelings would drive me crazy
butterflies and chills all over my stomach
I think about our future though
I wonder if we are meant to last forever.

Itzel Avila, Grade 7
Garfield Middle School

The Firefighter

3 AM and I'm awake again,
The lights beat red,
Faster, Faster here we go.
Fully engulfed, pack up, pack up,
I struggle with my mask.
Grab the line it's fully charged now,
Deep breath in we go.
Searching, Searching, praying to find,
While the angry monster roars all around.
Think, Think on my knees I kneel,
Reaching out and pulling near.
Calming, Calming I tuck her against me,
Shielding with my life.
Running, Running through the roaring monster again,
Thankful, Thankful I have the door in my sight.
No smoke, no monster,
Fresh air to breath.
Happy parents, of Elizabeth are relived,
And the monster is dead.

Shannon Haviland, Grade 7
Galloway Township Middle School

Nature's Beauty

The flowers that bloom after the rains of April
Invite the butterflies to sweet, fresh nectar
The roar of the thunder in my stormy sky
Makes the rabbits scurry in the blink of an eye
The cascade of a waterfall in a hidden spring
Is becoming to a deer who thirsts in the heat I bring
The music of a mockingbird echoes through the trees
Its partner, the firefly dances with untaught ease
The golds, crimsons and emeralds of the canopy above
Are a prequel to the empty branches on which perches a dove
The rustle of leaves beneath the tiger's paws
Warns the elk of danger's vile claws
The snow that falls from the crisp cold air
Cues the bears to bid the warm weather farewell
The thick warm fur on the back of an animal's pelt
Is the creature's protector from the cold's unwavering threat
The cycle once again repeats year by year
As I, mother nature show the beauty of seasons
That each living thing holds dear

Kalyani Parwatkar, Grade 8
Linwood Middle School

The Diligent Worker

Gnawing on a tree,
a beaver works intently to finish its dam
as the river flows on.
Spanking his tail on branches,
he makes sure the structure is sound.
Hacking down trees, hoarding sticks, squealing during the process,
a beaver works tirelessly to build its humble abode.
How extraordinarily diligent the beaver is!

Claire Alvine, Grade 8
New Providence Middle School

Air Trip

Up I go with my family to the airport
My feet trembling as I go
I was nervous as a tree needed water
Because it was the first time being in the sky

I bought bonus packs of peanut butter bits
That I was saving for the plane
Finally the moment had come
When I stepped on the planes surface

I knew the adventure was going to begin
But when the plane started to go
I felt I was a scaredy-cat
The plane creeped higher and higher

It sweetly steeped when I was sleeping
I knew I was wrong
Because the airplane is nothing to be nervous about
Until you have experienced it

Amy Yin, Grade 8
Westampton Middle School

Childhood

I look ahead of me and see flashing lights,
I look to my left and right and see rain flowing down the window,
So scared I wanna scream and shout,
My sister is a sleeping baby

I look at my mom she's as scared as a little bunny,
My dad says it's going to be okay honey,
The car goes up and then back down,
My sister wakes up and looks around and around

The car spins and spins,
While nobody makes a sound as the car slides on the ground,
Wishing and praying this isn't really happening,
Want it all to end

Finally the car comes to a stop,
While everyone is still in shock,
We are happy to be alive,
Never been happier in our lives.

Tatiana Casimiro, Grade 8
Westampton Middle School

I Love You Mom

I think of all the good things we do together.
We laugh, cry and even fight.
Thanks for making my life complete.
Thanks for turning the light on in my life.
But, you know I will never stop loving you.
I love the "love" you have for me.
I love you mom,
From the bottom of my heart.

Andrea Rodriguez, Grade 7
Battin School #4

Christmas Is Here

"Christmas is here,"
Is what they say,
Christmas is here,
Indeed it's a wonderful day.

Christmas is here,
Preparations have begun,
Christmas is here,
Decorations make this day more fun.

Christmas is here,
The fluffy white snow is falling down,
Christmas is here,
And there isn't a single frown.

Christmas is here,
It's just a moment away,
Christmas is here,
I just wish it would stay!

Jamie Jadav, Grade 7
Linwood Middle School

The Dance

The music starts, I take his hand
He takes my heart, I hear the band
I take a step and so does he
He takes another step closer to me
He pulls me in, I don't resist
He gives me a spin and then we kiss
I do not want to break this bond
I love him above and beyond
I close my eyes, the crowd gives a cheer
And I realize I've no fear
I open my eyes to see my dear
My eyes then fill with gallons of tears
The cheering stops, he is not there
A single tear drops and I'm all too aware
That I am lying in my bed
A pillow underneath my head
Night has become my new day
Ever since my love has passed away.

Martha Byrket, Grade 8
William R Satz Middle School

Music's Ability

Flowing steadily,
the music on the page comes alive
while the instruments play in unison.
Pulsing rhythmically,
the bass drum booms.
Filling the room, crescendoing gradually,
and penetrating the listeners' ears,
the sound emerges from the stage.
That's the power of music!

Catherine Canete, Grade 8
New Providence Middle School

The Delight Song of Sasha

I am the unique but beautiful snowflake that slowly falls to the distant ground.
I am the bright pink flower in the crack of the dim gray concrete.
I am the ray of sunlight gleaming into the deep, dark room.
I am the candle that would soon turn to the hot and blazing fire.
I am the drop of water that turns into a puddle on the ground.
I am the frigid wind that bristles through the bare trees.
I am, Sasha Rogenas.

Sasha Rogenas, Grade 7
Old Turnpike School

My Dream

Drowsing in my bed,
I, my head caressed by my soft fluffy pillow, fall asleep.
In lands composed of thought and emotion,
I am lost; I am found.
Flying on wings of blissful joy, swooping toward hills of bright vermilion, laughing as I go,
I am at peace.
Oh, I wish I could do this while awake!

Nicholas Arts, Grade 8
New Providence Middle School

Books

After being seized from the shelf,
The book travels to the counter.
Then slid into a bag.
The book is taken to its new home
Browsing the chapters, flipping the pages, and reading cover to cover,
Its new owner enjoys its content.
How boring it is to be a book!

Maggie Lust, Grade 8
New Providence Middle School

The Beach

Burning red was the sky
As the sun slowly started to descend onto the horizon.
Crashing on the shore,
The water was a soothing and steady rhythm to hear.
Spreading a red glow on the sky, washing away footprints, and spreading a salty breeze,
The sun and water contribute to the beauty of the scene.
At sunrise, the beach's beauty is ineffable and soothing to the mind!

Priya Vaishampayan, Grade 8
New Providence Middle School

Ocean

At the ocean you can see the crystal clear blue ocean.
You can hear the roaring crash of the waves and the cry of the seagulls.
When you walk you can feel the rough texture of the sand and the swoosh of the water.
Occasionally you can taste the salty water in your mouth.
If you take a big whiff you can smell the salty foam or the slimy fish.
Sometimes fish fly out of the surf to catch a fly.
Your senses come alive at the beach.

Connor Squier, Grade 7
Frankford Township School

The Second

Without Stalin's guiding hand, defeat seemed inevitable.
With weeks rolling by, terror was befalling and color was slowly draining from the Union.
Amid the chaos, disorder, fear and the useless, a leader arose.
Among the baffled and confused, Gerogy Zhukov lead, seemingly doing the impossible.
Against all odds he drove back the invaders of Germany, from one decisive battle to the next.
Throughout the motherland, color was returning, friends, lovers and family reuniting.
Off far away was a different setting. Punishment was to befall the treacherous Third Reich!
Onto Seelow Heights, Germany the Red Army boldly marches and fought; toward their goal of crushing Hitler's beloved empire.
Toward Berlin the Union marched, crushing all that had tried to withstand its might.
Across rivers and many miles of land, they finally made it. The parliament building now within their grasp.
For Mother Russia the soldiers shouted.
The fight and race was now on, to implant the flag atop the building to end the Second Great War.

Chris Choi, Grade 8
Clinton Public School

My Refund Please?

I try so hard to make it look like I'm happy but the more I stretch my lips up the more the tears roll in disgrace down my face. So on my own I cry alone. I cry until the tears are gone. I cry until the tears are dry, now angry I just scream. To whimper of the pain that speaks my name. I let you get the best of me so now my mind ignites with fury. After all the respect I treated to you, and this is what you do for me? You betray me discreetly in front of my eyes so now I roll mine in front of yours. When really you hurt others to make you happy, so the problems not really mine just yours. I try to throw a shadow over my true feelings but the night always turns back to day. And all my expressions are reveled by light unable to throw away. I try to cope with my thoughts so I soon begin to write. And then when I'm finished writing this poem, I will be all right. Because I now know who to stay away from and that you I can no longer trust. You kill me with your stupidity, so away I stay to stay alive because I must. I let you get the best of me, and I broke down to rise strong again. You sunk through my skin and drenched my mind, but this is now and that was then. Disregard for anything you have to say to me, your poison words are now useless. I've overcome so much in my life I refuse to let you make me be stressed. What you had thought to be funny has you now standing there with the crickets. So now that your show is over I'd like a refund for these tickets.

Ariana Barnhardt-Asbury, Grade 9
Montclair High School

All About Me

Joey
A Virgo, friendly, adventurous, funny
Brother of Kayla
Lover of camping, sleeping, and Internet
Who feels, anxious right before I get a test back, good when relaxing, happy when I'm around family and friends.
Who needs, food, shelter, and water
Who gives, donations to a food bank, Box tops to the school, community service to help those in need
Who fears, sickness, grades, terrorists
Who would like to get straight A's, be rich, and famous
Resident of East Brunswick
Silva

Joey Silva, Grade 7
Hammarskjold Middle School

Balance

Shooting long across, or exploring deep,
the roots of a tree are sturdy ones that hold their ground
Perpetually moving and yet unmovable,
the unseen base of the skyscrapers of nature is truly an impressive force
Aging, working, and never missing a beat,
they are the dedicated laborers of nature.
Astounding, how something so insignificant in the mind of the world can bring such balance.

Daniel Patel, Grade 8
New Providence Middle School

The Perfect Day

The burning sun,
smiles at me.
I grab my towel and iPod and race toward the car,
impatient to arrive.
I arrive at my destination.
I'm crowded by people,
short, tall, thin, pale, tan,
everywhere.

I search for an empty spot to lay.
I slowly fall asleep to the sound of the waves.
The laughter carries on.
I take a picture of my beautiful site.
I sit and let the water,
wet my toes.
The waves are calm,
yet big enough to knock me over.
I play in the water until I get knocked
by an unexpected wave.
I lay there and laugh.
I gaze at the sunset,
until the day ends.

Mariana Pereira, Grade 7
Schuyler Elementary School

A Walk on Halloween Night

As the full moon rises in the night,
the topic of conversations turn to fright.
As the fall crisp air turns cold,
the frightening stories are told.
The sound of screams,
turn into horrible dreams.
As the doorbells ring,
the candy bags begin to sing.
The scary costumes walk around,
and I want to throw myself in the ground.
I walk home to my house full of décor,
I quickly slam the wooden door.
I eat my meal of pumpkin seeds, warm cider, and apple pie,
I'm surprised I didn't cry.

TJ Haefner, Grade 7
New Egypt Middle School

Candy

As I eat candy, it melts on my tongue
When I go trick or treating, I eat the candy right away
When I eat candy, it's crunchy and chocolaty
When I eat chocolate, it's milky and creamy
When I eat Starbursts, it's chewy and sweet
When I eat Sour Skittles, it's messy but sour!
When I eat Jaw Breakers, it's hard but bitter
Especially with Licorice, it's sweet and delicious
When I eat cotton candy, it's fluffy and pink even blue!
When it's Halloween, I'M ALL CANDY SWEET!

Amanda Lou, Grade 7
Hammarskjold Middle School

Happy Thanksgiving!

Happy Thanksgiving is in everybody's mind,
on this happy holiday nobody's unkind.
It's hard to keep away from family on this holiday rush,
before we eat we must pray so everybody yells hush hush.

Grandpa tries to be the man and he cuts the turkey,
while the little girls are really perky.
While my uncle is already eating food,
my cousin is walking around saying "what's up dude?"

When the grownups clean up kids go outside and play,
all the kids jump for joy on this happy day.
Everyone sets up getting ready for more food,
parents tell their kids to wash up and now everyone's in a mood.

Everyone wants a bit of something,
after all dessert is the best part of Thanksgiving.
Everybody sips a cup of milk,
and everyone leaves happy in warm silk.

Tommy Haskoor, Grade 7
New Egypt Middle School

Halloween Creatures

I am a pumpkin with a big flare.
I hear kids laughing in the air.
I see ghouls and goblins stare.
I wonder if the kids really care.
I pretend not to stare.
I touch a ghost through the wind.
I don't think he really minds.
I hear his whisper in the air.
I wonder what he said right there.
I see something appear.
I hope it's not the headless horseman.
I now see that it's him.
I hear him ride and gallop through the air.
I wonder if he has a full head of hair.
I know the pumpkin queen will be out tonight.
I worry she will cause too much Halloween fright.
I smell the fear of children near.
I try to stop her every year.
I am just a pumpkin with a big flare.

Angela Feasel, Grade 7
New Egypt Middle School

Christmas Eve

Kids are waiting for Christmas to come,
Waiting for Santa late at night
Wanting presents to fill them with joy and delight
Testing the presents under the tree
Seeing if they're good, bad, or just maybe
What they want to see
The cookies are done the milk is ready
Now everyone is tucked in bed with his or her Teddy.

Michele Correggio, Grade 7
St Mary's School

All About Me

Kevin
Caring, athletic, generous, helpful.
Brother of Sabrina.
Lover of tennis, games, and animals.
Who feels happy when on vacation, sad when my pet dies, and bored during the summer.
Who needs to be more organized, to clean my room more often, and to be more talkative.
Who gives presents to my family on their birthday, people direction when they need it, and advice to my sister when she needs it.
Who fears rats, spiders, and big bugs.
Who would like to visit Hawaii, see a tornado, and be in a big snowstorm.
Resident of East Brunswick.
Daeninck

Kevin Daeninck, Grade 7
Hammarskjold Middle School

The Poem of Me

I am a sun, bright, shinning, and reliable to be on time…
I am a flexible piece of grass, swaying in the cool, refreshing breeze…
I am a chatterbox, wind me up and I don't stop…
I am a piece of candy, sweet as can be…
I am a stream, always running somewhere and getting over the obstacles in my way…
I am at times a gray shadow, secretive and mysterious…
I am a question being asked that has no answer…
I am an imagination, always thinking of strange and creative things…
I am a silence-breaker, laughing at a joke in dead silence that I was told yesterday and just understood…
I am a Swiss Army Knife, able to do many things…

Rachel Girardin, Grade 7
Old Turnpike School

Freedom

Soaring overhead,
Leaves twirl around with them in a crisp, clear blue sky.
Peering down to the open world below them,
The birds seem to have the world in their wingspan.
Using all their energy, gliding for a moment, then shutting two wings to land
Is the pattern that these animals seem to follow as they maneuver in their domain — the sky.
How easily freedom can come to them.

Elaine House, Grade 8
New Providence Middle School

Simple Little Seed

I am a simple little seed that will grow more and more each time I learn something new.
My roots are my home; it is where I start before my growing is through.
My stem will sprout and grow nice and strong; it describes my unique personality with every twist and turn.
My leaves are long and wide showing all of the places I've been,
And my petals, oh so many petals, represents all of my friends.
For now, though, I am just a simple little seed about to grow into a world of new opportunities.

Sabrina Rodriguez, Grade 7
William Davies Middle School

Movie Night

When you're in a movie you are quiet as a mouse.
The screen is tall as an elephant.
It's dark in a movie as it is at 12 o'clock at night.
There are lots of people as if you were at a football game.

Tyhirah Snow, Grade 7
Galloway Township Middle School

Pizza

Pizza crust is crunchy like a Dorito on the outside.
It's soft like cotton on the inside.
The cheese is like slime stretching with its meltedness
The toppings are pepperoni, buried into the soft cheese.

Richard Pugh, Grade 7
Galloway Township Middle School

As Snowflakes Fall

As snowflakes fall, I stop and remember
What happened the winter of 2000.
As snowflakes fall
I remember you standing right there by my side.
As snowflakes fall
I remember all the good and bad.
As snowflakes fall
I feel the breeze passing me by.
As snowflakes fall
I think about what a fun time we had that day.
As snowflakes fall
I realize you appreciate everything more after you lose it.
As snowflakes fall
I try to hold the tears back and stop myself from crying.
As snowflakes fall I start to cry because of all the memories.
As snowflakes fall
I wish you were right there standing by my side
As snowflakes fall...

Talia Ambrosio-Earle, Grade 8
Christopher Columbus Middle School

Soccer

Soccer is a sport of skill.
The black and white ball,
waits to be kicked on the green field.
The light blue sky looms over all.
There is the smell of enthusiasm in the warm air.
The players look excited to play the game.
The ball feels like hard leather.
Soccer,
a sport that makes fans sit at the edge of their seats.
The action begins.
The chanting of the fans fills the air with noise.
The players are enjoying themselves
as the ball bounces around from player to player.
The ball goes into the net.
GOOOAAALLL!
The exciting game continues,
the fun continues,
and the sport of soccer lives on.

Stephen Mourad, Grade 7
Herbert Hoover Middle School

Summertime

S unbathing on the beautiful beach.
U sing my favorite boomerang.
M usic blasting as I run around.
M y dog chasing me as I run around.
E verybody in the whole world having fun.
R unning on the beach as my feet burn.
T rying not to fall asleep at night.
I n my freezing cold pool all day.
M y family and I having fun every minute of the day.
E very day still reading even out of school.

Matt Lawson, Grade 7
Frankford Township School

You

Every time I hear your voice
I get shivers
That are indescribable.
Every time I think of you
I can't help but smile.
Every time I look at your pictures
Butterflies flutter round in my tummy.
Every time I see you
I'm at a loss for words.
Your voice is angelic.
Your face is gorgeous.
I like you. I want you.
I need you.
I hope for the day we meet.
It's impossible, I know.
You're a well known guy.
I'm a girl, that's a little shy.
But I don't know what to do.
I can't go one single day,
Without thinking about,
Y.o.u.

Shannon Sims, Grade 8
Good Shepherd Regional Catholic School

Thanksgiving

Taken out of the oven,
The turkey was deliciously cooked.

I inhaled the smell of the assortment
Of homemade cooking.

I have cherished this day for years,
Even since I was little.

Learning the recipes
Was a trait I learned by watching Grandma cook,

However this day is about family,
Being thankful for what I have and enjoying it.

Alex Shema, Grade 8
New Providence Middle School

Pennies

Pennies, pennies are everywhere
Worth so little and given no care

A little sparkly shine in Lincoln's old eye
To be on a coin he must have been a great guy

I pick them up when found on the ground
Brown and shiny, and oh, so round

Slowly but surely, I will bring them home to keep
Eventually, I'll have enough to make a giant heap

Wyatt Knapp, Grade 8
Township of Ocean Intermediate School

Phish

His small head shaped like an arrow
Slithers to its destination.

He watches —
Stares with beady eyes.

With his forked tongue he feels
And finds his direction.

His scaly skin cool to the touch
Sends shivers down my back.

He coils ready to strike —
Eyes fixed on his victim.

Ready, he attacks,
Strangles his prey,
And slowly cuts off his victim's air.

Quick as a whip
He gathers his prey
And swallows it whole.

The kill is over.
Lindsey Bean Collins, Grade 7
Galloway Township Middle School

Grounded

When the flowers started to bloom
Everything felt so alive
Winter had had its last hurrah
Land could begin to thrive

But there he was shut in a room
How was he to survive?
The window showed his bike staring
Asking for a test drive

"I can't leave, Daddy grounded me!"
"He's trying to deprive,
That little boy inside of you,"
The bike spoke with great strive.

The boy knew he could not leave but…
That bike sure could connive
Ugh punishment, you spoil the day
How was he to survive?

Should he listen or should he not?
Bees buzzing in their hive
Sun gleaming and shining outside
What would the boy decide?
Alyssa Caruso, Grade 9
Boonton High School

8th Grade: Looking Back

So it's the third and final year
I'm walking down your halls,
Treading over carpet floors
Passing faded, neutral walls

I've changed so much since I first sat
On hard, graffitied chairs,
And rushed into a musty gym
To find my best friend there

It's strange to think that I once cared
What those kids thought of me
When now we've grown so far apart,
Similarities are hard to see

It's not only my values
That have shifted over time,
So have my actions, thoughts, and words,
Into a style I call mine

So this time next year I move on
But I'll never be the same;
Middle school has given me
My friendships, face, and name
Molly Kuchler, Grade 8
Linwood Middle School

Three Hours Left…

Sit. Squirm.
Stand. Pace.
You're bored…real bored.
It shows on your face.

Hours on end
With nothing to do!
"I'm talking to myself!"
(Am I going mad too?)

There's three hours left,
Before you can leave,
Three hours of boredom…
Feels like an eternity

You're stuck inside,
Until your parents get home.
You want someone else,
But you're stuck all alone.

"Maybe a book,
Might get me through!
I might still be grounded,
But I'll have something to do!"
Alex Herrle, Grade 8
St James School

Dawn to Dusk

Trepidation is triumphed, hope rises anew
Dawn.
Hope is fading, fear slowly settles
Dusk.
Brilliant beauty, yellows and oranges
Sunrise.
Burning beauty, reds and purples
Sunset.
Hope is building, smiles glowing
Morning.
Tired and hungry, tempers flaring
Evening.
Heat of the day, hope is teetering, tottering
Noon.
It is easy to see the light of the sun,
But will you look for the light of the moon?
Michal Hirschorn, Grade 9
Bruriah High School for Girls

An Endless Debate

You took me from my home
To save me from a great unknown
But you had to take me all alone
So now my family is only bones
Every day and in every way
You get closer and cut away
All my past, it's gone today
My heart stripped bare in the fray
And now there's only room for you
Out with the old in with the new
Still, my mind will never construe
How I cared before I even knew
Passionate love and passionate hate
You get to me with your every trait
They burn within at an equal rate
Hate? Love? An endless debate.
Brigitte Lamarche, Grade 8
Assumption Academy

What Is Time?

Season by season
Day by day
Time just keeps going
So fast, yet so majestic
No turning back
Like a current of the mighty ocean
Like the wind of a swirling tornado
Just whizzing past our ears
Through every corner of the Earth
As I nestle myself in my warm, cozy chair
I think and I think, yet again
And come to the simplest question ever
Any scientist would want to have answered
What is time?
Tudor Tarina, Grade 8
Township of Ocean Intermediate School

Daylight in the Woods

I see the sun through the trees
As I walk through the den of leaves
It's golden and pretty all around
Colors are gleaming bright green and light brown

The birds all sing
They all make a different song
The critters all run
Here under the dim sun

The air is warm
Pine trees smell fresh
It's a great getaway
From every little piece of stress

From the animals running
The birds chirping
And the light through the leaves
No one can say this is not a magical place

Cassidy Wiltshire, Grade 7
New Egypt Middle School

The Hill That Could Kill

I woke up feeling the urge to accomplish something.
Even though my mind thought of nothing.
Eager, excited to find something cool.
Then it hit me, but people might think I'm a fool.

I should ride my bike without training wheels.
That should seal the deal.
Click! The sound of me putting on my gear.
Racing to my position everything seems clear.

I looked down the steep, deep, creepy hill.
Wishing my crazy thoughts would stay still.
Maybe I should quit.
But I shouldn't be a sore loser giving up like this.

I started to peddle as fast as a race car.
Hoping I wouldn't go too far.
But in a quick moment my head smashed the ground.
Instantly I was a baby crying with a loud sound.

Keina Thorpe, Grade 8
Westampton Middle School

Little Artists

Painting on pants,
grass creates a masterpiece
as if those jeans were a canvas.
Blending in the greens,
the colors decorate as a skilled painter would.
Emanating from fun, ravaging lawns, and draining bottles of Tide,
Their blades are their painting brush.
Those little artists have gotten the perfect touch.

Brian Charatan, Grade 8
New Providence Middle School

Gymnastics

Flipping, twisting through the air
When I am tumbling
I have not a care

Running, sprinting towards the horse
Power from the springboard
Gives me great force

Balance and grace on the beam
It is only four inches wide
So competing in this event is extreme

Swinging with strength on uneven bars
And feeling the chalk beneath my hands
I perform my dismount and reach the stars

So many things make gymnastics fun
But the best of all
Is getting the gold and realizing that I had won

Morgan Mostow, Grade 8
Township of Ocean Intermediate School

Music

Music is my life.
I love to hear it play
I listen to it every day

Music runs my life.
There is always a melody in my head
I'll be listening to it when I'm dead

Music is my everything.
People think it's just for fun
I treat it like my number one

Music is my all.
Every instrument in a song
A guitar, drums, and sometimes a gong

I love music no matter what
So I'm going to follow my gut
And do everything and anything with music.

Karli Conti, Grade 7
St Mary's School

Torn into Pieces

Before, this friendship was inseparable.
You would always understand me and how I felt.
I would understand you as well
But now, I don't see you anymore
I don't talk to you anymore
As I think about this friendship,
Tears roll down my cheeks.
Our friendship has been torn into pieces.

Karen Peña, Grade 7
Robert Morris Public School

An Enchanting Feeling

An enchanting feeling within me,
A soft whisper blown in my ear.
Just a whistling breeze calming me,
An aroma of fresh air I take in.
Rustle, crackle, rustle, crackle,
Leaves the shade of red and yellow,
Are being torn by the smallest footsteps.
However they're still lying mutually on the dying grass.
The days begin to grow shorter.
Gradually a night has approached before I know it.
Standing in this scene,
Feels like a spirit holding my hand,
And gently lifting up my soul,
Spreading out my wings,
Forcing me to glide in the still air.
There's no dreary acquaintance, not even if there's rain.
Rain drops are just tears.
Tears produced by an emotional, juvenile girl.
An enchanting feeling encountered me,
Awe-struck me, and made me believe that finally,
Autumn is here.

Ana Cardenas, Grade 7
Garfield Middle School

Food Chain Devastation

Observing the defenseless prey,
the wolf hovers over the astonished chick
that had just been hatched.
Licking its carnivorous jaws,
the wolf closes in on the paralyzed bird
and crouches to make its first move.
Hurled into a chasm of fear,
the chick focuses in on an exposed cavern
aligned with razor sharp daggers.
Driven into intense hunger, eyeing the juicy morsel,
sinking its piercing lances into the chick's delicate feathers,
The wolf doesn't even give the flightless bird a chance to blink.
Food devastation strikes again.

Daniel Hitchen, Grade 8
New Providence Middle School

Beauty Is Everywhere

Beauty is a pretty face pleasing to the eye
Beauty is a brand new vase made out of the finest china
Beauty is an oak wooden chair rocking along on a country porch
Beauty is a graceful smile of a beloved grandparent to a child
Beauty is a fragrant smell of newly cut pink roses from a garden
Beauty is dew on the grass gleaming in the bright sun
Beauty is a fresh-caught bass deliciously cooked right at your camp
Beauty is a moon in the night illuminating everything in its path
Beauty is a Chinese kite flying high in the sky
Beauty is the chirping of baby birds at the birth of nature
Beauty is sleek smooth skin of a nice toned body
Beauty that is true is found deep within a spirit

Derek Du, Grade 8
Township of Ocean Intermediate School

The Holiday Season

The frigid winter night, filled with obscurity
Contains enough snowflakes to drown a whole city.
Fluttering down from the sky
The snowflakes are as calming as a lullaby.

The street lights make the snow-covered roads shimmer
This is indeed the joy of winter.
Icicles hang from rooftops above
As snow hits the ground, white as a dove.

The winter air smells like evergreen
The Christmas lights are as bright as I've ever seen.
The snow cleared from driveways is tossed in a pile
The holiday season is sure to make anyone smile.

The caroler's songs fill the air with tune
The snow appears to never stop, at least not anytime soon.
The holidays are definitely near
But shortly after, all will be gone, including the holiday cheer.

Samantha Spence, Grade 8
New Egypt Middle School

The Lonely Stuffed Animal

I sit on the shelf in the stuffed animal aisle
I hate it up here, but I hope it may all be worthwhile
Someday, anybody, please take me home
To Paris, England, or maybe even Rome

We could go to all sorts of places
And maybe we would see some familiar faces
We could play games together and watch some TV
In my owner's arms I'd be as happy as can be

At the end of our day we would be really tired
It would feel so nice to finally be admired
We'd lay down in bed and cuddle up tight
Oh how that feeling would feel so right

But for now I'll just focus on getting out of here
Doesn't anyone want me? I'm beginning to tear
I see a little boy, I better sit up straight
He takes me off the shelf, it looks like this is my fate

Jamie Donovan, Grade 7
Little Falls School #1

If Love

If love is just a four letter word
why does it mean so much to me?
If only I can see past my heart,
maybe I'll be happy
The hurt and the pain put me through stress
I wish I could have somebody that will treat me the best.
I guess I'm going to have to go beyond looks
and maybe I'll find someone as great as the ones in the books?

Janelle Shepherd, Grade 8
Janis E Dismus Middle School

Lacrosse

The bell rang.
It was my last game,
My last chance to show my coach what I'm made of.
We got on to the bus, it felt like an oven.

I hoped it wasn't going to rain cats and dogs.
I hoped I would make my first goal.
I hoped my coach would feel proud of me.
I hoped for the best.

We were walking to the field.
I could hear the wind whisper in my ear.
The thought of making a goal floated across my mind.
My hands were shaking, I was a nervous mess.

The sound of a whistle came to my mind.
The game started.
The ball was in the air.
So I quickly caught it, and threw it into the goal.

Stella Lee, Grade 8
Westampton Middle School

Calling the Wild

you hear the birds chatting up a storm
As you walk into the sunlight
The trees swaying from side to side
In the winter wind…

The birds heading south
Into the cold air, and hot sun
The trees leaves just growing back
In the summer air…

The birds building their new nest for their young
As you walk into the warm air
Trees start to form buds
Creating new leaves…

The birds fly
The leaves fall and change
The wind blows from east to west
Calling the Wild…

Kesa White, Grade 8
Westampton Middle School

Tormenting Treat

Prancing in place,
my dog is unable to conceal his excitement.
Quaking and quivering,
he shakes with anticipation.
Sitting on the floor, holding his head high, fixated on my hand,
he hopes the good behavior will ensure him the prize in my hand.
As I open my hand, he springs up and pounces on the treat,
his torment is over!

James Burke, Grade 8
New Providence Middle School

The Seasons

Mother Nature is as spontaneous as ever
Even though it's not so clever
With all its different seasons
We can't predict the reasons

The season of summer is a time for sun
Summer is also a time for fun
Swimming in the deep waters
Also a time for mothers and daughters

The season of autumn has beautiful scenery
What is disappearing is all the greenery
The leaves start to fall
As they build up against the wall

Winter is a time for snow
Gently falling to and fro
Crystal angels in sunshine glow
Nutcrackers lined to protect them in a row

Sonia Routhier, Grade 8
Westampton Middle School

The Ocean and Me

The sound of crashing waves is soothing to the soul
Sea gulls chirping above my head
The ocean in full control

The smell of salty water is sitting in the air
The sun shining through the clouds
Water glistening everywhere

Seashells, sand dollars, fish and more
Swaying back and forth
All dancing on the ocean's floor

Keeping the sand warm and the sky bright
The sun sits over us
And will leave for the night

The ocean never ending, as peaceful as can be
I sit alone along the sand
Just the ocean and me

Briana Cruz, Grade 8
Little Falls School #1

Lacrosse

Racing up and down the field,
I guard the ball with my life as the defenders pile on.
Cradling it, passing to the attackers,
And capturing the ball as the time is running out,
I go for the goal.
Just as the lacrosse ball is sliding past the goalie,
The buzzer goes off.
We cheer for our victory.

Rebecca Blitt, Grade 8
New Providence Middle School

I Dare You

I dare you to laugh
    When everyone cries
I dare you to tell the truth
    When everyone lies
I dare you to run
    When everyone walks
I dare you to scream
    When everyone whispers
I dare you to be brave
    When everyone's scared
I dare you a lot
    Will you accomplish those dares?

Jasmine Gilder, Grade 8
George Washington School

A Winter Day

The winter is beautiful
the trees with no leaves
the wind blowing over my hot cocoa
Children with heavy coats
Kids playing in the snow
trying to make a snowman
getting a carrot from their house
to put it on the snowman
Parents getting mad because their car
is covered with snow
The Christmas is very happy and
time to say Merry Christmas!

Kerlyn Aviles, Grade 7
Garfield Middle School

Adrenaline Rush

This is now.
There are no lectures or imperative rules
roaming through my mind.

The clock skips seconds by five and time
may cause me future destruction.
But I don't care.

I have devoted my entire life
to create this rush of adrenaline
and cause my heart to beat faster than ever.

Mariana Loaiza, Grade 7
Garfield Middle School

Horse/Fish

Horse
Majestic, graceful
Jumping, galloping, rearing
Saddle, bridle, scales, fins
Gliding, twirling, flapping
Slimy, colorful
Fish

Rachel Hopkins, Grade 7
Frankford Township School

Halloween Night

Next week is Halloween and I'm having a party,
My friends will come over, hope no one is tardy.
They say their costumes are funny but not like mine,
When Halloween comes they will all look just fine.

Now it's the actual day of Halloween,
I actually hope I don't get seen.
Now it's the party the first person is here, their parents are king and queen,
My friend comes around the front and screams Happy Halloween.

Everybody is here and laughing at the costumes as we go to the first house,
My dad tries to scare me as quiet as a mouse.
My friends and I are talking about a pool,
But my other friends are talking about "TP-ing" the school.

My friend's little brother thought he looked cool,
So we told him to look in a mirror and he said I look like a fool.
Games, music and dancing, what a fright!
The house goes dark, wish them all good night!

Tré Gonzalez, Grade 7
New Egypt Middle School

Halloween Night

My bag was less than halfway full and I'm already out of breath,
It's getting darker and scarier now, I can sense death.
The kids are screaming and the doorbell is ringing,
People are waiting at the door to see what candy they will be bringing.

Everyone will say "trick-or-treat,"
Getting ready to collect some sweets.
Now to the next house hoping there will be a bowl of candy, oh my,
So you could take all the candy you want and don't be shy.

The scariest house of them all is waiting for us,
Don't get too excited and fuss.
I see some creatures waiting at the door,
As we got closer I heard a roar.

We got to the door and realized that they were just fake,
I took a bunch of candy, but apparently that made them wake.
Next time I'll be more careful too,
Or I'll just startle them and say "BOO!"

Alexa Winouski, Grade 7
New Egypt Middle School

Holidays

Ringing with melody,
Christmas carols play all day
To get people in the spirit,
Inspiring people.
Everyone gets very happy
Emanating happiness, glimmering lights, and encouraging gift giving,
The holidays bring joy to so many.
This is the best time of year!

Dominick Mellusi, Grade 8
New Providence Middle School

Sensing Life

A lone wolf howls in the dark night
The new baby cries from seeing light

I love tasting juicy steak
Spreading icing on the cake

Orange burning of a house caught fire
Little boy's blue balloon going higher

Rubbing alcohol burns my nose
Cigarette smoke clings to clothes

The smooth surface on a vehicle's hood
Rough edges on nails don't look good

Writing thoughts on a blank page
Meaningful memories start to age

So much around us, and we don't even know
Things as hot as the sun, or as cold as the snow

Rowan Bienes, Grade 7
Oxford Street School

Football

Every Sunday sometimes Saturday
You get butterflies in your stomach.
Coach gives you a pep talk.
He screams, "Are you ready?!"
We answer: "Yes coach."
But the truth is we aren't at all.
It's the time of the week where it's all or nothing.
You prepared for this team
All you could think is I better not mess up.
You step on the field
You haven't done anything yet but you're already sweating.
Turn around and you see the whole crowd cheering.
There's the whistle,
The whistle you've been waiting for all week.
First play the opponent scores
Suddenly your head goes down
Your teammates bring it back up.
You fall seven times, you get up eight times
This is what it is.
What is, is football.

Luis Lopez, Grade 8
Christopher Columbus Middle School

Disney World

I see people, rides, stores, and characters.
It tastes like popcorn, soft pretzels,
hot dogs, cotton candy, and ice cream.
It sounds like music, voices, screaming, laughing.
It feels crowded, fun, and humid.
Mickey Mouse's home

Erica Landau, Grade 7
Kellman Brown Academy

December 11th

Caroling coming from the east
Laughter coming from the south
The blizzard is like a silent beast
With hail drooling down its mouth
Snowball fight in the north
Hot cocoa being served in the west
Scarves and gloves provide many with warmth
Whereas others are under a woolen blanket taking a rest
At midday everyone is at their fullest
Even though this day just might be the coldest
The carolers from the east are now filled with pride
For they have done a good deed with nothing to hide
The laughter from the south is from the kids on the street
For the day was full of surprises they skipped a heartbeat
The snowball fight to the north is one to defend
But the children know the fun never ends
Hot cocoa in the west has danced its way into our tummies
"Thanks for the cocoa!" we say as we go hug our mummies
A kiss on the cheek is what every child needs
For a goodnight sleep, every child dreams

Jess Pritikin, Grade 8
New Egypt Middle School

Autumn at Its Best

After the intense heat of August comes September
A new school year begins, it'll be a year to remember
This is also the time when leaves begin to change
From yellow, to red, to brown, Oh what a wide range
Once September is gone, comes the month of October
This is the month when the mischief may occur
Halloween is around the corner, everyone beware!
You'll never know when you're in for a scare
Teenagers and delinquents stocking up on silly string
Sometimes they plan to do some serious egging
The end of Halloween brings the beginning of November
A holiday when Americans are appreciative and grateful
The entire family comes together as a whole
We feast on potatoes, turkey, and pie
In the end, however, we must say goodbye
All the trees have lost their leaves
A slight chill turns to a blistering cold
The signs of winter begin to unfold
Fall has gone and winter arrives
But the beauty of autumn will always survive

Donald Chu, Grade 8
William R Satz Middle School

Fall Joy

As I was awakened by a chilly fall breeze,
I looked out the window and saw colorful fall leaves.
They were all different colors, shapes, and sizes.
I went outside and noticed they have all different surprises.
The leaves looked so beautiful, unique, and plain.
Fall is my favorite season because the leaves change.

Aspen Jamison, Grade 7
Lakeside Middle School

Bosco and Dakota

I walk through the door,
two dogs jump on me.
Bosco fetches the purple chew toy.
I grab the other end,
and we play tug-a-war.

They're both black,
with white spots.
They destroy DVD's and Phone Books.
I listen to them bark and whine,
then I watch them do tricks.

Nicholas Springer, Grade 7
Schuyler School

School

The door is opened,
As we come into the school.
Our minds are turned on,
Ready to explore a world,
Of knowledge and attainments.

From that moment on,
The teachers begin their plan.
You know as they say,
You learn something new each day.
"Limits are nonexistent."

Kathleen Blehl, Grade 8
Assumption Academy

Costumes

I'm sitting on my porch
Watching kids go by
I see a little clown
Crying from his make-up eyes
I see a tiny fairy
Waving her magic wand
Some costumes are very detailed
Some are very poor
All the kids that go by are excited as can be
Which I don't understand because
It's the day after Halloween!

Alyssa Harvey, Grade 7
Hammarskjold Middle School

Colors

Colors, colors everywhere
Dancing in the wind
Watch them paint the sky
With colors that are within

Many colors interest me
What colors do you ask
I love every color of the rainbow
I will never change that.

Allison Sanders, Grade 7
St Mary School

The Soccer Game

The fans stream into the stadium
Laughing, talking, and chanting.
The smell of food fills the air.
The taste of hot dogs and cheeseburgers is enjoyed by many of the fans.
The players take the field under the glow of the bright lights.
The referee blows the whistle.
Kickoff!

The fans clap, chant, and cheer, urging their team on.
The players slip on the wet grass, catch themselves, and run on.
The goal keeper jumps and the ball sails over his head.
The referee blows his whistle.
Goal!

The referee blows his whistle.
Game over!
The fans leave, the cleaners sweep.
People taste their after-game snacks.
The smell of fresh air is everywhere.
The visiting team boards the bus to go home.
The lights dim in the silent stadium.

Matt Blomgren, Grade 7
New Egypt Middle School

Six Flags

Sounds of the roaring rides fill the air
Walkways crowded within, by people without a care
In amazement and awe people stare
At the mighty animals on stage that arrive with flare
Iridescent lights fill the night's darkness with color
Music blasts, giving a lively beat
The ride operator says over the loud speaker "step right up and take a seat"
For people experience the ride of their life, in this very park, on this very night
And even though some are filled with fright
Everything around is such a pleasant sight
A night filled with laughter and thrills
But sadly all will end, when it's time for the winter chill

Lauretta Lawlor, Grade 7
New Egypt Middle School

Dance

Among the crowd, there was cheering and applauding
Beside me were all my fellow dancers, jumping with excitement
After a while the crowd got quiet, and the curtain rose.
Towards the stage I leaped!
During the show I turned and turned.
With my feet, I jumped into the air.
Before the other dancers and I knew it, the show was done.
Throughout the dance, I smiled and smiled.
After the ballet the other dancers and audience members told me I was great!
Outside the theater, I was shivering from the cold.
Since I was tired, we started to go home.
On the way home, I started to get sleepy,
Underneath the covers in my bed, I dreamt about the performance then fell asleep.

Rachel Pedinoff, Grade 8
Clinton Public School

'Tis the Season

How beautiful the snow flutters from above,
'Tis the season for giving, caring, and love.
The snowmen come with cheerful greetings,
And we host our close family meetings.
Children's sleds glide swiftly down hills,
Snow hits my neck and gives me chills.
Snow angels engraved in every person's yard,
Bright, smiling faces on a Christmas card.
There's fun, exhilarating snowball fights,
And footprints carved in the pure white.
Sensational scents of warm cookies in the air,
Presents given, packaged with care.
People hum familiar holiday tunes,
For jolly old St. Nicolas is coming soon!
I hope you have the greatest December,
And this holiday season is one to remember.

Taylor Leonardo, Grade 8
New Egypt Middle School

Autumn Artwork

Once the summer days end,
Mother Nature begins a new painting,
A mural on the face of the Earth.
A work of art, filled with treasure troves,
Bursting with precious gems.
Priceless rubies dripping down upon the ground.
A canary molting its gilded feathers,
They flutter down so gently, softly,
Swaying and sweeping in the autumn breeze
Once decorated with the lush, emerald shades of summer,
The treetops have been set ablaze.
Like a torch, to guide the way for winter to make its entrance.
And, when the chill of the solstice sets in,
The glowing embers that light the autumn day slowly burn out.
The watercolor masterpiece begins to wash away,
And starts this never-ending cycle once again.

Claire Gates, Grade 8
William R Satz Middle School

Soccer

Soccer is a fast moving sport,
The black and white ball never stops moving,
The sturdy metallic white posts is the target,
Clumps of green grass sail through the air.
Your eyes are constantly on the ball,
While listening for the referee's whistle,
The forearms shoving each other.
Soccer is the number one sport in the world,
An energetic sport,
Kicking the ball into the net is the GOAL of the game,
Each player has a job to do on the field.
Sight is crucial in the game,
Teammates must communicate with each other,
Soccer is a fast moving sport,
In which you must have precision, focus, and teamwork,
Most of all just have fun.

Nickolas Lair, Grade 7
Herbert Hoover Middle School

My Old Friend Came to See Me

One morning day,
I woke up with a "hooray!"
An old friend, but someone new to see,
Came to greet me.
I went outside to see that he has changed,
His red, orange, yellow, and brown colors has been arranged.
My friend's aroma stayed the same as it always been,
The crisp strong smell of the pie in the pie tin.
My pal hugged me with his chilly wind,
I kissed him with a grin.
I can hear my buddy put all of his little critters to sleep,
He tells them calmly "Oh please do not weep!"
I know what will happen when December comes,
But my friend reminds me not to be so glum.
It is now time for my pal to leave,
But my good friend leaves another season to be with me.

Becky Fine, Grade 7
New Egypt Middle School

Puppy Mill

Tiny cages stacked floor to ceiling,
With small dogs stuffed in each one.

They dig at the doors of their tiny prisons,
Looking for a way out.
Each puppy's eyes telling a disastrous life story.

Lifeless and broken bodies lay at the bottom of each cage,
Illness had taken some, others crushed,
Like dead leaves in the palm of your hand.
Their eyelids dropped over their shattered crystal eyes,
Never to open again.

Ashley Fox, Grade 7
Galloway Township Middle School

Pumpkin Patch

Each and every day kids come and roam
To find the best one and take it home.
Rows and rows of orange are in plain sight.
You'll be amazed by the corn rows height.
Some are big and some are small.
They match the colors of the fall.
Kids carve happy and sad, mean or evil faces in it.
With or without a carving kit.
Place it on your porch, for people to see.
Trick or treaters walk up, and laugh with glee.
All the pumpkins you saw.
Came from the Pumpkin Patch!

Nicole Ielmini, Grade 7
Hammarskjold Middle School

What a Wonderful Day
Ah! What a wonderful day!
A wonderful time to go out and play.
When I look outside it all seems
So beautifully white and clean.
I go inside to drink a cup of tea
As I look out the window and see
Little children playing in the snow
There's a smile on my face as I whisper very low.
"I remember when I was only a child
I used to run around like I was wild."
As I laugh at the memory I say,
"Boy, what a wonderful day!"
I go outside to feel the cold breeze
I sit on my porch and feel at ease.
I take my book out to read
A wonderful story about a man that was freed.
As I go inside I have the need
For one last time I want to say,
"Ah! What a wonderful day!
A wonderful day to go out and play."
Ashley Muniz, Grade 8
Christopher Columbus Middle School

Holiday Time
Holiday season is the perfect time
Lights light up the shards of ice on the pitch black street.
Church bells ring their even chime.
Good citizens donate rice, gifts, and wheat.
Icicles are like tears
They drip slowly and appear this time of year
When divided families reunite…

I walked into the graveyard, with a wreath
The blizzard blows hard on my weather-beaten face, but I don't stop.
The snowcapped graves are lined up in rows
As my boots crunch along them.
I found what I was there for, a grave of a loved one
The etched white marble shone like the North Star.
I placed the wreath down, tears freezing to my cheeks
As I remember her dreadful fate.
I looked back only once as I strolled out the kissing gate.

We were united once more, that is all I cared about.
And that is why the holiday season is the perfect time.
Steven Wetzel, Grade 8
New Egypt Middle School

Stepbrothers
He isn't your brother.
He isn't your mother.
He is your stepbrother.
You're only half-related.
He is 50% brother, 0% friend, and 50% enemy.
You are enemies, but you are also brothers from different mothers.
Anthony Azzariti, Grade 7
Frankford Township School

Winter Has Fallen
Winter has fallen in one night.
White snow all around is such a delight.
Snowmen are being built
Snowball fights everywhere is so much fun.

Winter, oh how I enjoy you.
Christmas presents and family dinners.
New Year's Eve, the countdown is on
A new year will come, so hello 2010.

Red and green are winter colors
It's such a delight in how it brings happiness.
Hats, gloves, and scarves keep you warm
Rosy cheeks are what I adore.

Winter has fallen, so all be ready.
Christmas tree lighting and live concerts.
Parades are where I want to be
Shopping is every girl's dream.

Winter is a season for family.
Week off of school
Blizzards and hot chocolates
Christmas lights on your house
Glow like stars on Christmas night.
Naveira Paulino, Grade 8
Christopher Columbus Middle School

Popularity
Each time I blink, another second goes by.
Dilemmas shoot at me. Can my course go awry?
I need a helping hand, some nourishment or hope.
A foggy path approaches, now with this I have to cope.

Is it so that I chose the wrong route?
Why couldn't I have acted astute?
I did it just to fit in, to feel very chic,
I deserted my ways of being unique.

I remember memories of who I once used to be:
An innocent, little girl, but now I'm nothing but debris,
Of who used to be a leader, the commander, or the guide.
In the moment, my opinions are excluded and denied.

Why have I selected the dumbest of the choices?
I wanted to be popular like all the other voices.
Popularity is favored among the kids at school.
However, when we get older, it is no longer cool.

I've lost my closest friends,
And the list continues and transcends.
What is it about popularity that ties everyone in?
Once you join, you cannot fight it; it will win.
My advice for newcomers today: to popularity turn away
Rashelle Tsyrlin, Grade 8
William R Satz Middle School

Tiger

It runs in the night
But walks in the day
It creeps in the weeds
But attacks from the trees
It lives on land and doesn't like water
It is The TIGER!

It runs fast
But it sneaks slowly
It eats animals
And doesn't like humans
It grazes on rocks and likes to climb
It is The TIGER!
Quinn Mattos, Grade 7
Frankford Township School

Friendship

Friends aren't found every day.
But when they are I must say;
There's a special bond
A connection at heart,
Side by side
And never apart.

The laughs you share
The care that's always there.
You become one
And have so much fun.
With a good friend
Till the very end.
Daniela Losada, Grade 8
St James School

Friends

Friends are what keep people strong,
That's why I am writing this song.
Friends have their ups and downs,
And sometimes they may frown.
But they are always there,
Even if feeling despair.

Friends are there through thick and thin,
And, so is your twin.
So next time you befriend,
Always think of your best friend.
Alexandrea Soden, Grade 8
North Arlington Middle School

A Terrible Ghost

There once was a terrible ghost
Who was way scarier than most
He howled and screamed
As his body beamed
But the thing he did best was boast!
Danny Valencia, Grade 8
Christopher Columbus Middle School

Is the Pen Mightier Than the Sword?

Is the pen mightier than the sword? Is a poet stronger than a horde?
In my view word does damage; killing could cause mental baggage
War killing the innocent and guilty; sometimes killing royalty

Words can end a war; words can improve our core
Words saving millions; maybe saving trillions
Words in many peace treaties; can swords cure diabetes?

Can a sword save a life? Can a sword help your wife?
Can a sword do your job? Can a sword avoid a sob?
Can a sword remember feelings? A pen is not only for weaklings

Pens used in history; from Ben Franklin, to Hardy Boy mysteries
George Washington to George Carver; to Albert Einstein who always tried harder
Thomas Jefferson writing the constitution put that into consideration

Now don't you agree? A pen can do more, you see
Is the pen mightier than the sword? Is a poet stronger than a horde?
Tyler Wood, Grade 8
Cinnaminson Middle School

The Beautiful Beach

Children digging a hole in the hot sand.
Birds flying through the hot air.
Waves crashing onto the tan sand.
Fish swimming through the cool, blue-green water.
Sand moving as the wind blows along the beach.
People running along the ocean.
Children playing in the shallow, salty water.
Birds squawking as they walk on the beach.
Waves swallowing up people in the ocean.
Fish jumping out of the waves.
Sand becoming amazing sand castles.
People lying on the soft sand.
Children collecting many different sea shells.
Birds pecking at the sand to get their food.
Waves moving closer and closer to the dry, beach sand.
Fish nibbling worms off fishing pole hooks.
Sand compacting when you step on it.
People walking on the boardwalk after a wonderful day at the beach.
Taylor Malavet, Grade 7
Frankford Township School

Halloween Night

On Halloween night you hear the screams,
Of little girls and boys.
They run up to doors screaming "Trick-or-Treat!"
Then they go to there friends bragging about all their candy.
While the little ones run around happily you notice the brisk air that they don't mind.
You see the beautiful leaves then you too run with the little ones to get candy and toys.
After the night is over they all sadly return home.
They say "We should have stayed out longer, I don't have enough candy."
While they enjoy their treats they go back up to bed.
Before they drift off they wait in their beds eager for the next Halloween night.
Becky Kowalski, Grade 7
Hammarskjold Middle School

Christmas Time
Christmas lights shining like the northern star so bright
Hoping Santa will come tonight
In the morning you jump with glee
So excited to look under the tree
You tear apart the wrapping paper wishing it will be
The one present you wanted to see

Lots of snow covers the ground
Like diamond rings that surround

Snowflakes falling down from above
Walking up the driveway with the ones you love
You ring the doorbell everyone shoves to give kisses and hugs

As we sit at the table and pray,
Thanking God for this wonderful day!
Makenzie Magnotta, Grade 8
New Egypt Middle School

Flames
You scream when you touch
The heat burns you more than the sun
It hurts but you must
You pour your gasoline on the sticks
The dry grass nearby you add
New sticks become deposited into the pile
You rub the flint and a stick together hoping for sparks
Nothing happens so you take a deep breath
You rub even harder now and smoke appears
Your one drop of sweat burns out the little fire
Frustration occurs but you try again and hope to spark a broad fire
After constant rubbing an explosion of fire appears
Now my soul is on fire
Now my love for this fire is blazing
Now I shall smile
Now my fire is lit
Warrick Sabene, Grade 8
Township of Ocean Intermediate School

I Remember Halloween
I remember that night of terror and fear,
That comes on October of every year.
I remember the ghouls that came out to play,
Once the young children had gone away.
I remember the ghosts that shouted for joy,
As one of the goblins scared a small boy.
I remember a witch's shrill little cries,
That echoed through the air and up to the skies.
I remember the skeletons that clicked and clacked,
Making their bones very chipped and cracked.
Yes, I remember that night of terror and fear,
And I can't wait till it comes this very next year.
Nicole Girgis, Grade 7
Hammarskjold Middle School

Christmas!
When I wake up I scream in celebration,
I see the snow outside and I know what time it is.
I know what is coming next.
I know I'm getting presents because I've acted my best.
I go outside and smell the crisp winter air.
Then I go back in and see presents everywhere.
I see cookies and hot chocolate and go to snack.
I hear the fire cracking as my lips are smacking.
We all open presents and then it becomes night.
We celebrate the holiday and go to bed in delight.
Jason Hutchins, Grade 7
New Egypt Middle School

Jack
Atop the tree house sits Jack, trying to shoot me with his water gun.
Into the house I run; he can't shoot me if I'm inside.
Near the window I hide.
Outside, I can see him searching for me in the yard.
Inside the bathroom I stand; filling my own gun at the sink.
Over the screams of children outside, I slowly open the window.
Through the trees, I spot my target.
Across the yard, the water streams, target hit!
Without a warning, he screams "I give up!"
At last, I won the water war.
Abbey Carroll, Grade 8
Clinton Public School

The Delightful Song of Me
I am the tall tree by a clear blue lake.
I am a single pen used for the many tests.
I am a spice rack with many spices to me.
I am a single mouse chasing after a piece of cheese.
I am a rain drop falling to the ground below.
I am the singer to a new and improved band.
I am a star in the middle of the bright night sky.
I am a single strand of fabric on a shirt.
I am another proton in the nucleus of an atom.
I am a blade of grass in the field of weeds.
Joey Fernicola, Grade 7
Old Turnpike Middle School

The Delight Poem of Sarah
I am the softball of a new game played in the big stadium
I am the cool blue ocean waves crashing on the sandy beach
I am a snowflake that is so unique in my own way
I am the first flower to bloom before the snow melts
I am the single soft cloud in the sunny sky
I am the camera recording our many family vacation memories
I am the skier swishing side to side down the mountain
I am the swimmer who cannon balls into the pool
I am the first frog who leaps out of the pond
I am a photographer that loves taking pictures of nature
Sarah Egan, Grade 7
Old Turnpike School

My Little Flame

My little flame,
Burning within my soul,
It sparked to life
As soon as life touched me.

My flame dims,
As tears start to drench it,
But my strong little flame
Always burns.

My flame grows to glow
As bright as the sun,
When I reach each finish line,
Throughout my life.

My little flame,
Burning within my soul.
Alexis Kim, Grade 7
New Providence Middle School

Dancing

Dancing is my sport.
Pink ballet shoes,
Black leotard,
Pink tights.
I can hear the music,
I can feel the rhythm,
My mouth is thirsty to dance.
Dancing is my life.
Dance like no one is watching,
And I will succeed.
Practice and practice every day,
And I will get better.
I can see my feet moving to the beat,
I can feel my muscles working.
I know all of my routines,
Because I practice every day.
And I dance like no one is watching
Morgan O'Shea, Grade 7
Herbert Hoover Middle School

Winter Wonders

The holidays are coming fast
Though I thought fall would last
The scent of pine cones fills the air
While icicles hang everywhere
Mistletoes dangle all around
Snow falling gently on the ground
Winter is not far ahead
Though you still might see kids sled
I can't wait to see the first snowflake
Or to go ice skating on a silky lake
I think the holidays will be tons of fun
And don't forget that it's only begun
Brittany Miller, Grade 8
New Egypt Middle School

Karma

I was a bird,
That could fly away,

Leaving a mystery behind,
For someone else to unravel.

My white shaggy wings
Carry me forward,
On my way.

Did I make the right decision?
I turned around for a moment —
But it was too late.

I crashed in the water,
My wings dropped in an instant,
I crashed into water
As I drowned in my Karma.
Hannah Marr, Grade 7
Galloway Township Middle School

Winter

It's winter when it snows.
It's fun but although.
It gets cold and you know
Winter's such fun.
Snowball fights I have won
And shoveling houses gets done.
Always a time when,
You build a snowman and then,
Snowing comes to an end.
So you go back home,
And taste that nice
Warm hot chocolate
While you change your clothes that are wet.
And you relax just a bit.
Sit back and just watch it.
Snow falling into a fun blanket!
You can be inside with heat,
Or outside with that white sheet!
Stephen Gonzales, Grade 8
Christopher Columbus Middle School

The Big Black Monster

That big black monster's
One red eye, one small
Ear, and its big bloody
Teeth. Its big nose,
Its long green
Fingers. Its short
Red hair, and its four
Long legs. Its big fat
Belly. OH, that big black
Monster.
Esteven Eskasndar, Grade 7
Hammarskjold Middle School

My Hero

My hero is medium height
He has dirty blonde hair
He is very special to me
He looks strong

My hero is funny
He is smart
I hear him come to me

I feel safe and happy when I'm with him
He is fun to be around
My hero is my dad
Lauren Muller, Grade 7
Frankford Township School

The Truth About Bats

12:00 Halloween night
One will take flight
Then two then three
How hungry they will be
They fly above our heads
While some of us lay safe in bed
They are vampire bats
Also known as the winged rats
Take it from me
We should all flee
Small and harmless you may think
But it's your blood they want to drink
Gregory Youssef, Grade 7
Hammarskjold Middle School

Halloween

It is Halloween
A very fun time of year
Finally it's here

Taste the sweet candy
And see all the bright wrappers
Can't wait to get more

Kids run in the streets
And they ring all the doorbells
They yell, "Trick or Treat!"
Brianna Comforte, Grade 7
New Egypt Middle School

Fantastic Fall

Big, red, shiny apples on the trees,
Children playing in the leaves,
Big orange pumpkins in the patches,
Baseball players making catches.

Geese are flying in the sky,
While my mom is making yummy pumpkin pie.
The old oak trees are swaying side to side,
As I sit and sigh.

The bread is baking,
It's so cold that I'm shaking.
I smell the spice candle burning,
As the turkey in the oven is turning.

Thanksgiving dinner is ready to eat,
I sit and wait patiently in my seat.
It's time to dig in,
So, let the feast begin.

Rachel Stillwell, Grade 7
New Egypt Middle School

Thanksgiving Feast

Before a Thanksgiving Feast,
You might feel like a hungry beast.
You can smell the pumpkin pie,
As you can see it from the corner of your eye.

You can hear the corn fritters sizzle,
As it starts to drizzle.
Stuffing sitting on your plate,
Turkeys gobbling at your gate.

As your family piles in,
You wipe off your mean, sly grin.
As you eat and eat,
You might feel extremely beat.

Dessert is near,
So give a cheer.
Now you are hungry the least,
After that big Thanksgiving Feast.

Bianca Rinaldi, Grade 7
New Egypt Middle School

I Am Like

I am like a soccer ball
Rolling around and being kicked upon by my brothers and sister
I am like Bounty
Absorbing the new atmosphere

I am like the sun that shines on the Earth
But I shine the room with a great big smile
I am like the North Star
People come to me for help

I am like a violin
When settled down I become soothing
I am like an eloquent flower
Swaying in the air when I dance my way through life

I am like a beach ball
Always colorful and fun to have
I am like a mother
Taking care of my family and the ones I love

Jamie Marchesano, Grade 7
New Providence Middle School

Where Success Is Found

I was searching for success,
I was young; I was ambitious.
I climbed Mt. Everest.
Unsatisfied, I hiked Mt. Vesuvius.

I stumbled and I fell,
I bruised and I froze.
With every collapse I wanted to give up.
But I held my head high and struggled for the top.

Seeing the distance to go; I whimpered and sighed.
Each time I got hurt I wanted to cry,
I brushed the tears aside,
Moved on but didn't ask why.

At the top I looked below,
But not a single rock where I fell would show.
I realized those falls helped me reach my goal,
And true success is found in the journey of the soul.

Enrique Zalamea, Grade 8
St James School

Rain

Trickling across the surfaces,
it slides in a slippery path, causing destruction.
Drizzling my face,
little drops pop into bubbles.
Gliding on the floor, misted after the sun arises, humidifying the air,
a big rainbow appears on the horizon.
It can cause damage or help in need,
that's what rain is about.

Jod Prado, Grade 8
New Providence Middle School

Sunset

Glistening in the sudden darkness,
the sun begins to sink down in the sky
as I stare in astonishment.
Igniting colors in the air,
nature's beauty is shown.
Gazing up at the sun, reposing in the silence, enjoying every minute,
I see only half of the sun absent.
What a honorable way to end the day!

Ashley Amoia, Grade 8
New Providence Middle School

Vampires

They turn into bats
They soar through the night
You can't see them, they're out of sight
They look for a human to find a good bite
They glide down to you
Before they bite, you scream into the night
Suddenly, your eyes turn red and you feel a fright
Then you turn into a bat and fly away into the night
Can you guess what you've become on this Halloween night
A vampire of course, what else would give you such a fright
You wake up with a scream
It was just a spooky dream you had on this Halloween night

Watch out on Halloween for vampires yet to be seen
Happy Halloween!

Ryan Nasto, Grade 7
Hammarskjold Middle School

Today's the Day

The wonderful smell of everything cooking
The turkey just sitting there
It's calling people to come eat it
The feeling of your family being together
The love and happiness that everyone is giving off
Seeing people that you haven't seen in awhile
The aroma of pumpkin pie
All the smells making my mouth water
My grandma yelling at me for drinking too much apple cider
Having to wait another hour before eating
Going outside and playing football
Sitting by the fire
Listening to interesting and exciting stories
The best time of the year
When you are with the ones you love!!!

Samantha Rooke, Grade 8
Keyport High School

My Family

My family is everything for me
I love my family with my whole heart
My family is sad and happy and loved
Family is fun and painful and pretty
We have good times and bad times too
All families have love and happiness and tears
My family is the best in the whole world
I am very grateful that I have a family that loves me
My family is nice and kind
Sometimes we have arguments but we love each other
I am never going to stop loving my family
God is always with us no matter what
My life is great with my family
No one can replace them
They are the best for me.

Angie Salazar, Grade 7
Garfield Middle School

Autumn Events

Autumn is the time of year
When all the kids go back to school
When all the leaves fall off the tree
And as the days go by the temperature falls
When the jeans and sweaters start coming out
When the ghouls and ghosts hide under your bed
And when the pumpkins smile both evilly and crazily
When the pumpkins are harvested straight off the vine
When the corn is sweet and tender, ready to be picked off the stalk
When the apple trees are harvested for pies and cider
When the smell of cinnamon is strong throughout the town
When the aroma of turkey, mashed potatoes and gravy fill the house
And when all are merry and pleased with their meals
They enjoy all the delightful times that autumn has brought
And when the autumn festivities end with Thanksgiving
Everyone eagerly awaits the future years of autumn

Akaash Duppatla, Grade 7
Hammarskjold Middle School

Grapes

It's sweet and delicious
Lime green,
Lavender purple
And light red.
It's a great fruit,
The smell will make you feel warm inside.
The sight will make your mouth water.
It's a grape.
The fruit of summer,
It's in great numbers.
You feel the round texture,
You see it in the fields.
Hear the snap as you pick them off the vines.
Grapes are the best,
Amazing in taste.
How can you live without grapes?

Christian Mills, Grade 7
Herbert Hoover Middle School

Winter Wishes

The snow dances down from the sky,
resting on the window panes.
By each passing day there is more holiday cheer,
people running this way and that,
buying toys for family and friends.
Kids eyes are glowing,
meeting Santa in the malls,
parents tense while shopping and cleaning.
The smell of freshly baked cookies radiating from the oven,
sappy pine lingers in the air.
Trees are standing straight and tall waiting
anxiously to be decorated.
It's Christmas time!!!

Jenna Rodriguez, Grade 8
New Egypt Middle School

Living the Dream

A joy that could make your heart burst,
A joy that could make you scream,
"Thank you!" to the heavens,
A joy that could make you cry,
Seeing that faded chocolate ball of fur,
Being carried into my kitchen,
Into my house,
By my dad,
Making that faded chocolate ball of fur,
My faded chocolate ball of fur,
Made my heart burst,
Made me scream,
Made me cry,
13 years of waiting,
Begging,
Hoping,
Dreaming,
For the day to hear the clicking of nails against the wood floor
And to sit by the fire
Holding her tight and watching TV on that cold winter morning
To be a reality.

Elizabeth Thoresen, Grade 8
Cedar Drive Middle School

Winter, Winter

Snowflakes are being tossed on the ground
Making everything white as clouds all around
Children are sledding here and there
And icicles are hanging everywhere
The trees are a beautiful sight like newborn kittens
But you still need to make sure you have on your mittens
Snowmen are being assembled wherever you look
It's like you're looking inside a wonderful book
As the smell of cookies fill the air
Your mom comes up behind you and gives you a scare
You both run into your very large house
And see a cookie being eaten by a small mouse
You shoo him away and take a big bite
And your whole mouth is filled with delight

Annie Samis, Grade 8
New Egypt Middle School

The Loves of Our Dear Autumn

As days grow shorter,
The weather gets colder,
All the leaves change color,
Making the streets seem less duller,
The children step on leaves to hear the crinkle,
And from their mouths comes out a chuckle,
And let's not forget that Halloween rolls around,
And Thanksgiving when we all gain a pound,
So what's not to love about our dear friend Autumn,
She may not be as pretty as a blossom,
But in my opinion she's pretty awesome.

Jessica Kwak, Grade 7
Garfield Middle School

Rescued Kitten

Reaching his smoky gray paw through the bars,
One kitten waits while the others sleep.
Nuzzling up to my hand as I pet him,
Rolling over on his back,
And purring happily,
That kitten is the sweetest thing.
Gazing into his blue-grey eyes,
I want nothing more than to take him with me.
How could I not take him home?

Kirsten Peterson, Grade 8
New Providence Middle School

Thanksgiving Is Here

Thanksgiving is here,
Christmas is near,
Celebrate with Thanksgiving dinner,
Soon it will be the beginning of winter,
I like to eat pumpkin pie,
and to look at the dark cloudy sky,
I sit at the table happily,
and enjoy Thanksgiving dinner with my family.

Mitchell Berrios, Grade 7
Lakeside Middle School

Not Just the Willow That Weeps

Weeping over the grass,
the tree stood still before the storm.
Sobbing to itself,
it waits for the wind to pick up its legs.
Isolated, remaining on its own, perched on its stump,
the tree stays lonesome.
It wails for help, but the storm has already swallowed its cries.

Camille Ake, Grade 8
New Providence Middle School

Another World

Step downstairs and turn to the right. Hands out, taking it slow.
Black, everywhere in front of me, eyes are open, though only dull.
Useless, everything, nothing can help. Nothing.
Give up, it's what every person seems to do to me.
My parents, no longer here, abandoned me, now left alone.
Help me! It's all I say.
Down two more, straight, then left. Open door, finally, just wait.

Madison Gavornik, Grade 7
Old Turnpike School

The Silent One

I am feeling sad, can't wait to leave school.
Can't wait and can't contain this act anymore for the day.
My patience barrel is full, about to blast!
Their outspoken thoughts is like mini bombs,
waiting for me to blast!
Can't wait to be out
And express my controlled emotions!

Lexi Amadi, Grade 9
Teaneck High School

Winter/Fall

Leaves are falling from the trees,
My mom started cooking turkey and peas,
Eating a lot and having fun,
Thinking about the food makes me say Yum!
I'm hoping my whole family could come.
People eating and spreading cheer,
Like Halloween, there should be no fear,
Snow is falling and kids are riding down hills,
And I hope that I will not get the chills.

Jordan Canelo, Grade 7
Garfield Middle School

Thanksgiving Feast

A feast.
The biggest feast of the year.
On the 26th of November.
It's a day to remember.

The turkey is the main dish.
There are other foods from corn to fish.
These delicious foods fill our hunger
So we can enjoy the rest of the day then slumber.

Semi Eyuboglu, Grade 7
Garfield Middle School

Butterfly Fly Away

Anxiously awaiting its new life,
The butterfly frees itself from the cocoon
As it quickly attempts take-off.
Fluttering with its rosy pink and lavender wings,
The butterfly soars through the wind over the powdery yellow daises.
Fleeing from the old, drifting towards the new,
Gliding through the breeze away from the place where it began,
The insect floats across the sky.
Oh, how wonderful it is when a butterfly flies away.

Adrienne Cirrotti, Grade 8
New Providence Middle School

My Own Special Snow Globe

Soaring through the sky,
The first snowflake falls, slowly making its way to the ground.
Melting on the crisp terrain,
The snowflake disappears into the grass.
Glistening as it falls,
Descending upon the branches,
Knowing winter's approaching,
The ground starts to be covered with a thin sheet of white.
It is like being in my own special snow globe!

Dominique Iacovelli, Grade 8
New Providence Middle School

Winter Magic

The woodstove crackles,
The smell of Christmas cookies wafts through the warm air,
Little white flurries gently tickle the earth.

A robe of angels,
Sewn in Heaven,
The world is clothed in white.

Diamonds of unspeakable value,
Crystals of Christmas,
The world sparkles from their abundance.

Snowing, snowing, snowing!
Such a magical thing.
How lucky we are to be in its presence.

Jenevieve Ball, Grade 8
New Egypt Middle School

Monday

I'm not a fan of Monday,
I would rather it be Sunday,
The day goes by very slow,
If you go to school or have a job, you would know.
It's not quite a thrill,
You seem to never have time to kill.
I can tell not many like Monday by the way they look.
It all starts out when you pick up a book.
I can't help but just stare at the wall,
While half-awake faces walk down the hall.
I wish to avoid Monday, but it's just a day of the week,
I need to let it go by, even though it's something I don't want to seek.

Kelly Ann Turner, Grade 8
St Mary School

The Joys of Winter

Snowflakes dancing from the winter sky
The fireplace burns passionately
The aroma of cookies fills the air
While you sit there and cheer
Christmas carolers' melodies soothe the soul
Glorious gifts dressed in wrapping paper
Sledding down blankets of snow
When it comes to Christmas days
The room is filled with joy and delight
Hot chocolate as hot as a summer's day
Everyone is joyful in winter

Jeremiah Daniels, Grade 8
New Egypt Middle School

Mother

lovable, nice
playing, working, driving
She came from God
faithful, helper

William Troche, Grade 7
Lakeside Middle School

Kittens and Puppies

Kittens and puppies
Frolic and play
With a ball that's Lucky's
And some string of René's.

They will play tag
In the sunshine is the best,
Even when the other lags
They still never rest.

On rainy days
When they can't go out
They put on little plays
And are almost always sold out.

Meow says the kitten.
Woof says the puppy.
René is sitting on a mitten
And Lucky is, well, just being Lucky.

They always have fun
And that's the key,
Sitting in the sun
As happy as can be.

Kelly McHugh, Grade 7
Good Shepherd Regional Catholic School

Mother Nature

Merciful Mother Nature has created our earth
With it she added life, the best gift of all
Humans must work with her to keep this gift
Or into darkness her creation will fall

Mother Nature added wildlife and creatures
We must work hard to keep these things
Without cooperation they will cease to exist
It is away from us that these animals are fleeing

The rivers, lakes, oceans and seas are abundant
If action is not taken they will someday disappear
We have to correctly use what Mother Nature gave us
Or for our crystal clear waters, the end is near

On to the trees and forests that our Creator has made
Only we can keep them on the face of this earth
We must stop cutting and defacing them
And prove to everyone what they are worth

These are plenty of examples of nature's beauty
We need to put strenuous effort into preserving them
Civilization has only begun this daunting task
The world must treasure these marvels like a precious gem

Mark Zichelli, Grade 7
Little Falls School #1

1 of 6

My older brother Sam got many years
He and my parents had so much fun, so it appears
Seven years after Sam I came along
The 23rd of January was all about me, but not for long

I got a year and a half with my parents and brother
Until September, 1998 when along came another
Little Elizabeth Rose was her name
Stealing all the attention was definitely her game

She was adorable, fun, and bubbly
After two years together, along came Kadie, nice and chubby
Tiny baby Kadie was always wearing a grin
And for the biggest cheeks she would surely win

Three years later Fiona came into our world
One blue eye, one brown, and her hair grew in curled
She was the last, we didn't even question it
Then four years later things changed a bit

Eamon Stewart is our last and is devilishly clever
And this is my huge family, always and forever
I know what you're thinking, being one of six must stink
But it's never lonely and really great, at least that's what I think

Charlotte Cathcart, Grade 7
Little Falls School #1

My Halloween Death

I hear the sounds, all through the night
I hear the sounds that make me fright
To my left there's a cutting wrist
To my right there's a bloody fist

My parents don't believe me but I surely know
The principal in my school is only bone
I see it all but I'm no crier
Until I see the legs of a spider

Under my bed there's monsters to see
And vampires who want to suck blood from me
I see a witch flying in the sky
It's Halloween, are you ready to die

I see the devil when his red eyes shine
I get terrified when he looks into mine
Today is the day I look death in the face
For when I die there will be trace

My ghost will come back all wicked and creep
To haunt you now don't make a peep
Grab your pillow I'm the one out there
Who sure will be pleased to give you a good scare

Nora Sadek, Grade 7
Hammarskjold Middle School

Autumn
It is getting cold
Mom says to grab a jacket
Fall is almost near

The trees change colors
Orange, brown, yellow, and red
As they hit the ground

Kids run everywhere
To dress up and cause a scare
Join me if you dare

Not a ghoul in sight
Jack-o'-lanterns fill the night
Please don't get a fright

Apples in a pie
Turkey bakes in the oven
It always tastes good

Thanksgiving is here
Family comes near the table
A time to give thanks
Faith Schuetz, Grade 7
New Egypt Middle School

Gymnastics
Gymnastics has its ups and downs
We've got smiles and we've got frowns
It's dangerous and fun
But when you get hurt you're done

Competitions are hard
We all wear a leotard
Some in orange, some in blue
It's too bad some people have the flu

Everyone tries really hard to win first place
But when they don't they get a booboo face
I always try my best
And that's all that matters

Practice is totally different
We will still work hard
We still wear a leotard

Hope for the best
There's always another chance
For competitions and practice
We always show our best
Anna Farrand, Grade 7
New Egypt Middle School

Spring Time
Blue jays fluttering in the trees.
Blooming flowers will soon arrive.
Ladybugs crawling up my sleeve.
Rainbows appearing across the country.
Warm breezes and cool winds.
Freshly baked pies sitting in the windows.
Grass stained jeans in my laundry basket.
The smell of pollen and freshly cut grass.
My mom starts spring cleaning.
The sound of the lawnmower going away.
Ripe fruit falling form the trees.
Dogs barking early in the morning.
Spring is here.
Amanda Kelly, Grade 8
Keyport High School

Christmas Time
It's Christmas time!
Time to celebrate.
Hear the bells chime,
You could go on that special date.
There's the mistletoe,
hanging up high,
get your loved one,
and make that kiss, not say good bye.
It only comes once a year,
then everyone gathers,
they begin to cheer,
and if you are with your peers,
nothing else matters.
Peter Puzio, Grade 7
Garfield Middle School

Soccer
As the whistle blows
A 45 minute half begins
The pressure is definitely on
Trying to be the first to score
The never-ending sound of screaming fans
Encouraging coaches and chattering teams
Cluttering the silent air with commotion
Feeling tense and ready to play
The whistle blows again — it's half-time
Five minutes and our break is over
And the feelings start all over again
As we take the field to play again
Makenzie Oates, Grade 8
Township of Ocean Intermediate School

The Hallways
Madness, madness through the halls
A sixth grader runs, stumbles, falls.
Books scatter everywhere
Not one person stops or cares.
Rushing, rushing can't be late
Tardiness is something the teacher hates.
Shouting, shouting, voices are loud
We are a very big crowd.
Lockers, lockers open and slam
Pray the locker doesn't jam.
Teachers, teachers discipline and shout.
Are the kids listening? I highly doubt.
"Ring, ring!" the final bell chimes.
Every day it's the same old rhyme
Madness, madness through the halls.
Can't wait until that bell calls.
Kayla Santos, Grade 7
Garfield Middle School

Sitting in the Darkness
As I sat there alone
As silence filled the room
Everything went dark
I could not see
I felt blinded
Nowhere to go
No one to hug
I felt like a lonely slug slowly moving along
For the last minute I felt nothing
Finally the lights went back on
All my feelings came back to me
And I felt safe
My blindness left me
No more silence
No more darkness
Finally felt safe.
Abigail Gomez, Grade 7
Robert Morris Public School

Winter Thrill
Rushing, rushing down a hill
Fast as a cheetah
The winter snow begins to thrill
Wet as rain and cold as a freezer
Splashing in your face
Face as red as a rose
Toes soaked by the chilly ground
As you sled down the hill
Screaming with no sound
Heavy jackets won't hold you back
As you roll your very own snowman
Play and play all through the day
Up and down the hill
Rushing, rushing gives you a thrill
Abby Fennimore, Grade 8
New Egypt Middle School

The Beauty of Autumn
Here I am at the start of fall,
But most people do not like it at all.
Only second to spring,
Fall is a beautiful thing.

Sitting on a bench feeling a breeze,
Watching the trees sway with ease.
The first day of school was crazy,
But now I am lazy.

In fall you start to wear sleeves,
As I watch the swirling path of leaves.
I feel the warmth of my fire,
Seeing a sign for a leave raker for hire.

As summer comes to a close,
It is time to wear warm clothes.
As a season ends,
The light seems to bend.
Jason Donnelly, Grade 7
New Egypt Middle School

Cookies: The Sweetness of Life
Aroma of sugary dough
Sweetness permeating the air
Extraordinary sensation
Of cookies baked in the oven.

Hectic pace of the world stands still
Now transfixed by oven window
Spurs sweet scented memories
Of cookies baked in the oven.

No matter the day or reason
Ageless, timeless seasons of life
Sweetness erases needs, but one
Of cookies baked in the oven.

Quick hands dash to claim precious prize
Instant sadness, when nothing left
Turn to see another sweet batch
Of cookies baked in the oven.
Arushi Mittal, Grade 8
Thomas R Grover Middle School

Butterfly/Blossom
Butterfly
Colorful, camouflage
Flying, landing, spreading
Beautiful, quiet, plant, new
Blossoming, budding, rustling
Small, lovely
Blossom
Eryka Arroyo, Grade 7
William Davies Middle School

Piano Man
Gliding his hands across the keys,
he thought of what note he was going to play next.
Sounding out the right chords,
he composed a wonderful piece.
Singing to the melody, pounding on the keyboard, and fretting about perfection,
he continued onward to finish his piece.
A true piano man strives for perfection and doesn't settle for anything else.
Tom Fusillo, Grade 8
New Providence Middle School

Hawk
Spying its prey,
The hawk swoops down to apprehend the squirrel.
Missing by an inch,
The hawk flies back to its perch while the squirrel scurries under a bush.
Preening his feathers, disguising his motivation, searching again,
He races after another squirrel.
The hawk is victorious this time!
Chris Aman, Grade 8
New Providence Middle School

Snow
Drifting down from the sky,
the snow glistens in the morning sun as the sky turns white.
Gliding gently,
The flakes soon form a white blanket over the ground.
Playing with snowballs, building big snowmen, sledding down snowy hills,
I'm white with powder.
Everyone has a great time in the snow!
Jonathan Ebert, Grade 8
New Providence Middle School

Dinner
Gliding deep below the surface,
The flounder dwells, unaware of his near end, as the fisher sits on the skiff.
Cast into the water,
The lure bobs up and down, waiting for its time of glory.
Yearning for dinner, ascending the depths of the sea, nipping at the worm,
The flounder gnaws on his dinner and becomes mine.
Oh, how good he tastes!
Mark Sullivan, Grade 8
New Providence Middle School

A Great Present
Opening my eyes,
I'm staring at my sister's face.
Strolling out of my bedroom,
I listen to my sister waking up my parents.
Posing for the camera, anticipating what's inside, shredding the wrapping paper,
I rip open my first present.
It was just what I wanted!!
Robin Lauber, Grade 8
New Providence Middle School

Gingerbread Men
The mahogany colored cookies so pristine
They looked as if they were from a magazine

The icing was laid upon their head
As they laid in a cookie dough bed

The splendid smell spread through the house
Everyone could smell it, even a mouse

The cookies had a decadent flavor
And the cookies are what everyone started to savor

The cookies were laid out on a plate
But they didn't even know their fate

As the guests started to take their seat
The cookies started to disappear when everyone started to eat
Matt Knigge, Grade 8
New Egypt Middle School

Beauty Is a Day at the Beach
A day at the beach
Oh! Quite a beautiful sight
The multi color sun is rising
The sun warming my toes as they sink into the sun soaked sand
The ocean breeze blowing my long wavy blonde hair
A cool refreshing mist from the waves
Clear and foamy waves breaking
Dolphins jumping high into the sky in a row
Seagulls soaring above the sun bathers
Sailboats gliding across the ocean blue
Sea glass sparkling in the sand
Waves crashing against the rocky shore
Seashells along the wet and cold sand
Children laughing in the ocean
Fish jumping out of the water
The beautiful colored sun is setting
This extraordinary day at the beach is ending
Gabriella Hagerman, Grade 8
Township of Ocean Intermediate School

Shelter
Seek shelter in a story book, and live a life of ease.
You could be living happily, doing what you please
A life of sweet, sweet ignorance, the best treat of all
In a world of gentle fantasy, where life's always a ball
But sadly such a world, could not ever be true
For the world is full of depression, hate, and rue
Yet all of these challenges, which we have to face
Just teach to survive, in life at quickened pace
But if life were a storybook, the type that's always fair
We would be so bored, and nobody would care
A life without any consequence sounds like a party
But everything's so difficult when everyone's carefree.
Martyn Mendyuk, Grade 9
John P Stevens High School

Soccer Field
At the soccer field in spring
You can see the greenest grass you've ever seen
And look down to see the watery mud
The whistle blows and the game has begun
The fans are cheering having a blast
As the rain starts down pouring and really fast
You try to grip the slippery ball
And feel the beating rain as it falls
After the game you taste the snacks at the celebration
Sending your taste buds on an adventurous sensation

At the soccer field in fall
It's the place to do it all
The wind seems to whisper in my ear
And the fans go berserk as they cheer
The bitter cold seems impossible to bear
The wind whipping and ready to tear
The sweet scent of candy in the air
Grape, strawberry, cherry, and pear
Then get ready to have some candy to eat
And satisfied about the team you just beat
Nick Sample, Grade 7
New Egypt Middle School

Winter
Enchanted snow
Wind pleasures in sound
Cold air
Kind care
Friends give
Presents come
Christmas trees' smells refresh
Christmas breakfast delights
Family loves
Christmas joys
Time values
Winter snow is a white blanket that covers the ground
Winter
Kristen English, Grade 7
Frankford Township School

Texting
I love to text.
I text a lot!
I text nonstop like a robot,
My fingers race from one letter to another.
I hear the screams:
"Get off the phone!" by my mother.
Texting is on a daily basis,
In some of my texts I use smiley faces.
From family to friends I text all day,
At night time I have nothing else to say.
So, I text good-bye and turn off my phone,
Until the next morning before I leave my home
Ashbel Soto, Grade 7
Battin School #4

Forever Gone Mom

I see her face,
Bright as sunlight.
Her sparkling golden form,
Dissolving into light.
Her absence darkens
The midnight corners of my heart.

Blue makes me smile
All the while.
Her rebellious streak of Neptune
Is always showing through.
Tinting her hair,
Staining her lips.
Oh how I wish I could see her face,
Shining as the sea.
How I would give anything
For her to be with me.

Dara McClain, Grade 9
Phillipsburg High School

Friends

A friend is there for you
When you are alone
A friend is there for you
When you have bad days
A friend is there for you
When you have good days
A friend is there for you
Just so you can hang around together
A friend is there for you
A friend is there for you
To share secrets
A friend is there for you
To share time way from work
To share shopping time together
A friend is there for you
Always

Desiree Ortiz, Grade 7
Battin School #4

Being the Youngest

Being the youngest
Of two brothers in their 30's
Is really easy
Your parents
Spoil you
You get your own room
You don't have to babysit
Your younger brother or sister
But there is one bad thing
Being the youngest of 2 brothers
In their 30's
Is you don't get to see them
All the time

Angeline Suarez, Grade 7
Battin School #4

Music

Lots of lyrics that flow together.
Colorful covers,
Red for love songs,
Blue for gloomy songs.
You can dance to a song,
Listen with your ears,
Sing with your mouth.
Music,
Make your volume to the max,
Annoy your parents,
Listen to anything,
Rock out loud.
Dance with your body,
Listen with ear buds,
Sing with your vocals.
From one beat,
To another,
Note in the song.

Alfred Braza, Grade 7
Herbert Hoover Middle School

Snowing

White flakes in the air,
I think it's snowing everywhere.

Blankets of white on the ground,
it's so quiet, you can't hear a sound.

My cat likes to watch the snow,
what are those things? He'd like to know.

I look outside, I see it clear,
I am amazed, it's a baby deer.

I love the snow, it's so much fun,
and the winter has just begun.

I love the snow 'cause most of all,
school is closed, we just got the call!

Garrick Falcetano, Grade 7
Linwood Middle School

Winter

The cold snow
white and beautiful,
glistened in the sun

The sharp icicles
frozen and wet,
slowly melted off the tree

The delicate snowflakes
unique and fragile,
fell from the sky peacefully.

Bridget McCormack, Grade 8
Assumption Academy

I Hear Spring Singing

I hear spring singing,
I hear the bells ringing,
I hear flowers blooming,
I hear grass grooming,
I hear the wedding bells chiming,
I hear the boy rhyming,
I hear the birds humming,
I hear the ducks coming,
I hear the band playing,
I hear the church praying,
I hear the gardener digging,
I hear the dirt flinging,
I hear the farmers sowing,
I hear the life growing,
I hear the colors flying,
I hear winter dying.

Cameron Drake, Grade 7
Lakeside Middle School

Winter Sensation

The hot smell of chocolate
Fills the air.
When I like to eat cinnamon cookies
I share.
The smell of fresh snow fades
Watch out for the pine tree's blades.
Winter feels below zero degrees
I might as well freeze.
Snow is squishy
Wet and mushy.
Winter has a calm sensation
When you like a quiet vacation.
Winter looks completely white
Then, there are snowball fights.
I wish winter can stay,
Please don't go away.

Dayanna Maldonado, Grade 7
Battin School #4

The Four Seasons

Summer is gone,
And fall isn't done,
Until the leaves turn brown,
And everything comes down.

Then we will wait for winter,
Until the snow falls down,
And kids start to play,
Throughout the fun and amazing days.

After winter, spring will come,
And the snow will melt away,
But the grass will come out,
And that's what I'm talking about.

Stefanija Gjorgjioska, Grade 7
Garfield Middle School

Chicken

As wobbly as a penguin when on the farm,
Chocolaty brown,
Peppery black,
Hot sauce red,
It has the taste of spiciness,
The sight of it makes me full,
The smell from the seasoning makes me sneeze,
Thick chicken,
Juicy like an orange,
Crispy like fries,
Anytime food like cereal,
Tongue tingles when I bite,
Originated as an egg,
Grilled chicken,
Baked chicken,
Fried chicken,
Chicken sandwich,
Yearn for it when dipped in hot sauce and sweet and sour sauce,
Small and big,
Best part to eat is the leg,
Best part to get it is at KFC.

Fasia Amara, Grade 7
Herbert Hoover Middle School

Warm Gatherings

I take a seat on the soft carpet,
The warmth hitting my face.
My family surrounds me now,
Each holding a warm mug.

We blow the steam in every direction,
Put our cold lips to the mug, and take a small sip.
It feels good against our ice cold throats,
Giving us internal light…and warmth.

The fire burns higher and brighter like a ray from the sun,
Opening a new, deep meaning inside us.
Winter isn't about holidays,
It's about the warm gathering we share with our families.

Amber Steen, Grade 8
New Egypt Middle School

Furbies

Across the room the Furbies climb.
Until the Furbies and their googly eyes are inside the cave of pillows.
Within the hideout they discuss escape plans.
Over time, they invent a plan and move quickly.
Through the room and against the wall they scurry.
Beyond the rooms boundaries, Furbies scuttle timidly.
Off they go, they are searching for freedom.
Amid the house, Furbies meet many challenges.
Like grasshoppers, they keep hopping anyway.
Atop their beaks, a door can be spotted!
Outside their old lives, the Furbies will never be seen again.

Mackenzie Cowie, Grade 8
Clinton Public School

My Missed Brother

I wished you were here
because you were so dear
I looked up to you
in everything you do
I remember when you made funny jokes
About our old folks
I remember when we used to play
in any part of the day
You would have went to college
because you had a lot of knowledge
I remember when you had a fever
And when we picked up the receiver
I remember when you were in lots of hospitals
And they gave us sweet popsicles
They numbed the pain
When they stuck a needle up your vein
I remember when you could no longer fight the cancer
And when you could no longer answer
I remember when you died
And how everyone cried
I loved you so

Emily Sande, Grade 7
Battin School #4

Angels' Tears

The tears of angels, sacred and pure
Rain upon the world, thousands upon thousands
At a time, dancing and falling in rhythm
No one knows what forces them, sorrow or joy
Look up at the rain
They will cry for the rest of the world
In sorrow, for you out of joy
See the glass half-empty
The angels will cry for you in sorrow
Yet guide you into the light, letting you know
The rain will still not stop
But come down in sheets
Of one thousand drops
Each equally sacred and pure

Alyse Krug, Grade 8
Township of Ocean Intermediate School

Soccer

At game time I lace up my cleats.
Across the field parents and friends cheer!
Without haste the game has begun.
Between the two posts our goalkeeper stands nervously
By half-time the game is a zero to zero gridlock!
Amid the game one team must score.
But by whom them or us?
Toward the end I receive the pass.
Along the sideline I trap and then kick.
Near the 6-yard line the striker one-touches my pass.
Into the goal it flies; we win! Hooray!

Darin D'Ambly, Grade 8
Clinton Public School

I Am

I am a girl who loves to dance
I wonder if I'll be a professional dancer
I hear the flow of the music
I see the bright white stage lights
I want to be the greatest dancer in the world
I am a girl who loves to dance

I pretend to be on stage
I feel the rhythm of the beat
I touch my new dance shoes
I worry about messing up
I cry when I make a mistake
I am a girl who loves to dance

I understand when people don't like my dance
I say I CAN DO IT! I CAN DO IT! All the time.
I dream about my dance recitals
I try my best when I'm on stage
I hope one day I am the best dancer in the world
I am a girl who loves to dance

Sakai Young, Grade 7
William Davies Middle School

My Love for You

Can't wait to sleep and close my eyes
So I can see your smile and your face
On our journey through the night skies
While you hold me in your warm embrace
I'll feel the warmth of your touch
And the caress of your hands
It's a feeling that I've wanted so much
A feeling that only you understand
Sharing a love the only we know how
Without any borders or bounds
With history behind us, we live for now
As we follow our hearts and their sound
All our fears have disappeared
To another place, far from our reach
Our souls have again been cleared
With destiny's soft and tender speech
We'll fly forever together and always free,
My loves in your hands, your soul in mine
facing our worlds together, we'll never flee
Knowing we carry a love so pure, so divine

Glenn Baker, Grade 7
Good Shepherd Regional Catholic School

Halloween

The midnight bell rings on a silent moon
The goblins and witches will strike soon
Children are afraid and crying with fright
They walk down the dark street in the night
They get their candy; they're happy 'till noon

Deep Patel, Grade 8
Christopher Columbus Middle School

Games

Challenging, twisting,
Interactive, imaginative,
Having fun, wasting time,
Getting closer, happiness!

Internet, video, board,
All types of games,
Chess, hockey, Sorry;
Most you know.

Creative, colorful,
Educational, mind-bending.
All are forms of it,
All are fun

They're not about winning or losing
They're about how you play.
Having fun with friends
Or family, is what it's about.

When people are happy
Typically they're involved.
Being close is one thing,
But being a family and having fun, is another.

Bradley Borden, Grade 8
Little Falls School #1

Numbers, Oh Numbers

Numbers, oh numbers, how many can there be
Hundreds, thousands, millions there are many as you can see
How high will these numbers ever get
They may never ever end, I bet

Numbers, oh numbers, they are used everywhere
Even when used by a multi-millionaire
These numbers are said in many ways
To learn all of this would take days

Numbers, oh numbers, they are used every time
There are many types like composite and prime
Numbers can be used at many places
Driving distance, building, and for running races

Numbers, oh numbers, they are very essential
Numbers are important for existential
Without numbers we would be like cave men
Experiencing the Ice Age all over again

Numbers, oh numbers, without them we'd die
We would soon have to say our last good-bye
Numbers are an important part of existence
Recreating them would require extreme persistence

Suraj Shah, Grade 8
Little Falls School #1

Tomorrow
When the sun comes out and I look at the sky,
I started to sniffle and then cried.
Is it true that my tears will dry by the sun?
Is it true that my sadness would truly be gone?
When I woke up today I looked out my window,
I took a big cry on top of my pillow.
I later went swimming in the big blue ocean,
I just moved with the water and with the motion.
I touched my necklace and the moments came to me.
I remembered our first kiss how it was in the sea.
When he said goodbye, I tried hard not to cry.
We were at the beach on the dock,
And I remember it was four o'clock.
He hugged me, I hugged him.
You could really tell it was beautiful bliss
Before he left he said his love for me was granted
When he left I went crazy and frantic
The type of kiss you can't borrow
Was the last kiss we had filled with such sorrow
For we both knew I wouldn't see him tomorrow.
Jennifer Pimentel, Grade 7
Garfield Middle School

Success
Hopped on a plane, 4th of June.
They said we would be there soon.
I didn't realize I would leave my home land and go this far,
I didn't know that my friends and I would be split apart.

As soon as we got there, I felt an adrenaline rush.
I screamed "YES!" my mom says shush.
I felt so many emotions inside,
Happy, sad, and embarrassed like wanting to hide.

A car picked us up to go where we needed to be,
A house filled with love, and our family.
We arrived, and the house was full of happiness.
Cousins, aunts, parents, grandparents what a success.

Adjusting to the culture was hard at first,
Visiting back home was just what I thirst.
But now I can finally say, "I'm an American,"
And this is how my life long journey began.
Rhyza Lozano, Grade 8
Westampton Middle School

The Thirtieth Tree
Concealed from sight,
The perfect tree can take hours to find.
Creeping among the evergreens,
It waits for someone to discover it.
Inhaling the pine, stroking the needles, sawing the trunk,
I knew we had found the tree.
We had not gone very far either!
Jeffrey Paine, Grade 8
New Providence Middle School

Little Acorn
Crunchy little acorns under my feet,
Hard to crush and defeat,
Falling from a tree,
Begging a squirrel please,
Not to eat me,
In the fall they go away,
As squirrels store them for their long lay,
Little acorn oh little acorn,
Please fall from the tree,
So there are little crunchy acorns under my feet,
Hard to crush and defeat.
Amanda Leigh Simone, Grade 7
Herbert Hoover Middle School

Water
Torrential downpour from black clouds
A whirlwind of water going round 'n' round
Destroying houses in a sudden flash
Twenty feet of raging fury ready to kill
Demolishes everything in its path
Then becoming peaceful
The gentle pitter patter of falling off the roof
The calming sloshing of a stream
Peaceful and serene
Helping us and destroying us
Water
Raymond Morgan, Grade 8
William R Satz Middle School

Halloween Night
When Halloween night falls upon the sky
I shiver and shake for time to go by
Monster shadows haunting my room
Whispers of footsteps calling my doom
A squeak of the door holds me in fright
I'm blind without the help of my light
I go under my blankets blocking out all sound
And I knew at once I was fear bound
I uncover my blanket prepared to fight
And guess what I see,
MY LITTLE BROTHER SPOOKING THE NIGHT!!!
Vincent Cheng, Grade 7
Hammarskjold Middle School

Anxious
Getting ready to open presents,
We wait anxiously without care
As our parents take pictures.
Rushing forward,
We grab the boxes.
Shredding the glittery paper,
Ripping the ribbon, and creating a huge mess,
I see what I've been longing for.
Finally!
Jessica Mead, Grade 8
New Providence Middle School

Lady Gaga

Lady Gaga is the best retro artist.
Ever since her first song "Just Dance"
She always turns heads.
Her outrageous outfits and bleached hair.
Her connection to the gay community.
She's just a walking billboard.
To "Poker Face" and "Love Game"
Her inspirational lyrics take over.
No "Paper Gangsta" is my favorite
She's so unique and different
Star struck with a beat so sick.
But before Lady Gaga she was Stephanie,
A regular Italian girl from New York
Her dreams were to become a singer.
She is also the best pianist
But today she is the best singer.
She reached her goal of a singer
She is my idol and I love her.
I hope to one day see her.
I also hope to one day be like her.
Samantha Rios, Grade 8
Christopher Columbus Middle School

Winter Wonderland

Winter is like being in heaven
Snow as white as it can be.
Snowballs being thrown left to right
As love is being thrown back and forth.
Hiding in forts from each other
Laughing and tackling
In the white snow as you can see
It's our winter wonderland.
So let's spend it together
Let it run forever.
Winter wonderland, oh winter wonderland
Stay here till forever.
Memories fly by
As you and I fall in love
Sitting by the fire
Keeping warm as can be
Drinking hot chocolate
Wrapped in blankets
Making each other laugh.
Winter wonderland is heaven!
Samantha Wojtowicz, Grade 8
Christopher Columbus Middle School

Holland

Holland…
Below sea land
Riding Bikes, and windmills.
The home of my ancestry,
Lowland.
Matt Hoyt, Grade 7
Oxford Street School

I Am

I am kind and hard to figure out.
I wonder why we are put on Earth to live.
I hear things of my wildest dreams.
I see visions of war and peaceful land all across the world.
I am kind and hard to figure out.
I want to create peace between nations.
I am kind and hard to figure out.

I pretend to fly war planes.
I feel like I am already dead.
I touch the pool of happiness but when I do it turns to sadness and sorrow.
I worry about the death of a loved one.
I cry when animals die.
I am kind and hard to figure out.

I say life isn't always what you expect.
I understand that I will die at one point in time.
I dream of being a veteran.
I tried to concur my fears.
I hope the world won't end.
I am kind and hard to figure out.
Shawn Haring, Grade 7
Galloway Township Middle School

Fly High Little Bird

Fly high little bird, as far as you can go.
Be my eyes and show me the lands and lives I cannot see.
Be my ears and let me hear the songs the cities sing, even when all asleep.
Fly higher and higher and see the lights that sparkle across the cities.
Every day I wish to see what you can. Seeing all that's out there.
Be the wings I wish I had, and carry me far across the green and frozen lands.
And above the seas where the air is crisp.
When all is accomplished, return to me with a gentle song of all that you've seen.
Land with open wings to rest easy and dream of things anew.
Tomorrow is another day.
Brigitte Roos, Grade 8
Keyport High School

The Warmth Is Gone

As the warmth fades away,
The air gets cooler,
As the sun goes down earlier,
The world gets darker,
As the trees lose their leaves,
The ground becomes covered,
As the memories of lying in the warmth leave,
We know other delightful memories will be made,
As we look out our window and see the changing world,
We think of what will come in the days ahead,
As we think of the cold, dark, leave covered world,
It doesn't appear to be bad,
As all of these changes come,
I look at the world from my own perspective and think of how beautiful it has become.
Nicole Lavorgna, Grade 7
Old Turnpike Middle School

Holidays
Halloween smells like
There is fire burning wood
I love Halloween!

Thanksgiving is
Sweet potato pie
Turkey for my family
Very wonderful!

Fall comes
Chilly weather out
Leaves are falling about
Dark night's early!
Tyler Erwin, Grade 7
New Egypt Middle School

Halloween Party
Trees knock the window
Then the wind will let them in
The party begins

On Halloween…
Tonight brooms will fly
Tonight jack-o'-lanterns shine
Lights won't light tonight

Mischief Night
Wolves howl to the moon
The Jersey Devil will play
Halloween is here
Kayla Jacobus, Grade 7
New Egypt Middle School

Fall
Fall has arrived
The leaves are turning color
Day by day
The apple orchards are ripening
Week by week
The branches are snapping
Month by month
There are fewer trees
Year by year
Fall becomes more exciting
Decade by decade
Christine Beglin, Grade 7
St James School

School
Boring
It's not that fun
Can't wait till it's over
Brings tears to all students who go
Dreadful
Jack Nolan, Grade 7
Oxford Street School

Being Compared Is So Annoying
I'm tired of being compared
To my sister
Just because she gets good grades
And, became 2nd in the 8th grade
Doesn't mean I have to be like her.
Everyone says
"Oh! Now you have a goal to reach!"
But maybe I just don't want to get there.
I'm not as smart as Savannah
And I probably never will be.
Even if I get a good grade on a test
"You could have done better"
I don't like the comments
They make me feel
Like I'm not as important as her
I don't like to talk about school because of the teachers telling me about her!
It gets annoying all the time!
I don't get it!
Why can't people get it through their heads?
That I'm not like Savannah
I am ME!!
Brielle Riotte, Grade 7
Battin School #4

A New Language
After school I run towards the keyboard and sit down.
Above the keys my fingers tremble and get ready to move.
Along the keyboard my fingers leap and dance.
Past each page the music leaps off and surrounds me.
Beyond each song, I get to learn and explore a new one.
Into each song I hear and feel a new story and a new feeling.
Across the music I'm reading a new language or code.
Within each song it tells you about the person,
who composed it and what they were feeling.
Until it gets dark or my fingers fall off, I play for hours.
Beside the keyboard I stand and say good-bye until the next time we meet.
Jamie Kwasnick, Grade 8
Clinton Public School

My House in Winter
As the cold white snow falls from the sky,
You feel it hit your face as you fly,
On the sled down the hill,
The pain in your body as you come off the terrifying ramp,
When your snow gear becomes more and more damp,
As the frigid wind blows against your face,
You think about a warmer place,
Trying to walk up the hill to the house,
Your legs are tired, like a poor little mouse,
The smell of the fresh hot chocolate and cookies as you open the front door,
Your mom offers you some, and you replied sure,
Although the fun comes to an end,
You can sit and relax inside the den,
Now you can stay in the heat, and warm up your cold little feet.
Sarah LoRicco, Grade 7
New Egypt Middle School

A Winter's Day

Christmas time is near. Wintertime is already here. It's cold outside. It's warm outside. This season to me is very dear.
I love the cold. I love the snow and all the snowmen I come to know.
This season is not one bit frightful. To me this season is very delightful.
There are snowflakes on my hair. They are falling everywhere. To find me sad at all this time surely would be rare.
My excitement is like the snow. There's more of it than you know. I don't hold it in. I let it all out, I let my excitement flow.
It's wintertime today. Christmas time is near hooray!

Norman Johnson, Grade 8
New Egypt Middle School

2010

I'm not known for my poeticism or good use of rhyme, but when it comes to writing stories I have all the time.
The point of this poem is to tell you about the upcoming year, but I have no idea whether it will bring joy or tears.
But as far as I'm concerned, I don't really care, for to see into the future I would never dare.
What is in store for me? I'll find out when I'm there.
But as for right now I'll learn and I'll live, and I'll grant this next year all I have to give.

Nicole Sisco, Grade 7
Garfield Middle School

Shea Stadium

The hot, salty, buttery popcorn. The bright lights shining down on New York's team, the Mets. The joy of victory or the taste of defeat can all be seen in this picture. The scoreboard is as tall as the sky, and the lights are as bright as the sun at 2:00 in August. "Lets Go Mets" chants can be heard all the way from Flushing to the Bronx. The seats are hot like a barbeque. But the heat is drowned by ice cold soda and beer. That is all in this picture; along with the feeling "You Gotta Believe!" But looming, lurking in left field is Shea's replacement, Citi Field.

Kevin Brady, Grade 8
W.R. Satz School

The Words of a Judgmental Music Lover

Is love really all you need?
Mr. Lennon, I think we've proved you wrong.
But yet again, that was the 60's

Oh, the Bee Gees were wasting your time.
How and what were they staying alive for?
I bet it had to do with something green and Illegal.

"Michael Jackson thrilled me!" HA
The closest thing to a thriller I've seen from him
was his jerry curl.
Curse you 80's fads.

Did it really smell like teen spirit, Kurt?
Or was it just the girlie cologne going to your head?
No wonder you checked out early, you sang about B.O.!

Can I tell you what I want? What I really REALLY want!?
What the heck is a zig-a-zig-ah
and why do you want it so much?

And Gerard, are you okay? 'Cause if you're not,
you really shouldn't be writing a song about it.
Or name a band after a crush you have for your chemicals.
I think that's pretty weird, but that's just my opinion.

Joyce Canela, Grade 7
Schuyler Elementary School

Hope

Hope.
A very strong word
Said less than expected and surely rarely heard.

Filled with flowers and love,
The whole earth is hard to see.
Look around you, what do you see?
I may see you and you may see me,
But that doesn't mean we're the only ones here.

There's so much more out there.
Much more things to fear, rather than just fate
We may have it easy, but someone is asking for our help.
Our help, our love, and our hope.

There's so much more out there.
Things we may want to see; things we may not.
Others less fortunate call our names, but what do we hear?
Nothing.

We can't wait to be called.
And we can't wait to be heard.
But that doesn't mean we shouldn't help.
Someone is asking for our help.
Our help, our love and our hope.

Alexandra DeBonte, Grade 8
Lakeside Middle School

Change

Why is the grass green,
And the sky blue?
Why is the world as bad as it is?
These are just a few of the many questions
I ask myself daily.

We need to be different
If we want to see
Or even make a difference.
The real change
Can only be found
In you.

Why is the world as bad as it is today?
It is because
No one wants to
Take the first step
In making a real
Change.

Emmy Marroquin, Grade 8
Garfield Middle School

All Tied Up

Bounce, bounce, bounce
the ball is in my possession
Running, gunning, and pushing
to the hoop I go

I was just pushed down
Then the ref called "foul"
Cheering fans fantasize about
their favorite player

Up to the line faster
than a speeding bullet
The game was as tied
as my sneakers

The ball was butter in my
hands as I got ready to shoot
my hands up, the ball launched,
what will happen next

Amaziah Croom, Grade 8
Westampton Middle School

Baseball

Baseball makes my blood pressure fall
Watching the umpire make a call
When I'm up to bat
There's no looking back
Hitting the ball way out there
Hoping the umpire calls it fair
Making it to home plate
Hearing my team yell "We won first place!"

Stefano Cutillo, Grade 7
Garfield Middle School

"Chase(d)"

As the moon's shadows darken by the riverside,
the antelope peels away from the grass and sprints into the Oak Tree forest.
The antelope runs, she cries, she screams,
but no one can hear her as a rambunctious wild prairie dog chases her.
He howls, he barks, yet no one does a thing,
neither the trees nor the flowers pity the antelope.
Quiet, again,
the antelope runs briskly through the prickly vines and bushes.
Thinking that she is far ahead of the dog, she stops she smells the air,
nothing, nothing but the smell of stubbing milkweed from the ground beneath her.
Suddenly, the attack.
The dog.
Within seconds her spirit arises from her velvet body,
and forever holds peace.
The dog has finished his duties to his master, and goes back to being enslaved.
The end for them both.

Bethany Strong, Grade 7
Woodland Country Day School

Boston

I walked down the freedom trail and found myself immersed.
Immersed in the history and the culture of what our country was.
The coolness of the gravestones chilled my fingers.
Adams, Jefferson, and so many others buried here.
Closing my eyes, I took a deep breath.
The air smelled like fall and there was a slight chill to the warm summer breeze.
I could hear galloping:
The galloping of a particular horseman coming down the very street I stand on.
The wind then picked up and rushed by me.
As if something were running by at an accelerated pace.
It was so real; I could almost taste the dust in my mouth.
But when I opened my eyes I saw the streetlights and cars of today.
The fire lit lamps and carriages I had just so vividly seen, were nowhere to be found.
I shook my head and thought, "I guess some things never truly die in Boston."

Ashleigh Shay, Grade 9
Ranney School

Graveyard

Darkness all around me as I tip-toed through the graveyard.
I shiver as the wind blows by, I hear ghost sounds.
A ghost comes up from behind a tombstone.
"Boo!" it yells.
I laugh and run ahead.
Ding-Dong!
I ring the doorbell and the door creaks open.
A witch next to me cackles and a werewolf next to her howls.
"Trick-or-treat!" we yell together and candy gets dumped by our feet.
We walk out the graveyard and onto the street, without missing a single beat.
We all make spooky sounds and stomp loudly on the ground.
Down the road I hear a scream.
"Relax!" I yell.
"It's Halloween!"

Winnee Lee, Grade 7
Hammarskjold Middle School

Swing Set

I sit on a swing I'm ready to start,
I go back and forth back and forth just like the beat of my heart.
I feel free in the air without a care,
Just with the breeze running through my hair.
The sun's rays hit my face,
There is no pain not a trace.
If I was ever angry or ever filled with woe,
The swings would cheer me up and let happiness flow.
If I was ever confused or filled with fear,
Gliding through the air would make things clear.
Through the bad times and the good times they always been there,
Swinging is wonderful this I declare,
I go down to the earth and up to the sky,
When I swing I feel like I can fly.
When my heart's beat is off track,
The swings calm me down and get me back.
Some think swings are exciting some think they'll fall,
But I think swings are soothing like a waterfall.

Alexis Kerlin, Grade 7
St Raphael School

Volleyball

Who would be a volleyball who could help it?
Always the victim never the conqueror.
She's always being passed around like
A newborn baby who won't stop crying.
The startling slaps and noises,
Bump after bump. Set after set.
And our highest wishes: a spike.
She's a continuous game of "keep it up."
She would adore to forfeit if ever given the chance.
The crowd goes wild as she slams on the floor.
A quiet servant, following every order.
Finally, a moment of rest and retaliation,
Hearing the giggles as she is rolled away from the comforting closet.
She is like a guinea pig, always testing out new techniques.
When everyone's celebrating, she sheds a tear.
The tournaments are now over, and she is relieved.
The season comes to an end, and she is back in the closet.
Lonely and dreading next fall.

Tara McGowan, Grade 8
Clinton Public School

Fright Night

As I shiver in patience for Halloween night,
I can't wait to wear my costume that will send everybody in fright,
As the days get darker and colder,
I feel Halloween will be scarier, then the left pocket on my folder
I love Halloween, I love it very much,
Especially all the candy I get including the chocolate nuts,
As the days pass and Halloween gets near,
I can't wait to enjoy the day that will send everyone in fear,
With the parties and my dad drinking beer,
I can tell that this will be a great year!

Matthew Salvent, Grade 7
Hammarskjold Middle School

First Beach Trip

Sand slid smoothly into the water.
Seagulls scavenged salty snacks.
Wild winds whipped my face.
Beach balls bounce.

Boats honked from afar.
Waves crashed onto the land.
Seaweed sought refuge in the moist sand.
The boardwalk rested on the beach's edge.

It was no hassle to construct a sand castle.
Little kids screamed for cold ice cream.
I avoided horseflies while eating French fries.
Vibrant blue skies attracted my eyes.

Clouds were like cotton candy.
The air was as crisp as an oven.
Shells were jagged like shattered glass.
Umbrellas dotted the beach like a field of flowers.

Austin Pettit, Grade 8
Westampton Middle School

Days Pass By

I'm still staring out the window
As birds fly by
Even though it rains
The sky is full of clouds,
And my mood feels gray.
I hush my urge to cry.
I can still hear my mother's words.
"You're too young to love,
So you're too young to have your heart broken."
But this isn't a crush,
And I feel that pain.
I am young,
But why is this wound bleeding?
Being a child
It used to be better,
Scraped knees were better than broken hearts.
Bleeding on the outside
It seems like a scratch,
Compared to my bleeding heart!

Sabrina Hurtado, Grade 8
Christopher Columbus Middle School

Watch the Pretty Leaves

Watch the colorful, pretty leaves fall
Hear the leaves crunch on the bottom of your feet
As you pass on by, Crunch, Crunch, Crunch.
Watch the kids playing in the leaves.
Watch the parents rake the leaves.
Watch the wind whistle the leaves away from the trees,
Watch the squirrels gather nuts and seeds.
But most of all, watch the colorful, pretty leaves.

Lauren Nicole Hernandez, Grade 7
Garfield Middle School

Seasons

The time has now come
For the season to change
I watched the leaves change while sitting on my bum
The colors slowly began to rearrange

I watched the pretty, lovely colors
As they changed from one to another
Red, orange, and brown
I see them changing all around

This is a sign that fall has come
All I can do is sit on my bum
This season comes with so much work
But all this is worth it, if I get to eat pork

Overall, this is my favorite season
And I have many reasons
Although it's cold its so much fun
All this is worth the fun in the sun

Gabriella Coridon, Grade 8
Westampton Middle School

Truth or Dare

Why start if you know it would be hard?
This time no one is on guard
It infiltrates the body
Inhale exhale
Ahh...does that feel good?
You're killing yourself inside
Bet you didn't know that
The biggest abuse, smoking
Not to anyone but yourself
Did you know you can kill someone else?
Second hand smoking
Your kids, friends, and pets
Keep it up and they'll be next
Kids are known to follow in their parents' footsteps
Whirlpools of soot in your lungs
Every day is a new experience that is right
But are you willing to die just for a light?
Truth or dare
The truth is the dare will kill you

Dajsia Owen, Grade 8
Keyport High School

New York City

I came from a place in New York City called Chinatown.
When I'm sad, this place turns my frown upside down.
Dragon dances on New Year's Day,
Chinese people in every crossway,
The warm feeling of home included there.
That place is unlike anywhere.
The memories there, I will keep,
I can't wait to go back so I won't weep.

Wendy Chen, Grade 7
Battin School #4

The Light Which Shines

The light which shines down from the sky,
The light that illuminates our path,
It reflects off the puddles to make rainbows,
A true work of art and beauty,
That makes us awe at its site,
The light that illuminates our hearts,
When they are full of hate and distaste,
The light which comforts us,
When we are sad and have no faith,
The light which shines in a baby's eyes,
When a baby first sees,
It fills the parents with happiness and delight,
Yet, when the light goes out,
Things start to go amiss,
When bad things start to brew and stir,
When evil starts to creep about,
It starts to fill our hearts with misery and despair,
The light which shines will come about again,
To save us from our misery and despair

Raul Mendoza, Grade 8
Township of Ocean Intermediate School

True Friends

You tell each other just about everything
And have sleep overs galore
You turn the radio extra loud, and sing
Time together is fun; never a bore

A shoulder to cry when you're really sad
Going to the boardwalk, movies, and mall
She makes you feel good when you feel bad
There to catch you when you fall

This special person could never be replaced
Even if you searched the world and tried
Out of the crowd, that one special face
You go on vacations and really long car rides

They aren't just a friend; they are the best
You want her to be there until the end
If you don't know they're okay, you just can't rest
Whom could this be? Your true friend

Tatianna Leon, Grade 7
William Davies Middle School

Christmas

Ringing with great joy church bells
Christmas is finally here as December comes to an end
Awakening with great excitement that morning
To see what is under the big tree, I just can't wait.
Sprinting with happiness I leap under the tree.
Wrapped with colorful paper, big bows, and beautiful ribbons
The presents tease me.
I CAN'T WAIT TO SEE WHAT'S INSIDE!!!

Jack Scheader, Grade 8
New Providence Middle School

The First Snowfall

Tumbling down from the sky,
the first snowflakes float down to the Earth
with a chill in the air.
Glittering in the light,
the snow begins to build.
Blanketing the Earth,
magically transforming everything powder white,
and signaling the true start of winter,
the first snowfall brings with it the frosty days to come.
How wonderful the world looks laden in snow!

Mark Hays, Grade 8
New Providence Middle School

Exclusion

Like a glass wall separating them from me
The other side laughing with glee
I stand alone in the pouring rain
They are cozy and warm huddled under an umbrella's cane
They stare at me
Glare at me
Until their eyes get big and bold
While I stand there alone shaking in the wet frigid cold
Takes a while for the wall to shatter
If it takes that long, does it really matter

Emily Lang, Grade 8
Township of Ocean Intermediate School

Christmas Love

Presents are everywhere under the tree,
Even next to you and me,
Lights shining on and off, smiling at us.
No kid making a fuss.
Enjoying presents by the dozen,
The whole family is together even the cousins,
Sugar being baked,
While opening some presents emotions are faked.
Christmas time is here,
So give out a cheer!

Sierda Rodi, Grade 7
Garfield Middle School

Birthday

My birthday's coming up, oh joy, oh joy,
I hope I get Uggs and maybe a toy,
A new Barbie doll would be cool,
It would be awesome if my mom brought cupcakes to my school,
I can't wait to give them out to my best buds,
After one bite they'll all fall in love,
When I get home my presents are lined up,
I find a pair of Uggs, I have such good luck,
My family comes by and we have some cake,
I have to say this birthday was great!

Sabrina Kicaj, Grade 7
Garfield Middle School

Christmas

Christmas is almost here
There are people spreading Christmas cheer
Christmas trees and Christmas lights
It's always so cold on these cold Christmas nights
The whole ground covered with snow
It seems that the night goes by so slow
Decorations around the house
Everything seems to be as quiet as a mouse
The whole family around the table
Looking at the gifts, reading the labels

Samantha DeVuyst, Grade 7
Garfield Middle School

About Him

Everywhere I go I see him,
He always has a grin,
He never says "hi,"
He always says "bye,"
He's pretty smart,
But he's not into art,
His friends side by side,
I watch as my sister goes down the slide,
There's so much about him I don't understand,
However, I'm his number one fan.

Esilona Kristani, Grade 7
Garfield Middle School

Time

Time, it is beautiful, powerful, and oftentimes cruel.
It can weaken the strongest army, and throw presidents out of rule.
It freezes when situations are tough
and flies by when it's anything but rough.
Time, it hates us all and irritates us.
Makes us say "That happened just a while ago" and all that ruckus
So live life to the fullest and don't dare to cry
Because time will take life away in the blink of an eye
And don't whine, complain or let out a big sigh
because in time, it will make us all die.

Hubert Pietruszynski, Grade 7
Garfield Middle School

The Person Inside of Me

I am the first king in a brand new empire.
I am the risk taker standing alone on top of the mountain.
I am the only student in a group of jokers.
I am a cloud floating above everyone below me.
I am a puzzle piece different from all of the other pieces.
I am a goose struggling to get to the front of the flock.
I am an ocean wave crashing in the bright moonlight.
I am a tree slowly and gently shaking in the cold breeze.
I am a spark ready to ignite the ready to burn wood.
I am a football flying through the air just waiting to be caught.

Kyle Reiter, Grade 7
Old Turnpike School

The Game

I grabbed my ticket and headed out the door
I was ready for some action and a little bit of gore
When I got to the stadium
I smelled pretzels, food, and beer
And in the background I could hear the crowd cheer
The home team was running across the grass
Then they huddled together in one huge mass
I could feel the rumbling under my seat
As the college band played their steady beat
I bit into my hot dog that I had bought
And I could taste the mustard, it was spicy and hot
It was time for the coin toss
And the game to begin
I could sense in my bones that we were going to win
Then a whirling wind came
I could smell the crisp fall air
As the ball was kicked and soared through the air

Alex Sempervive, Grade 7
New Egypt Middle School

Christmas

It's a day of special holiday cheer
One of the greatest times of the year

Lights and sounds to always remember
It's a day in the month of December

Presents and gifts under the tree
It's a special time for the whole family

Everyone can enjoy it all together
In this cold and snowy holiday weather

In this month people shop for the whole day
While children go out in the snow and play

There's a big week off of school, all the children cheer
Looks like we'll see them in the New Year.

Ken Fedor, Grade 7
Garfield Middle School

School Year

In the hottest summer days, I stay out in my pool, but when September comes, I'm off to school. I'll try my best at math, and gym, and all those other subjects, but I hope that this year I'll hand in all my projects. School has always come along hard for me and I never turned out being the best of the best. But, hey, at least I can pass all those tests. So come on down and take a seat, because you're in for a really special treat. I always have a staring contest at the end of the period with the clock, but the only thing it does is taunt me with its tick-tock-tick-tock. And as soon as that bell rings, I say to myself, "I am so out of here." I leave the school, seeing it until next year, and I happily leave, without shedding a tear.

Michelle Chinalski, Grade 7
Garfield Middle School

The Blues Player

He sings for happiness, the ingredient for hope.
The recipe is adrift in his heart, tossed to and fro in the stormy seas.

As he sits on the corner, his dubious thoughts fill his head,
The memories of his wife leaving him come back into view.

The man is soused with desolation and yet,
He is also sober of happiness.

The blues follow him, love him and care for him,
Like it does to all other blues players.

He yearns for a second chance,
Another turn to roll the dice.

He walks away nonchalantly,
The look on his face tells that he is a true blues player.

Michael Marchese, Grade 7
Christ the King Regional School

Thankful

I am thankful for you
I am thankful for me
For almost everybody
Especially my mommy
And my daddy
Also my little brother
Even though he's sometimes a bother

I love them all no matter what
On Thanksgiving, it's not what we bought
But what we brought to the table

And love is what we have
It's not a label

The food we devour on this day
I am thankful to spend it with special people to this day

Sofia Agolli, Grade 7
Garfield Middle School

Squirrel

Scurrying up the tall oak tree,
the squirrel surveys the nearby area
as if he were its king.
Assuring himself that nothing is in its vicinity,
the animal carefully plucks
a nut off the tree.
Glancing at the acorn,
skinning the shell,
and popping it into his mouth,
the squirrel scampers into its hole
and takes a nap.
What a magnificent creature!

Andrew Scharf, Grade 8
New Providence Middle School

Around the Christmas Tree

There are many presents for thee
There are tears of joy,
And laughter caused by a baby boy.
Pretty young girls
With their hair all curled.
Everyone is very well-dressed
Some maybe even to impress!
Outside there are snowball fights
Inside there are tasty bites.
Around the fireplace
There's a decoration of Santa Claus's place
Music to fill the air,
But mostly with everyone's tender love
Snow around the doorstep
Because of people leaving footsteps.
Presents going around
Gift paper with the tearing sound
Family and friends
Together till the end!

Melanie Oviedo, Grade 8
Christopher Columbus Middle School

Beauty Is on Top of a Mountain

I stand at its highest points
And look to the land below
I don't see any signs of life
Just the view of the clean white snow

The mountain air is cool and crisp
The tall trees are brown and green
The longer I shall stand here
The more beautiful the scene

Last July, when I was here
The picture was different for me
Many animals scurrying about
Amongst the many grand trees

A prettier site I have never seen
My favorite place in the whole world 'round
I will come here whenever I can
Because I always love the sounds

Andrew Tobin, Grade 8
Township of Ocean Intermediate School

Sanctuary Stream

Sanctuary Stream
Cool, smooth, peaceful,
Flowing, dribbling, calming,
Swiftly sloshing silently; simply,
Giving me hope at night,
Standing, protecting, guarding,
Bumpy, rough, ragged,
Restful Rock

Chris Loos, Grade 7
Frankford Township School

Friends for Eternity

My friends are extremely unique to me
they always make me enthusiastic, joyous, and glee
we are always there for one another
and never leave out a sister, nor a brother
neither a human, or animal could break us up
we wouldn't even give each other up for a brand new pup
we have an abundant amount of delightful sleepovers
we watch continuous horror movies about zombie keepers
I yearn that we could interact, and play all day
but not everyone gets her own way
we will always be excellent friends for the entire duration of our lives
even when we are married, and are wives

Rachel Ghirardi, Grade 7
St Mary's School

Dance

Before the music plays I warm up.
About to teach I close my eyes and relax,
Until my students walk in…
Along the side I stand and watch as they themselves warm up.
Throughout the class kids fall but keep trying their best to get the dance done.
Through the practice my friend and I are spinning so much our legs hurt.
Without pain and sweat is when we know we aren't trying.
Among all the classes I teach FV is the best.
Neat a city that never sleeps…
I've been to that camp since I was 9, I love teaching there too.

Yamis Fernandez, Grade 8
Clinton Public School

Aunt Autumn

Ornamented with harvest red and fiery orange leaves,
The tree, which stood in the meadow, glowed in the windy, autumn morning.
Thriving in the rhythm of the wind,
The leaves spun and swayed stylishly
As though they were in a ballet.
Basking in the warmth of the sun,
Enveloped in burning leaves,
Generously letting go of her glory,
The tree stood in the lonely lane.
Oh, how elegant is Aunt Autumn!

Wajiha Khan, Grade 8
New Providence Middle School

Spring

The birds are flying in the sky,
They are singing into our ears.
Spring is here now!
The sun warms the ground.
The grass is growing.
The trees grow new leaves every day.
The beautiful tulips smell so lovely.
The rain pouring so beautifully onto the colorful flowers.
Splash! Splash! The rain stops, and the little sweet drops of rain get stuck on the flowers.
Oh wow! It looks like Spring is in another fresh and new wonderful world!

Rosalba Kapllani, Grade 7
Garfield Middle School

Alaska

Alaska is an extreme place
Winter or summer
With cruise ships, snow and rain
It never is the same
Alaska is warm and cold in summer
With cruise ships pulling up to docks
Rain pouring all day long, and birds flying in flocks

Cruise ship foghorns sound the city
Salmon get hatched and cooked
People fill the empty towns, and tours get booked
Alaska is much different in winter
You hear wolves howl in the night
There's emptiness throughout the state
And such big icebergs, what a sight

The frozen waters are so cold
Reports for snowstorms that you are told
On your cheeks you get frostbite
And there's more hours of the night
Alaska you can see is very unique, but never has a lack
And once you get there you will see
That you'll sure want to come back

Jen Manger, Grade 7
New Egypt Middle School

Summer '09

This summer
When I went to the shore and got out of the car
I instantly smelled that blue ocean smell
My nose started to tingle
Like a cat when it smells tuna
That's just one of the great feelings
You can get when you go down the shore

We were walking
And I was tugging on my little sister to go faster
But she just wasn't going fast enough,
I picked her up and started to run
Then we finally got there,
I got that nice feeling
When your feet touch the hot sand
As it goes between your toes

It's past that cold season
And now on to the hot
For just two months we had freedom,
Then as soon as you know, BAM!
It's time to go back to school
Goodbye summer.

Riley Burke, Grade 7
Schuyler Elementary School

Just Caity

I am the book, cherished and worn, tucked under a child's arm.
I am the journal, written in secret, holding memories.
I am the story, full of promise, waiting to be written.
I am the fingertips that reach for the never ending sky.
I am the bookshelf stuffed to the brim with fiction and fantasy.
I am the observer, sketching all I find interesting or strange.
I am the person who walks away from cruelty and violence.
I am the dreamer who conducts her own fate with a smile.
I am the teenager who still believes in fairies and soul mates.
I am the writer who refuses to conform to others' ideas.

Caitlyn Apgar, Grade 7
Old Turnpike School

Got Happiness?

People are all different
As all of us know
Different things make us happy
People find happiness in certain objects
An expensive item or a gadget
A whatzit or a thingamabob
But that is not true happiness
Happiness is within the heart
There's no need to find pleasure in useless things
Find the pure pleasure within

Alexandra Cros, Grade 8
Township of Ocean Intermediate School

Next Stop…?

At the train station, the ticket holder gave me a pass.
It reads: "destination —?", I told security and he just shrugged.
I got into the train and nobody was there.
So I sat near the window for two hours.
Then the outdoors disappeared and the announcement said
"Next stop…"
The train stops and I jump off onto nothing.
Then the train disappeared and I hopped into my
…Imagination.

Nathalie Velez, Grade 9
Holy Family Academy of Bayonne

The Delight Song of Toby

I am the first piece of elegant cake on a paper plate.
I am the unwanted man who speaks his mind on a soap opera.
I am the pencil sharpener in a stash of erasable pens.
I am the picture book lying next to a novel.
I am the baseball in a sport bag of air pumps.
I am Charles Darwin answering the door for Jehovah's witnesses.
I am the mud stain in Vera Wang's living room.
I am the light bulb in a dungeon of torches.
I am the egg man preaching in a church on Easter morning.

Toby Cozzolino, Grade 7
Old Turnpike School

The Breeze

My hairs on my arms,
Go stick up,
As the breeze hits me…

It feels like a wake up call,
A message…

I feel like an ice cube,
Frozen as can be,
Soon I start turning purple,
As a grape

My lips quiver,
As I shiver…

My breath can be seen,
In a form of a white puffy clouds

The atmosphere feels damp,
And silent…

Then I hear someone talk,
Mother nature…
Whistles through the breeze.

Raquel Lesser, Grade 8
Solomon Schechter Day School of Bergen County

Lesson of Life

Look out the window, see the sun shine,
Thinking everything will turn out fine.
Thinking the day will be divine,
Then come home, and end up cryin'.

Little boy, little boy, take a knee,
Here's a lesson you'll learn from me.
Life's all rules, we live by decrees,
Everything's not as simple as it used to be,

Life's not easy, not everything's good,
But that shouldn't stop you from the "can's" and "would's."
Make sure to make yourself understood,
Come out from under your hood.

Work each task out, one by one,
And continue 'til your work is done.
Even if, your job has just begun,
Even if your job is not fun.

Life may hit you, life may smart,
Life may land you with a broken heart.
Life may make you tear yourself apart,
Don't let that hinder your start.

Eric Tam, Grade 9
Parsippany High School

That Girl

Her style is vicious,
She is caring and kind,
She keeps her head up and her past for behind,
Her attitude is classified,
How she feels is most important,
She is in her right mind,
She is determined and confident,
Her word is the bottom line,
She isn't conceited or above else,
She also has a strong belief,
    "If you believe in yourself you can surely
achieve. Watch what you say and watch
what you do. Just trust and believe everyone
else will believe in you, too. Set a
standard and a goal to reach, and
if you succeed you'll have the world to meet."

Raven Butler, Grade 7
Lakeside Middle School

Michael

Dusk till dawn, I lay down in the meadow,
    only to ponder of the young little fellow.
His name is Michael only three years of age,
    and all ready he has made a difference in me.
I've learned to appreciate what I have and love.
    Anyway, nothing can stay long or forever.
Life is too short to keep sealed and hidden,
    so don't live it unnoticed, or unseen.
I am bursting with laughter and joy from
that little fellow who has given me more to live for.
From the day of his birth he has grown on me,
    and I love him more and more each day.
I love him every day of my life,
    and even though he gets me going,
I know that I can count on that little fellow
    to bring me back to my mellow.

Dana DeFelice, Grade 7
Lakeside Middle School

Autumn

The wind blows, the leaves fall,
    It's a nice autumn after all.
Many children are laughing with cheer,
    For Halloween is almost here.
"Jeez it's cold," yelled the class hooligan,
But his parents don't mind for school has began.
The school bell rings, the children moan,
The teacher say, "My, those children have grown."
    The day is done,
    All the children take off in a run,
        As the day draws away,
Those autumn leaves will still be there the next day.

Nicole Borowsky, Grade 7
St James School

The Everyday Life of Me
I am the last red drop of venom of death in the Black Mamba, watching its prey scurry over the hills at night.
I am the last crusty, stale, golden, expired Twinkie in a bomb shelter of W.W.II.
I am the shining, dazzling sparkly of joy in every winter snowflake white as a fluffy melting marshmallow.
I am the only red flaming candle on a birthday cake, older than the man himself.
I am the roaring engine of a silver Porsche Carerra GT flying on the New York, pot hole streets.
I am the lost mouse in a maze made of cheese from the moon with the brain the size of a human's brain
I am the crackling, glowing, explosive fire that burns throughout every night burning wood made of steel.
I am the explosion of a colorful rainbow that blinds the eye from the intense colors during a night sky.
I am the eye of the tiger, I am the thrill of my fight, I am my rival.*

*From "The Eye of the Tiger" by Survivor

Carl Pennella, Grade 7
Old Turnpike School

Halloween
During a cold night with crunchy autumn leaves, there are ghost stories and tales of creatures lurking.
Among us are vampires, witches, and more.
Throughout the night, people are screaming on the streets.
Within the hours of Halloween, people trick-or-treat to collect candy.
Concerning the trick-or-treaters is the story of the bad luck black cats.
Inside homes are parties and families gathering to have pumpkin pie.
Underneath a bowl of candy, sometimes a hand pops out to spook you.
Until Halloween night is over, all of this will be here,
Below the ground zombies are dying to get out.
Across the country, Halloween is a national holiday.
Without Halloween, what would October 31st be?

Hayley Doud, Grade 8
Clinton Public School

My Book
Worn out from thousands of page turns,
The book is my companion that is seen by the dim light of my flashlight, in the middle of the dark night.
Being read for the hundredth time,
It can still make me gasp and grin and refuses to bore me.
Having been lost under the soft sheets of the bed so many times as I sleep,
Being bent and creased time and time again,
Once again letting me forget all my stress and transporting me into the world within its pages,
It rests near my pillow, waiting anxiously to be opened again.
It's colors are faded and dull, demonstrating how loved it is.
Characters wait for me to read on so their life stories can continue.
The lives in my book are so vital to my own.

Kelsey Fama, Grade 8
New Providence Middle School

The Delight Song of Connor
I am the last line in Will Ferrell's comedy routine.
I am the man eyeing your cheeseburger behind you in the buffet line.
I am the last chapter in The Diary of a Wimpy Kid series.
I am the lacrosse ball that spins quickly into the corner of the net.
I am the elephant who fights his way through a pack of ferocious cheetahs.
I am the crack that you hear after a great hit on the football field.
I am the die hard Red Sox fan who is pounding his fists after a ball soars over the green monster for a home run.

Connor Cairoli, Grade 7
Old Turnpike School

Cold Hard Crash

Oh, what a sight
That vast, winter wonderland
Just right for a sled ride
My fingers froze as icicles overtook me
And I felt my fingers freeze to the sled
As I leap like a cheetah on it
And I start to ride down…

The sled overtook me
I couldn't stop it
The sled held me still
As I watched the world zoom by way too fast
As if an inebriated driver took control of the sled
And I saw a long brown thing
Right up ahead
I tried to swerve to avoid it, but…

CRASH!

I lay on the ground,
Watching the earth go by
And remembered my cold hard crash.

Billy Wetzel, Grade 8
New Egypt Middle School

This Man

He walks slowly in the rain
He has persistence, although going slow
He's knows some things we don't know
He is wise and wandering
He journeys the globe
He carries with him only his words
And his robe
He walks softly
But speaks softer
And he speaks kindly
But acts kinder

The trees wave to him as he goes by
The people come to meet him eye to eye
He is a stranger to many
But a friend to all
He walks with power
Elegant and refined
But this man is poor
And despite his standing
He still stands tall
And he leaves footprints; only footprints for all

Paul Bayruns, Grade 8
Good Shepherd Regional Catholic School

Summer

Summer is a time of fun,
Surfing and swimming with everyone.
Eating ice cream and drinking lemonade,
While sitting on a relaxing beach chair in the shade.
About Stone Harbor, Avalon and Cape May,
I have absolutely nothing bad to say.
In good old Spring Lake, Sea Girt and Manasquan,
I watch the lifeguard tournament and surf marathon.
The fireworks in Bradley Beach and Asbury Park,
Light up the sky when all is dark.
Summer is my favorite season
But that is because of only one reason.
I visit my grandparents at the shore
When summer ends I only want to stay there more.

Charlie Fritz, Grade 7
St James School

Fall

Fall fitfully flings foliage
Sipping chicken soup
Colorful leaves all around
Flying through the air

A patchwork of pumpkins pattern the streets
Big orange pumpkins
Green vines twisting all around
Bright brimming squash

Autumn annually announces approaching winter
In fall there is change
Trees lose their colorful leaves
For winter is near

Garrett Miller, Grade 7
New Egypt Middle School

Ghost in the Mansion

You're scared,
You're frightened,
Your skin may have lightened.
You're really close to crying or maybe even dying.
This place is rare to seek so don't take a peek!
I'm here but no I'm there.
BOOOO!!!!!! You're scared.
I win; I know I am not so fair
But I don't even care!!!!!!
Ha!!!!!!

Felix Rodriguez-Paulino, Grade 7
Lakeside Middle School

The Crack of the Bat

Baseball is a sport I love
As the bat breaks, the ball will soar
The ball flies over the monstrous fence
The crowd goes wild
The bases are circled, they add the score.
It's all tied up
The players are hyped, they're ready to win
With one out to go in the bottom of the ninth
The bat is swung as the ball flies again
Over the monstrous fence to win the game!

Cliff Nash, Grade 7
St James School

Where I'm From

I'm from the kitchen smelling of freshly baked cookies, and from delicious pasta at least one
night a week, and that surprise party where everybody thought I was going to cry.

I'm from mashed potatoes and people saying try them you'll love them, then two years later I
LOVE them, and from really bad ear infections and fevers to go with it!

I'm from my step mom teaching me how to sew, and taking goofy pictures with my best friend
Tara, and James Blunt blasting in the car on our way home from the shore.

I'm from my mom having my sister, Annabelle, and from Hawaii where my mom and step dad
got married, and really fun pool parties all the time.

I'm from collecting sea shells at the beach, and from taking my grandpa's ice cream cone away
from him and saying "I'm only using it!" and from my dad saying I'm proud of you, when I
have done something great, and from becoming a big sister of not only one but two baby sisters,
and from everyone calling me Winkler.

I'm from Italy and Hungary where my family was from, I'm from "Put your stuffed animals in a
bag, I won't throw them out!" I'm from that family tree that just keeps growing and growing!

Taylor Ann Winkler, Grade 7
Linwood Middle School

First CAP O-Flight

I still remember the first time I laid my hands on the controls of an airplane.
I was a scared little boy even though the wheels haven't even left the ground yet.
Then my experienced co-pilot jumped onto the other side.
We then started to go through the 5 million page checklist before we took off.

Then the engine popped as the pilot pushed the throttle forward.
We then started to gain our airspeed as we raced down the runway.
As soon as we got fast enough the wheels left the ground and it felt like the plane was a feather floating in the wind.
The pilot then handed me over the controls and told me to maintain an altitude of 2,500 feet.

While I was flying on course to the airfield in Millville I had to watch my speed, altitude, course and for other planes.
We finally saw the airfield over the horizon in the bright sunlight.
We then dropped our altitude and airspeed as we were coming in on our approach.
While we were doing that I had to call in for clearance for me to land.

I got the "ok" and handed over the controls to the pilot for the landing since he is more experienced.
As we got closer to the ground my stomach started to feel queasy.
As the wheels bumped onto the gravel I jumped a little.
After our flight was over I realized that I would like to get my pilot's license.

Brian Mumbower, Grade 8
Westampton Middle School

Garden

Strolling in a garden,
I feel calm and relaxed when I am stressed.
Overhearing the trickle of fountains
Combined with the crunch of pebbles under my feet are all delightful.
Reading on a bench, wandering aimlessly through paths, and inhaling the sweet fragrance of roses,
I discover that a garden is the perfect place to get away.
Oh, how much burden is lifted off my shoulders when I enter a garden!

Jackie Eisenberg, Grade 8
New Providence Middle School

Your Dreams

Dreams can be shattered by being put down,
Saying you want to be successful and be the joke of the town.

People say you can't when you know that you can,
When you're very successful they won't be saying you can't then.

If they still bother you then that is a hassle.
You just remember this quote, "When they throw stones at you, you pick it up and build a castle."

Dreams are your dreams not what anybody else think,
If you give in to the people that say you can't, then your dreams will sink.

You hope and pray that your dreams could come true,
And know that your dreams are what you want to do.

The people that tell you that you can't, will feel sorry when they know you are a success,
And that your dreams did work out for the best.

KeShawn Alexander, Grade 7
Garfield Middle School

Snow

The snow covered hill, like a white blanket wrinkled over the earth
Peaceful snowflakes started their descent from the crystal blue sky
The smell of the frosty air lingered in my body
The arctic icicles dangled from the shivering rooftops
The glacial hill seemed to never end
The runners sliced through the crisp field
The wind whipped my face into a knot
Everywhere I looked was colorless and smooth
When I began to reach the bottom of the hill I saw the green prickly trees, waiting to catch me
The sled sped up into a full sprint
I could not stop it, it was like a thousand horses were dragging me to the bottom
The lush tree was sucking me in like a black hole
Then I slammed into the brown bark
My head hurt as if I was smacked with a bat
Then everything changed, each delightful snowflake became a heavy brick falling from the gray sky,
And the once clear white earth became black.

Alyssa Bonavito, Grade 7
Old Turnpike Middle School

My Best Friend

Colby,
I remember you when you used to be so small
I remember how we grew together and wish we would live on and on
I remember how you would make me feel loved.
I remember how you could listen to me all day long
I remember when you ran around yelping just for me to come.
I remember when we played together and how we promised we would forever.
I still have you with me day-by-day and won't forget the memories and promises we made.
That would be because you will always be my best friend even if you have four legs.
Doesn't matter to me, I know you will always be there for me, watching over me and helping me.
You inspired me through my life and made me realize that you can make a difference in someone's life.
You will never be forgotten and will always be my best friend and my dog,
I love you, and I can't wait until I see you again, above.

Taylor Groves, Grade 7
Lakeside Middle School

Who Would Disappear First?

Strutting down the trail
Chirp Chirp
The mini crickets announcing they are here
Why am I here?
Can I go back?
Turned around to head home
A mysterious light appeared
What's that?
It grew larger
I stopped.
Hoping it would vanish
But it didn't.
It was coming towards me
The only thing I could do was run
My feet wouldn't move
Big, bright glowing yellow heading for me
I finally moved
It consistently followed
If it didn't disappear, I would.
I got curious
All I could do was wait.

Michele Ziobro, Grade 8
Keyport High School

Tasting Words

A bittersweet goodbye,
cannot compare,
to a sugary, flavorful "Hi!".
A luscious "I love you" rolls into the rain,
"I hate you" kills the flavor,
and leaves you with a feeling of disdain.
Let your words dance upon your tongue,
before they escape through your lips,
decide: sweet or sour? Speak or keep?
Before spicy phrases contaminate the air,
trap them in your mouth,
decide to leave them there.
Is it truly so absurd,
To think prior to your speech?
To choose to speak only a succulent word?
You could have eluded,
half of what was said,
You could have concluded,
that your words you should have tasted,
so you would be content,
and your words would not be wasted.

Pooja Parwatkar, Grade 7
Linwood Middle School

Candy

Candy on the floor
Butterfingers in my bag
I really want more

Jenny Barone, Grade 7
New Egypt Middle School

Halloween

Children trick-or-treating up and down the street,
in their funny, scary, and goofy costumes.

Kids dressed as ghosts, pumpkins, and pirates all carrying around
their bags full of candy.

The night is so cold, spooky and scary.

Fake blood on the door is dripping down slowly, as the bats fly back
and forth in such a hurry.

I find a weird piece of candy on the ground.
It read "Beware." I thought it was just saying that because it's Halloween.

It wasn't opened and it looked so good, so I opened it and popped it
in my mouth.

I felt woozy and oozzy; all of a sudden I heard a big poof.
Then I turned into a

WEREWOLF!

Kersyn Wood, Grade 7
Hammarskjold Middle School

Blueberry Muffins

The best afternoon snack or morning breakfast,
Crunchy on the outside,
Creamy on the inside,
And adventurous blue, I am hungry.
As I run inside,
I smell the sweet blueberries.
Blueberry muffins,
A sweet time of adventure,
And good, spirited fun.
I take the first muffin, excited for the delightful treat.
I take the first bite,
It is soft.
Mother leaves the kitchen,
So I sneak another one.
It is better than the first.
She still doesn't return,
And another one makes its way into my mouth.
Mother returns and I run away, so she doesn't ask about the missing muffins
And now my stomach is full,
Like a stuffed turkey on Thanksgiving.

Kirsten Yascko, Grade 7
Herbert Hoover Middle School

Snow

Snow looks cool, fluffy, and it's easy to throw
And if you didn't know it is really cold.

You have to wear gloves, a hat, and earmuffs to keep you warm and cozy
So you don't get frostbitten on your little nosey.

Aryana Rivera, Grade 7
Lakeside Middle School

To an End

You were the smile on my face
Even when I was blue
You picked me up, and held me in your arms
I knew I could always count on you.

Oh, why did you have to go
Your favorite season was coming around
We could have laughed and played in the snow
But no not now…you were alone.

As tears fell down my face
I remembered what a great person you were
And that I could never beat you in a race
The memories of you will never be far.

Although you are up above
You will always be my angel
I will never push or shove
And always remember I was loved.

Madyson Hawes, Grade 8
Township of Ocean Intermediate School

Football

Who would be a football who could help it?
Shaped like a ball, shaped like an egg.
Being kicked around like a can.
Kicking and tackling is what she goes through.
Reaching the end zone would be her greatest achievement.
She is used to the abuse the game has on her.
Field goals put her head over heels.
Flying through the air as if she could fly.
Going through the goal and landing on the ground at full force.
Nothing can stop her from reaching her goal.
Except for the player-manager foiling her plans.
Bruised and battered, cuts and scrapes.
Her skin peels like dandruff.
It seems that torment is all she knows.
But all this torture is for the love of the game.
Her old-fashioned design makes her easy to identify.
The wear and tear is like a story.
Telling people all she went through.
After all, she is a football.

Dakota Jones, Grade 8
Clinton Public School

The Delight Song of Ariana

I am the sun lighting up the entire world with joy.
I am a protein shake giving someone a burst of energy.
I am soap removing bad thoughts from someone.
I am a test with an excellent grade that is being shown-off.
I am popcorn giving the familiar smell off to everyone around me.
I am fire that burns all day and night.
I am a peacock spreading out my colorful feathers for all to see.
I am the energy that keeps everyone awake.

Ariana Licata, Grade 7
Old Turnpike School

Moving On

I set forth the day, for a path I won't stray;
The new life is nice, but leaving will make me think twice;
The friends I made, the happiness will pervade;
I want to move forward, but also go backward;
My expectations are high, but I will never fly;
Being a kid is fun, and I still need to stay one;
Life is a ride, that may make you stride;
Some may fail, some will prevail;
All will be a star, and some aren't far;
The risk of chance, may leave you in a trance;
The way I see it, the path is lit;
The road is smooth, and the warm sun will soothe;
If I lose way, my life will sway;
But it is time, time to shine;
I have to try to do my best, and leave behind the rest

James E. Barnett Jr., Grade 8
St Mary's School

My Feelings for Her

I get this feeling when you look into my eyes
Girl the things that you see start from deep inside.

And I never felt this way before
But when I'm with you it's a hundred more.

And you say we were only friends, but you like to flirt and play.
Ooh girl you make me say; I want to stay with you all day.

Because you are falling for me, and I'm falling for you.
And when we're to close we don't know what to do.
But you'll always be my boo because I love you.

When I speak it feels like everything was heard,
You finish my sentences when I stumble on my words.

Marshawn McShan, Grade 7
Lakeside Middle School

All of the Seasons

I love the seasons,
    yes I do.
They are God's gift
    to me and you.
I love fall for the colorful leaves
    that float to the ground
    and how they whirl all around.

I love the cool breeze of winter
    and the flowers of spring.
I love what they all seem to bring.
    I love the warm summer sun,
    who seems to warm everyone.
    I love them all in my heart.
I don't know what it would be if we were apart.

Anthony Lamancusa, Grade 7
St Mary School

I Am

I am a teenager with high hopes and dreams,
I wonder if I'll end up with a great life,
I hear my mother telling me to keep up my grades,
I see how much fun some jobs are,
I want to be successful,
I am a teenager with high hopes and dreams.

I pretend that one day I'll accomplish it all,
I feel myself proudly working hard,
I touch my future as if it's very close,
I cry of disappointment when I don't reach expectations,
I am a teenager with high hopes and dreams.

I understand that life isn't always fair,
I say to everyone what I hope to do in life,
I dream about how hard it will be to get there.
I try to have my life plan ready,
I hope that I will never give up,
I am a teenager with high hopes and dreams.

Jaime Ryan, Grade 8
St. Mary School

Summertime

As I sit with my love
Watching the clear skies above
I hear the waves roar
While watching the seagulls soar

I play with the white sand
I cannot believe I am here on this beautiful land
The wind howled in my ear
The waves splashed and I suddenly had a tear

I can hear children play
I wish I could stay all day
I splashed my feet in the water
I jumped up and down like a teeter totter

I couldn't believe my eyes
I was swimming as if a fish in disguise
This was the most peaceful I've ever been
I hope to do it again

Chloe Wimbush, Grade 8
Westampton Middle School

Sky

P ale blue roamed the sky,
A mazingly white clouds flying up high,
T racking the images as they pass,
R esting on the peaceful green grass,
I nviting sunshine welcomed me,
C reating a world only I could see,
I wish this moment will last forever,
A n everlasting dream, the greatest endeavor.

Patricia Vandergrift, Grade 7
Galloway Township Middle School

Summer

Summer only comes around once a year,
But when it does everyone screams and cheers.
Pools, friends, parties, and more,
Without summer life would be a bore.
Going to the beach is half the fun,
There is so much more to come.
Laughing, playing, singing all day,
Oh how we love to play.
Nothing could beat these summer days.
Birds chirping in the air, flying from here to there.
Summer brings us nice warm sun,
For swimming, fishing, and lots more fun.
For finding seashells in the sand,
For sunbathing to get a tan.
I have to go to bed by day,
Summer is different than winter in a way.
The hot summer days, gives us lots of days of play.
Eating freeze pops all day long,
And playing some Ping-Pong.
Hoping these days will never end,
So that school would never start again.

Brianna Knight, Grade 7
William Davies Middle School

Autumn

Outside the window air cools, getting ready for the new season.
Below the trees I sprint to the swing.
Behind me my friends follow.
On the swing Maria and Annabel tilt back and forth.
Off they jump for someone else to try.
Across the yard I dash then leap.
Past the highest branches I swing.
Over their heads I fly off the swing.
Into the ground I land with a thump.
Near me my friends stand, saying how frigid it is.
I tell them to follow me.
In the house we go through the front door.
For some hot cocoa, until we head back outside for more.

Jessica Fielding, Grade 8
Clinton Public School

Volleyball

Onto the court my teammates and I run.
Before the game, the team warms up.
Towards us the opposing team emerges.
Across the gym the parents sit in the stands.
Over the net my serve flies.
After they receive it we are on our toes.
Against the floor the ball slams.
Except them, everyone is happy.
Since we got the point we serve again.
During the game, my sister and mom cheer.
Up the ball went, I pumped and hit after the setter received it.
Regardless the score 21-25, we still left with a win.

Rose Burach, Grade 8
Clinton Public School

First Light*

Who am I? What am I? Unanswered are these questions.
Alone, locked in this shed, vacant of love or affection.
Have I a mother? A father? I did not know from the start.
The only thing they left me with, was an empty, broken heart.

My roommates in this damp, dark space are shovels, trowels and mice.
I grow alone in these trying times; only one friend would suffice.
It's strange how seemingly happy days, just leave me in disgust.
Today I celebrate my seventh birthday with fear, and darkness, and dust.

And as the earth trembles and the cacophony arises, I realize that I often cannot tell apart —
The gunshots and the thunder, the pounding and the shrieking, from the loud palpitations of my heart.
And the doors swing open, and I am quickly blinded, by this first light in so many years.
This man with a gun is shouting and laughing, and confirming all of my fears.

I am grabbed by the neck, and tied to a tree, and resignedly give up my attempts.
For my gaunt, fragile bones and malnourished limbs are no match for his fiendish contempt.
My body goes limp and my eyes glaze over; finally, there's nothing amiss.
In my posthumous thoughts, my worries subside; the birthday boy got his wish.

Jacob Samuel Gelber, Grade 8
Orange Avenue Elementary School
*A response to studies on the Holocaust.

The Puzzle

I've broken down into a million puzzle pieces.
Searching for the four corners;
That will make the completion that much easier.

Corner 1: You have no idea how easy I am to read.
You can tell what I'm feeling.
But I can act; a smile to falter your guesses
While my insides are crumbling to dust, they will leave with the forgotten air.

Corner 2: I take a long time to notice. People don't care
for the freak with the lame personality. She's never remembered.

Corner 3: Do you care that I'm dying? Tears overwhelm me, never to find a solution.
I hate every part of this world with a fiery passion that makes my raw insides burn with the
intensity of a volcano rushing to it's peak, destroying everything in it's path.

Corner 4: You're that much closer to discovering me. Don't lie; you can't stand even the mere thought of me.
It pains you to deal with me every day.

Put them together and your picture is an agonizing pain from your sick judgment.

Alexis Rodriguez, Grade 9
Absegami High School

Special Place

Whenever I close my eyes, I imagine a special place.
In this special place the bunnies frolic in the cool mountain breeze.
The perfectly green grass sways from side to side.
I turn around and I can hear the soft sounds of gravity forcing the water of a waterfall into a small pond below.
When I am in this place I feel a sense of peacefulness and serenity.
But, when I open my eyes once again, I am back in the real world and happy that I am back.

Maddy Hooker, Grade 7
Frankford Township School

My Grandfather*

My grandfather is a great man
And still is.
When he was younger
He walked from Portugal to France
Barefoot and alone!
A few years ago he had a stroke.
I was scared that day.
I wonder how he felt that day.
Was he sad?
Was he mad?
Was he worried?
Today he tries to walk.
He will always try his best.
He will always be important to me.
Christina Cerqueira, Grade 7
Robert Morris Public School
*Dedicated to my grandfather

R.I.P.

You've made my tears go dry
Because I've cried and cried
I won't lie
It was hard to understand it all
I'm left dark inside
I know you're in a better place
You suffered so much
I write this poem
To tell you that I miss you
I stay up at night thinking
Of how life would be
If you were still here
You are not here with me now
But, I still feel you near me
You'll always be in my heart
Melanie Donis, Grade 7
Battin School #4

Money

My favorite day of the week is
Friday!
It's allowance day!
I always save the FIVE dollars
My dad gives me
Because…
I really want to buy a car
One thing that always cheers me up
Is opening up my wallet and
Counting my
FIVE DOLLAR BILLS
Five…
Ten…
Fifteen…
Twenty…
Eric Nieves, Grade 7
Battin School #4

Wizardry

There are people beyond humans,
There are animals beyond the species,
There is magic beyond our own,
There are wizards in our home.

Why read about romance
When you've got Harry Potter?
Why read all that cliché,
When you can do magic every day?

Adventures with Harry,
Are never to be boring,
Romance with Harry,
Is just another story.

Hogwarts is the school I attend,
It is located in London.
I love their British voices.
I love all their wizard choices.

I was born to Muggles,
Which we call the non-magic people,
But still I wonder,
If they're magic way under.
Patricia DeJesus, Grade 7
Garfield Middle School

The End

I walk into her room
As my face shows gloom
She looks so weak
It seems she reached her peak

This is not what I planned
As I hold her hand
Giving her one last plea
Begging her not to leave me

Her smile, so weak
As a tear runs down my cheek
Turning my world grey
As the heavens take her away

I look at the nurse
Thinking things couldn't get worse
She was really gone
How can life go on?

Now I'm at her grave
Trying to be brave
As I put a flower by her name
The end which finally came
Zainab Kiyam, Grade 8
Little Falls School #1

He Came to Save Me

It's that time of year
When loving friends are near
Who come from all around
To see what we have found.

The fervent feeling of this day.
The mystery of what He chose to pay
Is more than I can say
As He lay
Upon the cross.
I know He is the boss.

He is the king of kings
I will praise and sing
I am jubilant
Because He came to save me.
Joelle Debrot, Grade 8
Koinonia Academy

Winter

Winter! Winter!
Not my favorite season
I prefer summer!
I love the hot sun hitting my skin
Laying on the warm sand at the beach
Is what I prefer to do.
Oh winter! This could've been you…
you just get too cold!
I only really like you
When Christmas starts.
Knowing winter is near
Is knowing Christmas is near
Also when you snow a lot
That's when I love you.
Not having to go to school
That's when you're really cool!
Angie Rodriguez, Grade 8
Christopher Columbus Middle School

Winter Has Just Begun

Snow is falling everywhere
People stop to look and stare
The snow looks like a blanket of white
Covering the ground packed very tight

Children then put on their gear
As they rush outside and do a winter cheer
Their faces are glowing
As the snow just keeps on flowing

Everyone sneezes
As the water freezes
Showing it is very clear
Winter is finally here
Casey Augustyniak, Grade 8
New Egypt Middle School

Life

It's not perfect,
It's not fair
Sometimes it's bad enough you don't care

It could be cool,
You could have good days
Sometimes in school
If not, find ways

Sometimes you will have bad days, anyway
It's good
It's bad
It's sometimes sad

It's Life!

But you have to go on,
no stopping here.
Because you never know if the end is near

Life can be scary, and we all have our fears
But life goes on and you have many years.
Nikaurys Espinal, Grade 7
Garfield Middle School

A Moment

She was walking down the hallway
and so was he
their eyes met and her heart leaped
she kept staring
not wanting to break the moment
it was precious
one moment that changed her life
don't look down
she told herself
don't lose this chance
but someone pushed her from behind
and she dropped all her books
everyone walked on
occasionally looking down at her
but no one said a word
they all went by
no one stopped to help her
except for the boy
who smiled at her
and bent down
to picked up her biology book
Alexandra Seneca, Grade 9
Ranney School

Japanese Cherry Blossom

Sweet scented Japanese cherry blossom
Daintily fluttering off branches in the wind
Aroma and sight are beautiful.
Heather Dupont, Grade 7
Frankford Township School

Mustangs

Who would be a mustang who could help it?
As swift and magnificent as a dove.
She plays her life like a song, dancing to the beat and changing the rhythm.
Nothing can stop her majestic movements and will to run forever.
The clouds close in, lassoing her away from her home.
Thrown in a dark dungeon, her song is silent. She is a quiet butterfly.
Pressed against others, she is afraid and trembling.
Ugly faces look in at her through cold, gray, bars.
They poke and prod her, scaring her to a back corner of the arena.
Suddenly, she is alone and is being chased by a killer, snatching at her with his long fingers.
She runs and calls for someone, anyone. But no one answers.
Thrown into another enclosure, a tangle of ropes is forced onto her noble head.
As the gate opens, and the light streams in, she thinks she is free.
Her spirits rising, she is a doe.
Too late, another monster chases her into another dungeon; this one is smaller.
Waiting for her to enter, it's gaping mouth is ready to tear her to pieces.
The darkness closes in around her, and she begins to forfeit.
There is nothing relieving about what she is experiencing.
Every bump brings her spirits lower and lowers until there is nothing left.
Finally the bumping stops, but she doesn't know. The aliens look in at her, excited.
But she is gone, running free, her song playing to the beat of her dancing hooves.
Jessica Barno, Grade 8
Clinton Public School

A New Start

The glistening sun is starting to slowly darken.
Its shining face leaves early every day.
Different colors are raining down onto the cold ground,
Forming a sea of which you will not be found.
Everyone going back to their daily habits,
Going to school or work, and even hunting rabbits.
You go to school, meet your new teachers, and catch up with your friends.
You get piles of homework and you hope that this will end.
Too bad that this has just started.
Hey, you can always look on the better side,
You can't wait till next year!
Daniel Chrostowski, Grade 7
Garfield Middle School

Skydiving

Fear: that is all I feel
what will it be like to fall into the unknown, unfamiliar void
no time to think, I must take the plunge
I step off, off the safety of the plane,
away from the security of the floor beneath my feet
I feel as if the ground will rush up to meet me,
but I keep falling, falling, falling into the abyss
the wind sounds like a wolf howling, trying to find his pack
I relate to his because I too, am lost, lost in the eternal sky
my chute jerks me back into reality, and it lazily drops me to the ground,
a sigh of relief escapes my lips
I fall to my knees,
this fearful venture did not only remind me of my love for land
it gave me something valuable-experience.
Jeffrey Diament, Grade 8
Township of Ocean Intermediate School

Dodgeball

You run, jump, duck, and cover as you
Avoid getting hit with a stinger that'll
Bruise you, you're all alone with your
Teammates on the sidelines watching
You get ambushed
As you run to pick up
A sphere shaped
Weapon to defend
Yourself from a
Raging army of an
Opposing class as
You're running, the wind
Flying through your hair
And you're being drenched by sweat
You almost run into a bullet,
Then when you're reaching to
Pick up defense, you feel a
Piercing blow that'll
Hurt in the morning and realize…
You're out.

Tyreek Sheppard, Grade 7
Buckshutem Road Elementary School

I Am

I am curious and intelligent
I wonder about the world
I hear my voice
I see an ocean
I want to know what I want
I am curious and intelligent

I pretend to answer this
I feel the breeze
I touch the water
I worry about school
I cry when I recall regrets
I am curious and intelligent

I understand some things
I say I am Catholic
I dream of the future
I try to find
I hope to understand more
I am curious and intelligent

Connor Kain, Grade 8
St Mary School

First Snow

Snowflakes are falling
A thick blanket to the world,
Snowmen are forming,
Snow angels are arising,
First flakes fell hours ago.

Erica Kelly, Grade 8
Assumption Academy

Hopes and Dreams Lost in the Wind

Tears sweltered in my eyes as I waved good bye, good bye to all my dreams
One swift action and they were all gone
I took out my hate, my revenge and now all is gone
What I gained I don't know what I lost was everything dear to me
Time and time again the sweet breeze on Cherry Street catches me
Digging up all my memories and dreams of the past
The breeze fills me up with the hopes and dreams I isolated
The path I chose…the path I chose…time is meaningless and life is dull
Every day I'm filled with so much regret
Wishing I could go back, back to Cherry Street
My hopes and dreams nestled in my hands I threw it away
A single smoke, bullet and betrayal is what it took
I've lost my family who once loved me so
Wishing to be back in my mother's warm arms
No one left to help me no one on my side to wipe away my tears
Wishing I could go back to Cherry Street where I belong
I had all I wanted I was vain; I used all and gave little
My people suffered while I rejoiced, how much pain I suffer now?
For those people are now rejoicing comforted by their families
If only I had been wise with my time for now it is dried up and gone with the wind
My life, dreams, hopes and family are all gone with the winds of Cherry Street

Habibah Arshad, Grade 8
Linwood Middle School

My Dream Rose

When I watch the stars go by,
I stop and think, "my do they fly."
I turned and found myself looking at the most beautiful thing I've ever seen.
It was a rose, a gorgeous red rose.
The rose looked like it was crafted by angels and the tears of mermaids.
It sparkled incredibly even though it was dark out.
When the rain hit the red beauty
It looked so graceful and beautiful, like the twinkling of diamonds.
Unfortunately I heard my mother calling me in.
Before I went, I looked back up at the sky and saw a shooting star.
My wish that I made was a little far, but I still wished.
I wished for another gorgeous red rose.

Victoria Hennion, Grade 7
Frankford Township School

The Beach

I see the immense waves crash on the shore
I hear the playful children running wild
I feel the sizzling soft sand squish in between my toes
I stroke the smooth shells lying on the ground
I feel the light summer breeze brush across my face
I relax on my colorful towel
I listen to my favorite music as I watch the waves come to an end
The sound of the children laughing slowly fades away, as I do too
I dream of riding the world's largest wave
I wake up to the blaring sun beat on my face
I spot the noisy seagulls fly over my head
I watch the beautiful sun of my colors, set over the bright blue ocean
I see the immense waves crash on the shore as I slowly walk away.

Alexis Ambrosino, Grade 7
Frankford Township School

Free

Look up into the summer sky
And see what your mind allows you
Even if it's dark outside
Let your imagination wander free

Whether it's a bird, plane, or cloud
Make of it what you want
Don't listen to anyone around you
Let your eyes wander free

Hearing the wind whistle around you
Or hearing a plane rumble by
Relax and close your eyes
Let your ears wander free

Look up into the summer sky
Make of it what you want
Relax and close your eyes
Let your freedom set you free

Max Bohm, Grade 8
Township of Ocean Intermediate School

My Family

My dad is fun and very silly
He laughs at nothing at all
Running around willy-nilly
Until we laugh so hard we fall.

My mom is not as nearly so silly
Cleaning, vacuuming, and such
She always says the house is chilly
And no one does chores as much.

My brother is quite crazy
He loves to play games of war
My parents say he's much too lazy
But he just yawns and plays some more.

I am of course sheer perfection
Who is kind and so sweet
I have a flawless complexion
To live with me is truly a treat.

Gabrielle Palumbo, Grade 8
Assumption Academy

Stefanie

S illy
T all
E nthusiastic
F riendly
A wesome
N ice
I nquisitive
E xciting

Stefanie VonWald, Grade 7
Lakeside Middle School

Video Games

A t Game Stop a boy sits and waits
B ehind the glass the game is on display
C ause he can't wait to get his new game even though he knows it will rot his brain
D ay after day he waits to play
E nding is near the doors swing open
F inally the game is his and ready to play
G ames are so fun they're way better than sitting in the sun
H appy to know that it can be played more than once

Kyle Horvath, Grade 7
Herbert Hoover Middle School

Anger

Grasping on negativity,
My hands clench into fists.
Ignoring the beauty around me,
A flower's fragrance is like a stench.
Recalling the good times, allowing depression to flood over me, trying to stop shaking,
I feel tears of frustration burn in my eyes.
How could my pet leave me alone in the darkness just like this?

Vaani Nanavaty, Grade 8
New Providence Middle School

Alec

I am the wrist watch upon your wrist that keeps you on time.
I am the first food you have in the morning.
I am the only Disney movie when someone doesn't die!
I am the sunset and sunrise in a foreign land.
I am the spark of a fire that is a great relief.
I am the shoe guy that says "how about an eight?" even when you said you're a nine!
I am the carpenter's pencil that stands out in a sea of regular school pencils.

Alec Johnson, Grade 7
Old Turnpike School

Basketball

Slicing through the net,
The basketball makes another trip while the scorekeeper puts up a point.
Ricocheting off the ground,
The ball is seized by the other team.
Soaring through the air, vaulting off the ground, and banking off the backboard,
It gives the other team two more points.
Basketballs have very repetitive motions.

Stephen Sangree, Grade 8
New Providence Middle School

Sewing Machine

Gleaming in its creamy white beauty,
The bulky metallic spider hums along.
Tripping over its own thread,
She tries to obey the groans of her mistress.
Buzzing over designs, spinning playful spools, slowing to a stop,
Unimaginable masterpieces are carefully pieced together.
Stitch by stitch the sewing machine is almost as brilliant as the dreams of its owner!

Laura Maxwell, Grade 8
New Providence Middle School

Halloween Bash
Halloween is full of boos,
The candy brings out yahoos!
Black cats are bad luck,
If you see one try to duck!

I like people that hand out Snickers,
It's scary when their lights flicker!
There are cool Halloween gowns,
But when there is no candy all you see is frowns!

Running from house to house is intense,
When you see a scary house you put up your defense!
Headless men freak me out,
When I see them I want to shout!

I always get a good outfit to wear,
But when I run fast I'm afraid it will tear!
Some chocolate is no good to eat,
Some old candy smells like feet!

Chase DiBenedetto, Grade 7
New Egypt Middle School

Surfing
Paddling out
Clear blue water
Tide's going out
Laying on my board
Leash on my ankle
Arms dipping into the water
Neck straining to see straight ahead
At first a ripple
Then it grows
Slowly at first
Then forming into a mound
Suddenly it shoots up
A growing opponent
I sit up, quickly turn around, and lay back down
Digging deep
Giving it my all
My strength is dwindling
But I feel the pull
I stand up, and ride the wave

Conor Mooney, Grade 8
St James School

Terror
The wind rushes in my ears as I go faster and faster,
Will I ever stop?
The trees, the sky, it's all a blur.
My breathing is increasing,
My chest may burst.
The fear is churning in my stomach,
Rising in my throat.
Will I ever escape this peril?
My legs burn,
My arms tire,
My eyes are tearing,
The speed, the cold, the complete terror.
I began to doubt my reality.
Why me?
Why now?
I began to say goodbye.
My life was ending.
All meaning was lost.
I succumbed to death.

Erin Wetzel, Grade 7
St James School

Fall
The leaves are falling
The leaves feel like their coloring,
They are coloring the grass that once was empty with nothing
And now all the kids are outside jumping.

All I hear now are the leaves cracking,
I see the car sparkling,
I smell the sweet smell of pumpkin pie,
It's time to go home, so I say bye

As I'm walking it seems like the wind is calling my name,
I think it's playing a game
I feel so warm,
I have that tone

I want fall to stay,
I want the leaves to make a bed so I can play
But it's time to go home,
I have that warmth in my throat.

Adriana Tapia, Grade 7
New Egypt Middle School

Christmas Time
Outside my window the snowflakes are falling from the sky,
To my cousin our Christmas tree looks so high,
The presents under the tree look fine,
I hope all of them will be mine,
It is Christmas Eve, what a blast,
Hope it will forever last,
When it gets cold I can sit and have some tea,
Christmas is the best time of the year for me.

Sabrina Gentile, Grade 7
Garfield Middle School

Cheerleading
It is something to do with much tumbling,
Many stunts and unique dance moves,
Lots of fun and smiles.
You are to be judged upon how well you do,
It brings much exercise and takes much effort.
I don't care who you are,
It's a sport,
It's cheerleading.

Michelle Cavallomagno, Grade 7
Garfield Middle School

The Biggest Feast

On Thanksgiving Day we went to the farm,
We were driving on Long Swamp road and saw the barn.
We went inside smelled turkey baking,
So Mom went to see what Granny was making.

The family was arriving we saw their trucks,
And each of the family members drove in the muck.
The family gave hugs and sat down to eat,
And Mom said 'thank God for this Thanksgiving feast.'

When we were done eating we cleaned up the mess,
And then Mom spilt gravy all over her Thanksgiving dress.
She looked in her suitcase for a change of clothes,
And put on her sun dress and pantyhose.

We had leftovers later that day,
And still smelled the turkey from earlier in the day.
We gave thanks and praise for this feast,
And then we ate the Thanksgiving beast!

Helaina Tilghman, Grade 7
New Egypt Middle School

The Last Day of October

Today is October 31 and it is Halloween,
I'm going to wear orange and green.
On this day ghosts and ghouls come out to play,
This is a fantastic day.

Lots of scary costumes all around,
There is always lots of strange sound.
When the monsters come out at night,
Don't run at first sight.

Under every step the leaves crunch,
Beware of goblins that might munch.
Tonight is the night,
Where creatures will bite.

You come home and take a bite of delicious pumpkin pie,
You could probably smell that piece of heaven from the sky.
That's all I have to say,
So, go out and enjoy your day.

Paul Hurd, Grade 7
New Egypt Middle School

In South Carolina

You can see the clear blue water
And taste the salt on your tongue
The sand feels as hot as an oven
And you see little children laugh and play
The mouthwatering seafood will make you want more and more
You can spend time relaxing down by the beach
You hear the high pitch squawks of the seagulls
In South Carolina everything is magic

Brittany Grau, Grade 7
Frankford Township School

What Happens on a Scary Night?

Trick — treat,
Come take a sweet.
If you don't I will cry,
So don't make a lie.

Come to my house on October night,
And you will get a fright.
I hope you will have no fears,
'Cause you will remember this for all your years.

All the kids will scream and yell,
All the demons rise from Hell.
Cauldron, cauldron, spin and brew,
Make these kids turn into stew.

Candy apples are so sweet,
They make a yummy treat.
Rose bushes filled with thorns,
Make your costumes ripped and torn.

Brooke Gatyas, Grade 7
New Egypt Middle School

Spooky Night

Spooky outfits roam the streets,
Kids getting a million treats.
Doorbells ringing door to door,
They all couldn't ask for more.

The town is lit with pretty lights,
This is the night of all nights.
Scary creatures will be jumping out at you,
They all scare you by saying BOO!

The kids have so much candy
But it always comes in handy!
When it's Halloween you may smell fresh candles,
It's almost too hard to handle!

At the end of the night,
They turn off the lights.
The kids catch their last house,
And go home as quiet as a mouse.

Brandilyn Wall, Grade 7
New Egypt Middle School

The Beach

Waves crashing on the sand,
Sand squishing between my toes,
The hot sun tanning my skin,
Loud planes soaring over my head,
Beautiful, blue dolphins jumping through the water,
Delicious Italian ice from the boardwalk,
Loud kids screaming on rides, like there is no tomorrow,
I always look forward to making great memories at the beach!

Alexa Smolen, Grade 7
Frankford Township School

Snow
Children's eyes gazed
Into the soft snow
Snowflake by snowflake fell

Bundling up
Coats and all
Snowflake by snowflake fell

Unlocking the door
Taking the first step
Snowflake by snowflake fell

A run for the fridge
Carrot for the nose
Snowflake by snowflake fell

Hours passed
Energy died
But still…Snowflake by snowflake fell
Laura Gleason, Grade 8
Township of Ocean Intermediate School

My Best Friend
She lifts me up,
When I am down.
She is always there,
When I need her around.

When I fall,
She stands me up right.
At the end of the dark tunnel,
She is my guiding light.

When I cry,
She brings me to a smile.
She would do anything for me,
Even swim across the Nile.

She is my best friend forever,
And I will never forget.
Meeting her in Pre-K,
Will never be a regret!
Victoria Thies, Grade 7
William Davies Middle School

The Holiday Season
H appiness
O verjoyed
L ovely snow
I nvigorating
D ecorations
A wesome
Y uletide
S easons
Nathan Morroni, Grade 7
Lakeside Middle School

A Wonderful Season
The colorful leaves are falling off the trees,
The branches sway side to side in the brisk wind,
Tattered scarecrows stand in fields of harvest vegetables,
Waiting for the wonderful season of fall to come.

Kids scurry to school as the piercing bell rings,
The blue jays whistle to the tune of the wind as it blows through the trees,
Pumpkins are carved into frightening faces,
The golden leaves scatter to numerous places.

The smell of pies baking fills the icy air,
Jack-o-Lanterns are waiting for kids to scare,
Children are taking out their hats and gloves,
Soon there will be snow falling from above.

The bright shy sun peeks through the white inflated clouds,
Children play outside, laughing and being loud,
All the excitement fills the air,
Fall brings joy to everyone, everywhere.

Out of all the seasons I have to say,
Fall is pleasant each and every day,
With the changes outside and its wintry features,
Fall will bring pleasure to all the creatures.
Justine Sendecki, Grade 7
Garfield Middle School

Me
I am from German food that is delicious at every meal.
I am from my mom's great Venezuelan food that takes you there.
I am from the meatballs and lefse that my Norwegian ancestors used to eat.
I am from same-day fresh salmon that I had caught,
And from that irresistible Michigan homemade fudge.

I am from Vikings in Norway,
from South Americans.
I am from Mark and Fina, Fa and Lita, and Grandma and Grandpa.

I am from baseball diamonds, tennis courts, football fields, golf courses,
And where anyone plays sports and has fun.
I am from Yankee Stadium, Giants Stadium, and the IZOD Center,
where the best sports teams in America call their home.

I am from trumpets and pianos that I can play beautifully for people to enjoy.
I am from the music of U2, Fleetwood Mac, Lynyrd Skynrd, Boston, Journey,
The Eagles, Eric Clapton, The Allman Brothers Band, The Doobie Brothers, The Beatles,
Genesis, Phil Collins, The Who, Jimi Hendrix, Van Halen, and many more.

I am from all the things in my own life,
from everything that I love.
My personality is one thing in my life that no one can change,
And I cherish that.
Kevin Urness, Grade 7
New Providence Middle School

Candy

October

I look around and what I see,
Is another chickadee.
Flying south for the hot,
Too bad they'll miss the candy pot!

Candy out for Halloween night,
And hopefully the costumes won't give me a fright!
I listen to the sounds around,
One thing I hear is the door's pound.

Trick-or-Treat;
I'll do it in a heart beat!
It's so much fun
Even though it's not in the Sun!

Leaves are falling left and right,
It's the perfect weather for flying a kite!
Windy, colder, almost snowy too
I love October, do you?

Valerie Iovine, Grade 7
Cinnaminson Middle School

Christmas

Christmas is the time of year
As little kids laugh and cheer.
Their excitement fills the air
You look around it is everywhere.
The tree is filled with Christmas spirit
The lights are bright for all to see it.
All the presents cover the floor
All the way out the door
As we sit down to eat
What I see is a feast.
The dessert was so yummy
It reminded me of milk and honey
Everyone is so nice
Exactly like sugar and spice
Family is the greatest for
Everything you want and more.
The night falls silent when everyone leaves
For Santa is coming after the Eve
I love the holidays
What's not to adore?
'Cause you're always welcomed through the door.

Alyssa Marquez, Grade 8
New Egypt Middle School

The Boardwalk

When you're on the boardwalk in the middle of the day,
Things tend to happen in a very different way.
You may see young children from ages ten to one,
Or you might see the ocean glisten in the sun.
Whether you hear a crane machine's whir,
Or a little kid's scream as a ride makes him a blur.
As you feel the buttons of an old arcade game,
You know that someone else had already done the same.
The smell of lunchtime enters the air,
As your stomach realizes something should be there.
You wolf down a burger, a soda, and fries,
And go play a game to try and win a prize.
Those of you who are attracted by the day,
Don't let other people stand in your way.

Edward Skirpan, Grade 7
New Egypt Middle School

When You Love Someone

When you love someone
You are always there for them
When you love your father
You always listen to his advice
When you love your mother
You always forgive her for nagging
When you love your sister
You always gossip with her about guys
When you love your brother
You always play with him no matter how busy you are
When you love your family
You are always united as one
Loving in general
Is what makes me smile

Blanca Cajas, Grade 8
Township of Ocean Intermediate School

Snow

Snow falls down upon the wet frosty ground
Snow stings your face like a bee
Snow gently falls to the ground covering the landscape
 in a powdery dust
Snow is as beautiful as a flower getting ready to blossom
Snow is soft like a rabbit's fur
Snow is gentle like a mother's touch
Snow is white like a sheet of paper
Snow is a winter wonderland
Snow is fun in the sun on a winter day
Snow is a day off from school

Glenn Davis, Grade 8
Township of Ocean Intermediate School

Candy Corn?

Sweet, colorful, and your teeth
Vary in size, sweetness, and shape
Shaped as a Veggie but do get warped
They come in white, to yellow, then orange
And rarely another
Sweet Halloween color
You may receive bags and bags of it on one scary night
While the wind whips your cape
And if you ask right
My hints are obvious for you to understand
For I imagined candy corn in my hand

Erica Sham, Grade 7
Hammarskjold Middle School

The Delight Song of Charlee Wood
I am the last goal of the game that won the Championship
I am the shining young smile of the Wood family
I am the happy playful puppy that every family wants
I am the funniest banana in the mixed bowl of fruit
I am the bright light among the dull dim candles
I am the sharpest pencil in a box full of pens
I am the pencil in which Albert Einstein wrote his problems
Charlee Wood, Grade 7
Old Turnpike School

Trying on a Dress
Sparkling like the ocean
The dress makes me smile as I zip up the back
Feeling as glamorous as a rock star,
I twirl around.
Looking like a diva, beaming with color, twinkling like a princess,
I step out of the dressing room.
I feel like an angel when trying on a dress.
Kimberly Morecraft, Grade 8
New Providence Middle School

Raindrops
Sparkling with evening sun,
the rain shatters on the boulevard as it ends its boundless journey.
Shimmering like silver glass,
droplets dance from aloft.
Plunging, plopping, splashing,
the playful drops fall everywhere.
Oh, what wondrous tears those gloomy gray clouds cry!
Nicole Garvin, Grade 8
New Providence Middle School

Paintball
The yells and roars of the enemy team
You can't imagine how mean.
I run up and hide, shooting wide
Shots coming in hard, within a couple of yards.
I peek out to shoot when…
BAM!
I'm out.
Trevor Kapral, Grade 7
Frankford Township School

Shells and Snowflakes
Shells are like snowflakes.
They each have a different figure.
Ridge edges and smooth centers make them unique.
When you hold a shell to your ear you hear waves crashing.
Snowflakes whisper your name as they fall.
Shells and snowflakes feel cold and rough.
Shells are like snowflakes.
Haley Gianattasio, Grade 7
Frankford Township School

The Gift of Winter
The ground is sparkling white,
Winter wonderlands are beautiful at night!
The trees are swaying and branches are frozen
Winter is the favorite season I have chosen.

There are *tiny* footprints in the ground,
But I don't hear any animal sounds.
The town is *silently* sleeping,
In the morning, there will be no weeping.

There used to be leaves on the trees,
And meadows filled with bees.
But now it's cold and pretty
I don't think that is a pity.

Christmas is an excitement to all
Time to give your relatives a friendly call
Icicles are hanging from lots of homes
While close to it children are building igloo domes.

Friends give gifts to your family and you
Your family says thank you and you do too.
On Christmas Eve you hardly sleep
but in the morning those presents are yours to keep.
Matthew Crepps, Grade 7
Cinnaminson Middle School

Actions Speak Louder Than Words
Be the change you wish to see
Because actions speak louder than words
Then people will come in herds
To make the change
Be the change you wish to see
Then you will become the queen bee
And everyone will follow you and Thee

I can see the headline two guys make the sun shine
And peace is here and there's nothing to fear
'Cause it's time to be the change you wish to see in the world
Time for no more cries
I can see the sadness in your eyes
But actions speak louder than words
So get that look off your face and be the change you wish to see

Head up, chin up
Stop spittin' in a tin cup
Let the dove outta the cage
and let there be love for this new age
Be the change you wish, want, need to see
In the world and you will see that
Actions speak louder than words
James Waring, Grade 8
Spring Lake Heights Elementary School

My Favorite Time of Year

It's that time of year
Christmas once again is here.
Carolers everywhere
Spreading holiday cheer.
Malls are packed
Santa fills his sack.
Gathering his reindeer
To make the biggest trip of the year.
Christmas truly makes my year.

Miles Townsend, Grade 7
William Davies Middle School

Unique Season

Bright red, orange, and yellow,
Autumn is very mellow.
Fresh air everywhere,
You'll live without a care.

When you walk you hear leaves crunching,
And on nuts squirrels are munching.
No more playing on sand dunes,
Because Autumn will be here soon!

Delani Pecchioli, Grade 7
Cinnaminson Middle School

The Heart of Autumn

The leaves fall off trees,
Losing their colors from May;
I walk a path, pensive,
Along my lonely way.

The birds have stilled their chirps,
They've quieted their loud calls;
My heart, alive in spring,
Is dead, too, in the fall.

Elizabeth Booth, Grade 8
Central Middle School

Finally Fall

Wind sweeps away the warmth of the sun.
In quick, violent gestures
It chills our faces, as if to say
"The wind has won."

It kicks the leaves,
And hides the beauty
Of what used to be summer,
Enclosing us in the gloomy depth of fall.

Marta Pobiarzyn, Grade 8
Garfield Middle School

Halloween

I hear the sound of a ghost or something calling me.
Whoosh! Whoosh! I can hear the wind.
Creak! Creak! The floors screech.
Now I am walking by the window.
I hear many noises that are creepier than scary movies.
My mom is calling me, but I can't find her.
Now I am by the door that enters the bathroom.
I am turning the knob and get a cold touch.
Now I am screaming because my mom is on the ground and there is blood everywhere.
I am running throughout the house to find the phone.
The phone is ringing do I dare pick it up!
On the other end of the phone I hear heavy breathing and screams.
Now I am running with the phone.
I find my room and go under my bed.
I am dialing 911 as fast as possible.
No one picks up.
The door bell rings.
I walk to the door.
I scream and a mask falls off the guy's face.
It was my dad the whole time.
It was just an act. HAPPY HALLOWEEN!

Danielle Sciacca, Grade 7
Frankford Township School

Blue

Blue
Blue looks like the sky on a bright sunny day
Blue sounds like waves crashing onto the soft powdery sand of the beach
Blue smells like a blueberry muffin fresh out of the oven
Blue tastes like a sweet sugary lollipop
Blue feels like happiness when I swim in a pool
Blue looks like a crystal clear lake full of fish
Blue sounds like a blue jay singing in the tree
Blue smells like a blueberry cobbler straight out of the oven
Blue tastes like a fresh round blueberry straight off the bush
Blue feels like the tranquility of a waterfall
Blue

Brendan Gifford, Grade 8
Township of Ocean Intermediate School

Baseball

Into the last inning the game is tied.
Out the dugout my friend walks.
During his at bat he gets a hit.
Toward first he starts to run.
Without stopping he heads towards second.
After my friend it is my turn to hit.
Behind me are the ump and the catcher.
Across the mound the pitcher moves ready to deliver the pitch.
Down the mound the pitcher goes throwing the ball at me.
Nearing the plate the pitch comes; swinging the bat I smack the ball out.
Onto the outfield grass it goes.
Across the plate my friend crosses.
On the field my teammates come jumping and screaming; we won the game.

David Mugavero, Grade 8
Clinton Public School

Grandpa
Oh, Grandpa, how I love and miss you so!
The fun that we used to have together.
The laughter and tears we had shared.
Oh, how the memories bring tears to my eyes!

All the times you were there to support me.
The softball games, the concerts
You were there for it all no matter what
And I appreciated it all.

You helped and loved us all
And how we loved you so!
You were very important in our lives
And you'll live forever in our hearts.

When you left, I couldn't help myself from crying
I'll never forget the holidays and birthdays we shared
You meant a lot to me and I didn't want you to leave
Since you died, I had a hole in my heart.

Be still my heart, for now you've gone
And now that you're in a better place
I hope we can reunite someday in Heaven.
For you I never wanted to leave
And I cry myself to sleep at night!

Courtney Perry, Grade 8
Christopher Columbus Middle School

A True Treasure
Happiness is a treasure
Where everyone in life is seeking pleasure
It can hide all around
And in very simple forms happiness can be found

For a child it could be a piece of candy
And that is what makes them feel dandy
Happiness for a teen could be getting a new shirt
Or being able to have their favorite dessert

But once you really think about where happiness comes from
You may think of yourself as a little dumb
Because happiness can come from the tiniest event
Even if there was no intent

Happiness can come from seeing someone you love smile
And it will make your time feel so worth while
Even just seeing someone succeed
Can give you happiness, indeed

The true feelings of happiness, you must never forget
Will come out when you need them, you can bet
It doesn't have to come from items you buy
For happiness is an awesome feeling you must never deny

Megan Rich, Grade 8
Little Falls School #1

I Miss You!
I miss the way you smile
I miss the way you hugged me
I miss the way we hung out on weekends
I miss the way you looked me in the eyes
I miss the way you said hi
I miss the way you said good bye

I know you still miss me
I know you still talk about me
I know you still smile when you hear my name
I know you still wish you were with me

Samantha Miskuff, Grade 7
Robert Morris Public School

Wonder of Nature
Glistening brightly,
The sun slowly sank into the sapphire sea
As though hiding from the anticipated darkness.
Dancing with eerie agility,
The rays of light bounced off the rolling waves.
Hanging high in the heavens,
Glowing with shades of pink,
Making its way across the horizon,
The evening clouds ornamented the sky.
What an ineffable wonder of nature!

Cindy Jiang, Grade 8
New Providence Middle School

The Beach
Resting by the shore,
I watch and listen while the sound of waves puts me to sleep.
Wishing I could stay here forever.
If I ever had to leave, I would surely cry.
Lying down getting a tan, watching seagulls fly around,
and feeling that nice and powdery sand,
I feel like the world is mine.
It's a great place for friends and family to meet,
and have a perfect day.
The beach is definitely something I can't live without.

Alexander Hocken, Grade 8
New Providence Middle School

Dance Recital
Waking up in the morning stomach sour like limes
Going over the dance about twenty times
Very hungry, but you don't want to eat
Doing your hair until it's perfectly neat
Putting on your costume as your hands tremble a bit
Hoping the dance will be a big hit
Walking on stage with no noise to be had
Looking out in the crowd and seeing Mom and Dad
When all is done and the curtains close
Flowers in your hands and joy from head to toes

Dana Zimmel, Grade 8
Township of Ocean Intermediate School

Thoughts

My mouth does not open,
Though it swirls in my head,
The questions I want to ask,
I am quiet instead.

Taken for granted,
Can't be taken away
Whenever I need you
You steal my heart away.

Thoughts are in my mind
As I write them down,
Rhymes do not come easily
I still don't make a sound.

"Food For Thought," I know,
And "If Pigs Could Fly,"
One day, I will stop thinking
If I really try.

Marissa Debrot, Grade 9
Koinonia Academy

Come Sail Away

Come sail away,
In the warm sun,
Come sail away,
And have some fun.

Come Sail away,
Along with the wind
Come sail away,
With a big grin.

Come sail away,
In the warm ocean,
Come sail way,
And feel the boat's motion.

Come sail away,
And go boating,
Come sail way,
And feel yourself floating.

Aaron Haegele, Grade 8
Cinnaminson Middle School

Ocean

Waves crash
Crabs crawl
Wind blows
Seagulls call
Sun shines
Claws click
People come to take a dip
Paradise

Emily Gear, Grade 7
Frankford Township School

Watching by the Window

Watching by the window; earth is turning, moon is changing
life goes on ever so slowly.
The glorious days of summer stretch on
indefinitely, before being caught — suddenly, by a flash storm.
Heavens open up and cry
big, fat tears splash — an endless scene of repeating gray.

Watching by the window; animals are hiding, creatures are resting
as Lightning lights the sky with her own display
Thunder fills the world with his music.
A glorious performance — well done!

Watching by the window; downpour becomes drizzle, sky peeks through clouds.
The worst is over — gotta keep holding on. monotonous drip, drip, drip
Is it over yet? Not yet, not yet.

Watching by the window; sunbeams are bursting, clouds are parting
to make way for the final act.
The Sun makes his way to center stage
in full knowledge of his superiority.
Though the storm is magnificent, the ending conclusion outshines it by far.

Watching by the window; endurance wins out
the end is near. the end is here.
Here. the end.

Sophia Wang, Grade 9
Hanover Park High School

Love

It never ends up as a happy ending
like Cinderella does it?
At the end no one leaves on a white horse
with Prince Charming

Boys are all the same.
They pretend to be something they're not.
Guys are completely different around friends.
They say they're going to call but instead forget and go out with friends.

Maybe Prince Charming isn't what Cinderella thinks he is.
He could be in love with her today,
but what about tomorrow?

Does he mean it when he says,"I love you"
or are they just a few more words?
Does he act like he loves her?

Did their dance at the ball mean anything,
or was it just another dance?

Are Cinderella and Prince Charming really meant to be,
or are they together because that's how the story is
supposed to go?

Camilla Teixeira, Grade 7
Schuyler School

A Lonely Rain
In the steady stillness of rain,
I sit and stare,
Solitary, yet for sudden
Sounds of splashing
Beneath my window.

Silently I watch,
Steadily I wait.
Alone I sit
By the window.

As the clouds storm
Fury and fear,
My tears in unison
Slide with the sky
Onto my window.

Sighing, I gaze,
Trembling, I muse.
Alone I sit
By the window.
Edyt Dickstein, Grade 9
Rae Kushner Yeshiva High School

Backwards
This is where I am,
Where the ocean plays,
Where the best is nonexistent,
And the worst plays with the happy ocean.

This is where I am,
Where the air brings me tears,
Where children laughing never ends,
And love brings tears to the air.

This is where I am,
Where the fire makes me icy cold,
Where shooting stars grant wishes,

This is where I am
Where I lay on the soft grass,
Where the birds song doesn't seem as sweet,
Where I find the rock is softer.

All is backwards.
I am home —
Devyn Adams, Grade 7
Lakeside Middle School

Snow
smooth, white
falling, sparkling, freezing
It's falling down out of the sky
crystal, flakes
Victor Bencosme, Grade 7
Lakeside Middle School

True Beauty Is from Within
A glimpse of beauty from an eye
Can tell us less and pass us by
But inner beauty within a soul
Can draw us in and show us more
Everlasting beauty deep inside
Destroys the looks with no surprise
A filthy mutt with tearful eyes
Is overlooked and placed aside
But its personality, so vivid with cheer
Overrules the thought of fear
So, beauty is an unseen trait
Which shows us more at wider rates
Kayla Klinger, Grade 8
Township of Ocean Intermediate School

Leaves
Walking down the street
I look at the trees
The leaves are changing colors
Transforming from green
To yellow, orange, and red
Falling so lightly
Floating like a feather
Summer is leaving
Fall is arriving
As the leaves fall from their trees
They land in a hush
With out a rush
Amber McConnell, Grade 7
Hammarskjold Middle School

Wishing Stars
Wishing is what I need
Looking at all the stars in the sky
Connecting the dots
Looking like a dog
Hoping I connected the dots right
Wondering what I drew
Should I start the countdown?
No I shouldn't, I should wait
Make a wish you really want
Thinking it very thoroughly
Count down from ten
3 2 1…now make your wish.
Samantha Oquendo, Grade 8
Keyport High School

My Spot
I rush out the front door.
thinking about
that one spot
where I can relax.

Questioning on
how I feel on that
exact spot
fearless.

As I run to the store
get some Jolly Ranchers
I take the pack and
pay the man.

I run as I sneak
through the trees.
To that little
hill by the
rusty tracks.

I study the graffiti
lay down and let everything
peacefully
fly away.
Kelsey Payano, Grade 7
Schuyler School

Technology Is Among Us
From games to business
Technology is among us
From difficulty to quickness
Technology is among us

TVs and computers
Clocks and phones
Electronic mailers
You'll never be alone

Add up with calculators
Charge up your battery
Listen to speakers
All made in a factory

Screwdrivers rotate
Vehicles transport
Videos can motivate
And many many more

So wherever you are
You'll know it by heart
Technology is around us
And that's just the start
Technology is among us
Kyle Robinson, Grade 7
Cinnaminson Middle School

Fall

Tis the season of Thanksgiving,
the warm smell of turkey traveling into your nose,
giving thanks to all of life.
The most beautiful time of the year,
as trees begin to die,
red, yellow, and green colors fall gracefully from the sky.
Wind howling on the streets,
birds leaving us behind
fleeing to the warmer areas,
Is this season good or evil?
All of mother nature leaving us behind,
all that good weather becoming opposite,
merely anyone is outside.
Skies are turning dark and gloomy,
heavy raindrops pouring from the sky,
feeling locked like in a cage,
I go on an outrage.
Tired quickly I lay down,
let all of darkness fall upon me,
I close my eyes,
and wait for another day's surprise.

Patryk Opilka, Grade 7
Garfield Middle School

Words of Love

Words are like the emotions we will speak
There is no way to describe words to thee
Words are gone but then come along to peek
They speak to us like whispering in me
Love is the word that I am telling you 'bout
It is the burning fire in your heart
When you would say this word there is no doubt
It's as if Cupid hit you with his darts
There will be that one person you love most
Your heart will be an angel in the sky
It is just like they were sent from above
You will never want to tell them good-bye
You'd first say those special words…I love you
Just know that they only come in a few

Cassidy Nalbone, Grade 8
New Egypt Middle School

Casualties

Across the room she lays
Beneath the veil she looks serene, peaceful
In my heart I feel hollow
Outside I mirror the rain and let my pain stream down my face
Below the umbrella, my family and I watch them lower her body
Underneath my act I want to scream
Out of the crowd I walk and gently place the flower
Among the dead the rose is out of place
From daylight to sundown I mourn the loved ones who were taken
Amid feelings of pain and sorrow I find hope
With luck she and others are in a happy place

Amanda Witwer, Grade 8
Clinton Public School

Backyard

Fall is filled with beautiful sights
Acorns, pumpkins and leaves fill the night.
Flowers grow along with crops
Acorns pelt the ground, people wishing it would stop.
Sports are popular this time of year
Hearing enjoyment and laughter, brings music in my ear.
Chilly weather is approaching fast
Better grab a sweater, sickness will be vast.
Fall is over don't shed a tear
Because winter is on its way, have no fear!

Good-bye Autumn, hello Winter
Chopping firewood, don't get a splinter.
Parkas, boots and mittens are worn
Santa in the fire truck, you can hear the horn.
Animals are hiding, from very brisk air
Making snow angels, getting snow in my hair.
The taste of hot chocolate is so delicious
Freezing cold weather, really vicious.
Winter comes only once a year
When it comes next year, let out a cheer!

Gavin Pritchard, Grade 7
New Egypt Middle School

My Best Friend

Today I found a friend,
Who knew everything I felt.
She knows my every weakness,
And the problems I've been dealt.

I reached out to this friend,
To show her that I care about her.
To pull her close and let her know,
That I really need her.

And I realized that this is a perfect friend that I found
And I'll never forget her.
Because she is like my sister,
And I need her everywhere I go.

Snezhana Damo, Grade 7
Garfield Middle School

Why?

You went and made a big mistake
that I hope you do regret.
Our whole team was left in tears
with that unbelievable news.
We had a trust
and I don't know where it went.
It was very upsetting, the big loss you gave us.
We are fighting to get you back.
Why?
Why is all I can say.
Why did you leave us on that day?

Margaret Horne, Grade 7
St Mary's School

Cats

I am playful and sleepy.
I wonder why I chase yarn.
I hear a mouse squeaking
I see toys and a litter box.
I want to be an acrobat.
I am playful and sleepy.

I pretend to be a dog.
I feel people touching me.
I touch curtains near a window.
I worry that people are going to step on my tail.
I cry when people don't give me food.
I am playful and sleepy.

I understand that I am cute.
I say that I want more food.
I dream of tons of squeaky toys.
I try to be brave when a dog barks at me.
I hope you will keep me.
I am playful and sleepy.

Sheila M. Rosado, Grade 7
Lakeside Middle School

I Am

I am a thirteen year old girl
I wonder what people think of me
I hear whispers in the wind
I see those whispers come alive
I want to be young again
I am a thirteen year old girl

I pretend I like being a teenager
I feel everything on my agenda getting bigger
I touch the memory of childhood, grasping it forever
I worry that I will disappoint my peers, my parents
I cry because I am overwhelmed
I am a thirteen year old girl

I understand that I have to deal with my problems
I say I can do things when I really can't
I dream about being five with attention again
I try to do my best in everything
I hope that some day I will forget that
I am a thirteen year old girl

Maggie Heinsman, Grade 8
St Mary School

The Delight Song of Niksson

I am the last page of a book in a series.
I am the last drip of red bull that still bubbles
I am the only yellow crayon in a box that I bought.
I am the last card in my collection that I love.
I am the last star that shines at night.
I am the only one who hides in the darkness.

Niksson Sanchez, Grade 7
Old Turnpike School

Oh, Nature

Oh, Nature
You're not hard to find
You're as pretty as a picture
You're fair and kind
With your diverse textures and a creative mind
You are a mixture of sights to see and find

Oh, Nature
You are a treasure
Some people may not like you, but I sure do
It is you we must protect from those who neglect
Without you, dear Nature, no human has a future

Oh, Nature
You have beautiful features
Grassy meadows and rolling hillsides
River ripples and ocean tides
Spring flowers in bloom
Glittering stars and a full moon
What wondrous scenes to see
You fill my heart with spirit and glee

Frances Min, Grade 8
Warren Middle School

Countryside Dream

A flock of birds fly high
In the beautiful dusk blue sky
Singing a soothing tune
In the middle of June

Trees sway softly in the breeze
As beautiful flowers decorate with ease
Warm sunlight glistens over the water in the stream
The scene looks like an absolute dream

Now it's over, the day is done
Red, orange and yellow are the colors of the sun
It's such a gorgeous sight
As the sun winks goodnight

Brittany Lewis, Grade 7
Lakeside Middle School

Phillies

October is finally here a time to relax and cheer.
The race is done and we had lots of fun.
The playoffs are here and the World Series is near.
It is basically in sight and to many a delight.
The champs are back with many new faces,
But they still have some small gaps and spaces.
They are very close and better than most.
You must carry your dream and bring it to your team.
It is all said and done and there is still more to come.
You bring it to your town and can now settle down.
The parade is here and all you can do is cheer.

Jacob Palmer, Grade 8
Good Shepherd Regional Catholic School

My Grandma

Purple, purple, purple was your favorite color
I knew that ever since I was smaller you had such a good sense of fashion!
With your leopard, cheetah and animal prints those were almost like your passion!
In the kitchen, that place was yours no doubt!
You made the best food and I would try to eat it all even if my stomach was about to bulge out!
At the dinner table funny stories were always told there was advice given out such as: "How not to get a cold"
Whenever going to your house there was always something to laugh about
Grandpa was always doing something sneaky and we would try to call him out!
No matter what you always had something nice to say! All day, every day!
Whenever I came over to your house you would always have a good book
It made me have the urge to read, sometimes cook!
You were also very good at sewing it was a task for you that was easy going
Me, Kelly, Amanda, Chloe, and Stevie
You always supported us from sporting events, dance recitals, swimming lessons, and theatre plays
It truly made all of our days
Remember the time when you got a fake white cat named Marsha? It was fake but we all thought it was real! Haha!
Remember all the times we went to the Morristown pool? It was so much fun and cool
Nice, wise, clever we always had the best times ever
Remember when we would all pretend to be a chef like you?
Or remember when we would have a blast playing wiffle ball on the beach? Wow! Time flew!
Time will keep flying, But the memories that we shared will forever be sealed

Caitlin Hammond, Grade 9
Hillsborough High School

Washington Crosses the Delaware, 1776

All was still that December day, the frigid iced air howled and bayed
And through the clearing, a long silence was kept, so the enemy soldiers peacefully slept
"Victory or death" was our motto in mind, for their treatment now wasn't an option of any kind,
And even though our morale was low, we knew that somehow, it would have to grow
To defeat the Hessians, setbacks would be there, as the task itself was no ordinary dare
Crossing the frozen river and marching beyond, awaiting the battle, waiting to respond,
And so slowly we crept atop the fresh snow, our feet all bare, bloody trails aglow
Yet we continued with the freedom dream's hope, swiftly making our risky elope
With inspiration in mind, we traveled on, in two columns through the dreary dawn
Quietly, nimbly we crept and attacked, the enemy's surprise was an accomplished fact
Alas! Now the moment had come! The raging battle now begun!
Guns exploded, cannonballs flew, missiles took flight out of the blue
And as the fight rose stronger and stronger, the battle grew faster and longer,
It was getting to be crystal clear, that successors were the Americans here
And so we claimed victory that Christmas day, with General Washington leading the way,
When news had reached far and wide, the feeling was beautiful, that sweet tasting pride
So today we look back and now we see, this is what history has led up to be
Just think what would happen if we didn't win, would our lives today come to what could have been?
Reflect and rejoice and know the glory, for we should now embrace the story
And know our history when we say
What happened on that still wintry day…

Juilee Malavade, Grade 8
Linwood Middle School

Maryland

Maryland is a very peaceful place. I can hear the ocean waves crash like an angry person. On the balcony I can hear the little kids
scream and laugh. At the beach in the sand there are many different kinds of people walking, laughing and playing. I love going
to Maryland. It's something that means a lot to my whole family — my whole family goes, it is a family tradition.

Rachel Orr, Grade 7
Frankford Township School

Winter Days

The freezing weather is coming around
Snowflakes and snow angels can be found
I pull on my gloves and my hat
The snowballs I'll throw will end with a splat

All my friends are snowball fighting
We will play until there is no more lighting
This oncoming blizzard is a pain
No matter how much I begged the snow still came

The cloudy sky begins to turn dark
Yet we continue to sleigh in the park
The freezing wind slashes through my bones
Then I realize it's time to head home

When I come home there are cookies on the table
Earlier today seems like a fable
I lay on the couch and fall asleep in the den
I wake up next morning just to do it again

Joseph Katze, Grade 8
Westampton Middle School

The Circus of Darkness

The Circus of Darkness has come to town
Where no smile doth reside on the face of a clown
Beware, my young children, this spectacle of fright
This ghoulish exhibition from a Hallow's Eve night

The Circus of Darkness, where it's black when it snows
Where light casts something sinister, along with their glows
The walk home is treacherous as it sleets and it hails
And demons call back to you with laughter like darkening gales

But remember, past the gloom, there is still but hope
Once you have mounted that final windswept slope
You will reach a place without darkness or strife
You will reach, my young children, the Circus of Light

So remember, my readers, through the good and the bad
You must keep on going even though you are sad
We all must cope with ongoing strife
Because the darkness is just part of life

Patrick Huggins, Grade 7
Little Falls School #1

Kindly Generous

Aiding everyone she comes across
With her admiring and generous conscience,
She mends the poor
With her altruistic volunteer hours, curing the sad
With a bighearted smile, she strolls hand-in-hand with God
She befriends the young, including me
There isn't one person she doesn't love
She is an angel from above

Kevin Maluso, Grade 8
New Providence Middle School

Christmas

Christmas has arrived allow yourself some happiness
Throw your worries out the window
Rejoice because Christmas has arrived
It's Christmas time again!
Everyone having a great time
It's that time of the year when we dance,
sing and party all night long.
Children unwrapping their presents
wondering what Santa gave them
laughing and cheering because Christmas is here
It's Christmas time again!
A snowy night full of love and hugs
Beautiful lights illuminating our night
Everyone with a big smile in their face,
remembering the good old times
It's Christmas time again!
It's just that joyful time of the year,
when everyone is wishing for bright days to come
Expecting a good new year to arrive.

Brenda Avila, Grade 7
Garfield Middle School

This Christmas

The Christmas joy fills the air
Christmas lights hang everywhere
In the houses the Christmas tree stands
Decorated with ornaments that were placed on by hand

As night time arrives, the kids lay in bed
Many thoughts keep running through their heads
What will they get, what will there be
When Santa Claus comes and leaves toys under the tree

When morning is here the kids fill with joy
They can't wait to run downstairs and see all the toys
When the last gifts are opened
The kids start to play, soon they find out it's been almost all day

They start to clean up
Their bed time is near
It's been such a good day
They can't wait until next year

Kristen Simunovich, Grade 8
New Egypt Middle School

The Delight Song of Me

I am a bright and beautiful, blue first place ribbon
I am a tiny butterfly, in a meadow filled with flowers
I am a dolphin, leaping happily in the ocean's waves
I am a bird, chirping cheerfully in the quiet morning
I am a single snowflake, drifting through the frigid winter sky
I am a warm quiet breeze, blowing the fallen leaves
I am a magnificent Christmas tree, decorated for the holidays
I am a beautiful little flower, waiting patiently to bloom

Faith Evers, Grade 7
Old Turnpike School

Golf

Golfing is new for me.
Have you ever tried it?
Come follow and see.
Gather my clubs — drivers, irons, and putter.
Balls, gloves, hear the cart sputter!

Getting started
I set up my tee; ready my ball,
Head down, swing, hit!
Watch it go or where is it?

In the fairway or the rough
Choosing which club is really tough.
Aim for the hole, swing through
Keeping the ball in view.
Heads up, fore! Uh oh!
Way over there, here we go!

On the green, near the end
Flag, cup, putter, and ball.
Counting my strokes, counting them all.
Bogey, eagle, birdie, par
I can't believe I got this far!

Brittanie Clarke, Grade 8
St Mary's School

Monday Restaurants

Restaurants on a Monday are not as busy as they can be,
You just hear some light chitchat and someone drop a key,
Utensils, food and money are basically what you need,
To enjoy a Monday meal and for your expectations to exceed,
You smell the aroma of your food coming,
And you are ready to relax and eat,
The food may taste delightful,
And you'll want another treat,
But don't come back on Saturday,
Or it will knock you off your feet!

Saturday Restaurants

Saturday nights at a restaurant,
The busiest night of the week,
Lots of people at every table,
Watching every TV while they eat,
Watching all the food go by,
Making you as hungry as can be,
So do not whine,
Or else your food may not come,
Listening to lots of talking,
Starting conversations.

Danielle DiMeola, Grade 7
New Egypt Middle School

The Delight Song of William

I am a fruit on the everlasting tree of life.
I am the last line of a gripping science fiction novel.
I am the first note played on a brand new Steinway piano.
I am the first gust of wind that blows in a frightening storm.
I am the last fruit to fall from a strong tree.
I am the mighty sword that struck the final blow.
I am the bright smile that lights up the world.
I am the warm happy feeling that you get on Christmas morning.
I am the peaceful moment before you fall asleep.

William Donoghue, Grade 7
Old Turnpike School

The House on the Haunted Hill

Long ago there was a house
That stood on a haunted hill
And in the window would stand a girl in a blouse
And her name was Jill
The little girl died long ago
And her spirit is trapped
With nowhere to go
If you enter this house, you will see
It is nowhere you would like to be

Chris Henry, Grade 7
Herbert Hoover Middle School

Thanksgiving Is Around the Corner

Seeing the leaves change colors on trees
As they fall, wishing that were me
Stepping in the leaves and hearing them crunch
Feeling the wrinkles of a whole bunch

Walking in the house and smelling the dinner
I taste it and say, "Mmm…I'm not getting thinner"
I sit by the window watching leaves fall near
Knowing now that Thanksgiving is here

Jennifer Weiler, Grade 7
Cinnaminson Middle School

The Sea

The inner glow of beauty
Is the waves on the sea shore
I want to show the beauty of the sea
I promise you I won't get bored
The everlasting love of the deep blue sea
Is something that can set you free
Best to have a connection with mother nature and its creation
Mother nature is what keeps the deep blue sea alive
And it is what keeps me free forever

Joshellin Olazabal, Grade 7
Garfield Middle School

Winter Is Great

I love winter
Winter is cold
Winter is white
Winter is fun.
My birthday is in winter.
Christmas is in winter.
Gifts in winter.
There's joy in winter.
Family in winter.
Hot chocolate during winter.
Vacation during winter.
Friendship during winter.
Snowy winter.
December, January, February
Ice skating in winter.
Going to NYC in winter.
Blizzards during winter.
Coals during winter.
Winter is snowboarding.
Winter is great!

David Lopez, Grade 8
Christopher Columbus Middle School

Christmas

Joy fills the streets
All the children cheer
A tree is decorated
Christmas is very near
The white crystal snow
The laughter's and joys
All the kids write to Santa
About all of their toys
The kids are extra good
And the parents shop all day
The Christmas decorations are up
For everyone to display
The family all joins
And sings their own Christmas song
They gather up all together
And celebrate all night long
Chocolate chip cookies
Warmed up milk is out
The family is together
And happiness is what it's all about

Jonathan Gonzalez, Grade 7
William Davies Middle School

Fast Cars

Fast cars are a jet.
A great thing in life.
Zooming and blasting by.
The sound of the exhaust.
Singing as an angel.

Marc Diaz, Grade 7
Galloway Township Middle School

Change

Change is what we need
Change is what we seek
Change is what might come
Change is not too far
Change is good and
Change is bad
I don't want an insignificant change but an extravagant change
Change, for my generation and future generations
Change, so my kids can be the difference and help out in this world with
Change, so homeless people will be in a home
And a beggar will have no need for begging
Change, when we can all unite.
Change, it will come when everything is all right.
Change, not one man will bring it
But millions of people.
Change, and I want to be in that number of people.
Me, my friends, and family,
We will try to unite
Set our differences aside and CHANGE!!!
"Change, we can believe in!"
CHANGE!

Oscar Gomez, Grade 8
Link Community School

Science

Science is veins, blood, and organs.
Science is hypothesizing, experimenting, and hoping to prove your hypothesis,
If not starting the process over again.
Science is animals and plants, how they live, what they eat, and how they interact.
Science is chemistry, and reactions like exploding, bubbling, and changing.
Science is like the weather, you don't know what will happen.
Weather is Science.
Science is a cookie baking in the oven.
Science is eating that cookie.
Science is everything in some way or another.
Science is life.
Science is death.

Michael Kelleher, Grade 7
New Providence Middle School

The Misused Purse

My mouth is always open because you barely close me up.
Sometimes you stuff me so full that my zipper gets stuck.
Lipsticks, money, gum!
That's what you shove into me.
You grab me, slam me, against doors when you are on a shopping spree.
You throw me into corners on the bare cold floor!
Once you even left me on the counter of a store!
Even though you misuse me I know you need me a lot
Without the money in my side pockets you can't buy anything you want.
Your student ID, your credit card, your diary, and your phone!
They all live inside of me, I am never alone.
So before you throw me against the wall and bounce me like a ball.
Remember that without me you can't buy anything at all!

Sayali Kirtani, Grade 7
Cedar Drive Middle School

It's Time

For those who have survived
For those who lost the battle
To stop worrying
And start believing.

Make a difference
For yourself
Your family
Your friends

Don't just watch
And wait for something
To happen

It's time to finish this battle
And make a difference
It's time to find a cure.

Emily Ehrhardt, Grade 9
Holy Cross High School

The Desolate Symphony

The neat row of ivory keys
The clean sheet of music
The patina of the piano

The pleasant quiet birdsong
The soft shafts of sunlight
The inviting aroma of cookies in the oven

Shattered by a song

Fingers fly across the keys
Playing a tragic tune
Illustrating the horrors
Of one whose heart; broken
Of one whose dreams; crushed
Of one whose only chance at fortitude is
To play a symphony

Rachel Schaefer, Grade 7
Thomas R Grover Middle School

Volleyball

Six people on each team
With a net in between
Volleyball is the game for me!
I don't like it,
I love it!
It gives me a rush.
Serving
Spiking
Diving
On the grass or in the gym or at the beach
It doesn't matter
As long as I'm in.

Maria Galvan, Grade 7
Battin School #4

Desperate Love

We are not connected anymore.
Now, you are nothing
But cold hearted toward me.
I thought I meant more than this to you.
I try to express my emotions to you.
But nothing comes out.
There is a wall between us now.
I tried taking you out of my heart.
But it didn't work.
You are always there no matter what.
Is this desperate love?
I always think about you wherever I go.
It is desperate love!
That no one can stop its power over me.
Only I can make it disappear.
Hopefully!
Someday it will dissolve and
Be positively directed elsewhere.

Elsy Muñoz, Grade 7
Battin School #4

Hawaiian Beauty

The sun rises and the moon falls
Oh! How beautiful is it all
Stars twinkling in the sky
Like a sparkle in a child's eye
Palm trees sway in the warm breeze
With the motion of the tranquil seas
Ocean waves, steady and still
Like a flower in a window sill
The cool sand beneath my toes
Feels soft like the petal of a rose
Birds flying gracefully in the air
As if singing a silent prayer
Tall mountains seen in the distance
Symbolize hope, no form of resistance
The horizon glows as the sun sets
Watching the sun fall puts my mind at rest
The sand, the sea, and the beautiful sun
The beauty of it all has just begun

Sam Green, Grade 8
Township of Ocean Intermediate School

Peering into a Heart

If you look deep into a heart with truth,
Emotions lie dormant soon to wake,
There may be despair or sorrow,
Or happiness and pleasure,
But it is who you are,
That really matters,
To really see,
What's inside,
Of a,
Heart.

Joy Li, Grade 7
New Providence Middle School

A Soft Snowfall

The white sprinkles start to fall
The soft touch of a flake hits my face
Mother Nature answers winter's call
I head inside to put on my jacket
The fireplace roars and lights with flames
Crackles and pops fill the room with racket
Little children are playing in the snow
As the snow starts to fall quicker
The tree branches all begin to blow
Winter is here at last
We can all play with our friends
Before winter passes by too fast

Caitlin Herod, Grade 8
Township of Ocean Intermediate School

Fall

The season is changing
And children are growing
The school year has started again
There are pumpkins and scarecrows
And new treasures to find
There are dried corn stalks
And already eaten apple rinds
The sun is dark
Like the beautiful night sky
And thousands of birds getting ready to fly
Fall
The best time of the year

Brooke Sutton, Grade 7
Frankford Township School

Swimming in the Air

My long tan arms open wide
Like a white plane flying high.

I am a bird losing my last flight —
Falling down losing control.

I splashed into the crystal clear blue water,
Swimming — swimming
The water overpowering me.

As the big wave devoured my body,
And I sunk to the bottom.

Maddie Maxwell, Grade 7
Galloway Township Middle School

I Am

I am a dancer
I wonder how far my life will take me
I hear the music within me
I see only what I want
I want to make the best of life
I am a dancer

I pretend there is no gravity
I feel words mean nothing to me
I touch freedom
I worry I won't do my best
I cry when rejected
I am a dancer

I understand practice is necessary
I say "I can do it!"
I dream about fame
I try to stay focused
I hope dreams come true
I am a dancer

Olivia Delaney, Grade 8
St Mary School

The Sun

The Sun rose and glared at me,
so strongly that I couldn't see.
It shone on me so strong and bright.
My eyes felt blinded by the light.
It made me marvel how lucky Earth was
to have a Sun that helped every cause.
It made the world so bright and warm.
Even the bees came out in a swarm.
It helped farmers with their crops
and let children enjoy their ice pops.
Then the clouds would cover the Sun
and the rain would stop the people's fun.
The clouds would then reveal the Sun
and brighten the day for everyone.
Then it would disappear over the horizon,
on the other side the Sun would be risin'
Soon everyone would go to bed,
on their pillow they'd place their head.
At seven the Sun will rise again,
and the whole cycle will start over again.

Naveen Setlur, Grade 8
William R Satz Middle School

I Am

I am a flower and have delicate petals
I wonder how long I will last
I hear the birds sing
I feel the raindrops
I want to sway in the wind
I am a flower and have delicate petals

Danielle Price, Grade 7
Frankford Township School

No Air

The book falls to the marble ground
Dropped open on its spine and nobody is there to hear it.
Where is the noble bookstand that should've held it up?
If only thin as a toothpick, the book would still be propped open, easily and triumphed.

Vindictive, they are, where brightness has yet to show
And darkness has yet to succumb to.
For now, the sky holds up
To let the water flow, over and under mountains
Round n' round, never stopping because there is no ending.

The sun is only an illusion, that even the courageous king must have an heir
to rule after himself
Continuing his reign and legacy, in a way, his life never ended.
But even they will fall apart, like a tree full of shriveled leaves:

A capture of the heart
A gaze
A word

In that well spun fable of lies.

Lucy Zhang, Grade 7
Montgomery Upper Middle School

The Weeping Child

The weeping child cries at night
Despair, emptiness, lies, and pain
All hope is gone
Within the mellows she lays to rest
Her heart is bleeding
She's all out of breath
Praying to God
"Dear Lord save my soul!"
Dying inside
Darkness can't let go
Every night she sings a sad song
Song of hate and fury
Scared and alone
All that's left is to worry
There's an essence of pain, hatred, and lies when you're around her
She is cold made of ice
Her heart is no longer
It seems that the pain just is stronger
She's a rock, bottles up everything
That girl she has awoken
Let me introduce myself; I'm a child and I'm weeping, that girl is me

Carmen Baldassarre, Grade 8
Keyport High School

Frustration

Conk! Conk! Everything was going around in my head.
Looking at the paper while it screams at me.
Everyone around me already half done the quiz.
I was going to do something stupid at one time like play with my pencil or twirl my hair.

Nicholas Camarota, Grade 7
Galloway Township Middle School

Wildwood

A city of delight,
foamy blue,
buttery vanilla,
sunshine yellow,
My throat is thirsting,
My feet are burning,
My skin is sizzling.
The wonders of Wildwood,
sandy beaches,
crowded boardwalks.
I see tandem bicycles,
and the smell of,
salty French fries,
and cotton candy,
whip through my nose.
Every year,
this makes me realize,
Wildwood,
fulfills my visions,
of Summer

Alexa Lubonski, Grade 7
Herbert Hoover Middle School

Dead Silence

All is quiet
As if nothing is happening
But I can hear something
Breaking the silence
I can't explain it
Nothing is making it
But I hear it
Maybe I can sleep it out
But I can't sleep
I still hear it
Ringing in my ear
Like a faded screeching
Someone stop it
Please
I can't take it
What is it?
I feel like I am being watched
But there's nobody here
What was that!
Make it stop!

Devin Rentas, Grade 8
Keyport High School

Halloween

Halloween is very fun
But it's better to trick-or-treat in the sun
People ask for candy at your door
Then they go and get more
Things are scary like witches and bats
But people walk around with funny hats

Ashlee Lail, Grade 8
St Mary School

Grass

Grass sways rhythmically to the soft, lingering breeze
It is everywhere; growing in plentiful amounts
Its bright green tips eagerly point upwards towards the heavens
Hoping to someday reach it
The fiery sun happily beats down its golden rays
And like a mother, urges the grass to grow
Grass is simple, delicate, and strong
It strives to survive, as it is constantly pounded by filthy feet that think nothing of it
It is looked down upon and stepped upon
When in reality, it is the foundation of our life
When grass is crushed, it climbs up off the dirt and gets back up
Unharmed; as if untouched
Still reaching towards the creamy blue sky
How can something so delicate and beautiful
Be so overlooked
Grass truly is a beautiful object of nature

Haa-Young Lee, Grade 8
Township of Ocean Intermediate School

Night and Day

Last night, conflict showed up on my doorstep.
I quickly pushed drama out the window so the two wouldn't meet.
I had more than enough to deal with.
After three hours of fighting, compromise arrived.
We talked, and compromise convinced conflict to leave.
I introduced compromise to gratitude.
The two walked out together.
I thought it was over until oppression called.
I tried to fend him off, but he persisted.
I hung up and cried to compassion, who held my hand.
Unfairness laughed through the paper-thin walls, and scorn joined him.
Then love walked in and hugged me tightly.
My heart relaxed and I fell asleep.
The next morning I woke up slowly.
As I stared out the window, I saw hope shining in.
Smiling, I ran out to greet tomorrow.

Rachel Hobble, Grade 9
Watchung Hills Regional High School

Friends

Everyone has a person, who's close to them, who's always there; basically a friend
A person who's been there from the beginning, and will be 'til the very final end,
never leaving your side, never back stabbing, never criticizing, you might not agree with
one another, but one thing's for sure you'll always have each other
You couldn't imagine a day without them, they're here to perk you up, or lead a shoulder to
cry on, just like someone I'm glad to call my friend… She's been there from the
beginning, and I hope the final end, she's always there to make me laugh or lend a
shoulder to cry on, she'll listen to my problems, and give out a joke or two
I'd never wanna lose her, cause she's all I really got
An amigo, amie, shinyuu, amica, filo
A friend No matter what you call it
A friend is a friend
You'd never want to lose
So hold on to them

Soler Nichols, Grade 7
William Davies Middle School

Winter Wonderland

The fall wasn't meant to last,
Now winter is coming on so fast.

The smell of cookies fills the air,
Friendly voices come from everywhere.

Children play games all day,
Too bad this season isn't meant to stay.

The snowflakes fall on the ground,
Decorations hung all around.

Tons of food and eggnog is so good,
Dad is filling the pit with wood.

Keep a smile on your face,
And watch Grandma cook with pace.

Now Christmas is here,
Everyone it's time to cheer.
Brooke VanDenBogart, Grade 8
New Egypt Middle School

Winter

I love the winter
The only thing bad is that
A lot of people shiver.
It is so cold and bitter
I love the snow
It is so fluffy and white
It looks like a bright white kite.
It is like a coat of feathers
It is such fun to have a snowball fight.
It makes your poor hands freeze
They feel like they are going to
Have frost bite.
I like making snow forts
Then like to run right
Through them and break it.
Also I like to have snow ball fights
With forts
One time I made a tunnel of snow
Another time I made an igloo out of snow.
I like winter!
David Fermin, Grade 8
Christopher Columbus Middle School

Excitement

Looks like a parakeet flapping in its cage.
Tastes like a peppermint stick.
Smells like a jasmine flower.
Feels like an invisibility cloak.
Sounds like people dancing the polka.
Christopher Cruz, Grade 7
Galloway Township Middle School

Cold Fall

I am cold and windy
I wonder why my leaves turn multiple colors
I hear wind whistling through the sky
I see dead trees without their leaves drained of their emotions
I want the leaves to sing a solemn autumn song
I am cold and windy

I pretend I am spring but then remember I am autumn
I feel cold and dark and the season no one likes
I touch the frosty autumn sky
I cry, I am the season no one likes and the season everyone despises
I understand I am only a three month season
I say to myself I am only a season, I will pass soon and next November I am reborn
I dream about everyone being happy and getting excited for me to come again
I try to make my season better
I hope for children to play outside for hours and hours on end
I am cold and windy and that is all I will ever be and for now it is only a dream
Now I realize that some people enjoy my presence!
Michael Moiseyev, Grade 7
New Egypt Middle School

Cat and Mouse

Nailed to the floor by the domestic beast.
My eyes bulged out of my eye sockets.
Lingering on the lonely dead streets,
under the luminous moon,
kept my exhausted body from sleeping.
Terrified and reluctant that this belligerent beast would soon kill.
Her heart was as slimy as a snake.
My muscles as strong as a wrestler.
Her speed as fast as lightning.
Her army of killers and assaulters covered my shaking and trembling body.
When I gazed into her eyes, fire appeared, mango-orange, crimson-fire.
Survival! I was a mouse and she was the shabby cat chasing after me.
The game began.
As the shabby cat showed her fierce claws,
I hovered in a corner.
She pounced on me.
The game was over,
and I lost.
Danielle Perez, Grade 7
Galloway Township Middle School

Field Hockey

Running, driving, dribbling, scoop, flick: score.
Catching your breath after running from one side of the field to the other.
Having the anxious feeling of trying to score a goal.
Always have your stick down and ready.
Counting on your team with positiveness.
Trying your best and don't give up on the ball.
Hearing my name being yelled out on the sidelines.
Running as fast as I can down the field protecting my forward line.
Having fun and loving it.
Running, driving, dribbling, scoop, flick: score!
Melissa Van Wingerden, Grade 7
Frankford Township School

Baby Bunnies

A cold rainy day, I see the poor shivering baby bunnies,
I check on them if I may, I do not find their pain funny.
One bunny dead, and I begin to dread, where is their mother, they need some cover.
The very next day, a nice lady will say,
"I will take them to the wildlife center," I decided it would be for the better.
Mother rabbit comes back, and practically has a heart attack,
All baby bunnies disappear, and she begins to fear.
All that was left was one dead bunny, and she did not find it very funny,
I head outside to check the dead baby bunny there, and all I could do was stare.
The baby's insides weren't there anymore, my heart felt sad right to the core,
I wish I could tell Mother rabbit I was sorry, and that she does not have to worry.
That her young baby rabbits were safe and sound, but by her they could not be found,
Tears begin to run down my cheek, I could not even speak.
Hopefully and hysterically hopping to every hole, she cannot find what I stole,
She must think I am the devil, I can't seem to help, but tremble.
I felt like a mime, right then and there, for there was news I cannot share,
I hear the pit-pats of the rain, and repeatedly told myself, I must stay sane.
A simple spring day seems so sinuous, full of curves and bends of events, that seems so continuous,
Are all these events supposed to be the natural flow, I wonder and wonder, and turn my back to the window.
My nose became runny, I could not tell her where her babies were sent,
Since our language is different from a bunny's, she will never know where her babies went.

Jessica Kerman, Grade 8
Westampton Middle School

I Don't Have All Night!!!!

Here is a poem that I had to write. I didn't get started until tonight
My dad got upset cause I waited so late He said "All you do is procrastinate."
Procrastinate is an awfully big word what does he think that I'm some kind of nerd?
When I said that to him he got really mad. Then I said "Chill out pops" this isn't so bad.
I'll think real hard and type really fast. He said yea you better or it will be you're… As-king
some questions what should I write? Times running out I don't have all night.
I better think quick and I better think now then it all came to me I'll write this stuff down.
I'll write about how I drug my feet when I knew this was due for the last 3 weeks
How I said to myself well it's not due yet now my times almost up and my dad is upset
Cause I know that if I don't get my work done Dad and I will have a meeting and that won't be fun
So my poem is finished there's nothing to say now come on Ms. S how about that A

Robert Ennis, Grade 7
Lakeside Middle School

One Star

A star, so bright, may twinkle in the sky and make the night come to life,
luminous, shimmering, alive
Not every star alike. Some bigger, some smaller
Some brighter, some duller, all part of the majestic, colossal sky
But what if one star, commanding and persuasive, changed the minds of some of the other stars, convincing them to hate and discriminate against the different stars. And what if the hate and prejudice led to the weakening strengths and fading lights of the alienated stars
There. Do you see? A star just fell, descending into the night, never to be seen again. But follow it, go back to the place where that star fell
It burnt out fearful and alone, with no other star there to lend a hand, to
catch it. Look up again. Another star and another, falling into
the petrifying, icy night
Put your hand out, and catch one. Two. Three. Small beacons of hope.
For all it takes is the saving of one star, and that night the endless, black canvas of the night sky will be one star brighter.

Meghan Carbone, Grade 8
Franklin Township School

Jenna Treen

J ust plain fun
E njoys life
N ot the one to say no
N ever down in the dumps
A wesome in so many ways

T reats everyone equally
R eliable to friends and family
E xciting all the time
E ager to help everyone
N ever gives up
Jenna Treen, Grade 7
Lakeside Middle School

Music

Music brings happiness to my ears
It can be played for all to hear
And all throughout the year
You can never stop learning it
It is a part of you
It's a gift that keeps on giving
It's a thing that's always living
You can play it together
There are endless possibilities
There are no responsibilities
Everything goes
Jesse Braun, Grade 7
Frankford Township School

That Little Green Monster

Your face turns red
It makes you stomp your feet with rage
It makes you want to explode
It's deep inside you
Waiting to come out
But don't worry
If you learn to control it
It will go away
As the saying goes
"When you get mad
A green monster grows inside you"
Gonzalo Gomez, Grade 7
Battin School #4

The Whipping Wind

The whipping wind
Was whispering around
The willow tree.
It was blowing
Willy-nilly near
The water of the sea
I wish and wish that I
Could see the whipping, whispering wind
By the water of the sea.
Anne Kitz, Grade 8
Assumption Academy

My Different World!

Living in a different world
Pretending everything's fine
Nothings ever fine
There's always something wrong
Fights, drama, everything

Living in my own fantasy world
Everything's fine there
The grass is the greenest
The flowers are beautiful
Everything's perfect
No fights, no drama, no everything

When I come back to reality
I wish I could go back
Back to my own world, back to my perfect life
But nothing can ever be perfect
I have to live in reality and live with what I have and deal with it
There will be fights, drama, and everything but I will have to live with it.
Amber Lombardi, Grade 7
William Davies Middle School

Where I'm From

I am from a quiet street with lots of laughs and long summer nights,
From the sound of my cats meow and the smell of Febreeze air freshener.
I am from a pale pink house with purple and white flowers in bloom every year.
I am from the dandelion invasion to stolen tomatoes.

I am from German parades and long eyelashes,
From Bucaria and Rastaetter.
I am from yelling in the car to cleaning up spills,
From, "I'm not made of money" and "Sweet Home Alabama."

I am from a catholic world,
From never going to church.
I am from Germany and Italy,
From apple pancakes to pizza.
I am from long hikes to Garret Mountain,
From Taco Bell.
I am from rock music and *Full House*.

I am an apple that hasn't fallen far from the trees.
April Rastaetter, Grade 8
Christopher Columbus Middle School

Sleep

Quickly jumping,
the cat got onto the coffee colored sofa,
as the children left the house.
Breaching soft pillows,
she made room to take a nap.
Licking her tiny paws, curling up into a tight ball, shutting her green eyes,
she falls asleep.
Oh, how peaceful she looks when she is tired.
Ryan Conklin, Grade 8
New Providence Middle School

Christmas
Christmas comes but once a year
Shining light and Christmas cheer

Singing carolers and Santa's sleigh
Don't forget the deer, who lead the way

Children playing in the snow
In hopes the winter will never go

The ground is covered in a blanket of white
Oh how I can't wait for Christmas night

Presents sitting under the tree
I can't wait to see if they are all for me

Christmas day was here and gone
Now the year must roll along
Kennard Taylor, Grade 8
New Egypt Middle School

Snow
It crunches lovely when it's tread
It's great for when you play
You could use it for a sled
Or enjoy it on a sleigh

It could be used to build a fort
Or to make a nice snowman
A snowball to the face might hurt
But it beats a summer on the sand

It makes a beauty on the landscape
It puts a blanket on the land
There's nothing about it one could hate
It really is quite grand

It's as white as a dove
And there's nothing not to love!
Andrew Levorse, Grade 8
New Egypt Middle School

Missing
You're the missing puzzle piece,
the lost sock in the dryer.
Nobody know where you are.
I send search dogs,
make calls day and night,
put posters up,
try to go on the air.
I ask all your friends where you are.
But no one knows.
But I want you to remember
that I still pray for you,
and hope to see you again.
Imelda Martinez, Grade 7
Robert Morris Public School

My Walk Home
The wind whistles in my ear
while my feet
splash in puddles.
The breeze gently
tousles my hair
as it sweeps newly colored
leaves off their feet.

Acorns stroll by my side
until they trip
off the curb.
The bottom of my boots
scrape the doormat.
I am welcomed inside,
away from all of my
tiny friends
blow, fly, and roll
with the wind.
Julia Coppola, Grade 7
Schuyler School

Family
Family is so close to my heart,
And no one could break us apart.
Family is all what life is about
And I know that without a doubt.
They are why I wake up every day,
From the people I care;
And everyone is aware
Family means a lot,
But to some people not.
We have good and bad days
And our feelings sometimes feel like more
We play and laugh
And we are close like staff
All my family is my second half,
Of my heart that's how important they are
And they shine just like a star.
Family is deep inside my heart,
And without them I'd get a heart attack!
Daniela Santos, Grade 8
Christopher Columbus Middle School

Ghost
I see a floating figure
I don't know what it is
The figure looks like thick, white fog
I scream in horror as it follows close behind
I hear a faint scream in the distance
I run as fast as I can
Then it just disappears
I start to shake and shiver
All of a sudden I recognize the figure
A GHOST!!!
Taylor Merwin, Grade 7
Frankford Township School

Baseball
A gorgeous,
Rough brown,
Metallic black,
Stained white,
Confident eyes,
Impatient faces,
Jumpy teammates,
Baseball,
The best sport there is,
Intense and exciting,
Interesting,
What I was made to do,
The sweetness of your energy drink,
The saltiness of sunflower seeds,
Baseball,
A long season awaits.
Jeet Ganatra, Grade 7
Herbert Hoover Middle School

Fraud
You hold me tight in your arms
You will say it will be alright
You talk to me like I'm grown up
You hug me when I'm down
You stick up for me
You care for me
You give me gifts and surprises
You let me be free
You are unstoppable
You let me grow up
You are there for me when I'm down
You are super-person
For I wish you and it were true
For you're only a myth of my imagination
For you're another dream I had last night
Natalie Moreno, Grade 7
Lakeside Middle School

Chocolate
Sweet chocolate,
Sweet brown,
Cloudy white,
And sunshine yellow.
Smells so sweet.
Tastes of sweet joy
Feels hard and creamy.
Chocolate
Chunky chocolate bar,
Blasting with nuts
Hear the crack in your ears
While you munch on it.
Chocolate oh so sweet.
Is the best,
Thing for me.
Billy Ippolito, Grade 7
Herbert Hoover Middle School

Pizza Rap

My head is aching because I'm standing in line.
It feels like I'm stuck in overtime.
I just can't take it anymore.
My stomach is growling right down to the core.
I've been waiting here with such ambition.
So I can finally finish my ultimate mission.
For me to obtain the food from heaven above,
It's the saucy, cheesy, doughy mixture that I love.
Its flavor will make your taste buds melt.
The most extraordinary feeling my belly ever felt.
Pepperoni, pineapple, peppers, or plain,
These foods are invincible, pounding my brain.
It seems like I need to be a browbeater.
Just so I can get my food, and be a "now" eater.
When it comes out of the oven, it feels like a dream.
Nothing's better than this, not even double fudge ice cream.
Even though I'm broke, I'm going to walk through the door.
My gut's a bottomless pit, and it's screaming for more.
Oh, the delicious concoction called pizza.
Is the best meal on earth for Alex Camisa.

Alex Camisa, Grade 8
Clinton Public School

Procrastinating Parents

Endless lines stretch from near to far
Many nearly grazing the closest star

Anxious parents who waited too long
Continuously hear the same Christmas song

Kids these days want many ostentatious things
Guess parents are going to have to pull some strings

Stampedes greet store owners when they open in the morning
Products fly everywhere without any warning

Hours and hours fly by
Only to discover that what they need is out of supply

The silly ones don't learn from their mistakes
And you see them rushing to find the perfect birthday cakes

You might receive a bruise here and there
But at least you have the joy of showing someone you care

Katie Solinski, Grade 8
New Egypt Middle School

Winter

W indy and cold
I nside drinking hot cocoa
N ever-ending day with snow
T he time is an hour ahead
E arly on Christmas morning opening presents
R unning around playing with snowballs.

Alexandra Dul, Grade 7
Garfield Middle School

The Diminished Life of a Leaf

Who would be a leaf who could help it?
Baking in the sun all day.
Bugs eating at his side,
There are holes everywhere.
Soon day becomes night, night becomes day.
He is watching as if something exciting will happen.
He changes colors from green to yellow.
Faded, old fashioned looking, he has no meaning.
Waiting, watching, nothing to do.
Then comes the wind, and rain.
The colony of leaves cling to the tree like it is the end of the world.
Soon the frost comes; it's like a blizzard to him.
It gets frigid and windier as Halloween arrives.
All his friends are getting plucked off one by one.
Now he is the only one left in the group.
All alone, cold and dismal.
Then, pop! He falls, down, down down, to his death.
There, the wounded soldier lies.
Only to get stepped on by passerby's.
The wind whips what's left of him into the sky like a feather.
He was a victim of a brutal crime who has been laid to rest.

Catie Hallstrom, Grade 8
Clinton Public School

From Autumn to Winter

There are many different color leaves on the trees
There's red, orange, and green what colors have you seen.

The season starts to change and the leaves do something strange
Their colors turn to brown and the leaves fall to the ground

The branches become bare and there is a slight chill in the air
The warmth is lost which soon begins the frost

The autumn becomes blurry as we spot the first flurry
The temperature drops quickly as the kids yell yippee

Autumn came and went with all the time we spent
Another season is near as winter creeps here.

Karly Mani, Grade 8
St Anthony of Padua School

Summer

As summer is beginning, all you can see
are the pretty, colorful singing birds.
As you pass through the backyard,
you see lush vibrant colors of the grass, leaves, and flowers.
What a gorgeous sight to see!
You might see cotton puff clouds
and the great summer sunlight as it twinkles in your eyes.
You come across the swaying of the pine trees
as they give off their fresh smell.
As I feel the leaves crinkle in my hands and the grass tickle my toes,
I know this is a summer to last!

Nicholas Pisani, Grade 7
New Egypt Middle School

LeBron and the Shot

During a cold Saturday night the Cleveland Cavaliers were waiting for a win.
Inside Quicken Loans Arena LeBron James and Mo Williams are about to hook up for a great play.
At the time the Cav's were down by 2 with 2.6 seconds on the clock in the 4th quarter.
Throughout the city of Cleveland, friends and family sat, watched, and worried about losing the game.
In my home in New Jersey I watched with my neighbor and Mom.
Before the great play, Rashard Lewis threw up a shot.
Below the net the players got ready for the rebound.
Under the net Zydrunas Ilgauskas leaps up to get the rebound and calls "Timeout!"
Behind the half court line the play is about to begin.
Beyond the 3 point line Mo Williams passes the ball to LeBron.
Within 2.6 seconds on the clock LeBron, who is triple teamed by defenders throws up a shot.
Atop the line he releases the ball and it glides through the air.
Inside Quicken Loans Arena the crowd is going crazy.
From LeBron's hand to the net the ball "swooshes" through the hoop for 3 points.
Out of the amazing plays I have seen that's the best and the Cav's won the game!

William Schneiderhan, Grade 8
Clinton Public School

Education

E ducation is the key to success.
D egree will take you to where you want to go.
U nder no circumstances should you drop out.
C areers is what this is all about.
A lways try to improve your grades.
T urn off the television, games and hit the books.
I mprove your mind through knowledge.
O pen a book today and read.
N ever settle for less only the best.

I nvention comes through education.
S tudy hard you will be a better person.

EDUCATION IS THE WAY TO GO.

T he key to the future is education.
H elp is always available so use it.
E xcuse is not an option.

W ork to the best of your ability.
A mind is a terrible thing to waste.
Y ou can be whatever you want to be.

T eachers are always there to help you.
O pportunity is there for you take it.

G o for the gold not the silver.
O nly you can stop you.

Christopher Clowney, Grade 8
Keyport High School

Baseball

Before the game the entire team prepares to play.
Outside on the field everyone is warming up.
Inside the dugout adrenaline is pumping through our bodies.
Until the game starts we sit patiently with win in our minds and hearts.
At the field the umpire arrives which means the game will begin momentarily.
Within one minute of the umpire's arrival we hear "play ball" and we take the field with excitement.
Upon home plate the batter steps into the batters box.
Behind him sits the catcher and the umpire.
Atop the pitcher's mound, he begins his wind up and his delivery.
Toward the plate comes the pitch and the batter swings and hits it right toward me.
On the ground the ball speeds at me, I snag it and throw him out at first base.
Beyond the fence the fans cheer with excitement.

Vinny Vitelle, Grade 8
Clinton Public School

The New Year

Days passed by quickly.
Days turned into 52 weeks.
Weeks turned into 12 months.
There are a lot of experiences
And decisions I made.
Keeping new friends,
Making new friends.
Memories to keep
Never fading away.
Now it's time to start all over
Adding new experiences, continuing old
Because the New Year is here to stay
For 365 days.

Stephanie Chaverra, Grade 7
Battin School #4

Halloween

A wicked witch over my head
And a monster or two
A white ghost under my bed
And vampires creeping too
What next! A goblin in pink
The colors! The creatures!
The good
The bad
The shiny cloth
The dark ones too
All zooming around from house to house
Taking candy all night
All here on the night of Halloween!!

Ruhi Shah, Grade 7
Hammarskjold Middle School

War

The sound of guns going off
Bullets zipping by
Bombs blowing up in our faces
The enemy charging us
The sight of a downed friend
The sight of fear in the opponent
The smell of gunpowder
It's like the eye of a hurricane
It's when a boy becomes a man
It's the most violent thing known to man
And no one wants to join it
It is called war.

Ryan Zvolensky, Grade 7
Frankford Township School

Haiku

Japanese poems
Made with seventeen moras
This is my Haiku

Kristal DeJesus, Grade 7
Lakeside Middle School

Rainbows

Who would be a rainbow who could help it?
They sparkle beautifully like pearls while they last,
But their lives are as short as a cold gust of wind.
Preceded by the rain and the cold dark, they are built by the sun and his rays.
She is sought out only because of her promise of gold.
Treasure hunters are a 24-hour storm that forever chases her.
But no men with red beards live at her ends.
Only dirt that has been torn up by the typhoon.
Her greatest fear is a fluffy white cloud,
His path in the sky shows a bias toward the sun.
He veils the golden disc's radiance for a moment.
She begins to forfeit her life to the wind; chaos races among her stripes.
The sun fights his way through the mist, but the damage has been done.
Colors of hers are a rusty sword, tarnished beyond repair.
Violet settles on top of the flowers.
Blue flies back into the sky.
Green crawls into the grass.
Yellow and orange sprout into leaves, and red bleeds into the cardinal's wings.
Her colors have gone back to their homes, and she fades away.

Jendayi Jones, Grade 8
Clinton Public School

Story of My Life

I feel like I'm wishing on a star that will never come into my gaze.
Reaching for the forbidden object on the top shelf that I cannot seem to reach.
Why you ask?
You're intangible.
Everything that I've ever dreamed of having,
and yet, too good to be true.
So, the underlying question
Was there really anything there all along, did those things actually happen?
Am I playing it out to be more than it was?
No — because you're intangible.
You cannot be held or touched.
In fact, do you even exist.
That question I know the answer to,
it's yes.
Although you can't touch nothing,
you can't love nothing, and that
means that you
are something.

Jamie Myhre, Grade 9
Southern Regional High School

The Delight Song of Riley

I am the soccer ball in a professional soccer game.
I am the cheese of a luscious gourmet cheeseburger prepared by the top notch chief.
I am the chosen one in the do or die hockey match.
I am the guitar The Beatles used for their first song.
I am the script Will Ferrell uses in the movie Elf.
I am the football Tim Tebow uses to get the winning touchdown in the finals.
I am the snowboard Shawn White uses to shred the half pipe.
I am the brain of Albert Einstein when he is inventing.
I am the Earth which we all live, eat on, and survive on.

Riley Parnham, Grade 7
Old Turnpike Middle School

Nature

Swaying back and forth
To and fro
Silent sounds it produces
Like someone whistling

Leaves falling to the ground
Waiting to be found
Turning different colors
Yellow, orange, brown

The trunk as brown as it can be
So rough and easy to see
So strong
Strong enough to survive

Its twigs so skinny
Its branches so strong
Even if you hang on it
It won't break at all
Jannicke Munford, Grade 8
Westampton Middle School

Fabulous Fall Fascination

The crisp, blissful leaves are amongst us
    Their spins are making us stare,
    The wind causes our bodies to shiver
    To shiver foreshadowing a scare

The trees are dancing in contentment
    The branches are beginning to sway,
    our coats are strapped on securely
    And away we scamper to play

The surprises of this blustery season
    Can be such a merry sight to eye,
    As our figures are delighted
    We can't stop but ask "Why?"

The universe is a box of surprises
And we will soon experience them all,
    But many of them are hidden
    Hidden in the joyous season of Fall.
Akshay Kamath, Grade 7
Linwood Middle School

Thanksgiving

Everybody with their family eating.
Everybody making and eating great turkey.
Everybody giving thanks to one another.
Everybody enjoying themselves
Watching a great football game on TV.
Everybody on a break of work and school.
Everybody waiting for Christmas to come.
Danny Perez, Grade 7
Garfield Middle School

Where I'm From

I'm from the asphalt driveway with the basketball hoop
I'm from the pool and the waterfall, from the basement and the movie theatre.
I'm from the three identical oak trees, that display, every fall, their plumage like a peacock.
I'm from the plants in the pond and the scooter with red and green wheels

I'm from Saroja and B.V.
From the two hundred year old swing in the family for six generations.
From playing the game of Palan Kuzhi with Pati
And learning that winning isn't everything.
I'm from Indian food and festivals, from prayers and offerings,
I'm from every personification of God, and knowing He exists in everything.

I'm from a family history of loving the Yankees, from Carole and Marty.
I'm from a place in the mountains called New Paltz,
From a loving home with baked stuffed clams and hugs.
I'm from crumb cake and elephant ears, from bonding and learning patience.
While fishing at Long Beach Island and learning that you only keep what you eat

In my room, on a shelf is a poster it has pictures and names which reminds me of who I am,
The names of the many people who lived before my time. I am these people.
The royal priests, the poets, and the musicians the policemen, the firemen, and the salesmen
A part of a long tradition from countries far away
From India on one side to Ireland on another
I am the boy who will carry my family name forward.
Jay Barry, Grade 9
The Lawrenceville School

I Ask My Mother to Help Me with My Homework

A child does not know the stench of misery.
The smell invades my home,
Battles with the smell of tomato sauce boiling in a pot.
I batter the red carpeted steps
That have become victim to my frustrated feet.

I kick my way into the room and enter choking on the smell.
She is too thin, a man's shirt billowing around her.
I yank on the sleeve and the collar almost strangles her slender neck.
My legs jump back, frightened at my power.
She leans on one arm, and weakly faces my tyranny.

I shove a worksheet into her bosom as waves of nausea shake her chest.
I force eyes tempted to close, to see
And try to strangle answers out of a mouth too tired to speak.
She tries to answer through the convulsions.

The face of cancer is beautiful.
A smooth milk chocolate with a tiny explosion
Of dark freckles scattered over sunken cheeks.
A rounded nose, one landmark before a set of dry lips,
Cracked like crevices in the ground, the bottom lip fuller than the top.
Cancer has curly hair cropped close to the head.
Beautiful, but it will not grow.
Charlene Francois, Grade 9
Livingston Sr High School

A Thunder Storm Strikes

Thunder rolls and cracks in the sky
The rain starts to pick up
So does the wind
The sky turns black

Lightning flashes in the dark sky
It lights up the whole town
The sky makes a loud boom
Tress blow furiously

The wind whistles throughout the sky
The thunderstorm was all night long
Flashes surround people everywhere
Loud cracks follow them

It rains cats and dogs
The wind howls
At last, it stops

Mallory Reburn, Grade 8
Westampton Middle School

Laughter and Bliss

L ivens the
A tmosphere, this
U ncontrollable burst of enjoyment.
G enerating
H appiness
T hat washes
E ven the most
R epugnant thoughts from the mind.

A lmost like a
N inja force
D estroying the pessimist in you.

B eautiful and
L oveliest way of living
I n the moment without a
S econd thought about the
S hrouded future.

Akshitha Ajayan, Grade 7
Linwood Middle School

Silence

Subtle signs of silence
sweep away my thoughts.
Staring in solitude,
I suffer so solemnly.

Some say silence is stillness,
a soft tranquility.
But silence screeches,
like a squeal or sharp shrieks.
So…LOUD.

Danielle Cole, Grade 8
Assumption Academy

Lunch

Eluding the hawk,
The gray squirrel leapt to a branch mantled in frost after the morning dew.
Growling with hunger,
The squirrel scurried to find food before the first snowfall.
Bounding through the dead grasses,
Scampering into the underbrush,
Stumbling upon its acorn cache,
The squirrel found its lunch,
And it savors it in peace.

Stefan Olesnyckyj, Grade 8
New Providence Middle School

A Walk Down Stream

Against my toes and soles of my feet the mud slithers.
Along the river the bullfrogs chirp and croak their songs.
Beneath the banks a refreshing river flows and I step into it for a walk.
Above the trees, the birds and bugs soar.
Below the water, fish slice through the ripples.
In the crisp, clear water my feet rest in the gritty sands.
Past all the tall grass along the banks is where I walk.
Throughout the whole entire world, this is my favorite place to go for a walk,
down this little stream.

Tori McDermott, Grade 8
Clinton Public School

The Beach

Packed with soft, warm, golden sand,
the beach lures many travelers from all over to stay there as long as time allows them to.
Crashing small waves in the warm water
bring tourists into the water to cool off and take a rest.
Lurking, climbing, then plunging onto the wet sand,
the clear, blue waves of water bring an exciting thrill to everyone.
A place to have a good time and relax,
the beach is always a great place to spend a summer week!

Miller Gorny, Grade 8
New Providence Middle School

The Delight Song of Natale

I am the vibrant Evergreen among naked Oaks in the winter.
I am the detailed, sparkling snow crystal hidden in the snow fall.
I am the only polar bear left swiftly swimming in the Arctic Sea.
I am a red present standing out next to invisible white gifts lying under the Christmas Tree.
I am the last yellow lily picked in the flower field.
I am the brightest star in the open, midnight sky.
I am the last drop of rain that finally stops the storm.
I am the roar of a lion in the midst of a quiet crowd of crickets.

Natale Swick, Grade 7
Old Turnpike Middle School

Zoom Zoom Zoom

It's amazing how fast this can go,
In a few seconds,
And come to an immediate stop.
Just sit there motionless,
And jump forward with speed.

Just chasing something,
Until they go and find it,
And go back home and rest.
When it stops, just sitting there waiting to go out tomorrow,
To go out for another run.

And when it's ready,
It roars, ready to zoom all around,
Ready to go here and there,
Stop and wait then speed up once again.
Repeating this cycle every day.
Every day a new road to travel.

Mark Hodges, Grade 7
New Providence Middle School

School Vacations

Once in a while we get off from school
Relaxing at home or in a pool
You can do anything you want to do
Until the day of school which you are sad and blue
No homework or assignment needs to be done
Just try to lay down under the sun
You can play video games until you have won
Being off from school is very fun
At school everyone is tired
Their brains need to be rewired
Sometimes after people are finished with the days off
They stay home an extra day by faking a sneeze or cough
It's tough having to do work all over again
Also, having to do manual labor with a pencil or pen
This happens a lot of times every year
Going back to school gives you terrible fear
No need to worry because you'll have another vacation real soon
Then you can look down upon the grass and stare at the moon

Ala'a Damrah, Grade 7
Garfield Middle School

Poetic Justice

I hold my pencil in my hand.
I try to write, but my words are bland.
I rack my brain for something poetic,
But all my thoughts are useless and pathetic.
As I try hard to ponder
My mind begins to wander
To when I danced under the brightest star
Knowing that any danger is far.
Then splashed in the salty ocean
Shrieking at its strong motion.
So as I hold my pencil in my hand
My heart and mind are in a faraway land.
Those vivid summer days
Set my eyes ablaze
In the land with no formality,
But it's time to come back to reality.
The summer memories come rushing out
And now I know what to write about.

Amanda Pra Sisto, Grade 8
St Mary's School

Winter Mountain

I walk up the mountain and I see a snowy town.
Waist-deep snow is all around.
I see very few people and not many animals.
Leafless trees stand tall,
towering over me.
I hear a strong wind blowing and growing.
My hand rests on an ice cold rock,
it seems that my hand is locked.
I jerk my hand away and continue my journey,
stepping through icy sticks and logs.
I feel frost bite,
in the middle of the night.
The snow is coming down,
but I hear not a sound.
The frigid air enters my lungs and I can taste it too.
I taste the frigid air.
Walk up a mountain in the winter,
if you dare.

Jonathan Mitchell, Grade 7
New Egypt Middle School

My Precious Angel

Baby screams echo as my cousin hands me
A precious angel sent to save us.
He stops crying, and a hint of smile swung across his face,
As if a boy just compliments a girl.
A blush flows along on his white flesh,
While I rock him like the soft breeze hits a rocking chair outside.
He squirms around as I cradle him to sleep.
I kiss the baby's small forehead,
And its warmness rushes through my veins.
His eyes slowly shut, leaving me staring at his small, fragile body.

Brittany Aponte, Grade 7
Galloway Township Middle School

Snow

Snow is a crystal white.
Snow is like a cup of joy.
Snow is the taste of a snow cone but without the juice.
Snow is the smell of cold in your nose.
Snow is the sound of light drizzling rain on the sidewalk.
Snow is the feeling cold and happiness.
Snow is lots of fun to play in during Christmas break.
Snow is joy falling from the sky.
Snow is the happiest season.
Snow is everything that you have ever wished for.

Christine Fox, Grade 7
Frankford Township School

The Chilled Winds of Fall
As the chilled winds blow,
Now I finally know,
That fall is near,
Which is my favorite time of year.
When all of the spirits are about,
You see many spiders climbing up each spout.
The leaves sing as if an opera, as they fall among the ground,
Falling near each pumpkin, big, fat, and round.
Now for Halloween, kids are out and about.
Collecting much more candy, than those who sit and pout.
Thanksgiving is the highlight of each and every year,
No more having to fear.
Eating turkey, gravy, and rolls,
Everyone having so much fun while cleaning up the ghouls.
As fall comes to a stop,
So do the apples that usually drop.
Hanging heads to say goodbye,
To all of the birds who usually fly.
Here comes winter, another great time,
But sadly ends my story and all of my rhymes.
Courtney Soden, Grade 7
New Egypt Middle School

The Autumn Crisp and Cold
I am autumn crisp and cold
I wonder if kids will go trick-or-treating
I hear leaves crackling
I see leaves falling from trees
I want to be a scary pumpkin
I am autumn crisp and cold

I pretend I'm a ghost
I feel the coolness in the wind
I touch the crisp big colorful leaves
I worry my season will be over soon
I cry when I don't see happy people
I am autumn crisp and cold

I understand it's very cold
I say hip hip hooray when my season starts
I dream my season would be year-round
I try to make a scary noise like a howling wolf
I hope everybody enjoys me
I am autumn crisp and cold
Ryan Simoes, Grade 7
New Egypt Middle School

My Bus
I see dirty, ripped seats and stale food in the cushions,
It tastes like a dump.
It smells like someone was smoking.
It sounds like Lady Gaga, Sean Kingston…in my ears.
It feels like a long journey…a very long hour.
Stink bomb
Mollie Baruch, Grade 7
Kellman Brown Academy

Bright and Colorful
I am bright and colorful.
I wonder why I'm changing colors?
I hear the crunch of the leaves.
I see kids running and playing ball!
I want to be a big maple tree!
I am bright and colorful.

I pretend that I'm invincible to hide from the winter frost.
I feel the crisp cold air.
I touch the brightness of the sun.
I worry that kids will jump on me.
I cry when I see little kids get hurt by falling on acorns.
I am bright and colorful.

I understand that I will fall.
I say "oh gosh, I'm up high!"
I dream of never falling.
I try my very best to hang on.
I hope I'll be ok after I fall.
I am bright and colorful.
Dan Fernicola, Grade 7
New Egypt Middle School

Frights in the Night
I am a jack-o'-lantern.
I wonder if children are scared of my carved out face.
I hear bats fluttering in the dark, spooky night.
I see darkness around me and the children running about.
I want to be able to trick-or-treat.
I am a jack-o'-lantern.

I pretend to be a zombie pumpkin.
I feel like everyone is watching me.
I illuminate the dark night.
I worry that rats will eat me alive.
I cry when I start to rot.
I am a jack-o'-lantern.

I understand that Halloween doesn't last forever.
I say "muahahahaha!"
I dream about tasting delicious candy.
I try not to get frightened by all the ghosts and goblins of the night.
I hope Halloween comes again soon!
I am a jack-o'-lantern.
Nikkie Martire, Grade 7
New Egypt Middle School

I Will Miss My Caring Brother
I will miss my caring brother
I wonder if my brother will join the military
I hear gunfire and explosives when I think of it
I see him being a great fighter and war hero
I want him to overcome his love for our country and stay home
I will miss my caring brother
Mark Garrett, Grade 7
Hammarskjold Middle School

Book

Captivating stories bound together,
Ink black,
Dull white,
Beautiful rainbow.
I listen to the storyteller's voice,
With breathless anticipation.
I read the words,
And my imagination
Starts to wander.
A book
A deep well of knowledge,
A vast sea of entertainment.
Reading page after page
Time flies by.
I hear the faint sounds
Of others flipping the pages.
Everyone is far away,
Lost in the world,
Created by books.

Shreya Shirodkar, Grade 7
Herbert Hoover Middle School

A Ride Round the Merry-go-round

You walk to the line
Cotton candy in hand
You have waited in line for 15 minutes
For a ride 'round the merry-go-round

Your baby brother is with you
Standing with his hand in your hand
You have waited in line for 18 minutes
For a ride 'round the merry-go-round

You watch the horses race up and down
Holding your tickets patiently in hand
You have waited in line for 21 minutes
For a ride 'round the merry-go-round

You watch the conductor stop the ride
You place the tickets in his hand
You have waited in line for 25 minutes
Finally, my ride 'round the merry-go-round

Maddie Fabricant, Grade 8
Township of Ocean Intermediate School

The Beach

Crashing on the shore,
The midnight blue waves wet the sand
As I stand at the shoreline.
Laughing happily,
The children play.
Jumping, diving, swimming
In the waves, I entertain myself.
How can you not love the beach?

Emily Surman, Grade 8
New Providence Middle School

Macaroni and Cheese

A combo of macaroni and cheese.
Mustard yellow,
Dim yellow,
Dark yellow
The look of it,
Makes my mouth water,
Just waiting for that spoon-filled mac and cheese to land in my mouth.
Macaroni and cheese,
So cheesy,
So delicious at its sight,
And so scrumptious when it is eaten.
Everyone spots that fresh smell,
coming right from the oven,
as the mac and cheese is taken out and placed onto everybody's plate.
Finally, the time has come,
I and the rest of my family put in a mouthful of macaroni and cheese.
At that moment a heavenly taste rushes onto everyone's taste buds,
leaving a smile on each and every face.

Vidya Venkateshwararaja, Grade 7
Herbert Hoover Middle School

The Life of Chopsticks

My extensive frustration
is the opposite of elation.
Is pencil form so hard to keep?
The way people form my posture makes me weep.
Soy sauce is my friend,
Ramen noodles will be with me to the end.
Plastic or bamboo I come in either,
When it comes to picking up sushi I'm an overachiever.
I'm proud of my identity just so you know,
Chopsticks are who I am and I'm letting it show.
I have a life that isn't so grand,
For example, I can't be in a restaurant that features a mariachi band.
From this I am truly offended,
I work better than utensils that are pointy ended.
My fury is on the back burner,
When I'm picked up by a curious learner.
They use me correctly and treat me with care.
My enthusiasm puts heaps of joy in the air.

Rebecca Van Vliet, Grade 7
Little Falls School #1

A Poem Of Me

I am the bright sun warming every corner of the earth.
I am the last snowflake in a cloud high in the sky.
I am a sunset in the Mexican sky in July.
I am a cucumber seed in a field of pumpkins.
I am a delicate blue bird making children smile around the world.
I am the last star fruit in the bowl God picks from.
I am a dragon in a cave of bats in Greece.
I am the first ripe apple on my tree every year.
I am the gentle bird of paradise floating in a breeze.
I am the only bioluminescent fish that can see in the darkest corner of the sea.

Sierra Yetka, Grade 7
Old Turnpike Middle School

A Ring to Remember

As I look at my hand, I see a ring with a stone. I also see my reflection, but I know it holds so much more.
There was a moment of friendship, an argument, a fight
A "Best Friends Forever," a really fun night.
A beginning, an ending, and so much in between,
A teardrop, a laugh and turning fourteen.
There in that ring, I see a reflection
Of how much we've accomplished starting section by section.
The yearbook, the pictures, the frozen moments in time,
Will have so much meaning to last us a lifetime.
It's a symbol of our childhood, an engraving of our pride,
As we place each ring upon our finger stirring memories inside.
You often hear that if you love one, put their name inside a circle, not a heart
For a circle has no end to it, and can never come apart.
A graduation ring is that same circle, with so many souvenir's inside,
A graduation ring has no end to it, and always shines off the wearers' pride.
It's also a time for celebration, to look back on lessons learned,
A time to praise yourself on goals achieved, and dreams that were not burned.
It's a sign that a new beginning's facing you, bringing challenges ahead
But it's not a fact to dread about, but bring joy to you instead.
So put your memories inside a circle, for a circle never ends,
And wear your ring forever more, because memories are your true best friends.

Katerina Nozhenko, Grade 8
School Number 14

I Love MaMa Cat

So lovable and sweet, MaMa rubs against my leg especially when she's hungry, she never begs;
Her food bowl is always filled with her favorite food
It's crunchies for MaMa, no canned or seafood;
She loves to rub against me, and I just want to hug her
She's lazy and fat, yet every day she seems bigger;
I once called her Skinster, she was a skinny little thing
But now she's a big girl, in our house she's a queen;
We call her our MaMa, she had seven kittens, we found them homes and I sure do miss them;
MaMa is an imp, she annoys my only two birds
I hear tweeting at night, it's their protesting words;
MaMa is as soft as a kitten, as round as a beach ball.
When she runs you can hear her breathe down the hall;
Oops, I have stepped on the MaMa cat too
Thinking I stepped on my soft, comfy shoe;
No bugs for MaMa, it's crunchies for her.
She loves them so much, just listen for her purr;
But my MaMa cat will never ever stray very far
I think she's afraid to be hit by a car;
I'm glad I found MaMa, she's a part of my life
But I've got to cut those nails, they're as sharp as a knife!

Delaney Koch, Grade 7
Herbert Hoover Middle School

The Splish Splashing Wondrous Beach Day

Scattered seashells in the beady, hot sand, pricking your little toes while walking in the calm, cold ocean water. Seeing small
children run to the ocean, quickly gathering water in their pails to make a huge sandcastle. Relaxed and soothed by the sound
of the waves, gently crashing together and hitting the deep, moist sand. Even if the salty water burns the eyes, the coolness of the
water makes you feel like you are floating and letting everything drift away. Many wonderful memories take place at the beach,
but the ones that are best are ones which are spent with family and friends.

Mitali Gupta, Grade 7
Herbert Hoover Middle School

Walking

Dancing leaves around me
the air smells as sweet as candy
my cold red nose
my numb frozen toes
and whistling birds
all about me

I see a couple far ahead
they're so precious, hand in hand
it makes me wonder when
my sadness will ever come again

I keep walking
past the shops
boutiques, cafes, and homes bordering the town
my eyes fixed on that couple

I walk farther still
into the woods
that's where they stop
and unlock the door to our home

Tommi Schieder, Grade 7
William Davies Middle School

Epoch

The shrouded patriarch,
whose tails oft lead astray,
the set man traversing
on his incognizant way.

The assiduous bystander,
whose shifting eyes riled
the earthly father, arrogant,
yet unknowingly beguiled.

The perdurable eidolon,
whose three hands encased,
have the saint lifted
on his humble foray.

Benjamin Glass, Grade 8
Solomon Schechter Day School of Bergen County

Fall Is Among Us

As the wind blows,
And the leaves change,
The summer season is over,
And fall is upon us,
As the degrees plummet,
As the warmth trickles away,
As children run for school in their heavy fall coats,
We are in the midst of fall,
As the leaves slowly fall from the monstrous trees,
As children play in the leaf mounds,
Fall is among us.

Connor Foor, Grade 7
Ocean Day School

Winter Fun

Jackets and snow is a sign of the winter
It's cold and icy everywhere you go.
Some kids go snowboarding in the park
Enjoying the time until the snow is no more.
Winter could be fun and could be boring.
Fun and exciting holidays
Come during the time.
It only comes once a year
So enjoy it while it comes.
Christmas is what I enjoy most.
Colorful lights are on the house
And gifts that are under the Christmas tree
Family comes together and enjoy the day
Having fun, singing and dancing
A memory that I will never forget.
But let us not forget snowball fights.
Throw a snowball at your friends or make snow angels.
It's fun to play and all were happy
Just think of all these things that you can do.
Winter has never been better.

Ronald Poliquit, Grade 8
Christopher Columbus Middle School

Gym Class

Gym Class is such an amazing blast
Gym Class makes me really fast

Mr. Dempsey lets you play games
Some of them are really lame

Gym class let's you go outside
It feels like you're on a really big ride

Gym class makes you run at last
And when you do it feels like a flabbergast

Every Wednesday and Friday it's always the same
He says the same people's name

After gym it feels like you are going to die
And when it's over you hear a big huge sigh

Isn't gym class so awesomely great?
Unless when we have it right after we just ate!

Anthony Silva, Grade 7
Oxford Street School

Forest Flutterbug

This is a Forest Flutterbug
It lives in forests, flowers, fruit trees, flawless factories
A Forest Flutterbug eats figs, flower petals, fudge, and food
Flying, fooling around, flicking pollen off flowers, frying
It flees, flops, fights frenemies, fails
My Forest Flutterbug flew away and fled to a far away forest.

Helena Sirken, Grade 7
Kellman Brown Academy

The Song of Kutin

I am the sun in the bright summer day.
I am the light from the lamp in your room
I am the first note on the musical scale
I am the last crumb from the cinnamon muffin
I am the last page of your favorite book
I am the brightest flame in your campfire
I am the shine of your brightest Peridot
I am the smile that brings joy to your life
I am the roar of the mighty lion
I am the heartbeat which keeps you alive

Kutin Manu, Grade 7
Old Turnpike School

Halloween

Between the cracks in the road witches' juice is bubbling.
Among me tons of ghosts and goblins run.
Across the street people are laughing and screaming.
Around me kids with funny and scary costumes scamper.
Beneath the ground monsters rise.
Underneath rooftops people are eating candy and pumpkin pie.
During trick-or-treating mom and dad never see you.
Along the way I am in and out of orange and black houses.
Within the night moans and groans I hear.
After this night I will never feel the same.

Jake Blazovic, Grade 8
Clinton Public School

Music

Music is the sound I wake up to
It's the melody I focus on, while on the bus
Music frees me when I listen to it
I can escape from my thoughts
Music makes me happy even when I want to cry
Music is not noise, it is a sound
Words with a meaning, a purpose
Some people think it's just a nuisance
Those who care for music take offense to that
Music completes me in many ways

Rebecca Fackenthal, Grade 8
Township of Ocean Intermediate School

The Delight Song of Meghan

I am the horse running in the meadow at sunset.
I am the last drop of water in the hot desert.
I am the cool breeze of wind on a hot summer day.
I am the first glistening snowflake on a soon to be winter morning.
I am the first grand present being opened on Christmas morning.
I am the last colorful fall leaf hanging on an oak tree.
I am a vibrant rainbow on a gloomy day.
I am the first spring tulip blooming on a May morning.
I am the brightest star in a midnight sky.
I am the bright yellow sun shining over the horizon.

Meghan Whaley, Grade 7
Old Turnpike School

The Delight Song of Liam

I am the steps in the writing process that help you write
I am the staples in a stapler that might come in handy
I am the bear at an abandoned picnic with lots of food
I am an elf making toys for kids around the world
I am the bull chasing the man in the red shirt
I am the strong, fierce jaguar running in the open fields
I am the paper flying freely in the clear skies

Liam Morris, Grade 7
Old Turnpike School

The Trap of the Fromage

Anticipating his cheese,
The petite mouse hides behind the desk.
Gazing at the cheese,
The mouse scurries forward.
Dashing to the chair, vaulting on the legs, diving toward cover,
He grabs the cheese.
Snap! The trap behind him springs and cuts off his tail.

Joe Masucci, Grade 8
New Providence Middle School

The Delight Song of Meghan

I am the shining apple of everyone's sparkling, little eyes
I am the dramatic feeling of a strong, powerful sentence
I am the rose petal that gently floats to the ground
I am the crack of your bone when you tripped
I am the notes to a beautiful song of classical music
I am the seam of sunlight peering through the ajar door
I am the last cherry on the cherry blossom tree

Meghan Olsen, Grade 7
Old Turnpike School

Eternal Waves

Crashing on the beach,
The waves create a steady rhythm.
Splashing and diving,
Children and adults of all ages wade in the icy blue ocean.
Rising up, splattering down, running through the cycle endlessly,
The sea never tires.
Neither do I, watching the beautiful waves.

Kathryn Paris, Grade 8
New Providence Middle School

The Delight Song of Matthew Gilbert

I am a giraffe in the middle of a herd of zebras.
My smile is the sparkling star on the Christmas tree.
My sneaker could be a vacation home for The Little Family.
I am a part of a school of fish riding the waves.
I am a coffee bean roasting in the summer sun.
I am a bear hibernating in the cold of winter.
I am the skis that swoosh down the mountain in winter.

Matthew Gilbert, Grade 7
Old Turnpike School

The Last Hope

The boat, the Fuhrer, the Reich
All else has failed we are told
Our tanks, our guns, our countrymen
We are the last hope they say
It came from the blackness.
No one knows how but everyone knows why
The low rumble, a shadow of death
Then the light, a blinding light
They have come for us
We dive, down to our only refuge
The splashes, doom descends upon us and then the wait
The Allies say they fight for freedom
What do we fight for? An empire?
One that slaughters millions as justice?
Is this what we are fighting for?
Is this what we are dying for?
Then the explosions Doomsday is upon us
The crack, the final splitting of the hull
Down the dead hulk goes
Its final voyage down to the crushing abyss
The boat, the Fuhrer, the Reich

George Li, Grade 8
Thomas R Grover Middle School

October Days

My toes crunched against the rough leaves,
while my golden-brown hair blew in the wind.
Trees were waltzing with the breeze,
swaying to the rhythm of the music.
Leaves were singing to them,
while rusting on the bitter soil.

My bare feet swished through
the faded-green grass.
The sun playing hide-and-seek with the clouds,
swallowed by the moon and dark sky.

A breathtaking October day.

Emily Silver, Grade 7
Galloway Township Middle School

Baseball

Baseball is the greatest sport.
Not only to me but to people who play.
Baseball is a talent.
It takes time and a lot of effort.
Baseball is not just given to someone.
You have to love it.
Or you have to hate it.
Not only is baseball a sport. It is also a career.
One that you can be really successful in.
Baseball is hard and a challenge.
But when you step to the plate.
You feel unstoppable.

Evan Morales, Grade 7
Battin School #4

Up, Up and Away

As we reach the top of the hill,
butterflies are fluttering in my stomach.
The only thing holding me down,
a blue metal bar.

Hard to keep yourself from peeking down,
the curiosity overpowers my fear and I take a quick look.
The people look like ants,
it seems as if the buildings came out of a dollhouse.

The coaster cars slowly crept over the hill,
and we could see the drop.
Then, all of a sudden,
ZOOM!

I let out a loud scream,
and the butterflies flew away.
A huge smile formed across my face,
I had conquered the 22 story beast, Nitro.

Sarah Wain, Grade 8
William R Satz Middle School

Love

His eyes met mine — fireworks burst in the dark sky.
His soft, warm hands were blankets,
protecting me from the brutal wind.
Tears dropped down from my eyes.
They plunged onto his shoulder,
making complete silence.
He held me closer, and closer, but still
we were miles apart.
He whispered, "I love you," as he held me
close to his heart.
His heartbeat pulsed rhythmically.
The ripple of his heart was the drums to the music
we were building out of our devotion
to each other.
I squeezed his hand as it came up to my cheek
to wipe away the tears.
The moonlight wrapped around us
as our arms locked together.
We were unbreakable, unyielding and everlasting.

Colleen Garrison, Grade 7
Galloway Township Middle School

The Jets

The mighty green machines
Who won the Super Bowl in 1903
The Jets are the team for me
When they score a touchdown I scream in glee
The Jets are the team for me
I hear the fans screaming for the Jets
I can see the tackles
And I know the Jets are the best team for me.

Derrick Banfield, Grade 7
Frankford Township School

Wintertime

I wake up with the chills
Walk to the warm fireplace
See the snow flowing through the air
Announcement on the news saying
No school. Kids laughing and smiling
Walk outside to the deep fluffy
White snow. Steep steps
Dad's complaining traffic everywhere
Sale! Sale! Sale! Commercials on
Every channel; time for Christmas shopping.
Walk to the backyard Frosty the Snowman
Standing in every corner.
Jingle bells jingling through the streets
Missing hats and scarves flying through the air.
Sweet cinnamon aroma filling the house
No cries but laughs, grins, and happiness.
Happiness fills in the month of December
Rips, tears from Christmas presents
Family hugs and happy cries
How winter and its holidays fill me with joy!

Samantha Ruiz, Grade 8
Christopher Columbus Middle School

Army

Bullets fired like a downpour on the pavement
while flame throwers incinerated like fire on gas.
Rockets propelled like a bow and arrow.
Nearby blood sprinkled on the floor
as explosions corrupted the Earth.
Ashes streamed on the landscape
as dust drifted on the horizon
and grenades erupted the charcoal terrain.
Battle after battle —
war after war —
kill after kill.
Soldiers, accept your fate!

Riyadhul Taher, Grade 7
Galloway Township Middle School

Typical

The morning air is crisp and cold
Like a summery day in Antarctica
I pull up the covers
Look out the window
And see
Snow fluttering gently to the ground
A white blanket of snow hugging the wintery earth
Children laughing like hyenas
Snowball fights starting
Forts and snowmen being constructed
Grown-ups tediously shoveling the snow off the driveway
And all I can think about
In this perfect chaos
"Is school closed?"

Johanna Poedubicky, Grade 8
New Egypt Middle School

Mystery in Music

As you hear the sounds,
they are different from each other.
But in a way they are both the same.

It sings to you every day.
But the sounds you hear may not
be what you think.

The music is played from two different voices,
if that's what you hear.
This is the mystery in music,
which will be heard from a different ear.

They may not be the same to you,
but to me it is pretty clear.
The mystery in this music,
from both things that we hear.

Emily Erdenberger, Grade 7
New Providence Middle School

Trick or Treat…If You Dare

We all went out, on this dark creepy night,
Dressed up as goblins all full of fright.

We went to each house, every single one,
It was a great time — oh what fun!

Door to door on all of the streets,
We stacked up the candy and all of the sweets.

My trick or treat bag was filled to the top,
We started with one candy then just couldn't stop.

We got so much candy, almost too much to take,
I woke up in the morning with a bad stomach ache!

So I won't be in school, please tell Ms. Green,
Just blame it on having an awesome Halloween.

Demitri Krempecki, Grade 7
Hammarskjold Middle School

Civil War

I want to crumble the thought as if I were a sledgehammer.
What has this world come to?
Cannonballs burst past me, smoke billowing off every one.
Each explosion pounding my hearing; I can only hear
The cries of the wounded sons and fathers.
The rattling ground shakes my vision
Searching and searching —
I found my brother,
Nose-first, his head sunk into the fertile-black soil.
As I hold him, his blood stained my hands,
Dripping onto the torn up dirt.
For eternity I will carry his blood on my hands.

Domenic Maggi, Grade 7
Galloway Township Middle School

My Personal Adventure

I wave at people who come my way
Little sea creatures are with me every day
I'm never alone but I'm scared out of my wits
That is the truth and I'm not afraid to admit

Someone is taking the lid off the tank
Should I go for it, or is it a prank?
It's my only chance, it's time to climb
This feels so wrong, like I'm committing a crime

I'm at the top now and it's time to jump
Somehow I land in a bucket, with hardly a bump
I'm free! I'm free! Oh, yes I am
I promise to be as quiet as a clam

I realize a small girl is holding the bucket
Swing, swing, ugh! Am I going to Nantucket?
Looks like she's putting me in the car's back seat
It's hot back here, I'm feeling the heat

Finally the car stops and I see the ocean's waves
The little girl thought that I should be saved
Someday I'll remember to tell my son and daughter
How this little red lobster escaped from the slaughter

Amy Greene, Grade 7
Little Falls School #1

The Big Day

With all the wedding preparations,
There were bound to be a few complications.
From problems with the wrong-sized dresses,
To all the other messes!

But the big day is finally here.
The one that felt so far, rather than near.
Hear those wedding bells ring.
Listen to the choir sing.

Watch the people walk down the aisle,
All wearing their best and brightest smiles.
Here comes the bride and her dad;
He can't help but look a bit sad.

He hands off his baby girl to her soon-to-be groom.
Everyone becomes silent in the room.
The couple exchanges their wedding vows.
The big moment is finally here, right now.

"You may now kiss the bride,"
The priest says as he steps aside.
As the newlywed couple walks back down the aisle,
All those watching can't help but smile.

Coleen McDonald, Grade 8
St Mary's School

Boardwalk

During the day I see many things at the boardwalk
I see small groups of people
I also see a bright yellow sun
I see cops and people on bikes

During the day I hear many things at the boardwalk
I hear the loud waves crashing
I hear the kiosk employees trying to get customers
Lastly I hear the annoying seagulls screeching

During the day I feel many things at the boardwalk
When I go mini golfing I feel the soft clubs
I feel the rough splinters in my hand when I sit on a bench
And I feel the sand blowing in my face

During the day I smell many things at the boardwalk
I smell the salty ocean
Then smell the delicious hot wings
And the barbecuing of the hot dogs

During the day I taste many things at the boardwalk
I taste the sweet samples of fudge
I taste a grilled cheeseburger
And I taste warm crispy french fries

Mark Dempsey, Grade 7
New Egypt Middle School

A Crush to Remember

We whisper by a tree in each other's ears,
So this must be love or so it appears,
I'm at home thinking of you,
Knowing a true love must always be true,

In school, I study your eyes and not my book,
When I first saw you my heart nearly shook,
You don't know what you want till it's gone,
You'll never notice till she moves on,

Because it was hard to hear you when my glass heart shattered,
It's not like my feelings for you never mattered,
With all the stuff that you've put me through,
I still want to be with you, yes it's true,

And you know that I really like you,
And how I wish that you felt this way too,
If you say that I'm your friend,
Being more I guess would have to pend,

Please give me that green light to go,
Just tell me when I should know,
I want us to be that flame that turns into a fire,
You're one that I admire, but even more the one I desire!

Sara Rose Callow, Grade 8
Westampton Middle School

School

School can be fun
sometimes it can't
For some it makes them jubilant
and for some it makes them cry
Why do we go?
Because it's important
but we all hate it
For me,
I jump up and die
at least in my thoughts
but we all have opinions
As long as we're smart
it's great for us!

Jakub Duma, Grade 7
Garfield Middle School

My Favorite Day

A rainy day
I sit inside and read a book
Drip, drop
The rain hits the front window
The smell is like a brand new car
My favorite day is a rainy day
I hear a loud rumble
I look out the blurry window
I see a bolt of light dash through the sky
The lights suddenly go out
My favorite day, a rainy day
Has been turned into a thunderstorm
My second favorite day

Erika Fleming, Grade 7
St Mary's School

Christmas

It is snowing outside
Kids are having fun!
The Christmas tree is up
Hot chocolate is smoking hot
The decorations are shining
The kids are smiling
People are caroling
Others are putting the star on the tree
Finally at last it hits 12 o'clock
Everyone unwraps presents
Yet they can't wait for next Christmas

Natalie Gonzales, Grade 7
Garfield Middle School

Fall

Warm weather moves south,
The wind gives trees a hair cut,
Children rake outside,
Squirrels stock food for winter.
Colors blend in the thin air.

Bradley Anderson, Grade 7
Oxford Street School

Seasons Pass

The fall season comes all too soon replacing summer and its heat;
Winter follows — cold as the moon spring arrives and the chill retreats

In autumn, the leaves will all fall red, orange, yellow from tall trees
The wind will beat on your house wall and people go on shopping sprees

As jolly holidays draw near, the winter frost coats everything
Many hope Santa will appear…set out cookies he'll be finding!

"April showers bring May flowers" everything starts to bloom, and then
You see a colorful river that in winter was once frozen

The summer heat looms in the air the water is warm! Just jump in!
The sun makes a powerful glare vacations galore will begin

The fall season comes all too soon replacing summer and its heat;
Winter follows — cold as the moon spring arrives and the chill retreats.

Karen Sun, Grade 8
William R Satz Middle School

Music

A paper filled with notes
The sad blues
Rocking red
And exhilarating green
Impatient hands waiting to play the instruments

Eyes wandering about the paper;
Already predicting the beautiful sound
The piano, hi-hat, and bass drum creating a melodious loop,
filled with surprises awaiting its journey to the audience
The tasty jam foreseeing the awesome reaction from the crowd
As the music is being played the jubilant people tap their feet in a content manner
The song ends,
The musicians take a bow,
The crowd applauses
Just some music to you…
Genius being born to me.

Parth Rishi Brahmbhatt, Grade 7
Herbert Hoover Middle School

Summertime

"Tick-Tock! Tick-Tock!"
I can just hear the summer parties and endless beach days calling my name.
The calls get louder and louder after every second passing by.
"Tick-Tock! Tick-Tock!"
I am so close yet so far from getting in touch to summertime.
I am so close yet so far from three months of no stress.
I am so close yet so far from making a big splash in the pool.
I am so close yet so far from —
"Ding-Dong! Ding-Dong!"
I finally have a connection with summer.
I now have three months of freedom and relaxation.
Get ready summer; I'm ready for fun!

Emily Hoang, Grade 7
William Davies Middle School

The Race
Stretching on the pool deck
Waiting for my race
Tension rising as time passes
Then up on the block
It's my turn to swim
The buzzer goes off
Until the end
Nothing else matters
Except getting to the end first.
Kari Shankle, Grade 7
Ocean Day School

My Sunlight
Where has my sunlight gone?
Why has it been ripped away?
Where has my sunlight gone?
The question haunts me day by day.

My sunlight was never gone
It was merely a distance away
My sunlight was never gone
It is here, with me, today.
Milena Chorzepa, Grade 8
Garfield Middle School

Grades 4-5-6
Top Ten Winners

List of Top Ten Winners for Grades 4-6; listed alphabetically

Hailey Benesh, Grade 6
T J Walker Middle School, Sturgeon Bay, WI

Anne Cebula, Grade 6
Intermediate School 239 Mark Twain for the Gifted & Talented, Brooklyn, NY

Zari Gordon, Grade 5
Walker Elementary School, Evanston, IL

Helena Green, Grade 5
Hopewell Elementary School, Hopewell, NJ

Kristin Kachel, Grade 6
Discovery Canyon Campus, Colorado Springs, CO

Carrie Mannino, Grade 5
The Ellis School, Pittsburgh, PA

Mariah Reynolds, Grade 4
School for Creative and Performing Arts, Cincinnati, OH

Jeremy Stepansky, Grade 5
Hillside Elementary School, Montclair, NJ

Anne-Katherine Tallent, Grade 5
Providence Academy, Johnson City, TN

Claudia Zhang, Grade 6
Rolling Ridge Elementary School, Chino Hills, CA

All Top Ten Poems can be read at www.poeticpower.com

Note: The Top Ten poems were finalized through an online voting system. Creative Communication's judges first picked out the top poems. These poems were then posted online. The final step involved thousands of students and teachers who registered as the online judges and voted for the Top Ten poems. We hope you enjoy these selections.

To Mom

I miss a lot of things
But I mostly miss you
I miss your smile, your laugh
Everything about you
I know I need food and water
But I mostly need you
You know I want a lot of things
Like toys that do me no good
But I mostly want you
Though I don't remember
Every tiny detail
I remember my last words to you
"Good night Mom! I love you!"
I remember how you smiled at me
And closed your eyes to go to bed
And I can tell you this
I love a lot of things
Like gymnastics and my friends
But out of everyone and everything in this world
I love you the most

Angela Son, Grade 5
Little Falls School #1

In My Dreams

When I am in my dreams, I never know what will happen
There are twists and turns
I sometimes crash and burn
Only in my dreams
I could be super woman, a super villain or anything in between
I may go unseen
Or be loud, scream and shout
Or I could have a friend with a pig snout
Only in my dreams
I could be ruler of the made up world Pindia
Live anywhere in the world somewhere like Rome, Paris or India
Hey, I could even live underwater!
Or be a queen of an unknown land with three young daughters
I can laugh or cry
Or roll up in a ball and die
Bad things could be here
I would run and cry out "OH DEAR OH DEAR"
But then they would go away because remember, it is only a dream
Only in my dreams
I can do anything

Jordin DeSenzo, Grade 6
St Mary's School

Planet

If I were a planet,
I'd spin and twirl.
I'd get close to the sun,
and start sweating because of joy!
The best part of all…
The bright silver stars right next to my door!

Tiana Rahi, Grade 5
Bartle Elementary School

Life

What is life?
Life has many emotions
Love
Fear
Anger
Happiness
Things happen unexpectedly in this life of ours
Things that may bring up many emotions
Then you think to yourself…
Your life is so much more difficult than others
You may be wrong
Every day a life is taken away by the clutches of death
Or a life reborn by a loving and caring mother
But…the world is unfair and so is life
As absurd as this may sound,
This is a lesson I have learned.

Gabrielle Cruz, Grade 6
Garfield Middle School

The American Demolition

On September 11, 2001 the American demolition was done.
There were people on the run as the four planes spun
     When the American demolition was done.
The buildings fell as people would yell.
On that day you could tell no one was feeling quite well
     When the American demolition was done.
The heroes rushed while the city was hushed,
And those who had lost loved ones were crushed,
     When the American demolition was done.
The pilot of the plane was absolutely insane
Trying to wreck our honored name
     When the American demolition was done.
But the man up in the plane did not wreck anything but the plane
And so our honored name will remain and remember…
     When the American demolition was done.

Ryan DeSane, Grade 6
Township of Ocean Intermediate School

Mr. Fox

Mr. Fox Mr. Fox
He really is the boss
He has the power
He has the strength to save us all
He is smart and brave and really has a brain
to help us and protect us from people that we
don't trust
The three mean farmers will never catch that fox
for he could outsmart them for years and years
He has all his friends
He has his family
The farmers and the people will never catch his sight
They call him king
They call him the soldier
They call him the best and their hero Mr. Fox!

Lia Choi, Grade 4
Edward H Bryan Elementary School

Summer

I am a crazy girl who loves the sweet sensation of summer
I wonder why summer seems so short but still enjoyable
I hear still the light, fresh summer breeze dancing around me
I see the old dry heat waves from the summer passing by
I smell the sizzling grease from the grill with puffs of swirling gray smoke spinning up my nose like a slithery black snake
I am a crazy girl who loves the sweet sensation of summer
I want it to be summer again forever on
I pretend summer is a couple days away
I feel the soft sand rushing through the ocean in and out sliding in between my bar toes
I touch the silky ocean floor with my wet feet stirring up sand, POOF!
I worry summer won't come again and we'll be stuck in school for eternity
I cry that this is my last visit at the shore for this never ending year to come
I am a crazy girl who loves the sweet sensation of summer
I understand that we have to go to school day in and day out
I say that I don't want to go back to being trapped in the classroom, glued to my seat
I dream that one day the gorgeous ruby red, sparkling blue, and grape like purple flowers will grow forever
I try to make it through the long, new, tough school year
I hope summer comes quick like a shark at the swarming fish around him
I am a crazy girl who loves the sweet sensation of summer

Sami Oriente, Grade 6
Olson Middle School

Me, Myself, and I

I am a lacrosse player and try my very best
I wonder who will win the game
I hear the refs whistle for fouls the loud screechy noise
I see the goal post and the goalie as I get the ball to run to the net
I am a lacrosse player and try my very best

I pretend to be the best
I feel the wet grass coming through my cleats
I touch my cold water bottle when it flows down my throat as cold as a winter day in the snow
I worry what the score will be after the game
I cry when I get hurt when the ball hits me fast and strong in the face
I am a lacrosse player and try my very best

I understand it's not all about winning
I say it's ok when we lose the game
I dream of lacrosse every day
I try my best in the game like when I cradle down the field staring at the goalie
I do the best I can
I am a lacrosse player and try my very best

Tori Mattia, Grade 6
Olson Middle School

Fog Over My Eyes

Fog over your eyes prevents you to see.
Nothing but the seen or just plain awfully.
You must open them up to discover, what's always meant to be uncovered.
The wind and rustles will be profound, you'll shiver and shake when you hear the next sound.
This is a disease that will take advantage — of the one that only peers, not the one who has no fear.
Before it's too late lift open those eyes and say peek a boo! It's time to say good bye to you.

Nicole Lenino, Grade 6
Patrick M Villano Elementary School

Things in the Winter

Snow
Cold, ice, water, round
It always turns out on the ground.

Hot chocolate
Hot, liquid, torrid, brown
In the winter it cools me down.

Snowball fight
Fun, snowy, amusing, game
This thing is not very lame.

Vacation
Relax, enjoy, play, breaks
At that time don't have any dates.

Ice skating
Entertaining, glee, frolic, great
Sometimes they do figure eights.
David Cummings, Grade 5
Hillside Elementary School

My Father

My father is quite special
He does lots of things for me
He helps with my homework
He's like a worker bee

He always goes to work
He does not miss a day
Dad buys me food, toys, and clothes
With the money from his pay

He likes to watch TV
Especially *Star Trek*
When I watch it with him
He gives my cheek a peck

He sends me to school every day
He gives me a hug and a kiss
Believe it when I tell you
That opportunity he does not miss!
Morgan Lunsford, Grade 4
Marie Durand Elementary School

9/11

Crashing airplanes
Burning buildings
Running people
Rushing firemen
Bright lights of fire
Lost loved ones
A terrible time
9/11
Rebecca Ruben, Grade 6
Township of Ocean Intermediate School

School

Spelling, reading,
Library, lunch,
Art, gym, and it's time
for fun.

Math, pre voc,
science, and social studies.

What comes next?
It's time to get nutty!
OXE, social skills,
And in Music we lose it.

But there's one more thing
We love the most —
At dismissal
It's time to go!
Julian McCrea, Grade 6
Ocean Academy

A Snowy Day

Today is a snowy day
I can't wait to go out and play

The snow is falling softly and
the ground is really white

My friends are outside waiting
for me to go out sleighing

When I finally go outdoor
the weather is good to adore

My friends are calling, "Come on!"
I'm yelling, "Okay!"

I laugh out loud and sled down a hill
Oh what fun that is on a snowy day.
Minji Kim, Grade 4
Edward H Bryan Elementary School

K'Janei Bates

K now it all
J unior of girl scouts
A thletic
N ormal
E xcellent
I mpatient

B owler
A ctive
T all
E xcited
S mart
K'Janei Bates, Grade 5
Mckinley Community School

Fireflies

A flash here, a flash there
Fireflies are out tonight
I dash outside with jar in hand
And catch them one,
By one,
My jar grows bright
As lights dance before my eyes.
A flash here, a flash there
Fireflies were out tonight.
Madison Kartoz, Grade 4
Village School

What Has Happened?

What has happened in this world?
So corrupt and full of war.
What has happened in this world?
So many people without jobs.
What has happened in this world?
So full of hate and evil.
What has happened in this world?
So many crooks and drugs.
What has happened?
Abe Plaut, Grade 5
Hillside Elementary School

Broken Hearts

Broken hearts are like
Melancholy tunes

They crack like dynamite,
But are as delicate as rose petals
drifting in the breeze.

Broken hearts make me feel like
Teardrops on a pillow
Maya Boateng, Grade 4
Village School

Flounder

Tastes like chicken.
Sounds like "Puck-Puck-Puck."
Smells like smelly sharks.
Looks like a colorful butterfly.
Feels like a soft skinned baby.
Fahid Shah, Grade 4
Chelsea Heights School

Soccer

Racing through the wind
Chasing the ball down the field
Want to get a goal
I now have the ball
Dodging the other players
I just got the goal
Emma Enright, Grade 5
Catherine A Dwyer Elementary School

Oh, Crocodile

Oh, crocodile, it's been a while.
Ever since I've seen that smile, oh, crocodile.

Oh kitty, it's such a pity.
I haven't noticed you've become so pretty, oh, kitty.

Oh, bat, you're such a brat.
Chasing that ol' helpless gnat, oh, bat.

Oh, pig, you're so big.
Eating all of the tasty figs, oh, pig.

Oh, bunny, you're so funny.
With your sticky paws full with honey, oh, bunny.

Oh, crocodile, it's been awhile.
Ever since I've seen that smile, oh, crocodile.

Jack Motherway, Grade 4
Hillside Elementary School

Christmas Time

In the season of Christmas
Many things go on
The bells on Christmas trees jingle
And make a lovely sound
Swish
The winds are very strong tonight
I look out the window
Snow is falling gently on the ground
I think when Santa will come tonight
He'll come from the chimney
BOOM!
Will be the sound it'll make
Tomorrow I'll run down the steps in a hurry
Creak, creak
And find a stack of presents
Mom says, "Shush let's go to sleep.
Tomorrow you'll find a bunch of presents beneath the tree."

Pooja Patel, Grade 5
Frances DeMasi Elementary School

Where I Live

I live near the woods,
They creep me out,
Especially when it is dark,
Once I saw a fox,
It gave me the chills,
But I have to say,
It is the best to live near
the woods,
Because when it snows
I love going sledding
down the hill.
I love where I live.

Anne Del Colombo, Grade 4
Good Shepherd Regional Catholic School

Autumn, Autumn

Cold yet gentle breezes
Blow as the wind
Comes to knock off
The pigmented leaves,
From their pitiful hemlock tree.
Autumn, autumn, what a rainbow of colors!

As dusk comes forward,
The bright burning sun
Is setting in the distance,
Going down as fast as a rock drowning in a pond.
Autumn, autumn, what a rainbow of colors!

The festivity of autumn
Is in the brisk air.
Exotic smells floating around
On the huge sale tables.
What a wonderful feeling autumn is!
Autumn, autumn, what a rainbow of colors!

Sharing with my closest family and friends,
Is how autumn makes me feel!

Marianna Poccia, Grade 5
St Rose of Lima Academy

The Bad Part of Thanksgiving

T he bad part of Thanksgiving is
H aving stomach aches.
A t Thanksgiving dinner you eat too much and
N ow you look like a ball.
K ind people keep serving you more.
" **S** o much food," you say. What will you do?
G etting up and leaving would be
I nappropriate. You don't want to
V omit. You think it was so good, but
I t's coming back up right now!
N ext, is dessert, but you don't want to eat,
G uess that is what good food does to you, and you're beat.

Chase Hartnett, Grade 6
Riverside Middle School

How to Make a Bum of a Brother

Take an older brother, some video games, and some showoff-ness.
Put in some screaming girls.
You need to combine in some laziness, and
Blend until you feel kicking.
Don't forget to add a frog for the ugliness.
Fry the head until the cell phone rings.
Set the temperature to 100,000 degrees.
Then stop when his arm grabs you and says "Stop hitting yourself."
Then chop it off and put it in again.
You can tell it's done because you hear pig squealing sounds.
Let it watch TV until it cools.
That's how you make a bum of a brother, but a happy one.

Clarissa Miranda-Simmons, Grade 5
Roosevelt Elementary School

Life of Nature

Part I: The Sky

The day sky, a brilliant blue
A cloud passing by birds sing cuckoo

The night sky, deep and dark
Sparkling stars are the voices of heaven

The sunrise sky, lit by the sun
Our giant candle spreading warmth throughout the land

The sunset sky, beautiful, bright
All the colors, pink, orange, red, blue
The leaves of heaven fall, covering the skies
In a blanket of colors

The stormy sky, gray and gloomy
The bright lightning claps the loud thunder
God's anger flares the angels cry
Their tears fall to Earth

Then it's over and a rainbow forms.

Ethan Bull, Grade 5
Bartle Elementary School

The Storm

Darkness fills the sky and flowers start to die,
Alone I hear the town's cry.
I go to the window to admire the beauty of this storm,
Raindrops glide down the window pane.
The thunder roars as I head out the front door.
With the whole town inside, I stand alone in the storm,
With no one by my side.
The whole town's waiting for tomorrow.
The storm is dreadful to the town,
But the raindrops kiss my face,
And fill cobwebs with an elegant lace.
It is only me who notices this beauty.
The thunder roars its last roar,
And the lightning strikes its last shot of light.
Now the sun shines brightly through the breaking clouds,
And birds start to sing and fly through the clear blue sky.
A gentle wind whispers to me, and I see the trees wave happily.
I hear the town's people give a cheer for the storm is no longer here,
A smile rests upon my face
Because the town has learned from their mistakes.
The storm was not dreadful, it was only nature.

Erin Sawadzki, Grade 6
Hartford School

Flying

Flying gives the delight of swooping, gliding, and soaring
to feathered birds and leathery bats
when they slice the air with their magnificent wings.

Sam Murphy, Grade 5
Bartle Elementary School

Thanksgiving Fun

T urkey is good at Thanksgiving.
H arvest moons are beautiful.
A pple pie and whipped cream is on my plate.
N ative Americans taught Pilgrims how to survive.
K asey is 500 pounds overweight after Thanksgiving!
" **S** tart eating your turkey," said Mom.
" **G** reat turkey Dad," I said.
" **I** 'm as fat as a bat!"
V isit my siblings at night.
I hate squash!
N ot many people hate turkey.
G et more turkey, now!

Kasey Getz, Grade 6
Riverside Middle School

Turkey Night

T urkey is good to eat.
H arvest moons are bright at night.
A pple pies with whipped cream are on my plate.
N ative Americans and Pilgrims created Thanksgiving.
K nives are used to cut the turkey and ham.
S aying prayers before eating.
G iving thanks for good gooey giblets and everything we have.
I n the kitchen my dad is cooking.
V anilla ice cream on top of a pie, with a cherry on the very top.
I n the dining room we are eating.
N ever be disgusted while saying our prayers.
" **G** et ready for bed," Dad said.

Evan Howe, Grade 6
Riverside Middle School

Thanksgiving Is a Great Holiday

T hanksgiving is for the thankful, with
H aving a feast with family and friends.
A lso, enjoying turkey throughout the day, and
N ever forgetting a moment to pray.
K icking your feet up under your chair, while
S taring at the table of foods to share.
G iving thanks to the willing preparers, for
I f you're there, and pray, you'll always have a say.
V ery eager am I to eat all leftovers and treats. For
" **I** n our house the feast has begun!" Joe said.
N ever to take this day for granted, for
G iving thanks is all it takes.

Marquis Thomas, Grade 6
Riverside Middle School

Flowers

Flowers are one of God's many beautiful creations.
They color the Earth with their wonderful colors.
We become happy and relaxed when we see them,
They have a smell that is indescribable,
Their petals are as soft as a blanket.
Flowers bring our world brightness and joy.

Christina Puntiel, Grade 6
Perth Amboy Catholic Upper Grades School

Leaves
Zipping up my jacket to go outside
Thinking of the season and what I might find.
I finished putting on my gloves
I ventured on the trail looking above.

The leaves are crunchy as I stepped
The trees are swaying and they crept.
A leaf is flying, swooping through the air.
Then it gets tangled in my long, dark hair.

They are all brown except one up so high
That one is red and dancing like a butterfly.

I love walking all around
Thinking of the season, and what I have found.

Holly Huff, Grade 5
Central School

September 11, 2001
September 11th was a day to remember
The Twin Towers held many
With the sun shining
They stood tall and made us so proud

On that day some enemies
Our planes they used to destroy us
And blew the towers away
Our world changed forever in that moment

We learned many names after the flames
And our hearts will always be saddened
In tragedy our country united
And promised to be strong, and unified against
Terror!

Kristian Morales, Grade 4
Marie Durand Elementary School

Christmas
The day that I've been waiting for all year is coming!
All of the fancy presents that I get.
Christmas is coming!
Christmas is coming!
It's the best day of the year!
The next day when I wake up
I sit on the steps
Until my dad tells me I can come down.
I race down the stairs.
I ask if I can open my presents and I can!
I rip the wrapping paper open.
I never know what I am going to open!
If you look at your presents sooner
Then there will be no surprise!

Andrew Phillips, Grade 5
Zane North Elementary School

Heather
H appy describes my mom no longer with me.
E xciting was the way she lived.
A merican Mom was her title.
T eacher by profession.
H elpful to me in every way.
E ager to provide assistance.
R egretfully she passed away one day in May when I was only six.

Halle Brown, Grade 5
Hillside Elementary School

Yo-yos Are Amazing
Yo-yos are awesome,
Yo-yos are cool,
Yo-yos are the coolest thing in school.

Yo-yos are fun,
They're great too,
They're very useful when you have nothing to do.

Garrett Pahl, Grade 5
Hillside Elementary School

My Puppy's Wonderland
My puppy frolics in the snow
Wandering freely, wherever he pleases
Icy crystals pelt down on his head, but this does not stop him
He loves to explore the snowy Wonderland
Barking at the squirrels, chasing them up trees
The only way you can tell he was there
Is by a trail of paw prints left behind in the snow

Grace Carolonza, Grade 4
St James School

Dolphins
A beautiful light blue color,
The sound "Eeh-Eeh" just makes me wonder.
One bit of it might taste like salt water taffy,
The smell of it makes me happy.
It looks like a big piece of the sky,
Sometimes dolphins make me shy.
…DOLPHINS

Myah Jabbar, Grade 4
Uptown School Complex

Candy Corn
Candy corn, candy corn, orange, yellow, and white.
If you eat too much you will stay up all night.
Candy corn, candy corn, lying on the post.
If you leave them out too long you will find a ghost.

Candy corn, candy corn, everywhere and in between.
When you see that candy corn, then it's HALLOWEEN.

Betsy Ferra, Grade 4
St Joseph's Regional School

My Mighty Companion

Oh, the moon shines so brightly in the dark cloudless night sky,
giving back the light that it borrowed from his day time companion.

Oh, the moon, your mysteries make us all think and wonder
from such a distance rocking our mighty oceans.

Oh, the moon will always shine cheerfully for me
at the darkest hour when I'll need a guiding light
Oh, the moon

Yuval Thuroff, Grade 6
Christa McAuliffe Middle School

Fantastic Lime

On the outside you look like my step-dad's green eyes.
You feel like slimy silly putty.
When I peel you, you sound like an egg is being cracked.
When I slice you, you sound like a rubber glove.
Inside you look like green parts of the earth on the globe.
You feel like something rubber.
You smell like a ripe lemon.
You taste like the green sour patch kids.
Tell me, do you ever want to just be sweet, not sour?

Katelynn Perez, Grade 5
Roosevelt Elementary School

Winter Won't Wait

Winter is a beautiful thing
Filled with snow and tunes to sing
Christmas is coming, you know it won't wait
So put up your tree and don't be late!

On Christmas Eve, you'll go to bed
With thoughts of presents in your head
When you wake, presents are spread
So, go get your parents out of bed!

Jessica Aumick, Grade 5
Durban Avenue Elementary School

Christmas Thoughts

Christmas comes just once a year,
Bringing with it loads of cheer.
Food, toys, games and fun.
There's a present for everyone!

We think about the little Christ child,
With His face so kind and mild.
He came to Earth to save us all,
The strong, the weak, the great, the small.

Robert Sears III, Grade 6
Perth Amboy Catholic Upper Grades School

Moon's Night Sky

As I strolled outside I witness planes flying by
crickets chirping in the bushes
as I glanced up I saw the moon shining on me
the smoky odor of the chimney drifted into my head
crunch, crunch went the leaves under my feet
wind swirling around blowing leaves off the trees
witches wildly whipping around the moon
wolves howling at the glorious glow of its shine
stars as bright as the sun rising on a summer day

Brandon Pallonte, Grade 6
Christa McAuliffe Middle School

Football

Football, football it's all you hear
All the fans cheering and making it clear
All thirty-two teams competing for gold
Buy your tickets or they will be sold

Football, football the best time of the year
Everyone knows when the Super Bowl's here
Now it is over for next year again
I wish football would never ever end

Kenny Vesey, Grade 6
St Mary's School

Baseball, Oh Baseball!

Baseball, oh baseball, how's the season so far?
Can't those batters hit the ball hard?
It might even fly to the stars!
Those pitchers can throw the ball so fast.
They strike out every batter, first to last.
Jeter can hit oh so fine.
Whenever he hits the ball, it goes straight down the line.
Baseball, oh baseball, it's so fun;
To watch and to play for everyone!

Drew McDonald, Grade 5
St Mary's School

Hope

Hope is what brings the leaves to trees,
and the stings to bees
Hope brings the stars to the sky,
and the buzz to a fly!
It is full of smiles and imagination,
for it can even bring you on a good vacation!
It's features are like magic that fly like a dove,
because hope is full of love!

Rakhi Kundra, Grade 5
Hillside Elementary School

Winter

Calming sounds of the wind,
Snowflakes drifting slowly down,
Glistening white snow.

Olivia Chen, Grade 5
Bartle Elementary School

The Beautiful Moon's Shine

The moon so dazzling,
It's glow so radiant,
That no star compares

Even a glimpse upon its brilliant shine,
And your jaw will drop in awe.
The bats rejoice at its shine
And praise it by dancing in the night sky

Every night I ponder and ponder,
Oh! The moon is such a glorious wonder
Though some nights it may rain and pour,
The moon is something I will always adore.
Marianna Palumbo, Grade 6
Christa McAuliffe Middle School

Impatience

Impatience is
A storm cloud
Suspended over my head.
Like a barbell
About to plummet.
The longer it hangs
The more infuriated
I get.
Suddenly, CRASH!
The barbell drops.
My patience explodes.
It makes me want to
SCREAM!
Joe Durie, Grade 4
Village School

Buddy

I have a new dog
His name is Buddy.
He loves to play outside,
Sometimes he gets muddy.
He loves to play and run
He just doesn't like to be shunned.
He eats his food and loves his treats
But he also loves to lick our feet!
He's six months old and is small
But he can still fetch a ball.
He's a new member to our family
We all love him and
HE LOVES ME!
Sean McGourty, Grade 6
St Anthony of Padua School

New Jersey

The rivers are cool
The Kittatinny Mountains
There are wet beaches
Peter Gurecki, Grade 4
St Peter Elementary School

Half a Moon

As I gaze upon the sky
I see the greatest moon of all
A shiny, silver half a moon
Much more than just a crescent
Much less than a full moon
There it sits like half a pie
above the tall pine trees
Surrounded by faraway stars
Beside the bushy gray clouds
When people think of the moon
they think of perfect crescents
or completed circles
But I think the best moon of all
is just half a moon
Nicholas Iorio, Grade 6
Christa McAuliffe Middle School

Questions

How do birds fly through the sky?
Or why do people eat pot pie?
Does the president ever lie?
Oh, so many questions.

Why are rabbits very quiet?
How come Nancy's on a diet?
When do teachers make a riot?
Oh, so many questions.

Why are boxes always square?
When do nurses truly care?
How come horses are called mares?
Who will answer all my questions?
Caroline Creaser, Grade 5
Hillside Elementary School

My Parents

The stars are bright
Just like you
Having a mother
Is awesome too
Your eyes sparkle
Like the moon
Either way
You're great too
Now it's time
To talk about
My father
To let you know
He is the human man
The superhero of my life
Fabiana Caballero, Grade 6
Garfield Middle School

Next Grade...

Third grade
Has come to
An end.

Going to fourth grade
It's going to start,
Begin again!

Next thing you know
Middle school,
Halfway there.

Changes, changes
I'm going to enjoy,
Or am I?
Marissa Cole, Grade 4
Greenwood Elementary School

Wise Owl

The wise owl
sleeps through the day
and seeks at night for prey,

Animals come to him,
desperate and sad,
full of questions,
seeking advice or truth,
about their small lives.

He answers,
noble and wise,
one at a time,
Finished with the questions,
goes silently to sleep.
Sophia Hernandez, Grade 5
Richard E Byrd Elementary School

I Don't Understand

I don't understand…
    School
    Latin
    French

But most of all…
    Why there was the Holocaust
    War
    The reason for 9/11
    Violence

What I understand most…
    Math
    The twinkling stars
    The bright moon
April Lange, Grade 6
Lounsberry Hollow Middle School

Autumn Wonderland
Autumn is like a cool breeze
That blows through your hair.

The leaves of red, orange, yellow,
And brown fly
From one place to another.

The squirrels scamper about
To get ready for hibernation
Gathering nuts for the winter.

What an autumn wonderland!
Yooha Kim, Grade 5
Bartle Elementary School

Thanksgiving Day
T hanksgiving is wonderful.
H am is good to eat.
A ngela said, "I love pumpkin pie!"
N aps are good for after eating.
K ids love their families.
S tuffing goes in the turkey.
G iving hugs to friends.
I ce cream is as cold as Alaska.
V illagers eat food on this holiday.
I have good friends.
N ever forget your family!
G ive thanks.
Angela Azevedo, Grade 6
Riverside Middle School

Thanksgiving
T urkeys are good to eat.
H am is really salty.
A pples are really sweet.
N uts fall from the trees.
K nives are used to cut turkey.
S moked duck is good to eat.
G iving thanks to friends and family.
I 'm booing the Cowboys. Miss
V illeco, my teacher, likes turkey.
I also like turkey.
" **N** o one likes fish," said Dad.
G rapes are my favorite fruit.
Robert Alfred, Grade 6
Riverside Middle School

Passionate Love
Shall I decline the nature's balance
Of spring's
Delight and beauty?
I dare to say that all I see is
Art made by
Thee love and passion.
Viktoriya Abakumova, Grade 6
Memorial Middle School

Tatiyana
T errific
A mazing drummer
T alented
I ntelligent
Y oung
A thletic
N eat
A wesome gymnast

D rummer
A dmirable
N oble
I maginative
E nergetic
L ovely
Tatiyana Daniel, Grade 5
Hillside Elementary School

I Don't Understand
I don't understand
Why teachers give homework
Why fatty food tastes so good
Why people hunt for sport

But most of all
Why people are rude and nasty
Why people lie
Why people steal
Why people kill

What I do understand is
Why the sun rises
Why it rains
Why the leaves fall
Staci Trezza, Grade 6
Lounsberry Hollow Middle School

Teacher's Brain
Go inside a teacher's brain
See its glory and its thoughts.
Perhaps you'll find a dictionary.
Maybe a train of words.

Perhaps you'll see a brainstorm
Zooming right above her head.
Perhaps you may find something odd
like a goofy side
or a worn out joke book.

So now you have an idea
About a teacher's brain
Maybe next time you'll take a look
only if you dare!
Allie Strouse, Grade 4
Village School

My Grandma
My grandma is very kind.
She walks me to my bus stop each day.
She greets me when I walk in
She is nice in every way.

My grandma tries to buy me what she can.
She cares for me when I am sad.
A day with her is always fun
When I'm with her I'm never mad.

My grandma exercises each day.
She watches what she eats,
But when she gets a break,
She'll sometimes sneak some sweets.

My grandma works as a nurse's aide
She really loves her job.
But when she tells me stories,
They make me want to sob.

My grandma really loves me
I love her just the same.
So when I hug her in public,
I don't feel any shame.
Kiana Oliveras, Grade 4
Marie Durand Elementary School

The Big Game
I step onto the field
Everyone's shouting my name
Their team is undefeated
Get your head in the game

We run to our places
The whistle blows
We begin the chase
Our excitement grows

I kick the ball
I score a goal
The crowd goes wild
Feels like I'm at the Super Bowl

The score is 2-0
My team might actually win
We've worked really hard all season
I cannot help but grin

The whistle blows
Our team has won
Can't wait to play again
Playing soccer is so much fun
Ysabel Tullis, Grade 4
Little Falls School #3

Daddy

The best man in the world is my dad
He always makes me happy not sad
He works hard, gets home late
That's okay 'cause he is great
That wonderful man I call my dad

Ava DelForno, Grade 4
St Mary's School

Pigs

Friendly pigs
rolling in the mud
from day to day
on a farm
cooling off in the hot sun

Madelyn Gonzalez, Grade 5
Bartle Elementary School

Cows

Bad cows
mooing loudly
at bad times
on a farm in New Jersey
because they are hungry

James Kjer, Grade 5
Bartle Elementary School

Can I Fly?

There once was a guy I don't know why
But he said I could fly
I said, "No!"
He said, "To you I'll show"
And from then on I could fly

Anna Gottesman, Grade 5
Hillside Elementary School

My Naughty Hamster

I own a hamster who bites.
I took her to see some sites.
She escaped from me,
Then bit a flee.
She got in so many fights.

Claudia Stagoff-Belfort, Grade 5
Hillside Elementary School

The Girl Who Loves to Write

The smart girl who wants to fashion write
Her ideas and thoughts are really bright
She writes every day
She eats off of a tray
She barely sleeps during the dark night

Antonia Bellavia, Grade 4
St Mary's School

Red, White, and Blue

What is red? A rose is red for a love unsaid.
What else is red? An apple is red nestled in its tree bed.
What is white? The moon is white during the dark night.
What else is white? A cloud is white all puffy and light.
What is blue? The sky is blue where eagles soar far from view.
What else is blue? The ocean's blue where dolphins play each day anew.
These colors together mean so much to so many,
Red, white, and blue together stands for the land of plenty.

Melissa Fletcher, Grade 6
St Anthony of Padua School

Threatening Tiger Tickle Tummy

This is a Threatening Tiger Tickle Tummy.
It lives in Tiberia, Tasmania, Tennessee, and Texas.
A Threatening Tiger Tickle Tummy
eats tangerines, turnips, tomatoes, and teddy bears.
It likes tanning, teaching, talking, and tickling.
It threatens to tickle tiny tigers and terrorize teddy bears.
The Threatening Tiger Tickle Tummy told me that if I took his tomato
he would tickle me until I was too tired to talk.

Jonah Barnett, Grade 6
Kellman Brown Academy

My Brothers

I have two brothers named Jake and Nick.
They can get so annoying.
They will mess up when I do projects
Or bother me when I'm doing homework.
They will be rough and wrestle
Even when I tell them to stop!
They will make my room
A disaster area
And try to take my possessions.
We will get in fights
But that's what we do.
I have told you all bad things
But they are not all bad.
They cheer me on
They make me glad.
They make me laugh (sometimes.)
They are the best
And they're not bad.
And I'll love them always
No matter what!

Lauren Patetta, Grade 5
St James School

The Terrible Terrorists

The terrible terrorists
Tried their hardest,
But they didn't defeat us.

The terrible terrorists
Knocked down our towers,
But they didn't defeat us.

The terrible terrorists
Killed our people,
But they didn't defeat us.

The terrible terrorists
Came on planes,
But they didn't defeat us.

The terrible terrorists
Didn't come again
Because they knew,
They didn't defeat us.

Alison Chomsky, Grade 6
Township of Ocean Intermediate School

Touchdown!

I'm sprinting away from the defense.
Running with the offense.
Ready for the kick off attempt.
It came straight to me and I ran
and ran and ran.
Soon I was at the end zone and touchdown!

Lawrence DiCoio, Grade 4
Lincoln Park Elementary School

Dogs

Dogs are so much fun
They really like to run
All they want to do
Is play with friends, old and new
With a ball, they like to play
All the night and all the day

Dylan Lattuga, Grade 5
St Mary's Prep School

Leaves

Green, red, yellow, and brown,
They are all over the ground.

Leaves let out a crunch.
They come in a bunch.

As you jump in leaves,
There is a cold breeze.

You have a blast,
Fall comes and goes fast.

Green, red, yellow, and brown.
They are all over the ground.
Julia Owens, Grade 5
Durban Avenue Elementary School

The Moon

Oh the moon
It sits
All
Alone,
Only stars to
Keep it company.
As it watches
Through the
Night,
Across the
Country, I wouldn't
Be surprised
If
It saw me.
Chris Raimondi, Grade 6
Christa McAuliffe Middle School

I Love to See the Moon

The moon is one thing I love to see.
Shining and staring back at me.

Bright between dark grey clouds.
Shining down to illuminate the ground.

I see the moon as a balloon in the sky.
Reflecting light and rising high.

The moon sits on a great chair of clouds.
Just sitting there staring down.

Rising above the tall grey trees.
The moon is one thing I love to see
Jason Wojcik, Grade 6
Christa McAuliffe Middle School

The Pink Ribbon

Pink is the color for us,
And no one makes a fuss.

It is scary to face,
So people go at their own pace.

People try to fix the cause,
There is no time to pause.

My mom has the pink cancer,
How could she be fancier?

She is not only a fighter,
She is almost a survivor.
Samantha Cytron, Grade 5
Hillside Elementary School

Best Friend

I had a best friend,
Her name was Red.

I saw her every day,
'Till she melted away.

Then she grew in my room,
Into a pretty red bloom.

I talked to her every day,
'Till she faded away.

But I could not bear to let her go,
So I drew her again into my heart.
Chista Behbin-Guirand, Grade 5
Hillside Elementary School

Allergies

Blow your nose, cup your hand,
this unpleasantness is not grand.
I lay in bed, red forehead,
I'd rather suck on pencil lead.
As I huff a powerful sneeze,
eyes tearing, I want to wheeze.
I pull my covers up high
and yelp a powerful cry.
I say "Tissue please!"
Uh oh, here comes another sneeze!
My body is sore,
I could take it no more!
Well, allergies come for a reason,
it's the time of the season!
Isabella Zorich, Grade 5
Hillside Elementary School

Halloween

Halloween is sweet and scary
People give out lots of candy
Mummies roam,
Witches fly,
All throughout the midnight sky
Black cats out and all about
Hear the kids all scream and shout
Kids dress up,
Pumpkins lit,
Baseball players use your mitt
Dorothy and little Toto
Let's all take a Halloween photo!
Shannon Revelant, Grade 6
St Mary's School

Yearly Beauty

As the day drags on
I wait for the end
The new month
Morning feels like years
Afternoon makes me sleep
Night finally comes
I wait for this yearly beauty
To strike the sky
Its orange look
Is much better than the sun
Here it is
An Eclipse
Raven Wesner, Grade 6
Robert Morris Public School

Francisco Vazquez de Coronado

I was born in 1510, in Spain.
In 1554, I went to seek my fortune.
I found a horse,
and tried to ride.
It got mad
and kicked with a good flick.
I fell off,
and it kicked again.
It kicked me right
in the head.
A few minutes later
I was pronounced dead!
Ashley Marie Miscia, Grade 5
Roosevelt Elementary School

The Moon

The moon was like
A bowl of soup,
A few nights ago,
and now it looks
like a slither of
white melted snow.
Cameron Goodwin, Grade 6
Christa McAuliffe Middle School

Life

Life
There's one path that leads to
A dark black hole
Unwelcoming and frightening
Sucking you into its ways
Imprisoning you like a slave
Rainy days that endlessly pours down on you
Biting down on your bare skin
Days without the warm sun
Nights without the guiding stars

Life
There's another path that leads to
Where the greenest grass grows
Where the most astonishingly beautiful flowers prosper
And birds sing with felicity
Grins, laughter, and gratification
Spread across the world

Life
There are two paths
What will you choose?

Kristine Reithmeier, Grade 6
Hartford School

Thanksgiving

T hanksgiving is a happy time of year.
H appy children play outside.
A ll of our family gathers at our house.
N ew gifts are exchanged each year.
K ids are happy to see their cousins after a long year.
S ticks are seen everywhere I go.
G ames are played all day.
I love to see my cousins.
V icious stomachs growl like a dog as the feast begins.
I nside, all the food is gone as the football game begins.
" **N** otre Dame is my favorite team," Kush said.
G ifts are exchanged with happiness at the end.

Kush Patel, Grade 6
Riverside Middle School

A Christmas Joy

A joyful Christmas
We have together
We cheer when we see
That there are toys under the tree
Happiness and cheerfulness fill the room
Beliefs that Santa was there that night with delight
The boys have toys and the girls have pearls.
Together they share their joys.
The boys play with their toys with tons of joys.
The girls wear pearls with tons of twirls
In their curly hair
This Christmas

Shae-Lynn Jarozynski, Grade 5
Zane North Elementary School

Lime

You look like a sour patch pack on a hot day.
You feel like a rubber glove when I feel you.
You sound like a rubber band when I peel you.
When I slice you, it sounds like a guitar.
Inside you look like a soft caterpillar.
You feel like a soft pair of socks.
You smell like the lime soap called Ajax.
You taste like a sour lollipop.
Don't you ever get tired of getting eaten?

Nicole Silvey, Grade 5
Roosevelt Elementary School

Christmas

C ome all gather around
H aving fun at all times
R ight outside I can hear Saint Nick
I n a winter wonderland
S anta will be proud 'cause I've been so good
T oday shall never end
M erry Christmas to one and all
A mazing things happen on this special day
S adly this day has to end

Amy Linser, Grade 4
Springfield Township School

Christmas Tree

I look at your light
With lots of delight
No it does not give me a fright
I would like a bite
Of the little gingerbread men sitting on the tree
All of them with a smile on their face filled with glee
I've always wished to be the bright, yellow star on the Christmas tree
O, Christmas tree I love your gleaming yellow light
It makes me filled with joyous tears on Christmas night

Tim Rittinger, Grade 5
Hawthorne Christian Academy

Beach

The boiling sun covers the beach with light
The waves splash down like bombs
The soft sand sizzles as the cool wind blows
The horizon of the water and the sky combine
together and make a warm feeling
You stare at the beautiful ocean and it clears your mind
What a beautiful sight have you found?

Darko Budinoski, Grade 6
Garfield Middle School

A Bear's Goodnight

The tired bear gathers food for the starting winter.
Going through a forest of white.
Gliding through the snow, like a bird through the sky.
Going to its den to say goodnight.

Tate Mikula, Grade 5
St Rose of Lima Academy

Dixon

Dixon the prettiest reindeer,
She lived in stable number 111.
She fancied her number 111.
Her eyes were as bright as light.

She lived in stable number 111.
Dasher had a fancy for Dixon.
Dixon's eyes were as bright as light.
Dasher thought 111 was for the best.

Dasher had a fancy for Dixon
He loved her freshly washed coat.
Dasher thought 111 was for the best.
Dixon was the head of the training school for flying.

He loved her freshly washed coat.
When Dixon was flying, she crashed.
Dixon was head of the training school for flying.
Luckily she crashed…right into Dasher.

When Dixon was flying she crashed.
She fancied number 111.
Luckily Dixon crashed…right into Dasher.
Dixon was the prettiest reindeer.

Hilja Stamper, Grade 4
Zane North Elementary School

My Autumn Feeling

As the last school bell rings
I am walking to the field,
I place my backpack down,
And lay on the dark green grass.

I see the beautiful changing leaves
Some sunset colors, apple red and banana yellows,
I get my bag and open up my peanut sack,
A squirrel comes by to steal my snack,

I laugh and stare at the baby blue sky,
I feel the breeze whisk across my face,
My mind is empty, for nothing is there,
I hear the sound of geese, flying so high.

I think of how they migrate
To a nice warm place,
Where the cold is no match for the heat.

I sit up to see a small house,
The children are getting ready in their costumes,
I smile, thinking of Halloween,
My mind is now excited,
With thoughts of my autumn feeling.

Nicole Davino, Grade 5
St Rose of Lima Academy

Amidst the Storm

As I stepped on the cool, wet sand
I felt a strange chill in my hands
The sound I heard could be detected from faraway lands
it sounded like the clashing of a dozen bands

The wind, oh how it blew so loud!
It could blow away all the clouds!
I lifted my hands up to my face
As the wind howled in a steady pace

The sound was like the sky cracking in half
The heavens giving a merciless laugh
And as I heard the rain starting to pour
I started to sprint away from the shore

A deafening "Boom!" came from the sky
The light — its laws it seemed to defy
Rain droplets started to pitter patter down
In harmony with the wind's pound

I finally reached the cover of shelter
Away from the water's pelter
I looked outside and this is what I could see:
The furious thunderstorm's beauty

Sharon Lin, Grade 5
Indian Hill School

The Lonely Book

I'm sitting here all alone
On this bookshelf, as still as stone
No one ever comes near me
I'm as lonely as can be

I'm the only book in this row
The last time I've been read was quite a while ago
I never understand why I am here
Nothing ever seems to be clear

Finally someone comes close to me
I think this is my chance to really be free
They pick me up and look me through
Then my wish finally comes true

He brings me over to his home
It really feels like I'm in Rome
I finally got a few breaths of clean air
Then he reads me through in his chair

He read me and enjoyed my story
By then I felt so much glory
By the look on his face I felt so much delight
I knew this place would be just right

Sagar Shah, Grade 6
Little Falls School #1

Full Moon

Full moon
How much I love you.
You're the brightest thing,
In the night sky.

You make me cherish you,
So I will never ignore you.
Please moon,
Never stop smiling at me.

I wish I can tell you,
How much
Everyone and *everything*
Loves you!
But since you're so famous,
You already know.
Konrad Kropiewnicki, Grade 6
Christa McAuliffe Middle School

The Disappearing Act

I am bright
Lighting up our world
Slowly slipping away at dusk
And then my friend, the moon, comes along
Keeping watch of the night
When the moon gets tired, his shift is done
It is my turn once again
To light up our day
Keeping watch of our world
12:00 is my highest point
But slowly the moon reappears
He is the guardian of our night
Hanging high up in the sky
He is slowly disappearing
It is my turn to rise
I am the sun
Yelena Stuherck, Grade 5
Little Falls School #1

Down the Chimney

Christmas comes once a year,
Trees are out, very bright,
Santa's sled led by reindeer,
In the windows, candlelight.

Santa squeezes down the chimney,
Kids in their rooms fast asleep,
Presents are set under the tree,
Alarm clocks ready to beep.

Children jump out of beds,
Unwrapping presents morning to night,
Lights hung above their heads,
Christmas is really a sight.
Abby Henderson, Grade 5
Durban Avenue Elementary School

Father Jacques Marquette

Father Jacques Marquette
Did not want to get wet
So he sailed in a boat
And it started to float
Down the mighty Mississippi River.

He sailed with Joliet
For many a day
On the Arkansas River
With his arrows and quiver
Which made the French happy.
Amaya Tillman, Grade 5
Roosevelt Elementary School

My Cousin

My cousin is the best
We never ever rest
We are always on the net
We cannot even budge
By the time we come out
We feel like eating fudge
My cousin's name is Sid
He thinks like Billy the Kid
He always likes "the spice"
But forever I will think
I will think he's always nice
Ishan Bhalgat, Grade 5
Frances DeMasi Elementary School

The Clouds and the Moon

The clouds are like
huge black waves
that are drowning the moon
out of the sky.
Without the moon
the sky is black.
It seems
the moon forgot to wake up
and slept in instead.
I think the stars
decided to stay home too.
Joseph LaBianca, Grade 6
Christa McAuliffe Middle School

My Bird, Fluffy

Under the sheet
Without any warning
Despite its chirp
Upon a perch
Within the cage
With a door
Down in the dark
During our visit
Accepting our gift
Jeremiah Sanchez, Grade 5
Hawthorne Christian Academy

Summer

You can play outside
You can run in the sun
You can stroll on the beach
And have lots of fun!

You can play in the water
You can jump on the land
You can use lots of buckets
And make a castle of sand.

You can do lots of sports
With an inflated beach ball
You can do all of this
Instead of going to the mall.
Marian Gallo, Grade 6
St James School

Summer

Summer is fun
It is fun for everyone
You can splash in the pool
While everyone is keeping cool

You can run in the park
Until it gets chilly and dark
All around you the birds fly
While they chirp in the deep blue sky

I hope the fun never ends
So I can play with all my friends
Everything is so much fun
Playing in the big yellow sun
Jonah Rausch, Grade 4
St James School

My Xbox 360

This is my Xbox 360
Sleek, shiny, and black,
Hours of fun
When playing I also attack.

This is my Xbox 360
In my bedroom I play,
Call of Duty and *Battlefield 2*
I could stay all day.

This is my Xbox 360
My stepdad gets beat,
When challenged at boxing and racing
He hates to admit defeat.
Jordan Field, Grade 5
Bartle Elementary School

Autumn Colors

Autumn has colors here and there,
and leaves are plummeting through the air.
The happy family is so strong,
as they're raking, raking all day long,
till their backs and bones ache from head to toe.
Big piles scattered to and fro.
The wind picks up and blows everything around,
leaves flying everywhere on the ground,
and in the air,
having to rake once more.

Colin Haines, Grade 5
Central School

Skittles

If I were Skittles,
I'd be colorful and proud like a spectrum in the sky.
I'd be in a bunch,
crowded like people at a concert.
We'd be eaten one by one in line.
We would get smaller and smaller,
until there was only one left.
If I am blue, I'm sad.
If I am red, I'm mad.
I am a Skittle!

Yahia Chahine, Grade 5
Bartle Elementary School

A Recipe for Disaster

First, take a cup of people.
Put in a pitchfork and a plan for the riot.
Then put it in the biggest pot you've got.
Mix with a big machine until you hear them planning a riot.
Pour them in a big bowl.
Cook at 9,000 degrees until you can hear them yelling.
You can tell when it's done when they're red with anger.
Add fire on a stick.
Don't taste it.
Throw it outside!

Ryan Moncada, Grade 5
Roosevelt Elementary School

The Amazing Apple

On the outside, you look like a young green leaf.
You feel like a newborn face.
When I peel you, you sound like a man cutting wood.
When I slice you, you sound like somebody making fire.
Inside you look like a tundra.
You feel like the dirt in the park.
You smell like a tree.
You taste like sugary goodness.
Tell me, where were you born?

David Tobar, Grade 5
Roosevelt Elementary School

Joy

Joy looks like a patch of flowers in
    Floaroma Town;

It sounds like the breezy wind
    whistling through the trees;

It smells like homemade pumpkin pie
    with cinnamon and whipped cream;

It feels like a soft, cuddly pillow
    waiting for you to sleep over;

It tastes like my grandmother's
    delicious buttermilk pancakes.

Adrian Genao, Grade 5
Perth Amboy Catholic Upper Grades School

The Great Bambino

In the 1932 World Series
The Bambino went to the plate.
All the fans were on their toes
To see the Great One meet his fate.

He was ready at the plate
Boom! A home run that's out of the park
Rounding the bases happily as can be
That ball went out like it was scared of a shark.

With his teammate Lou Gehrig at his side
Years later, the Bambino died in 1948.
We will always remember him with pride
We call him "The Sultan of Swat."

Alex Medina, Grade 4
Marie Durand Elementary School

Earthbound

The winds are flying,
Laughing gaily too,
They send butterflies to tickle my face,
One thousand leaves to paint the ground.

The rushing river's leaping,
Rushing far ahead,
The fish parachute through the currents,
One thousand fish that make no sound.

The sun is shining,
Smiling down to friend or foe,
The lights show through a blind one's glasses,
One thousand rays fall forth earthbound.

Gabrielle Friedman, Grade 6
Lawton C Johnson Summit Middle School

Fourth Grade Kid
I am a kid
Eager to be,

Don't know
What's coming for me?

Maybe something
Exciting or sad!

Maybe something happy
That'll make me glad.
Nelson Delgado, Grade 4
Greenwood Elementary School

Olivia Lowe
O utstanding
L ovely
I ncredible
V ery kind
I ntelligent
A great best friend

L ucky
O livia is great
W elcome to come to my house
E xcellent
Lilah Givens, Grade 5
Hillside Elementary School

Holiday
I jump up and down with glee,
Right next to the plain Christmas tree.

After we finish making it pretty,
Then I play with my new little kitty.

On go the ornaments and tinsel too,
Then there's the star, the best part to do.

I never had such a great holiday,
Now I have to go and play.
Prairie Fiebel, Grade 5
Hillside Elementary School

Christmas
C arloads of presents
H ot cocoa
R acing sleds
I ndoor fires
S chool's out
T he most wonderful time of the year
M erry good time
A wesome days
S led rides over the powdery snow
David Kuhn, Grade 5
Catherine A Dwyer Elementary School

Dream
Things on earth are horrible!
It brings my heart such pain.
I wish paradise was here.
We would be treated fairly.
No more being judged by our skin type
Paradise would be wonderful for all!
That's my dream!
Thomas Perren, Grade 4
Marie Durand Elementary School

Seasons
Spring paints the flowers
Fall paints the leaves
Winter paints the ground
But what does summer paint?
You ask.
Summer paints a glowing smile
On your face!
Aarushi Gupta, Grade 5
Village School

Colors
Red are roses in the sun.
Blue is the large, lasting sky.
Orange is a sweet smelling flower.
Yellow is the big, bright sun.
Green is the plants, trees, and grass.
Indigo is the berries in a bush.
Violet is gum, sweet and small.
Andrew Quesada, Grade 5
Bartle Elementary School

Walk Away
Walk away, and if you do,
I will walk with you.
If I walk I hope you will too
we support each other
we walk together.
walk away and if you do
I will walk with you.
Skylar Guica, Grade 6
Home School

Speak/Below
Speak
State, declare, express, voice
Think before you make your choice.

Below
Beneath, a lower level, under
Reading books make you wonder.
Samantha Chee, Grade 5
Hillside Elementary School

Can You Imagine?
Can you imagine?
A story without words,
A world without birds
Or a cowboy boot without spurs?

Can you imagine?
A clock without hands,
A celebrity without fans,
Or a kitchen without pans?

Can you imagine?
A chair without legs,
A dog that never begs,
Or a cat that lays eggs?

Can you imagine?
A brother that's not a pain,
A horse with no mane,
Or a rain forest without rain?

Can you imagine?
Michigan without the great lakes,
A cake that doesn't bake,
Or that this poem's a fake?
Rachel Paroff, Grade 5
Hillside Elementary School

The Beautiful Moon
The moon is high in the sky,
out and about.
The moon will hide,
then soon come out.

The moon plays hide and seek
with stars and clouds.
The moon beams bright,
looking so proud.

The moon, oh the moon
is what catches my eye,
when I look up
to the never ending night sky.

The moon lights the night
with its gleam and glow.
When shining in the sky,
it puts on a show.

The moon is such a
beautiful sight,
on this cold, late
fall night.
Taylor Serad, Grade 6
Christa McAuliffe Middle School

Eyes on the Clock

At my desk with my eyes on the clock
All I can think about is the hole in my sock
I'm waiting for the clock to strike three
But then I realized it's not only me

As I watch the minutes slowly go by
I let out a really big sigh
With my eyes peeled on the clock
There I am still thinking about that hole in my sock

Tapping my pencil on my head
Trying to break that dirty piece of lead
All of a sudden it was thirty seconds to three
When I let out a big "yippee"

That's when my teacher really got mad
And said I was being very bad
My punishment was twenty pages of homework
But I just gave a really big smirk

She asked me what that smirk was for
And I began to laugh as I headed for the door
The next 2 1/2 months was summer vacation
Turns out I wasn't in a bad situation

Nick Martinelli, Grade 4
Little Falls School #3

My Own Land

Outside my window I believe there's more than sky
There's a distant land that's not so dry
The ocean waves are orange and red
I'm liking this land; there's nothing to dread

Some of our people could get there by spaceship
It would be a long and fascinating trip
On the way they might pass a planet like Mars
Or maybe something special, like twinkling stars

When you step off the ship you don't need an air tank
On this planet there's lots of air, and that's no prank
There we would be able to start a new life
A place where husbands could bring their family and wives

In this land there's nothing to worry about
For animals will live and plants will sprout
There is no problem because this land is green
The animals would be happy since this place is so clean

As you can see this world is so new
The clouds are puffy and the sky is so blue
At least I can still dream about this magical land
And so can you if you try to understand

Rosa Mazza-Hilway, Grade 6
Little Falls School #1

Snowflakes

S anta comes in this season
N ow everyone is happy
O ooooooh no she got coal
W eeeeee yippie look at the big presents we got
F ollow the track there is more presents
L ook at all the kids playing outside
A t last Christmas is ending
K ids are going back inside
E veryone is happy for what they got, but
S nowflakes are always falling

Jessica Logan, Grade 4
Springfield Township School

The Race

On a Saturday morning it was cold and snowy.
I walked outside and the wind was very blowy.
I called my friends Jacob and T-Bo.
We raced outside to hear the man yell, "Let's go!"
We quickly got our huskies and ran across the snow.
Once we got set up, the man yelled, "Go!"
The sled racers were off to a slow and steady pace.
It felt so cold when the snow hit my face.
It was almost over and the finish line was near.
"We have a winner!" the man yelled loud and clear.

Kristen Greco, Grade 5
Roosevelt Elementary School

School

School starts with thinking students writing at their desks.
Soon will come a test.
Students do homework with challenging questions on it.
After that come uniforms, oh, I hope they fit!
Science, reading, math are always easy to do.
The tough part comes when it's something new.
I passed my first test because I got a ninety-six.
School is fun now and I'm getting my kicks.
Here comes the weekend, it's the end of the week now.
I smile to my teacher and then I take a bow.

Sonam Mistry, Grade 5
St Rose of Lima Academy

Nicole

Nice, caring, helpful
Wishes to do something important that will help the world.
Dreams of running like a puma, but never getting tired.
Wants to write a book that will win a Newbery medal.
Who wonders if one day it will start to rain food.
Who fears going in a maze, but not finding my way out.
Who likes the flavor of cold lemonade on a hot summer day.
Who believes that wishes on shooting stars come true.
Who loves living on a clean and healthy world.
Who plans on making something that people will need.

Nicole Gomez, Grade 5
Bartle Elementary School

Why?

Why can some birds never fly?
Not even half a mile high,
Maybe if they really try,
They can fly two inches high.

Why do bears look so mean?
Maybe because they're really keen,
Or maybe they've recently seen,
Something that is very, very mean.

Why do kittens look so kind?
You will see it's hard to find,
A kitten with a very small mind,
One day you will find, everything is one of a kind.

Caroline Koschik, Grade 5
Hillside Elementary School

Making Strides

M aking strides
A n exciting cause to help.
K eep women alive
I ncredible organization
N othing gets in its way
G etting monies to help with cancer research

S earching for a cure
T alking to others
R eaching out to kids with mothers
I n a battle to beat the disease
D aring people to walk
E xtra care for those losing hair
S tarting a revolution

Isabella Jo Boyko, Grade 5
Hillside Elementary School

Life

Life is cruel,
Cold,
Bright,
And bold.

Loving life is like
A soft dove
That comes
From above.

It answers our hopes
And dreams,
But I wonder what it means.
Does it really answer our hopes and dreams?

Rhiannon Bender, Grade 5
Durban Avenue Elementary School

My Mom the Nurse

Sometimes
I think Mrs. Vazquez is an angel in disguise
Really I do
She is like an angel with invisible wings and a halo
So gentle, caring, and good.
She is always helpful and kindhearted to other people
Even when everything is frustrating
All around her and in our world
Sometimes
I think Mrs. Vazquez is an angel in disguise
And I am thankful I am one of the lucky ones
Who gets touched and hugged
By such a special spirit
My Mom, the Nurse

Briana Martinez, Grade 4
Marie Durand Elementary School

Edward H. Bryan

E very year we have many interesting events.
D on't do drugs.
W hen you work hard, you will get prizes.
A lways smiles in here.
R ead and write.
D o great job.

H ot red color in school color

B ulldog is school mascot.
R ight way we always take.
Y oung people are learning from teachers.
A lso there are lots of fun in here.
N umber 1 school in NJ.

Mirii Muto, Grade 4
Edward H Bryan Elementary School

The Best Time of the Day

When the day gives over to the night
When the chirping bird solemnly silences itself
When the day lily gently closes its buds
The best time of day has begun
When the crickets come out and begin their song
When the lightning bugs brighten up the night
When the darkness conquers the evening sky
This is truly the most pure and delicate time of the day
When a lull of sleep overcomes my mind
When I'm rocked to sleep with my dad's lullaby
When the night gives over to the day
When sweet dreams take over my night sleep
When the clock tower strikes its twelfth chime
Then and only then has sweet morn begun anew

Fatima Anwar, Grade 5
The Ellison School

Soccer Is So Much Fun

Soccer is so much fun
Blocking, kicking, running
Across the field.
Trying to get past the goalie,
And not yield to his defensive moves.
I like to play this game.

Dez Gopaul, Grade 5
Hillside Elementary School

No Poem

I sat up half the night
And couldn't think of a thing to write
I asked my mom and dad
They said it's time to say goodnight
So this is what I have
I hope that it's all right!

Amanda Morales, Grade 4
Ethel M Burke Elementary School

Seed

It starts out very small,
Then it grows until it's tall.

Then it's there growing slow,
And drops more seeds to grow.

Nick Venanzi, Grade 5
Frances DeMasi Elementary School

Cows

The black and white cow
chewing on green grass
for her morning food
in her private field
she is very hungry

Henry Streblo, Grade 5
Bartle Elementary School

Foofoo

Foofoo is a black and white bunny
He likes to hop around and play.
He chews on everything but people,
And is very friendly and cute.
I love Foofoo!

Michelle Chow, Grade 5
Hillside Elementary School

Mr. Bunny

The bunny in the prairie is white
When night falls he's always out of sight
He is always eating
And when I am reading
He thinks my book page is a delight

Emma Steiner, Grade 4
St Mary's School

Up at Bat

Another person on the base, I guess I better get ready
Adrenaline pumping, my back is slumping, I try to hold the bat steady
I walk to the plate and hear the crowd all calling my name
I step in the box, take my smile off, and get my head in the game

Try to take the bat off my shoulder, whoosh it came too late
Oh no, I missed it, I need to swing before it's over the plate
I try to forget what had just happened, get my bat back in place
Here comes the pitch, crack goes the bat, I start to run to base

I think I really hit it hard, it is nowhere to be seen
Look, there in the sky, the ball is the size of a bean
All the outfielders look to the sky
They don't notice me as I run by

I touch second base and check for the ball
It doesn't look like it will fall
My head's looking forward, my coach says don't stop
I now touch third base, I'm on my way to the top

I'm heading for home as I reach for the base
I shut my eyes when I heard him say I was safe
I got a homerun, the crowd was calling my name
Believe in yourself, and you too can have fame

Alexandria Dutkiewicz, Grade 6
Little Falls School #1

The Legend of the Man in the Moon

There once was a man on the moon.
The man still lives there today.
Except back then he was lonely and blue, and the Earth was a bad shade of gray.

One day he left the moon to go for a stroll through the sky.
He met a gorgeous woman, it was love at first sight.
So they walked and they danced and they sang every day, except for that one horrid night.

The night when he had to go home.
Back to his home on the moon.
He longed to go home, yet, he did not want to leave so soon.

So together they made up a plan.
A special plan where they could be together.
A plan where they could be with each other, but stay in their homes forever.

When the man went back to the moon,
The woman went to live on the sun.
They frolicked and played. Together they had tons of fun.

Again the moon shines bright.
In reflection of his love, the sun.
Together they lit up the world, and life on earth had soon begun.

Erin Deluccia, Grade 6
Christa McAuliffe Middle School

The Forest

Looking out on the cliff
Watching the blue water
Listening to the chirps of blue birds around,
Watching the red, orange, and yellow leaves
Flowing through the trees
Into a nearby lake

Walking around listening,
To the crunching of the fallen branches
Wishing I could stay longer

But it's getting dark and
I have to leave.

Emily Glenning, Grade 6
Buckshutem Road Elementary School

Because of You

When you said you loved me
I really thought it
When you said you'd be there
I really believed
But then you betrayed me
And this is what happened
Now I am heartbroken
Because of all the lies you said to me
I will never believe anyone
Because of you
I will never think I can be loved again
Because of you

Shayna Navarro, Grade 6
Garfield Middle School

Thanksgiving

T hanksgiving
H aving a good time
A pple cider is the best
N ative Americans shared their food
K ind people all around
S our apples taste so good
G ravy on the amazing turkey
I mportant family members come to visit
V ivid memories of that day
I ncredible stuffing
N ever take what you have for granted
G oing to have a great time

Christopher Agugliaro, Grade 5
St James School

Cool Rock

Nice rock
Is nice and green
It is from a cold stream
It is beautiful and pretty
Nice rock

Dylan Decker, Grade 4
Springfield Township School

Soaring…

At Greenwood School
In fourth grade
My favorite subjects
Math and science.

It's hard this year
But I like to
Test my brain!

Great teachers
Are nice
And caring.

Helping me to listen
And pay attention,
All to learn new ideas!

Tinnoh Blayee, Grade 4
Greenwood Elementary School

Ice Cream

One spoon, one bowl
Like juicy meatballs on a roll
Circular snowballs go plop
I do not think I can stop!

A cold icy dream
All flavored up to a radiant beam
Easy to eat on hot summer days
Or a luscious treat in a cold winter haze!

Ice cream, oh ice cream
You are not what you seem
Delicious, you know
but if I eat too much, I will…

BLOW!

Hannah Crisafulli, Grade 6
Great Meadows Regional Middle School

A Windy Day

A wind blew up one dark cold morning.
And joined us in our play.
Chasing us around the playground today.
Blowing all the basketballs away.

It knocks on our window
The wind blows quickly through.
It found our teacher's pile of papers too.
And the papers blows, and blows.

Then everybody runs.
As we hear our teacher shout,
"Quick! Shut the doors and windows
To keep that awful wind out!"

James Vorrius, Grade 5
Durban Avenue Elementary School

The House

In this house
the floor creaks
and the roof leaks.
There are cracks in the walls
and the stairs make you fall.
The couches are lumpy
and the beds are bumpy.
In this house.
The lights flicker off
and the drafts make you cough.
In the kitchen there are mice
on the pillows there are lice
The locked doors I fear…
won't get me out of here!

Zack Marzulli, Grade 5
Hillside Elementary School

Friendship

A ring is round,
It has no end.
That's how long,
I'll be your friend.

Trusting each other
When we tell secrets
That could change
Our lives.

A ring is strong,
Like a metal pole
That stands through
War holding our flag.

Christian Escobar, Grade 5
Durban Avenue Elementary School

My Chess Set

This is my chess set
Pieces made of clay
My dad and I love it
We could play all day

This is my chess set
Although it's tiny
It feels heavy
Looks very shiny

This is my chess set
I keep it in a glass case
A present from my aunt
It would be hard to replace

Esteban Cardona, Grade 5
Bartle Elementary School

Winter*

Winter	Winter
Glistening	
	Freezing
Magical	
	Uninviting
A kingdom waiting to be discovered	
	My nose turns red like a clown's
Sipping hot chocolate by a fire	
	Messy hot chocolate, chopping wood for the fire
Christmas presents, waiting under the tree	
	Worrying about what gifts to give
Spending time with my wonderful family	
	Spending time with my horrible mother-in-law
Snowboarding down gleaming, white hills	
	Breaking a leg skiing
Winter: It's wonderful!	Winter: It's horrible!

Dana Schmeltzle, Grade 6
Great Meadows Regional Middle School
*A poem for two voices

Fall Will Soon Rest
The sun smiles down on the rolling hills and warms up the land.
Its rays hug the animals before it leaves for its slumber in the cold dark winter.
The trees hang their heavy heads and let their leaves fall down.
They smile as they see their young ones get picked up and blown off the ground.
The pine trees are sprinkled with berries like the ornaments on a Christmas tree.
The squirrels wait for the teasing nuts to fall so they can finish their game of tag.
The air is singing, "Over the River and Through the Woods" and is soon joined by many more.
Hungry bears splash in rivers looking for unlucky fish to feed themselves before hibernation.
Kittens purr by the fire while quiet ladies rock.
The radiant colors of leaves are like a rainbow blossoming with joy.
The swooping wind and birds dance and perform the best ballet.
Fluffy chipmunks chatter over one fallen nut when there are many more.
The squawking geese depart the lake in a V formation and head south for warmer weather.
Sunflowers smile up to the sparkling sun until night, when they rest.
The swirling leaves race the wind, but only to fall again.
Aromatic pine trees are being cut down, the season is coming to an end.
The first frigid frost has come, and fall rests its head with the setting sun.

Ursula Beesley, Grade 5
Hopewell Elementary School

No Moon Blues
The crickets are chirping. It's six past nine. I look outside and there's no moon in the sky. I got the no moon blues, where's the face I see in the night? Just wondering because all I see is stars.

A couple days later, I'm looking in the sky. The moon is there and as full as an eye. Don't got the no moon blues, now that my friend's back in town. Don't got the no moon blues, just because the moon is found.

Another week later, I'm gazing at the stars. The moon is gone and the blues are back again. I got the no moon blues why did that light disappear?

I got the no moon blues
Everybody
We got the blues!

Andrew Seney, Grade 6
Christa McAuliffe Middle School

Wonderful Winter

Moist snowflakes,
falling from the sky.
Little kids,
sledding down the hill.
Young couples,
watching a movie.
Snow, love, fun
Wonderful winter!

Hot cocoa,
after shoveling.
Bundled up,
in coats and snow pants.
Lay in the snow,
and make a snow angel.
Snow, love, fun
Wonderful winter!

Ellie Koschik, Grade 5
Hillside Elementary School

A Glimpse of the Moon

I look up into the dark night sky
But no glowing moon
Not even a glimpse.

I look up into the night sky
I see a small sliver
Oh so thin and very sharp.

I look up into the night sky
I see half of the moon
Just like the half of a pizza pie.

I look up into the bright night sky
I see a full moon
So round like a cookie
Craters are the chocolate chips
And the stars shimmer and shine.

Louis Sansone, Grade 6
Christa McAuliffe Middle School

I Don't Understand

I don't understand
why people fight,
why we have 4 seasons,
why I have allergies.
But most of all
why we get old,
why people have to die,
why we have friends.
What I understand most is
why my family loves me,
why I was born,
why the sun shines bright.

Maggie Felker, Grade 6
Lounsberry Hollow Middle School

If I Were a Soccer Ball

If I were a soccer ball,
I'd watch someone's foot kicking me,
not knowing where I'll land!
I'd be getting thrown back to someone,
when I crossed a line I wasn't supposed to!
I'd be watching myself get kicked into a net,

If I were a soccer ball!

Harrison Smith, Grade 5
Bartle Elementary School

Love

Love is a feeling
you get from your heart.
You can get it when you're with someone,
or when you're apart.
Love is very strong
it can last a whole life long
and when you're filled with love
nothing can go wrong!

Madison Mastellone, Grade 5
Village School

Bubbles

Bubbles are cool and they are clear
And they have tiny colored rainbows
Shining brightly inside of them
Bubbles come in many sizes
And if you touch them they will pop
When you blow up a bubble or two
They will stick together like glue

Thomas Nevius, Grade 4
Marie Durand Elementary School

Nature

Green leaves drifting in the air
Towering trees swaying to and fro
Grass rippling with the wind
Spring birds chirping
And me
Standing there as it all
appears

Madelyn Gostomski, Grade 4
Village School

If I Were a Planet

If I were a planet,
I'd revolve around the big and bright sun!
I'd sweat and have my tongue out,
because I'm hot from the sun's heat!
I'd provide people with a place to live,

If I were a planet!

Joshua Mayfield, Grade 5
Bartle Elementary School

When It Rains

When it rains
I think God is crying
because someone
died or got hurt
When it rains
I love to go outside
to play in the puddles
When it rains
I wonder and wonder…

Grace Accardi, Grade 6
Garfield Middle School

My Dog

My dog is fluffy
She's always dirty
She has big floppy ears
When she walks they flop
She likes to play with her toy
She likes to take walks
She loves me the most
I rub her belly
I love my dog just the way she is

Gina Smith, Grade 5
Frances DeMasi Elementary School

Forest

Clang, clang, clang
Such a hollow sound for a tree
Of owls knocking on it
While leaves spick, sprickle my legs
I feel what the trees felt
When the owls made holes in them.
Pain we don't feel, but we fear.
So we must stand to face it,
Because if we don't we can't get rid of it.

Yuriy Prots, Grade 5
Bartle Elementary School

Why War?

Why do we have wars?
I hate it no matter what!
Killing and fighting
Only sadness can survive
But the brave ones bring us peace.

Andrew Nocilla, Grade 5
Richard E Byrd Elementary School

Snow

Snow is falling down
Snowball fights, igloos, shovels
Sledding 'til it stops
I drink hot cocoa
Mittens, heavy coat, pants, hat
Let's go to sleep now!

Rushi Patel, Grade 5
Catherine A Dwyer Elementary School

The Impressive Elements
Beryllium gives you berylliosis,
But mercury makes you mad.
Molybdenum is friendly to the environment,
But chlorine just pollutes.
Copper can be ancient,
But radon is current.
Phosphorus is vital but deadly,
But nickel can cause a rash.
Vanadium is divine,
As is gold.
Cesium is alarming,
Whereas hydrogen is reassuring.
The elements are impressive,
Do you think they are not?

Shannon Foreback, Grade 4
Nut Swamp Elementary School

Love
Love is something everyone needs.
Love is for anything, I'm sure you would agree.
Love is for anything at all.
It can be for an elephant or a puppy that's small.
Love can be a person and I'm sure.
It can be a spouse, a cousin, or family galore.
Love can be for one person or more.
It can be even for the floor.
Love is for anything you like.
It can be for your bike.
Love is something you share.
With love, you can show people you care.
With love, you can find the right person for you.
You find them with love, which is what you should do.

Maria Herrle, Grade 5
St James School

Summer
Summer is cool
you play in the pool
Inviting some friends to have some fresh air.

Eating and laughing
with family and friends
This makes my day always the best.

Sometimes we relax on the chair
'til my dad says "OK" it is time for a snack,
So I jump from my chair and grab some snacks

That is why I like summer because it is fun
you spend some time with your family and friends.

Jillian Zupito, Grade 4
Good Shepherd Regional Catholic School

Joy
Joy looks like the first soft snow of winter;
It sounds like church bells ringing on Sunday morning;
It smells like a forest of pine trees;
It feels like a soft, fluffy kitten;
It tastes like an ice cold glass of lemonade in the middle of July.

Tomasz Kasztelan, Grade 5
Perth Amboy Catholic Upper Grades School

You're Lucky
Some people don't have the possessions you do,
Some people don't have nutrition like you,
Some people don't have water to drink every day,
Some people don't have a soft, cozy bed,
And some people don't get any love from a family.

Meredith Busch, Grade 5
Richard E Byrd Elementary School

A Wonderful Moon
On this dark, dreary, damp night,
    I look to the heavens for a comforting sight
The moon's sliver of a crescent
    plays hide-and-seek beneath the clouds
Its smiling face is watching me tonight!

Brendan Tye, Grade 6
Christa McAuliffe Middle School

Happiness
Happiness looks like the first snow of winter;
It sounds like a bat hitting a ball in summer;
It smells like chestnuts being roasted;
It feels like a soft pillow;
It tastes like hot chocolate on a Christmas Day.

John Nunez, Grade 5
Perth Amboy Catholic Upper Grades School

Love
Love looks like a fluffy, white cloud;
It sounds like the beautiful song of a humming bird;
It smells like the sweet fragrance of white roses;
It feels like a warm, white cashmere scarf on a cold, winter day;
It tastes like caramel filled chocolates.

Alexandra Jerez, Grade 5
Perth Amboy Catholic Upper Grades School

Ode to the Moon
Moon, moon shining so bright.
    You look like a big glistening ball of glitter
Shining bright in the sky.
    You make me happy when I am feeling blue moon,
moon what would I do without you?

Alexa Torre, Grade 6
Christa McAuliffe Middle School

Puppy Love

I have a puppy who loves me so,
He's the only one who understands.
He'll lie there on the floor,
His two paws in my hands.

His soft brown eyes look up at me,
His damp nose sniffs the air.
His rough wet tongue licks my face.
We are the perfect pair.

He whimpers when I go to school,
But when I'm home we run and play.
He smiles when I pat his fur,
I love being with my dog all day!

I love my dog, and he loves me.
We're meant to be together.
We always have so much fun.
We'll be the best of pals forever!

They call this PUPPY LOVE
Sydney Miede, Grade 5
Hillside Elementary School

The Burning Light

I plod my way
towards the town's edge.
I smell smoke in the air.
I pass church grounds,
and watch
poor people, beaten like cattle.
Rows of houses
fade away —
so does my soul.

I look at my white, blood stained hands:
30 lashes.
I deserved punishment.
Poisoning my master was not tolerant;
that is what I've done.
I see a glimpse of light
in the outstretched field.
Light turned to fire.
Fire's flames,
burned with pain —
so does my soul.
Ian Wasserman, Grade 6
Hartford School

Summer

Swimming around
Humid and boiling day
Playing, swimming, fanning yourself
Delight
Lillian Smith-Mullen, Grade 5
Bartle Elementary School

Trick or Treat!

Autumn is a wonderful season,
And I have a good reason.
Halloween! Aren't I right?
Watch out, the ghouls might bite!
Run away, run away!
The ghosts are out to play!
Bags full of chewy candy,
Isn't that really dandy?
Halloween is over; everyone is sad.
Next is Christmas; I hope you weren't bad!
Erika Bulger, Grade 5
St Rose of Lima Academy

Iris Reyes

I mpatient
R espectful
I ntelligent
S mart

R esponsible
E xcellent
Y oung
E xciting
S hy
Iris Reyes, Grade 5
Mckinley Community School

My Birthday

It was my birthday,
   everybody came.
   I got lots of gifts,
no two were the same.

   It was very fun,
   we had some cake,
   I played in the sun.
Today was the best day
they could ever make.
Alysia Camacho, Grade 6
Garfield Middle School

School

Another day of school
I miss my pool
I walk to my bus
as slow as dust
just catching the bus!
Sitting next to a girl,
that loves to twirl.
I have butterflies in my stomach
   for…
   the first day of school!
Gabriela Beyda, Grade 4
Yeshivat Noam

A Seed

I am very very tiny
And I'm the color green
I am not very shiny
I'm so small I can hardly be seen

Someday I'll be a redwood tree
I will be planted in the ground
A place where I can feel so free
With soil all around

There is nothing for me to worry about
Except if my owners water me
It is something I cannot live without
I think you will agree

Great! I am now a sapling
And I'm growing very fast
It looks like I'm always napping
I'll enjoy it while it lasts

It's ten years later than before
And now I'm really very tall
I see the birds fly as they explore
Can't believe I used to be so small
Nicole Gallegos, Grade 4
Little Falls School #3

World Peace

A feeling of nonviolence
Flowing through the air
Peace, happiness, and joy
Harmony everywhere

Discussing our problems and issues
Love is in the air
Doves singing in the breeze
People showing they care

All hatred is gone
For now and forever more
Fighting with guns no longer exists
And there is no such thing as war

Everyone has equal rights
Please bring home our troops
All I see are smiling faces
With the world not split into groups

Now I want to make a wish
I wish that peace will soon be here
Everyone who inhabits our earth
Will live in harmony every year
Tara Daly, Grade 4
Little Falls School #3

All About My Sister

K arla is smart
A re you?
R eady to yell at me
L ying and screaming, blaming me!
A re you sure you are my sister?

Kerlyn Garcia, Grade 5
Mckinley Community School

The Night Sky

Starry skies
The moon's always shining
Not once, not ever blinking out
Never leaves us, not 'til dawn
Our moon

Michelle Hillock, Grade 5
Richard E Byrd Elementary School

Rain

Pouring
a small drizzle
water falling from sky
parachuting down from gray world
cold, wet

Sydney Mangaroo, Grade 5
Richard E Byrd Elementary School

Tiger

Tiger
Orange and black.
It leaps in the jungle.
Ferociously surprises prey.
Big claws

Liam Roth, Grade 5
Bartle Elementary School

Falcon

The falcon
Dives fiercely
During the afternoon
In the valley
Searching for food

Shivam Agrawal, Grade 5
Bartle Elementary School

Change Has Come

Change has come to America,
And to the streets,
And to the community.
Since Barack Obama
Took the presidency.

Amir Chavis, Grade 5
Hillside Elementary School

Life

I am a person who will change the world.
I wonder about life and what it has in store for me.
I hear the sad stories of tragic deaths on TV.
I see a world full of evil that needs us to change it.
I want a better life for all of us.
I am a person who will change the world.

I pretend that the shootings that happen on TV don't but they do.
I feel like the world depends on me to change it.
I touch the tip of a pencil and begin to write about the problems of the world.

I worry about what will become of life years from now.
I cry for the people that are less fortunate than me.
I am a person who will change the world.

I understand that I can't change people that don't want to be changed but I can try.

Sean Hill, Grade 6
Olson Middle School

My Favorite Place to Be

My favorite place to be
Is up in a tree
Up in a tree
There is you and me
And my pet bumble bee
Up in my special tree
There is so much to see
A little robin's nest
Looking at me
Across the street
Up in my tree
My neighbor Nelly
Is looking at me
And that is why
My tree is special to me

Sydney McDonald, Julia Aasmaa, Kiersten Stewart, and Abby Borin, Grade 5
Wildwood Elementary School

Things Come and Go*

Things come and go even if you don't want them to.

When people are living they're like the seasons to me.
They come and go just like the sea.
The sea is the ocean true fact indeed,
the waves will come to your feet and leave.
Just like a boyfriend,
you're pretty sure you know him until he walks out on you.
Of course I wouldn't know that,
I'm a kid you see!
An average 11-year-old kid,
just like you,
and me!

Nevada Simonetti, Grade 6
Memorial Middle School
*Dedicated to anyone who has lost a loved one or has been through a lot

Black Panther

Soft, black
Growling, toying, hunting
Claws and paws trying to get a fish
Fierce.

Andre Baldini, Grade 4
Ethel M Burke Elementary School

Cats

C ats are cuddly,
A nd very lovable.
T hey can be over active.
S ometimes, a little SCARY!!!

Kelsey Gonzalez, Grade 5
Catherine A Dwyer Elementary School

Dog/Friend

Brown, white
Barking, jumping, running
My neighbor's dog is black.
Friend.

Ali Khan, Grade 4
Ethel M Burke Elementary School

Goal

Physical, fast
Pass, skate, shoot
Hollydell Hurricanes on a breakaway
SCORE!

Shane Ewing, Grade 4
Ethel M Burke Elementary School

The Movie Blue

Very cool, wicked
Scaring, swimming, surfing
Sailboat float with sharks.
Video

Shivam Patel, Grade 4
Ethel M Burke Elementary School

Dusty

sneaking
around at night
up the attic stairs
waiting to pounce on her favorite toy

Mara Rose Myers, Grade 5
Bartle Elementary School

New Jersey

Moderate climate
Middle Atlantic Region
Neither hot nor cold

Justin Palmieri, Grade 4
St Peter Elementary School

The Dancing Couples

The fall leaves are like fireballs on the ground.
But how do they get there?
They dance with the wind.
When they dance with the wind they do somersaults.
But the leaves die because when the wind stops
They fall to their death.
When the leaves fall,
The wind cries with its roar of tears
But the sky cheers it up.
The wind makes the leaves die when they hit the cold hard autumn ground.
The leaves get scared because creepy, crawly critters crawl all over them.
But the wind picks them up and throws them away.
The leaves want to dance again, but they cannot move.
So the wind finds new crimson and scarlet leaves.
The turquoise sky dims down to an indigo shade
And the wind gets tired and goes to bed.
So the leaves wait for the wind to come once again.

Thomas Davis, Grade 5
Hopewell Elementary School

Life Has Struggle

I am a mature farmer's daughter.
I wonder when the raging war will end.
I hear laughter, like bells ringing, but it's just my imagination.
I see a perfect life, one without tears, sadness, and with a happy ending.
I want an easier life, and for people to see how hard it is to be me.
I am a mature farmer's daughter.
I pretend I can do anything and everything, and that I rule the world.
I feel incomparable to any other soul.
I touch a sick person and they are healed.
I worry I will never find myself and open my mouth when I must.
I cry only when I have had enough of being driven to extremes.
I am a mature farmer's daughter.
I understand my life may not get easier.
I say nothing is impossible, and never say never.
I try to open up and express my feelings and myself.
I hope my life will be easier, more flowing.
I am a mature farmer's daughter.

Gabrielle Russo, Grade 6
Olson Middle School

Eating on Thanksgiving

T hanksgiving is when I help my mom cook and prepare the table for
H appy family members to enjoy.
A pple pie is for dessert, but
N obody eats until we get our drinks.
K evin my uncle eats like a pig, but
S ally my aunt rarely eats at all.
" **G** race" is said before we eat. Then
I have turkey, ham, macaroni, and other things too. My sister yells,
" **V** eeou," because she burned her tongue. So,
I wait for my food to cool down.
N ow, I dig in and eat everything I can.
" **G** ulp, gulp" is what you hear from me.

Dominic Dreadin, Grade 6
Riverside Middle School

Go Inside a Star
See its soul like fire glowing
Perhaps you'll find wise genies
Perhaps sacred saints praying
Perhaps an unknown land of fortune
Perhaps you'll find a gift waiting
Rajitha Pulivarthy, Grade 5
Village School

Sweet Sounds of the Sea
The sea so peaceful
every day the sea so nice
the sea so calming
the sound of the ocean sleeps
the sea sounding like heaven
Michael Blando, Grade 5
Richard E Byrd Elementary School

Happy
H appiness
A pplause
P izza
P arty
Y o-yo
Kelly Martins, Grade 6
Roosevelt Elementary School

My Blue Special Friend
Whale of the blue sea,
Come sing to me with your spout,
Upon this gray day.
Humming and projecting,
Wanting the day to end.
Nina Goodman, Grade 6
Kellman Brown Academy

If I Were the Waves
If I were the waves
I'd be happiness moving back and forth.
I'd be opening a whole different world.
I would make everyone feel free!
I am the waves
Alia Dene Underwood, Grade 5
Bartle Elementary School

Beautiful Winter
Leaves are falling,
It's getting cold outside.
Days getting shorter,
Snowing lots…everything turns white,
White color covers the town.
Haruki Shigeta, Grade 5
Richard E Byrd Elementary School

I Don't Understand
I don't understand
why people dislike each other
why some people stay inside all day
why there are different languages in the world.
But most of all
why we don't have peace in our world
why people murder innocent others
why our economy is so bad
why so many people are out on the street when we're the richest country in the world
What I understand most is
why the sky is blue
why people stick up for each other
why school is important
why the sun sets
Jordan Barany, Grade 6
Lounsberry Hollow Middle School

Fall Enigma
Brightly colored leaves fallen on the ground
Some kids playing outside with light coats on
A park with fluttering leaves
In colors of red, orange, brown, green and yellow
Crunchy bright colored leaves
Crunch crunch under my feet
A little squirrel full of nuts in her mouth seeking to her house
as her famished babies wait for her
Everywhere are leaves like a carpet of leaves
The wind arching its way shaking the bare trees
A woman sitting on a bench dreaming a reverie, slowly sipping the hot coffee
Fall is a big colorful enigma
This is a wonderful season fall!
Nehal Patil, Grade 6
Pond Road Middle School

Moon
I strolled outside and the moon caught my eye.
The fire horn going off.
Planes going through the glow of the full moon.
The stars are like light bulbs surrounding the moon.
The cool breeze sends a shiver down my spine.
The leaves crunched under my feet as I walked.
The cars flew by my house like race cars.
The trees are rocking in the wind while the dogs were howling at the moon.
When I strolled outside and the moon caught my eye.
Tyler Melnick, Grade 6
Christa McAuliffe Middle School

Out the Window
The clear blue sky with no cloud in sight, the big bright sun brighter than I've ever seen!
People honking their car horns angrily.
A little girl across the street from where I am gazing out the window.
The night club with the big round light bulbs.
NYC is very, very busy on Thanksgiving.
Amelia Wilkerson, Grade 5
Bartle Elementary School

New Jersey's Pinelands
New Jersey's Pinelands
Forests of endless pine trees
Oak and cedar, too
Ryan Ferdinand, Grade 4
St Peter Elementary School

The Beach
The beach is awesome
The beach is a perfect place
It will steal your heart
Elizabeth Beaver, Grade 4
St Peter Elementary School

New Jersey
I like the Pinelands
New Jersey is exciting
New Jersey is mine
Christian Pascal, Grade 4
St Peter Elementary School

Lenape
Friendly Lenape
William Penn was fond of them
They were peace-makers
Maureen Dymond, Grade 4
St Peter Elementary School

Waterfalls
Pretty waterfalls
I love waterfalls so much
Exciting and fun
Lauryn Adams, Grade 4
St Peter Elementary School

New Jersey
Awesome New Jersey
The lakes are glacial and clear
Fun in New Jersey
Gabriel Rouse, Grade 4
St Peter Elementary School

New Jersey
Wide sandy beaches
Beautiful rivers and lakes
Pine trees and farmlands
Christian Belz, Grade 4
St Peter Elementary School

Stars
Stars light the dark night,
Stars are an amazing sight,
All stars are different.
Thomas Notaro, Grade 6
St Jerome School

A Thanksgiving Feast
" **T** hanks for coming," my uncle greeted me.
H onestly, I was only paying attention to the delicious smell from the kitchen.
A s I walked through the door my cousin looked like a clown with his big smile.
N ext to me was my whole family at the giant table.
K nives cutting into the turkey are all they would do.
S o, I knew the only way to get any food was to find an empty seat.
G ravy decorated the mashed potatoes and butter covered the corn, it looked yummy.
I was so grateful for everything I got to eat.
V anilla cake, pumpkin bread, and pumpkin pie were served for dessert.
I was surprised we had no leftovers.
N o one could even take another bite because they ate so much.
" **G** ood night," I said to everyone as I joyously walked out the door.
Alexis D'Amico, Grade 6
Riverside Middle School

Thanksgiving Is Finally Here!
T hanksgiving is for everyone to spend time with family and friends, and to
H ave fun with each other. "We all should be thankful, grateful, and
A ppreciate the Pilgrims and Indians," Mama said kindly.
N ow everyone is eating a nice turkey dinner. I
K now when dinner is cooking, I love when Mama makes her famous moist
S tuffing for the turkey.
G iving thanks is what Thanksgiving is all about.
I t's all about fun. There will be a lot of
V arieties of food. I can't wait until Thanksgiving.
" **I** enjoy spending time with my family," said Mama.
N ow, everyone is happy with the nice yummy dinner.
" **G** obble, gobble!" to everyone!
Destiny VanEmburgh, Grade 6
Riverside Middle School

Wishing for the Moon to Show
Oh how I wish for the moon to show to see its beautiful glow.
There are so many stars
Zoom zoom the cars fly by
There are so many constellations
Orion's Belt is so bright and sparkly
The wind is so fine shaking the top sign across the street
The sky is a tie-dye of purple and blue
I can see a shooting star leaping across the sky
Oh how I wish the moon would show to see its gorgeous glorious glow
Julie Renee Gall, Grade 6
Christa McAuliffe Middle School

How to Make a Big Brother
Take 3 spoons of love, 5 pounds of tallness, and a packet of meanness.
Put all of the ingredients into a big pot.
Blend until he says "Mommy!"
Cook at 120 degrees for 2 hours.
You can tell it's done when he cries.
Let stand until he's asleep.
Add sprinkles.
Slice him into 15 pieces.
Blah!

Joseph Pastor, Grade 5
Roosevelt Elementary School

A Wonderful Sight
I watch as the wind
Blows the leaf down
Onto the mossy green waters
Of the canal
As I see the turtles head
Rise above the cold water
As the birds chirp from the tree above
A family of ducks waddles by
Heading for the wet grass
As I hear the frogs croak
I think
What a beautiful sight.
Adrian Rodriguez, Grade 6
Robert Morris Public School

Dance
To speak with your hands
To speak with your arms
To speak with your legs
Expressing feeling without moving your lips
Gliding across a shiny floor
Spotlight following you
To talk without speaking
All you have to do
Is
Learn the language of
DANCE.
Jessica Korhumel, Grade 6
Mount Laurel Hartford School

Dreams
I love to dream
When I fall asleep I see
beautiful things.

In my dreams
I can be anyone I want
It's like I am in a whole other world.

I keep them close to my heart
So the next time I fall back to sleep.
I will dream all over again!
Jordan Tobolski, Grade 4
Marie Durand Elementary School

Starfish
It feels so rough
It tastes so weird
It looks so strange,
like an old man's beard.
It smells so salty
It sounds like, "WOOSH!"
Then it dives up the water
with a great big, "SPLOOSH!"
Camara Wimbish, Grade 4
Martin Luther King Jr. School Complex

Ode to the Moon
Like a light bulb
The moon goes through cycles

When a new moon comes out
The sky is as dark as an alley
At midnight

As if someone doused
The only light we have
At night

Have you ever wondered why
Wolves howl at the moon

Is it because the moon is
Speaking to them or are
They calling to the moon

If it's speaking, why can't we hear it.
Is it warning us?

That something might be coming
Should we be scared…?
Samantha Dykes, Grade 6
Christa McAuliffe Middle School

Halloween
The cold night air whistles by,
A prowling wolf gives a cry.
The vampire's corpse rises from the grave,
A swarm of bats comes out of its cave.
The pumpkin king floats from the field,
A ghostly knight raises his shield.
So always remember on Halloween night,
The crisp night air is filled with fright.
It's Halloween.
Matthew Nicolls, Grade 6
Great Meadows Regional Middle School

My Bear Blanket
This is my little bear blanket
It's very warm and fluffy
Wrapping myself in it
Makes me feel stuffy!

This is my little bear blanket
It is a bit old, maybe
I still love to lie on it
Especially when I feel lazy!

This is my little bear blanket
It's colorful, but mostly blue
If you slept under it each night,
You'd love it too!
Michelle Fan, Grade 5
Bartle Elementary School

The Journey You'll Never Forget
Take out a book
Read it in bed
Let it take you on a journey
You'll never forget
Through mountains and rivers
And magical lands.
Be back in a jiffy
By your fireside bright.
Rachel Mellicker, Grade 5
Hillside Elementary School

December
D ashing through the snow
E njoyment
C rowds cheering
E njoying the holiday
M erry Christmas
B est time of the year
E xcellent presents
R acing over icy ponds
Farahnaz Pourmoussavian, Grade 5
Catherine A Dwyer Elementary School

Henry Hudson
The Dutch built settlements
Then Henry Hudson claimed the land
He said, "It's mine!"
With the wave of his hand.
He was so adventurous
He couldn't wait
That he discovered
The Hudson Bay, River, and Strait.
Megan Ternay, Grade 5
Roosevelt Elementary School

Winter Love
Oh joy it has come
Frost covered hills
Gingerbread men
Grinning with joy
Snowmen all happy
Cold to your toes
The winter phase
Has just begun
Laura Belovs, Grade 5
Catherine A Dwyer Elementary School

Aniyah
A bsolutely fantastic
N ever gives up
I ntelligent every day
Y o-yos are my favorite toy
A lways perfect
H appy all the time
Aniyah Talbert, Grade 5
Mckinley Community School

The Fine Line

There's a fine line between what's real and what's not,
What's given and what's taken,
What's done and what's thought.

It separates courage from cowardice,
Good things from bad,
And most things that you know of,
Thought about, or had.

The line is very strong,
But can be bent to fit.
It can disappear from your eyes
Even when the room is well lit.

So when you face hard choices
Do not be trouble's pawn;
Think of the fine line, and decide,
Which side are you on?

Jeremy Stepansky, Grade 5
Hillside Elementary School

The Images of Autumn

The colors of autumn are as bright as a rainbow.
The leaves are swooping down as fast as the speed of light.
The trees are letting loose their leaves as each fall day goes on.
The cold air blows against my face as I walk.
The trees are waving their arms at me as I slowly stroll by them.
As the leaves fall, it seems like a rainbow falling from the sky.
The leaf piles in autumn are like playground equipment
As children run and jump and play.
Fall is a time to get outside and enjoy the fresh, crisp air.
Fall is a time to create memories with family and friends.
In the early morning, the dew sparkles on the grass and trees.
Fall winds make the leaves fall in a frenzy.
The colorful leaves happily dance down from the trees.
The sun goes down earlier in the autumn
And the sky gets darker in the day.
When the wind gets good and strong
The shivering trees sway to one side.
These are the images that autumn paints in my mind.

John Lewis, Grade 5
Hopewell Elementary School

Swirling Leaves

Branches shaking,
Leaves falling,
There's a cold breeze in the air,
Telling children fall is coming,
Piles of colorful leaves begin to fill the land,
Wind blowing them gracefully past summer leaves,
They twirl like children playing at the park,
Leaves are unique to see,
Reminding me of butterflies flying in fresh air,
Leaves tumble all around.

Victoria Spangenberg, Grade 6
Great Meadows Regional Middle School

I Don't Understand

I don't understand why dogs and cats dislike each other
why kids have trouble in school
why the sun rises in the east and sets in the west
But most of all
why people hurt one another
why people marry then separate
why some people are mistreated because of their skin color
why the world can't be at peace for two seconds
What I do understand is
why dogs bark
why it rains
why I have friends
why my family loves me

Jenna MacDonald, Grade 6
Lounsberry Hollow Middle School

Playing in the Park with Friends

T hanksgiving is a time for memories, and
H aving fun outside with your friends is awesome.
A great day to go to the park, because
N o one ever stays inside.
K ids are throwing leaves into the wind, and
S ome try to jump in a pile of red ones too.
G etting in trouble for messing up people's yards,
I t's really fun for everyone, and sometimes
V ery good to do.
I n the end it's late and we must go home,
N othing is better than a Thanksgiving dinner and
G iving thanks for this great day we had.

Johnny Tapia, Grade 6
Riverside Middle School

Halloween Night

The moon is glistening lighting up the town,
    telling children to come out and trick-or-treat.
Vampires, werewolves, Frankensteins, and many other ghouls,
    all of them are only children dressed in costumes and masks.
Gooey and sweet treats there are,
    vast amounts of them to go around all night.
Disgusting and nauseating goblins are everywhere,
    lurking through alleys and streets.
Witches flying all over the sky,
    injecting spells into the stormy night.
There is only one possibility,
    it must be Halloween night!

Justin Morris-Marano, Grade 6
Great Meadows Regional Middle School

Santa

S eems to be a very unique person
A fter climbing down the chimney he fills our stockings with goodies
N eatly he swallows delicious cookies
T akes time to deliver presents to us
A very elderly man gets the job done

Doug Reinisch, Grade 4
Springfield Township School

Emotions

Happy, sad, and mellow.
Mellow as in calm.
Happy as in joyful, and sad as in blue.
These are emotions
That come from me and you.
Some you may like
And some you may not.
These are emotions
That you feel through the day.
Happy when you wake up.
Mellow when you come to school.
Sad when you have to leave your friends.
This is all I'm trying to say.
We all have emotions
And feelings all through the day
Yes each one of us
And all through life.

Evan Collier, Grade 6
Harding Elementary School

Magnificent Moon

The sky holds numerous objects
That catch my eye
The sky holds the moon,
Clouds, stars,
   But most intriguing is the moon.
The moon, reflecting sunlight
Has a magical glow,
One the stars will never know.
I hope the moon will never go,
Will never leave our view.
I hope the moon will always stay,
Keep near me and you.
The moon is the enchanting gleam,
   In the heavens, like a gift from a god.
   I watched the moon as it nods,
   Agreeing with me,
   For this is my ode to the moon.

Taylor Hughes, Grade 6
Christa McAuliffe Middle School

Halloween

Spiders spin their webs and creep.
   Bats swoop down and sneak.

Owls fly in the night and whoooo.
   While ghosts scare and boooooo.

The moon up above will glow.
On dark, dark graveyards below.

On Halloween night.
You might get a fright.
BOO!!

Nick Zeliff, Grade 5
Central School

Halloween Craze

H ave a great time
A t the Halloween party
L ove all treats
L ots of people get dressed up
O h! That costume scared me!
W e all go to people's homes
E ating lots of candy;
E w! Their house looks haunted
N eed to go home now, it's almost midnight.

The moon is full; did you hear a howl?

Michelle Hsieh, Grade 5
St Rose of Lima Academy

Champions

Time is running out!
It is our ball
We have to make a score
to break the tie
5, 4, 3, 2
Then at the last second
We…
Score!
We win
We win
We win the championship!

Meredith Karback, Grade 4
Lincoln Park Elementary School

Nature

Flowers red and gold
lined down beside the sidewalk
looking beautiful

Birds most blue and red
chirping and flying up high
then come diving down

Trees the color green
bark climbing up the wide trunk
standing tall and strong

Audrey Somalwar, Grade 5
Bartle Elementary School

Slip, Promise, Shy

   Slip
Stumble, stagger, fall, fault,
To slip may cause a somersault.
   Promise
Intention, assurance, pledge, guarantee,
Make these promises to your employee.
   Shy
Throw, toss, hurl, pitch,
A wayward ball may land in a ditch.

Yuki Nakayama, Grade 5
Hillside Elementary School

The Twelfth of March

Under an indigo moon,
upon the twelfth of March,
unto the town we will march
over many a dune.

Upon the entrance to the town,
sat a picture of a clown
just above the gate,
and below it were words inscribed on slate:

"Under an indigo moon,
upon the twelfth of March,
we marched over the fountain
on the mountain and saw,
in the shape of a picture of a clown,
an obelisk." On its slate could be read:

'Under an indigo moon,
on the twelfth of March,
we marched to Rome,
and on its great dome
we read a slate that said…'
"That's all that could be read."
And no more on the subject is to be said.

Benjamin Hantho Smullyan, Grade 5
Hillside Elementary School

Children in My Eyes

See the children laughing,
We're thought to be rebellious and cruel,
But we aren't always naughty!
Mostly we are caring!
We love and laugh and play,
We accept those who are different,

See the children walk from church,
They smile from ear to ear,
They know they must be good and kind!
Mostly we let others in,
No wonder we're so diverse,
We love and care and know,

See the children playing,
Their group grows and grows,
Like their respect for each other,
When given the chance we donate money,
And toys and other things,
Out of and to charity,

See the children kind and joyous,
We're full of charity, love, and joy,
We're good people too!

Spencer Hess, Grade 6
Olson Middle School

Crunch!

It's autumn and I fell
CRUNCH!
Why me?
The wind howls and lifts me off my feet
I soon move into someone's yard
At least I'm not lonely
CRUNCH!
Again, I am the unlucky one
Now it is winter
I feel the bitter cold air and get buried in the snow
Will the cold ever end?
For weeks I lay here frozen
Finally I feel water, not snow
That means it's melting
The warmth is like my home
I have come a long way
But things change
Someone will take my place
As I leave this earth
I will always miss the crunch sound
But it will always be in my dreams

Francesca Zumpano, Grade 5
Little Falls School #1

The Scary Land of Below

Auburn branches sway in the twirling wind
Like tall grass in a storm.
Arms reaching far and wide
Catching the last glimpse of the summer sun
And the fall tree stands proud and lush
It whispers to the leaves, "Hold on tightly. Don't be in a rush."
The sky is a zebra of fuchsia and azure
Misty clouds fill the horizon as the daylight starts to die.
And the fall tree stands proud and lush
It whispers to the leaves, "Hold on tightly. Don't be in a rush."
When cool air begins to stir
Like hungry witches around their cauldron,
Fuzzy animals scurry to hibernate
And the fall tree stands proud and lush
It whispers to the leaves, "Hold on tightly. Don't be in a rush."
But when the first frost comes,
The tree knows what has to be done.
It whispers to the leaves, "Relax and let go. The time has come."
And all the stained glass leaves of crimson, iridescent, and gold
Swiftly swooping silently to land softly on the sheer, silk blanket
To the scary land of below.

Sabrina Schrader, Grade 5
Hopewell Elementary School

The Night of Halloween

Halloween, Halloween, oh what a night
Trick or Treat, Trick or Treat, all through the night
The fantasy of Halloween is enough to make you scream
But do not fear Halloween is not coming near

Alex Tsemberis, Grade 5
Hillside Elementary School

Mmm Food Time

T hinking of all the food
H as put me in a good mood.
A s soon as my mom started cooking,
N othing ever looks disgusting.
K eep thinking of the rest of the day,
S o your hunger can finally go away.
G ood looking desserts like
I ce cream and pie, and
V ibrant flowers set up high.
I 'm finally in my seat, and
N ow it's time to eat. I'm
G rateful for Thanksgiving Day and I wish, you could stay.

Nicole Lallo, Grade 6
Riverside Middle School

Thanksgiving Feast

T hanksgiving is a great time for living.
H ave an awesome time with friends and family.
A pple pie, pumpkin pie, oh what a good time!
N ever say never, eat all you want.
K illing turkeys is not nice but it's delicious with rice.
S even turkeys said Kenzee, "Yum, yum, yum!"
G obble, gobble, gravy is good.
I ncredible it is to bake turkey as a cake.
V ery talented, as my aunt makes a turkey costume.
I love turkey a lot better than jerky.
N ever eat too much you don't want to throw up.
G obble, gobble, wobble, wobble.

Kenzee Hudson, Grade 6
Riverside Middle School

Dance

Ballet, jazz, hip-hop, and tap
Pirouettes, double lindies, Russian turns, and Cincinnatis
Grand Jeté, shorty George, jazz square, and Maxiford
Recitals, costumes, music, and friends
Fun, fun for everyone

Talent, patience, attitude, and enjoyment
Watch us leap across the stage
Dance recitals are all the rage
Cameras, roses, flowers, and pictures
Fun, fun, for everyone

Jeté Flinn, Grade 6
St Mary School

Victims and Heroes

Victims and heroes died on 9/11 and everyone was sad.
Some people lost the only families they had.
Unfortunately, the people that caused the terror did not feel bad.

People cried as they came together to help clear the land.
Terrorists thought they had the upper hand.
But, were they surprised when together as a nation we did stand.

Lauren Tresente, Grade 6
Township of Ocean Intermediate School

Cheese

Stinky, gross
Cut, chew, package
I will never eat it!
Milk
Talia Hoffmann, Grade 4
Ethel M Burke Elementary School

Homework

The sky is so blue,
and apples are so red.
I need to get my homework done,
Before I go to bed!
Angy Kim, Grade 5
Bartle Elementary School

My Sister

My sister is in college
Because she has a lot of knowledge.
She is oh so smart
And she is tucked in my heart
Sophie Claman, Grade 5
Hillside Elementary School

Poet

P eople's
O utrageous
E motional
T estimonies
Terrell Yaya-Nash, Grade 5
Hillside Elementary School

Pizza

Firey, flavorful
tossing, splattering, baking
super taste bud excitement
Italian
Max Broggi-Sumner, Grade 5
Bartle Elementary School

Sky

Blue, cool
Float, drift, wing
The sky is everlasting air
Soar!
Alexa Stetser, Grade 4
Ethel M Burke Elementary School

Clouds

Gray, white
Rainy, small, big
Fluffy, dirty, smelly, wispy
Clouds are really cool.
Conor Osborne, Grade 4
Ethel M Burke Elementary School

What Comes Out at Nighttime

At nighttime ghosts and ghouls come out,
Causing little kids to shriek and shout!
Their sharp, long fangs and eerie eyes,
Under your bed is where that monster lies!
Teeth and jaws,
Paws and claws,
Coming out of your closet,
Kids screaming *"Aaaaaaaaaaaaaaah!"* in a frenzied fit!
Mom rushes in and the monster scoots away,
Leaving the unfortunate kid with nothing left to say,
The kid explains,
Mom complains,
When mom leaves the child STOMP…STOMP…STOMP…they're alone again indeed,
Leaving the kid in their bed with nothing left to do but plead.
The monster prowls around the shadowy room,
Under the dim light, shining in from the moon,
It circles, it lurks, it swarms,
The kid can only, sobbingly warn!
At nighttime ghosts and ghouls come out,
Causing little kids to shriek and shout!
How do I know this? You see…That scared little kid happens to be me!
Marisa Salvia, Grade 6
Great Meadows Regional Middle School

It's the Best Time of the Year

T hanksgiving is a time to feast.
H olidays are celebrated at a place called Maggiano's.
A ll stuff themselves with ham and turkey, and Mom says, "Oh, I am so stuffed!"
N icole is excited to see her family.
K ids are acting like crazy people after dessert.
S oon it will be time to leave.
G iving thanks is all about this time of year.
I love spending time with my family. I am
V ery happy to have quality time with them!
I know I am having a blast tonight!
N ow, it is almost time to leave.
G oing home is the worst time of this holiday.

Nicole Evans, Grade 6
Riverside Middle School

A Masterpiece

The sky grabs its paintbrush and all of its paints
So that it can draw our graceful flickering Fall.
The sky seizes its paintbrush and plunges it into a colossal palette
Overflowing with blushing carmines, shimmering saffrons,
Animated apricots and charming chocolates.
The sky snatches its paintbrush and loads it full of color
Then lobs it at the chartreuse tree and thus autumn begins.
The sky reaches for its paintbrush but lets its arm fall to its side
It sits there, sighing as Fall carries on.
The sky grabs its paintbrush and one of its paints
It scoops up a load then again lobs it toward Earth like a bullet from a gun.
The snowball hits the flaming trees,
And thus autumn ends.
Liv Olcott, Grade 5
Hopewell Elementary School

Robert LaSalle

Robert LaSalle wanted to sail
so he got his crew and decided to bail.
Deep in the ocean with a crew of three
he made it to his destination and shouted with glee.
They slept outside for quite some time
and told stories about their childhood lives.
Robert LaSalle was first to speak
he was born in 1669
and decided to become an adventurer
by the time he was nine.
On the way back to his homeland
Robert LaSalle died.
People looked up to him
and so have I.

Pharoh Allah, Grade 5
Roosevelt Elementary School

Where Are My Gifts?

I'm searching and searching under the tree.
But I don't see a gift for me.
I looked on the tags and inside the bags.
Maybe in the attic? Lets go see.
Not in the attic. Maybe in the basement?
I'm beginning to get fumb-ly.
It's not in the basement either.
I went to my mother and to my brothers
And they gave a weak chuckle.
"Is there anything for me?" I said with a burst.
"Heh. We forgot about you honey
because you were the worst."
So I walked away slowly
'Cause now my heart hurts.

Ky'Oanna Lee, Grade 5
Zane North Elementary School

My Shadow I See

The sun goes down behind the sea I see
While the wind goes through my skin
The cold breeze and the silence echoes cold to me
I see nothing else than my shadow
My shadow I see
My shadow I see glowing through the sea
And while all that happens
I see my shadow and it reminds me
Of all the things I have done, bad or good
I know I've learned something
Even if I don't realize it
It's only my shadow
My shadow
My shadow that I see glowing through the sea

Genesis Cintron, Grade 6
Garfield Middle School

The Day the U.S. Stood Still

America, America, the beautiful sound
What an amazing country to be found
But then one September morning,
The U.S. stood still
Firefighters climbing up that hill,
Trying to help others will
We all tried to help a nation attacked
The day the U.S. stood still

My country so brave in so much of us all
Those two tall buildings standing tall
But the day that one great tragedy occurred
The day the U.S. stood still

Come brave ones like you and me
To help our nation's terrible catastrophe
Though the U.S. stood still, we stood tall
Hoping for peace, love, for one and all
Though the nation was hurt from those terrible people
We still have peace in our hearts, and we stand so tall
Lives were lost but our men and women made the call
To help a nation seeking help,
The day the U.S.A. stood still.

Evan Maccia, Grade 6
Township of Ocean Intermediate School

The Diamond in the Sky

The moon is like a ball of light
    That keeps the dark at bay
        The moon gazes down at all of us and sends its light our way

The moon is like a diamond in a tar pit
    He's white and yellow and gray
        The moon loves to show himself
            He shines all night and day

Of course the moon loves to frolic
    He's always ready to play
        The dark gray clouds like to take him hostage
            They like to cloak him away

When the moon is on the job
    He wears a jolly face
        The moon's grand face is oh so bright
            It lights up the whole place!

Some say the moon is made of cheese
    But I don't think that's true
        Such a splendid sight to see at night
            And that's why I love you!

Christopher Murphy, Grade 6
Christa McAuliffe Middle School

Thanksgiving Is a Time for Family!

T hanksgiving is a time for family to be together.
H ow does Thanksgiving bring family together?
A ll the cousins, aunts and uncles.
N othing better than family all around.
K ezia, Judson, Debbie, and Larisse are having fun.
S miling and waiting for dinner to come.
G iving thanks to the Lord.
I love the food.
" **V** ery good turkey," I said to my mom.
I 'll play in the leaves, then jump as they crunch into little pieces
    that are faster than a train.
N othing but family is surrounding my every corner.
G iving the gift of family is excellent.

Kezia De Souza, Grade 6
Riverside Middle School

Inside the House on Thanksgiving

T urkey is baking in the oven
H am is inside it too.
A nd don't forget the sweet potatoes, because
N ever can we eat pumpkin pie yet. Hunters
K ill that poor turkey for us to eat.
S itting there waiting for that "Beep, beep, beep."
G ive the pots to the person next to me, while we
I nvite family members to eat…with us.
V ery warm is it in the kitchen,
    but it smells as good as the food we are about to eat.
I ce cream is delicious after dinner, "Yum!"
N obody left a piece of pumpkin pie for me, but
G iving thanks is the best part of all.

Haylee Loveland, Grade 6
Riverside Middle School

Halloween

H appy you can go trick or treating
A lot of delicious sweets
L ots of scary decorations
L aughable costumes
O ffering candy to little children
W itches, goblins, ghosts and spooky graveyards
E xciting costumes to wear and see
E mpty candy wrappers in the garbage
N oises that are eerie and creepy

Kalyna Leshchuk, Grade 5
St Rose of Lima Academy

Hero/Villain

Hero
Strong, fast
Flying, fighting, saving
Protective, powerful, clever, destructive
Destroying, flying, fighting,
Fast, smart
Villain

Izac Cruz, Grade 4
Katharine D Malone Elementary School

War Song

Oh my! How horrid, how bad.
So horrible, it makes me sad.
So many dead.
So many hurt.
So many peoples' heads,
Feel like they've been stuffed in dirt.
But why?
For what?
Can't treaties and agreements ever be enough?
Why?
Why must I sing this war song?

Why?

Maya Jenkins, Grade 5
Hillside Elementary School

My Teddy Bear

Your brown fur that's been worn out from so many hugs
Your red bow that's been torn and sewn back on so many times
Now it's being held on by a headband
8 years ago she was still with us,
But I have you to remind me she's still here.

She gave you to me,
I've loved you ever since and I'll never stop.
I can't go a night without holding you.
I can still hear her voice as I lay on you telling you about my day.
You're the only thing I have left of her.

And I called her, "Mommom."

Michaela Thomas, Grade 6
Buckshutem Road Elementary School

Barracuda

It looks like a small log.
It sounds like "shccaaa."
It feels like many little knives.
It smells like blood.
It tastes like fish.
    Now
        that's
           a
             Barracuda!

Delano Hendrix, Grade 4
Dr. Martin Luther King Jr. School Complex

Race Car

If I were a race car,
I'd zoom down the track and into First Place!
I'd drive quickly to the pit stop and back to the track!
My eyes would be the windshield,
My arms would be the doors,
My feet would be the tires, and
My nose would be the hood!

Angel Holguin, Grade 5
Bartle Elementary School

If I Were a Floor
If I were a floor,
I would hold
everything up

I would be strong,
but sad —
to always
be stepped on,
to never be paid
any attention

I would moan,
and hurt,
but I still would
stand strong,
holding everything up.
Holly Beske, Grade 4
Village School

New School
School is good,
well it could,
but this one is great
and not just because no one is late.
This school is new and all
but everyone is having a ball.
We play four square
with everyone aware
that Shannon and I are new.
The food is fine,
and the sixth grade is being kind.
We feel like we have been here a long time.
We were welcome when we stood on line.
So far it is better than my old school.
That's why it's so cool!
Katianne Dunay, Grade 6
St Mary's School

My Lost Puppy
I lost my puppy
and don't know where he went.
I looked at the funky, punky hotel
and I checked by my funky monkey's cage.
I had a bad slip
from my funky monkey's banana
on my downstair's floor.
So I looked in the cookie store,
found him eating cookies
in the flooky jar.
He was in it
but got stuck
so we called my Uncle Flooky
and my Aunt Peggie
who helped get him out.
Kathleen Corzo, Grade 5
Roosevelt Elementary School

Cocoa
Hopping all around,
She loves to jump everywhere.
Sniffing the flowers,
They smell good to her.
Her name is Cocoa,
She likes to bite paper.
I love Cocoa!
Hannah Strickland, Grade 5
Hillside Elementary School

Jumping and Tumbling
Standing in the middle of the mat
Stretched out and ready to go
The music starts
I do a back handspring,
Then a backbend kick over,
Finally a handstand flip over,
And the 1st place prize!
Dominique Coiro, Grade 4
Lincoln Park Elementary School

The Big Backstroke Race
There I go,
Pushing off the wall.
This is the backstroke race,
My best stroke.
Legs kicking,
White water behind me,
I know I can win.
Gregory Pise, Grade 4
Lincoln Park Elementary School

Greece
What a place to be.
Nice people.
Great oceans.
Awesome seafood.
If you're lucky you can go surfing.
Greece, what did I say?
It's the place to be!
George Riginos, Grade 5
Frances DeMasi Elementary School

Feelings!
I feel great to be in the race
I can feel the wind blowing on my face…
I also feel excited to race for a trophy
I can't explain how I feel
I am excited because I get lots of food
I never felt like this before
This is the best time of my life…
Jaison Mendez, Grade 5
Roosevelt Elementary School

NyAsia
N utty
Y oung
A nxious
S low
I ntelligent
A nnoying
NyAsia McMillan-Ruffin, Grade 5
Mckinley Community School

Can You Imagine What's Up There?
Can you imagine what's up there?
Can you imagine what's in space?
Is something behind suns or stars?
Are there some aliens on Mars?
We will continue to wonder, you see
For it yet remains a mystery.
Michael Pisciotta, Grade 5
Hillside Elementary School

God's Wild Pets
Hungry otters eating fish
Passed away piggies on our dish
Kangaroos jumping up and down
Slithering snakes on the ground
I see crabs on vacation
All of the animals are part of God's creation
Nicholas Leonchuck, Grade 5
St Mary School

Santa
Santa, Santa come my way
I know you have a heavy sleigh.
Santa, Santa come and rest
My delicious cookies are the best.
Santa, Santa job well done
I know you had a lot of fun!
Madison DeSantis, Grade 4
Ethel M Burke Elementary School

Kicking into a Goal!
Running across the field.
Sweat on my face.
The ball is coming my way.
Blood racing through my body.
I kick as hard as I can.
I kick it right into the goal.
Chiara Totoli, Grade 4
Lincoln Park Elementary School

Life
Love, family
Mom, Dad, Richie
Playing games is the best
Energy.
Julia Paglia, Grade 4
Ethel M Burke Elementary School

Puppies

Puppies are playful and fun,
They bring joy to everyone,
They love to roll and tumble,
Sometimes they even stumble
Puppies always want to eat,
It seems that they love meat
In the day,
They want to play,
But at night,
They seem to get a fright
About a ghost or two,
Many do
And then they'll turn to you,
(You'll know what to do)
You'll read them a story,
About happiness and glory
Then you will tuck them in bed
And give them a kiss on the head.
Mary Carolonza, Grade 4
St James School

First Love

First love is a very special time
Love is more a game,
than it is a rhyme

Love can be found
in the toughest of times,
Love is the key,
to all of life's crimes

Cry, cry, cry,
Feelings not divine
included in the package,
is sorrow on the climb

Love, you should cherish
Love never lies,
Love is the point,
Passion never dies!
Katalina Pieger, Grade 5
Old Turnpike School

A Thing of Amazement

I run
For the spring board
And jump
Hoping I make it.
I flip off the vault
Land on bars,
Swing off,
Cartwheel off the beam,
Do a front handspring
And stick it.
Lily Lombardi, Grade 4
Lincoln Park Elementary School

Music in My House

Music in my house surrounds me
Almost every day
Piano, guitar, drums and cello,
That is what we play.

One brother works intensely,
His fingers fly so fast,
He plays no matter the time of day,
And makes the music last.

Just climb the stairs so softly,
And you might hear the sounds
Of cello strings singing out
A song you're glad you've found.

I rush into the house each day,
And grab my sticks to play away,
A joyful, noisy rhythmic power,
My hands could play for endless hours!
Maya Stepansky, Grade 5
Hillside Elementary School

Picture

A picture is…
A flash in time,
When time stops
So you can remember,
What it was like,
In that picture.

So still in its frame
So we can see,
Our smiling faces
Looking at me.

The lens I hold in my hands
Breaks away time,
For a second's hand
It captures the moment,
Flashing away,
The magical camera
I hold in my hands.
Madisen Siegel, Grade 5
Richard E Byrd Elementary School

How I Got Home

Hitting then running to first base
Excitement and the wind hitting my face
Stealing 2nd base hearing the ump yell
He yells out, "Safe" I know I did well
Next batter bunts the ball through the yard
Beat out the throw while I slide real hard
One more batter with a great rip
Running to home, completing my trip.
Austin Sultzbach, Grade 5
Catherine A Dwyer Elementary School

I'm Worried

What is it?
What's the answer?
I know this answer
I studied so hard
Why don't I know it?
I feel my heart pounding
Like a big heavy drum
I'm starting to sweat
All this pressure and
I'm only in fourth grade
I suddenly remember
I hope I am right
Here you go
I've tried my best
Test back already?
I can't believe it
Like a miracle, 100% on my science test
I'm so proud of myself
Next time I'll try not to worry
Alyssa Suvino, Grade 4
Little Falls School #3

Not My Fault

My dog ate it
Stranger came to take it
Fell in the shredder
Toilet, toaster or the blender
Left it at school
I'm too cool
Was too busy
It attacked my friend Lizzy
Might have grown legs
It laid eggs
Got all wet
I got upset
Broke my arms
Was raiding farms
Was in a long coma
Guess I should have told ya
Wait —
We had no homework?
Nathan Roberts, Grade 5
Frances DeMasi Elementary School

A New Day Awaits

Twilight is here,
The stars are shining,
A new moon is near,
All lights are combining.

An eclipse will be tonight,
There is little light abound,
In the far distance, see the beautiful sight,
As dawn is breaking around.
Gabrielle Harrison, Grade 5
Durban Avenue Elementary School

Happiness

Happiness looks like presents on Christmas morning;
It sounds like the last bell for dismissal;
It smells like fresh cinnamon buns;
It feels like my fluffy cat purring on my lap;
It tastes like hot chocolate on a cold winter day.

Erika Orellana, Grade 5
Perth Amboy Catholic Upper Grades School

Stars

Stars feel like a whole other dimension.
It sounds like wands waving.
Stars, stars are what make it all worth while.
It's sparkly and bright to make your day a delight.
Stars are one in a million.

Desire Dortrait, Grade 6
Perth Amboy Catholic Upper Grades School

Tree

One single tree
In a forest of trees
A tree of life

Birds live here
Bugs live here
Ants live here
Mice live here

One single tree
In a forest of trees
A tree of life

Then came a group of workmen
Sawed the tree down
The forest shudders

No birds live here
No bugs live here
No ants live here
No mice lives here

One single tree
In a forest of trees
A tree no more

Tara Liu, Grade 6
Hartford School

My Skateboard

Knee pads and a helmet
Shoulder pads and my skateboard
Sleek and so cool
Riding my skateboard
I feel the wind on my face
Going faster and faster
Freedom on my skateboard

Edwin Cruz, Grade 4
Marie Durand Elementary School

A Silly Salmon Story

A salmon swims solemnly up the stream
Its mother's caught and gone
The water boils and begins to steam
Anger fills the fish and pond

"Oh why, oh why has my mother left?"
The son calls to all the fish
But because of this water's huge depth
No one hears him a miss

So off in search of his mother he goes
Rushing down the waves
He bumps his head and begins to doze
Twirling through a misty maze

Through his nightmares he says the same,
"Mama! Oh Mama, you're missing!"
In the fish's head lights a flame
and the salmon starts wishing

His wish is finally obeyed
As his mother comes into view
"Why are you so afraid?
I said I'd come right back to you."

Rachel Lyons, Grade 6
Paradise Knoll Elementary School

Wind Woman

Once the Wind Woman
was a caring breeze,
that cradled seeds
over the whole world.

Once she was a harsh hurricane
destroying,
everything
in her path.

Now, the Wind Woman winds
through limbs of the
Old Oak.
As a rotting branch falls
THUMP!
She whistles on
and on.

Until,
she stopped.
The Wind Woman
is now only
a memory,
a tragic memory.

Maddie Strouse, Grade 4
Village School

Apples
Apples are delish.
They are sweet and sour.
Apples are nutrish.
Matthew Notaro, Grade 4
St Jerome School

Changing Trees
The trees are now clean
Soon they will be white as snow
Then it melts away
Eamon Logue, Grade 6
Lounsberry Hollow Middle School

Yoffi
Yoffi is my dog.
He likes to lick my dad's feet.
He makes me have fun.
Danielle Sklar, Grade 5
Hillside Elementary School

White with Love
White spotted new deer
The snow rabbits all in white
We cuddle with Love
Julia Blando, Grade 4
Richard E Byrd Elementary School

Trees Help Us Breathe
The nice big thick trees
give us oxygen to breathe
can't live without trees
Matt Smith, Grade 4
Catherine A Dwyer Elementary School

Rain
Rain is falling down
Put your umbrella up now
lightning is striking
Ava Holtzer, Grade 4
Catherine A Dwyer Elementary School

The Friend
My best friend and I.
Sitting on a wooden bench.
Talking together.
Lila Taylor, Grade 5
Hillside Elementary School

Flowers
Flowers are pretty
There is different colors, cool
They have many shapes
Victoria Aspiazu, Grade 4
Catherine A Dwyer Elementary School

Enchanted Autumn
On a motionless fall night the trees stand tall
With the whispering moon from afar
Until the golden, saffron sun awakes from his rest
And the sapphire sky embraces the light.
The leaves brag about their glistening colors.
They dress in beanies and mittens of scarlet, crimson, and gold.
They show off their dances while rustling and playing, "Hold-on-Tight."
No match for the wind, they parachute
down, down, down, one by one
to be tickled by metal rakes.
The trees are now naked and
Birds' nests once hidden are now in plain sight.
The bare branches are grasping the last sunset of colors
Primrose, infrared, teal, salmon and violet —
Painting brilliant rainbows above.
The flickering colors take their last breath and
The swirling, sweeping, swooshing wind closes the day
The night creeps in as quiet as a mouse and says,
"Autumn has passed and Winter has come."
Kelly Schorr, Grade 5
Hopewell Elementary School

A Work of Art
Autumn is a work of art, the trees are where it starts
With wonderful, whirling, wispy leaves
Transforming from emerald to vibrant golds
Then slowly turning into a dull hazelnut
The sign that autumn is here.
Autumn is a work of art, the howling wind soars in next
Pulling and prying perfect leaves off the trees
For them to dance, swoop and swirl
Slowly down onto an enormous green carpet of grass
Like a bird gliding gracefully down onto a tree.
Autumn is a work of art,
Next comes the amazing animals. Squirrels silently gathering acorns
To put in their tiny holes. Bears preparing for hibernation
And the cold harsh winters, like busy beavers building their brilliant nests.
Autumn is a work of art, now the harvest jumps in.
It is an explosion of various fruits and vegetables
Autumn is a work of art, soon it gets colder and colder.
Autumn is over and winter creeps in.
Eliza Bell, Grade 5
Hopewell Elementary School

The Lemon's Friend, the Lime
On the outside, you look like a green, rolling hill on a grassy plain.
You feel like clay just taken out from the earth.
When I peel you, you sound like the crackling of fire in a fireplace.
When I slice you, you sound like a light, trickling waterfall by a forest trail.
Inside you look like the rays of a sun on a hot, summer day.
You feel like the soft tickle of grass on the bottom of my feet.
You smell like freshly cut grass.
You taste like a Sour Patch candy, just made.
Tell me Lime, don't you ever get tired of acting so sour?
Kami Beckford, Grade 5
Roosevelt Elementary School

Cake

There once was a cat named Jake
He liked to eat cake
One day this cat
Got very fat
And didn't eat for his sake

Simon Will, Grade 5
Hillside Elementary School

The Great Big Fall

There once was a boy who played baseball
He made a great catch by the stone wall
All the fans really cheered
As the other team sneered
Just before he had the great big fall

Steffan Peterson, Grade 4
St Mary's School

Ocean

O pen space
C lam shells
E njoyment of the sea
A tlantic
N ature all around

Rachel Goldman, Grade 5
Catherine A Dwyer Elementary School

My Favorite Friends

My favorite friends comfort me a lot,
They help me with homework on the spot
Sometimes they make me mad,
Forgive, forget, don't be sad.
We are always as tight as a knot!

Skye Stripeikis, Grade 4
St Mary's School

Football

Football is a sport that I enjoy
It is a game that will bring fans joy
Hut one, two, down set hike
Pick your team, get so psyched,
A fun game for a girl or a boy.

William Syslo, Grade 4
St Mary's School

Smooth Rock

Smooth rock
Golden smooth rock
A nice texture to feel
As sparkly as a crystal
Earth rock

Ben Hirthler, Grade 4
Springfield Township School

Family Time

T hanks for the good food. I am
H appy when I am around my family. It's
A wesome to spend time with my lovely family.
" **N** ini was running like a wild turkey," said Ahmir.
" **K** icking and Screaming" is the movie we watch every Thanksgiving.
S ometimes the turkey is dry.
G iving great stories at the dinner table is cool.
I n the fall my cousin and I play in the leaves, then go inside when dinner is done.
V ictoria cooks a good turkey.
I n the house we play lots of board games.
N obody says "No" to my banana pudding.
G ravy with mashed potatoes is good too.

Ahmir Palmer, Grade 6
Riverside Middle School

My Family

T hanks to my family for all they do for me.
H appy are the gifts we receive.
A unt Sue gave me a Wii and asked, "What game do you want?"
N eat and tidy is the house for our guests to enjoy, so Mom will not scream.
K ind is my family.
S traighten up for the party, because gifts come next. I am
G rateful for my gifts.
I love when family comes and stays over.
V ibrant people I share the holidays with.
I love my family so much.
N ever will I forget this day.
G iving thanks to my family is what it's all about.

Stacey Levy, Grade 6
Riverside Middle School

How to Make a Little Sister

Take 5 pounds of love, 3 cups of brattiness, and a tsp. of klutziness.
Put all the ingredients in a shiny bowl.
Blend with a hand blender until bratty.
Pour the mixture into a small, cute pan.
Cook in an Easy-Bake oven at 200 degrees until she hits you.
You can tell it's done when she calls you names.
Let cook until she acts like you.
Sprinkle on a head full of hair and rosy, red cheeks that turn red when she smiles.
Cut and serve in a cute little outfit.
Taste and smooth her in your arm.
For the best result, kiss and love for all eternity.

Skyler VanDiver, Grade 5
Roosevelt Elementary School

Reading

R idiculous when it comes to "Falling Up"
E xciting when reading "The Spiderwick Chronicles"
A mazing authors like Holly Black, Tony DiTerlizzi, and Shel Silverstein
D iTerlizzi and Black co-authored "The Spiderwick Chronicles"
I believe that Shel Silverstein was the author of "Falling Up"
N ow "The Ravenmaster's Secret" is a good book too
G oodness, aren't almost all books great

Elizabeth Gleason, Grade 6
Cinnaminson Middle School

I Don't Understand
What I don't understand is…
Why boys wear skinny jeans,
Why dinner is at night,
Why our flag has red, not orange stripes

What I really don't understand is…
Why we have war,
Why we are so unkind to the environment,
Why snow is cold,
Why flowers are all different colors

What I do understand is….
Why leaves change colors,
Why girls are cooler than guys,
Why I love to read
Why people love music
Ashley Salamone, Grade 6
Lounsberry Hollow Middle School

I Don't Understand
I don't understand…
    why dogs are man's best friend
    why we don't believe in aliens
    why animals can't talk

But most of all…
    why people steal
    why it matters if you're black or white
    why we litter
    why friends become enemies

What I understand is…
    why Earth revolves
    why we need close friends
    why we forgive
    why we need to learn from our mistakes
Harley-Nicole Rubenacker, Grade 6
Lounsberry Hollow Middle School

This Is Mine
This is my baseball mitt
I love that mitt
It's just the right size
When I play with it

This is my baseball mitt
My dad gave it to me
I spilled water on it
The color changed look you can see

This is my baseball mitt
I catch fly balls
They go real high
I catch them all
Lucas "Lucky" Trevor, Grade 5
Bartle Elementary School

The Toy Train
I bounded down the stairs
On wonderful Christmas Day
And on some chairs
My presents lay

I took one down
And shook it too
It made a thump sound
And I had no clue

I opened it up
And took a small peek
Lying there in a box
It's a toy train that I seek

I put it together
and turned the train on
I loved it very much
And played with it
'Til the day was gone.
Sam Schoch, Grade 5
Zane North Elementary School

Moon Man
The face on the
MOON
Beamed at me.
Like he was saying, Hello, Greetings from
SPACE.
The moon man is a commander
Of every single
STAR.
The bad thing is that the
CLOUDS
Control the sight of our
MAGNIFICENT
Earth.
The man on the moon tells
EVERYONE
What to do.
He is the
RULER
Of everyone and
EVERYTHING.
Leszek Gronowski, Grade 6
Christa McAuliffe Middle School

Falling for Fall
I like fall very much.
It's when all the leaves change colors.
The football season finally begins.
It also means Halloween is coming.
We gain one hour of sleep.
This is why I like the fall.
Zachary Steiner, Grade 6
St Mary's School

The Forest
The wind — it whispers
to the trees.
The bubbling brook
just laughs at me.
The birds — they sing
their pretty song
inviting me
to come along.
The crow just croaks
unhappily;
the wind-blown grasses
bow to me.
The wary rabbit
stares at me,
unlike the friendly
bumblebee.

Of all the places,
big and small,
the forest is
the best of all.
Maura Cahill, Grade 6
St Dominic School

Shots
Scared,
    shivering.
I'm going to the doctor,
                to get a *shot*.
Feeling,
    trapped.
Like an animal, surrounded by,
    hunters.
Frightened, when the *image*,
    of a *needle*,
        appears on my,
            brain.
The image, thumps on my *heart*.
The *tears*,
    that I cry,
        cannot be taken back.
The voice in my head,
        keeps saying,
Shots,   Shots.
That's all I think about,
    Shots.
Abigail Merton, Grade 5
Knollwood Elementary School

My Pet Rats
Active rascals
Sniff and sniff
Playfully scamper
Nocturnal noises
Mackenzie Miller, Grade 5
Catherine A Dwyer Elementary School

A Lemon

On the outside, you look like a ball of fire.
You feel like the roughness of asphalt.
When I slice you, you sound like ripping paper.
Inside you look like the inside of an orange.
You feel just like you were a flower petal.
You smell like sweet raspberries.
You taste like sour gum.
Tell me, how do you like to be sliced?

Michael D'Emilio, Grade 5
Roosevelt Elementary School

Winter

The snowflakes drop and the snow feels soft.
I wish the snow piles would let me climb to the top.

So when I'm done outside I sit by the fire.
Then I go to sleep, I'm so tired.

When I wake up I do it all again,
And I love to go outside in the snow and rest my head.

Evette Oyola, Grade 5
Hillside Elementary School

The Lonely and Friendless Mouse

In the small and quiet house
sat the little lonely mouse.
He may have been quite very nice
yet he did not like other mice.
The little thing attempted wiggling his tail
yet all of his tries ended in deep fail.
He tried and tried and tried some more but —
without friends, life's such a bore.

Simone Rembert, Grade 5
Hillside Elementary School

I Have a Passion for Singing

When I get on the stage,
I'm free to do anything I put my mind to do.
Sing, dance, cartwheels, handsprings, anything.
And when I'm sad I sing alto,
And when I'm happy, I sing soprano.
Singing,
It's a great way to show my feelings.

Mckenzie Stephens, Grade 5
Hillside Elementary School

Love

Love looks like a beautiful wedding
    dress that was just bought out of the store;
It sounds like a flock of hummingbirds singing
    on a beautiful sunny morning;
It smells like melted chocolate in a warm pot in your home;
It feels like a comforting hug that will never end;
It tastes like a fresh baked chocolate cookie from the oven.

Vanessa Suriel, Grade 5
Perth Amboy Catholic Upper Grades School

Christmas

I go to get my Christmas tree,
While my mom goes on a shopping spree.

Santa goes to get my presents,
He goes down my smoking vents.

I sneak downstairs in the middle of the night,
While my parents were in a fight.

It is December,
What a Christmas to remember.

Matthew Comini, Grade 5
Hillside Elementary School

A Dream of Snow

The night was cold, the moon was bright,
And in my eyes there was a light.

I had a hope, I had a dream,
That in the morning it would seem,

That clouds would let loose their silver treasure,
The heaps of snow would be beyond measure.

When I woke up, I found it was true,
The snow was falling: white, against the blue.

Katie Murphy, Grade 5
Hillside Elementary School

A Recipe for a Fire Drill

Take a drill, fire, an alarm, sensors, a pot, a bowl, and a spoon.
Put the drill in, then add the fire in a pot.
Stir with a spoon until all the lamps are gone and it will be red.
Pour it in a bowl and mix it well.
Bake it in the oven at 360 degrees until it is hard as rock.
You can tell its done when it starts to shape into an alarm.
Let it cook until a minute has past.
Sprinkle on a little bit of sensors.
Slice it and serve it to the school.
It tastes bad because you cannot eat it.
"Warning! YOU CANNOT EAT IT OR YOU WILL DIE."

Sandra Escobar, Grade 5
Roosevelt Elementary School

Copier

If I were a copier,
I'd print all the things people put into me.
My fingers would be the buttons.
My eyes would be the screen blinking letters on my eyes.
I would not copy what I do not like.
I would spit out the papers,
and that would be my mouth.

If only I were a copier!

Kevin O'Brien, Grade 5
Bartle Elementary School

Lost

Where did I go?
Am I home?
It feels like home.
But it is not.
Where am I?
It's nowhere I know.
Where did I go?
I'm not home.
A mystery.
The answer I will never know.
Where did I go?
I do not know.
Is this a fantasy?
Is this real?
Am I lost?
This is crazy.
I'm imagining.
Yes that's it!
My imagination.
Raymond Fry, Grade 6
Robert Morris Public School

Ireland

I am from beautiful, green Ireland
where leprechauns hide their gold
at the end of the rainbow.

I am from beautiful, green Ireland
where clovers are planted for luck,
and for hope to all the people.

I am from beautiful, green Ireland
where people have fun
dancing the Irish Jig.

I am from beautiful, green Ireland
where bakeries cook Irish Soda Bread,
the most delicious thing in the world!

I am from beautiful, green Ireland
where the land is beautiful
end to end!
Noah Callahan, Grade 5
Bartle Elementary School

Autumn Nature

I step outside
I inhale the fresh chilled air
Crunch, crunch goes the fallen leaves
Beneath the rubber soles of my shoes
I listen to the chirp of birds
I watch the rainbow colored leaves
Shimmer in the golden sunlight
All is still…and I am happy
Na'eem Ghee, Grade 5
Bartle Elementary School

My Mommy

My mommy is special
She is very, very pretty
She loves me very much
And she is so witty

Mom loves me no matter what
Even when I get in trouble
I know I can count on her
She is always there on the double

My mom loves to cook
She lets me share her measuring cups
As long as I will promise
To always help her clean up.

My mother and I like to cuddle
And be close like two bugs in a rug.
We love spending time time together
While drinking hot chocolate in a mug!
Sierra Flores, Grade 4
Marie Durand Elementary School

Wolves

Among tall trees
And growing fern
Racing through meadows
Wading through shallow creeks
Are wolves

On dark nights they gather
Few in number
But strong
Dark as night
Silver gray like the moon
Lifting their heads
To sky

Among tall trees
And growing fern
Racing through meadows
Wading through shallow creeks
Are wolves
Catherine Hodgson, Grade 5
Village School

Spring Time

The birds are singing
The flowers are in bloom
The sun is shining
The wide open spaces give you all the room.
The butterflies are flying
The bees are buzzing around
I am really trying
To make a springtime sound
Loren Donnelly, Grade 4
St James School

This Hand

This is a hand
That can be seen
Nail polish is
Bright and shiny.
Yes, this hand
Is germ free.
No stitches, no scars.
Does it have control
Over me?
Jenna Iachetti, Grade 6
Great Meadows Regional Middle School

Football

F amily game day
O ut come the tailgate snacks
O utstanding defense
T ime to put our jerseys on
B rowns are going to bring it
A rizona Cardinals are fantastic
L ions scored a touchdown
L eaving the party after cheering too much
Dominick Inzitari, Grade 5
St Rose of Lima Academy

Iditarod Racer

When I was in
the brutal Iditarod race,
I was trying to imagine
a happy place.
My hands were freezing
my toes were numb.
But all was well
when the race was done.
Zion Perry, Grade 5
Roosevelt Elementary School

Slap Shot

Snapping my helmet on,
Getting my stick,
Roller blading to the center.
Ref drops the ball.
Everyone attacks it.
Passing up the court,
Taking one shot,
We score!
Kyle Kerwin, Grade 4
Lincoln Park Elementary School

My Sister and Cousins

I have a sister named Gianna
And a baby cousin Briana
A cousin named Chelsee
The girls drive me crazy
I want to send them to Montana
Anthony Gesimondo, Grade 4
St Mary's School

Snow

Snow is white
Snow is bright
White snow is everything I wish for
It covers the earth with a white, silver blanket
Snow allows children to play and have fun
Snow is so cool
It's fluffy and bluffy
Snow is fuzzy and sparkling but it's cold

Yaileen Gomez, Grade 4
Marie Durand Elementary School

Bears

Bears I love them
Bears come in all shapes and sizes
Bears are different colors like black or brown
I love to see them dance around
Bears are such beautiful creatures
And have such powerful features
But one thing I know about bears
I love them!

Brianna Stevenson, Grade 4
Marie Durand Elementary School

Perfection

I believe that what comes first is family.
We should all live in harmony.
I believe in a perfect day,
That it's not the end till everything's okay.
I believe that living is the greatest prize,
No matter our shape or size.
I believe that we are created differently,
Yet we all should be treated equally.

Victoria Zayas, Grade 6
Perth Amboy Catholic Upper Grades School

Changes

I looked out the window and to my surprise
The bright green leaves that brushed the skies
Had fallen upon the marshy ground
And in their place here's what I found.
Leaves of orange, brown, and red
Swirling high above my head
Our Earth is changing every day
All the time in every way.

Raegan Davies, Grade 5
Central School

The Race

I'm a dog handler
The day gets colder and colder
I give my dogs love and shower them with food
They slow down after we hit a tree
At last we win
We win!

Abisola Atilola, Grade 5
Roosevelt Elementary School

Christmas Tree

Christmas tree! Christmas tree!
You are so bright
So pretty
And so quiet

You are so bright
So big
And so quiet
You light up the night
Christmas tree, you are so grand

So strong
But not for long
Christmas tree, you are so grand
At the end of Christmas we have to take you down

But not for long
So pretty
At the end of Christmas we have to take you down
Christmas tree! Christmas tree!

Jacob Heinel, Grade 4
Zane North Elementary School

Bumpy the Pumpkin

Hello! My name is Bumpy
That's my name because I'm lumpy

I live in a patch
Where pumpkins almost match

Some can be dirty
And some can be nerdy

A little girl takes me off the vine
She says, "Daddy! Daddy! This pumpkin is fine"

He says, "Okay we'll carve out a face"
And then we were driving out of that place

Then I saw him get out a knife
I thought to myself this is the end of my life!

He started to carve gently into me. It tickles!
Just to think I only cost a few dollars and a couple nickels

Rachel VanLenten, Grade 5
Hawthorne Christian Academy

Wind

If I were wind
I would make sure kites could fly in the air.
I would whirl so hard that everyone's hat would blow away.
Then I would make everyone hungry,
as I blow the smoke of barbecue in the air.
If I were wind.

Amani Sherman, Grade 5
Bartle Elementary School

His Creation

God made the earth
God made the sky
God made the animals
and the birds that fly
Flowers, animals, trees so tall
God made it all
the earth and the sky
He needed one more thing
to complete His creation
So He made you and me
and now it's perfection.

Cecilia Wiggington, Grade 5
St Mary School

Pumpkin

Pumpkin
Pumpkin
Big and round,
Small and lumpy,
Orange, green and brown,
Autumn's here
For pumpkin season
Big ones, small ones
Round ones, too
Pumpkins are finally here
Wahoo!

Alyssa Cole, Grade 6
Great Meadows Regional Middle School

Greg Mortenson

Greg Mortenson
Was quite a man
Who had much care
For the completely bare.
They had no school.
The people thought it would be very cool
If they had one.
Greg knew this could definitely be done.
He raised the money he needed.
The school was built.
Mortenson knew he had succeeded!

Shalin Shah, Grade 6
Township of Ocean Intermediate School

Santa's Hat

Santa
puts me
on his head.
I warm his head
with my fleecy inside
Santa puts me on his head
He stretches me out. I'm surprised
I make it through the holiday after
seeing Santa's BIG BALD HEAD!

Lauren Howitz, Grade 5
Zane North Elementary School

Albemarle, NC

Fun and excitement.
Kids and adults outside
On the porch.
Nice warm weather,
Love in the air.
Kids eating big chunks
Of orange cantaloupe.
And adults drinking
Smirnoff.
No place like home.

Davina Thompson, Grade 6
Buckshutem Road Elementary School

Go Inside a Dragon

Go inside a dragon
Look through his noble eyes
Soar into the sky and
Breathe the terrifying fire,
Slash with sharp talons
And feel his hatred
For those who think him evil
For inside this dragon
Lies a heart of
Gold.

Sammy Liao, Grade 5
Village School

Tiny Dancer

Tip tap, tip tap —
Goes the dancer
On the roof.
Tipity tap, tipity tap —
Goes the tiny dancer
On the window.
Drip, drip, splash! Drip, drip splash!
The rain stops and
The tiny dancer takes a bow
To a rainbow of applause.

Anchala Rao, Grade 5
Village School

Shoot and Score

As I am running to my position,
With a basketball in my hand,
I dribble toward the net.
In a throwing position,
I jump up high
Above the ground
My arms over my head.
Letting go of the ball.
It lands into the net!

April Zanfino, Grade 4
Lincoln Park Elementary School

Gingerbread Man

Being baked in the oven
As brown as can be
People waiting to eat me
Kids wanting to
Take a limb from me
I don't know why
It makes me cry
I come out of the oven
All gold and hot
You better eat me
Before I rot
My limbs are crunchy
As a potato chip
I am so tasty
You will flip
My arms come off
As my leg is bitten off
I taste so good
You will have a fit

John Bonder, Grade 5
Zane North Elementary School

The Unusual Snowy Owl

I am white
And in the snow
I cannot be seen
For I am in camouflage

I am a raptor
A bird of prey
I eat other animals
Like rodents and fish

I live in open fields
Or a tundra in North America
I like it where it's cold
That's the weather for me

My nest is a small hole
In the ground to be exact
I am awake during the day
And that makes me unusual

Alyssa Kline, Grade 5
Hawthorne Christian Academy

Light Bulb

Always loyal
Never stopping
Always working
No time to rest
Working, working
Till they fade away
Get replaced
Start over again

Alexander Hermann, Grade 5
Frances DeMasi Elementary School

The World So Far

The world so far…
Filled with failure and tar.
The world so far…
A place of things that don't belong, like a golden hat.
The world so far…
The moon hides behind a cloudy shield.
The world so far…
In current time, the world is full of crime.
The world so far…
Different things that don't need to match.
The world so far…
Filled with failure.
The world so far…
Nothing is the same in the world so far…
Unknown things,
No real truth,
The oddities of things in
The world so far!

Tobias Rayside, Grade 5
Bartle Elementary School

The Grumpy Old Man

How I hate Christmas Day!
"I hate it so much!" I say.
All that joy and jolly.
Also, how I hate that holly.
Everyone gets presents, SO
Who cares about that mistletoe!
All those cookies and cake
I know I wouldn't want to bake!
I don't like the giving
In fact I prefer the getting.
Everyone's happy on Christmas Eve
Even my uncle, Old Man Steve.
How I hate Christmas Day!
Instead I like it MY WAY!
All you should get is coal
And all you should eat is a gumball in an empty bowl.
No more Christmas trees
That would be the best Christmas to me.

Evan Royds, Grade 5
Zane North Elementary School

Snow Falling, Snow Melting

Snow falling.
Gloriously sleeping on the ground.
Glistening to the beat of the sunshine.
Glittering like a diamond soaked in water.
White like a pillow case and soft like a cloud.
Stuck to the ground and still falling.
Slowing down.
Sprinkling.
Stopping
Melting…

Kaitlyn Philipsen, Grade 6
Great Meadows Regional Middle School

Food

T hanksgiving is the best time to eat very delicious food.
H aving fun is making pie crust.
A nd it's a wonderful smell after crushing the cranberries.
N ana and Pop-pop said when they called, "We got the turkey!"
K ids help with seasoning the turkey.
S un shines through the window as we cook the bird.
G etting the desserts ready for dinner is nice.
I can't determine what we should name our turkey this year.
V ery delicious is the cranberry sauce!
I see people digging into the wonderful food that was made.
N ana and Pop-pop and everyone else get ready to leave.
G iving is the best time of year.

Karleigh Haller, Grade 6
Riverside Middle School

Thanksgiving Memories

" **T** urkey is very good," said Jacob.
H anging out with the family is fun. I have
A bout nine juicy pieces of turkey on my plate.
N ice people are all around me.
K inship is good to have. I am
S haring and having fun with my friends.
G ravy on biscuits is next to my turkey.
I love Thanksgiving!
" **V** ery good dinner," said Jacob.
I hate when this day ends. I
N ever want this day to end!
G iving thanks is what it's all about.

Jacob Green, Grade 6
Riverside Middle School

What Holiday Is It?

T urkey is good to have on this day
H oliday joy fills the house.
A ll of the food makes me stuffed,
N ovember is a colorful month.
K itchen noises like "bang" and "clang" are loud as
S tuffing fills my stomach.
G iving thanks on this day,
I ndians and pilgrims who started this holiday.
V oices of family makes me happy, while
I n the kitchen there are boiling pots.
N ever going to eat again,
G iving thanks on Thanksgiving Day.

Zoe Adams, Grade 6
Riverside Middle School

L Is for Lantern

The Lantern lights the way
It helps you see well like the day
It shines the place up with a bright light
So a path can be seen in the dark night
A Lantern is helpful for everyone
Because you can see with it when there is no sun.

Elise Chomiczewski, Grade 4
Good Shepherd Regional Catholic School

Smiles

Smiles are free, I know it's true
There's always someone smiling at you
You may notice their eyes, you may notice their teeth
But smiling will help you get rid of your grief

I tend to laugh when I'm filled with glee
Like when I see someone smiling at me
Whether you're angry or maybe even sad
Having a smile on your face makes it never that bad

You can cheer up a friend with just a smile
Give it a try, it will be worthwhile
When I smile at someone it usually makes their day
It speaks to them in a unique way

I call it a smile, some people call it a grin
It all looks the same, no matter where you've been
Smiling is free, you never have to pay
Go ahead and smile if you have nothing to say

Jared DeCesare, Grade 6
Little Falls School #1

The Alluring Night Sky

O moon, o moon every night
you light up the dark and dreary night
you outshine the stars
with no doubt you conquer all
when the sun falls into its deep slumber you rise
You shine like the biggest flashlight
Even the sun's rays cannot compare to you
We crave and desire your light during the night

Without you there is no reason to be:
Cheerful, pleased, or delighted
instead we are
Depressed, mournful, or crestfallen

O moon, o moon you rise every night
that is why I wrote this ode
to you
Moon

Solomon Watkins, Grade 6
Christa McAuliffe Middle School

Shining Star

I shine above the Christmas Tree
I am bright as the sun
People stare at me when I am shimmering
I light up as bright as night
I see Santa sneak in the house to give presents
Santa eats cookies and milk
When you leave them out.
I am still hanging on until Christmas is done.
I will be up on top next year!

Olivia Egbert, Grade 5
Zane North Elementary School

Animals Are Weird

Bats will sleep upside down in trees
And elephants are the only mammals that have four knees
Clams start out as boys and become girls later
But crocodiles do not become alligators
For dinner, an aardvark will eat a termite
And cats can see better than humans at night
A hummingbird is the smallest bird and the only one who can fly backwards
Did you know that a camel has three eye lids?
And mosquitoes do not prefer to bite kids
Almost without limits you can hear a lion roar from five miles away
Most ants are dead by their sixteenth day
A poor little owl can't move it's eyes
And if a parrot eats chocolate it will die
These are a few things that I have learned
You won't see a dog or a cat with a beard
But if you ask me animals are weird

Ella Hamburger, Grade 4
Edward H Bryan Elementary School

Poems Hide

Poems hide at the bottom of your heart
In your pocket
In the eyes of schoolteachers.
In the rich
The poor
The fancy and
The people who are living a comfortable life
They pop out at you
They say what's on your mind
They're happy
Sad
Glum
Dull
They help you become more confident
Feeling good about yourself
And that's where poems hide.

Hallie Lerner, Grade 5
Bartle Elementary School

B Is for Best Friends

B is for best friends,
They stick together and play forever,
They play all the seasons away,
They ring the bells of happiness.
As the years fall away they still want to play,
But you have to remember that there's still more time.
When they grow old and wise,
They'll remember those great times,
When they would play all year round,
When their feet hit the ground.
They remembered those times when they
laughed and cried,
B is for best friends and nothing can change that.

Shannon McHugh, Grade 4
Good Shepherd Regional Catholic School

It Takes Two

To form an army,
it takes a million!

To build a bridge,
'bout sixty men.

To play some ball,
it takes eight kids.

To play cards,
'round four.

But to form a perfect friendship,
it takes
just two.

Nora Peachin, Grade 5
Village School

Fun Snow

White as cotton balls,
As they fall from above,
Blowing with cold air,
There is enough to share.

Every kid smiling,
Enjoying the day of snow
Until comes the night,
When kids sleep with delight.

Hoping to wake up
To another snow storm
Like tomatoes red, ripe,
And ready to be picked.

Patrick Aufiero, Grade 5
Durban Avenue Elementary School

My Piano

This is my piano.
I was very glad,
when I got my new piano.
Thanks to my dad.

This is my piano.
On it, I often play
a beautiful song.
"That sounds great!" my dad would say.

This is my piano.
It's dark mahogany brown.
Every time I look at it,
I smile and never frown.

Joan Hong, Grade 5
Bartle Elementary School

Autumn

Crunchy leaves falling down
Don't worry they don't make a sound
Hiking in the woods
Campfire songs, the sights you see
On this autumn day.
Wait a second and you will be;
Very happy.
Thanksgiving Day, you smell so much
But later we will take a munch.
Raking leaves
And falling in
Now they're in the trash bin,
I go inside
And then I hide
Later I say "hi"
To my friends that rode by.

Cyan Vasquez, Grade 6
Great Meadows Regional Middle School

Winter

Snowflakes are falling
Snowballs are flying
Ice skaters are skating
Ice fishers are fishing
The lake is icy
The sky is blue
The wind is blowing
Angels are dancing
The leaves are snoozing
The animals are hidden
Kids are laughing
Hot chocolate is cooking
Cookies are baking
My nose is bright red
The sun is going down
And I say goodbye to all my friends

Brittany Polizzi, Grade 5
St Mary's School

The Swift Owl

Her talons are sharp
Though she is a whisper in the wind

Her disc-shaped face
And broad wings

She takes a swoop at any sound
Just a clutch in her silent flight

She's ready and in position
Her feathers like a knife's side in the air

The prey is caught and unaware
And she flies to her owlets

Rachel Rubio, Grade 5
Hawthorne Christian Academy

Where We'll Be One Day

Can we make it through the winter?
Who says we can't? No one!
When we come together,
We will survive, we'll make it through...

Just think of the possibilities,
We'll make it through,
Just think of where we'll be one day,
We can do it, just do it, do it together!

Just think of the possibilities,
We'll make it through,
Just think of where we'll be one day.
We can do it, just do it, do it together.

Devin Bellotti, Grade 5
Durban Avenue Elementary School

This Is My Snail Ninja

This is my snail ninja
He is black and small
When I feed him
He goes on the wall

This is my snail ninja
He is a little green
He has a ton of friends
And they're not mean

This is my snail ninja
He is shiny and can crawl
Even though he's a snail
He looks like a brown and black ball

Monica Aspy, Grade 5
Bartle Elementary School

This Is My Tree

This is my tree
living for 35 years
it's a strong and tall maple
towering over its peers.

This is my tree
you're welcome to climb
near the leaves that sound
sweeter than the most merry wind chime.

This is my tree
with a tree house on top
no sides makes it exciting
boring my tree is not!

Josephine Heibel, Grade 5
Bartle Elementary School

April
April flowers bloom
Filling the air with joy
The peak of spring is here

The birds chirp the day away
While warm breezes
Usher the chills away

Majestic oaks become
Home to
The critters that
Emerge

April is a time of the
Renewal of life
Mother Nature awakens
And embraces
Her springtime realm
Sruthi Katakam, Grade 4
Village School

Just a Dream
Where am I?
I wonder as I open my eyes.
But when I do I see only blue skies.
I stand up and look around.
But there is only hard ground.
I am on a large square.
I know I am on a building,
But where?
As I look down I start to fall.
Help help!
I call.
A strong wind blows my hair.
I look for a landing.
I look everywhere.
I start to panic.
I start to scream.
But then I realize.
It's just a dream.
Lily Feinberg, Grade 4
Hillside Elementary School

The Out That Never Happened
There I was on the pitching mound
Two outs
3 balls
2 strikes
Last inning
Championship game on the line.
I go to throw the last pitch
And fall flat on my face.
I have enough sand in my mouth
To build my own beach.
Nikki D'Ambrosia, Grade 4
Lincoln Park Elementary School

Montclair
M y home town is number 1
O ptimistic
N ice people
T ogether we make a great town
C amp is fun here
L ooks like a big family
A lmost everyone is nice
I love Montclair
R oot for Montclair
Melanie Noel Flowers, Grade 5
Hillside Elementary School

What Is Autumn?
Autumn is not too cold or not too hot.
And lots of leaves falling down.
I wear a long sleeve shirt and a jacket too.
There is Halloween and Columbus day too.
But don't forget to have Thanksgiving!
I see animals getting ready for their sleep.
And see snow on the mountains.
I see people turning their heaters on.
That is Autumn.
William Chung, Grade 4
Edward H Bryan Elementary School

Marco Polo
This Italian explorer
Sailed across the sea.
Searching for riches,
Spices, and tea.

He traveled through Asia,
And wrote a book.
Treasure he wanted
It is what he took.
Rukiya Billups, Grade 5
Roosevelt Elementary School

The Sky's Moon
The moon
Shining pretty
Hanging low in the sky
Rotating around mother earth
Breathless
Steven Ayers, Grade 5
Richard E Byrd Elementary School

Thanksgiving
I love Thanksgiving
It is the best holiday
We have fun on this special day
It's nice to be with my family
We have the best time celebrating
I love Thanksgiving!
Yamesse Lopez, Grade 4
Marie Durand Elementary School

Music
Music is a gift from God,
To be able to make
Such a beautiful sound.
It brings joy to the world,
And makes our minds happy.
And to more than most people
It's not just a hobby.
From drums, to flute, to clarinets,
To many different shapes and sizes.
Music is my favorite thing
That makes my heart sing.
Kristen Russo, Grade 6
St Mary's School

Christmas Night Is Coming!
Kids asleep,
Dreaming of dancing sugarplums.

Santa stuffing stockings
That dangle from the wall.

Children dreaming of everything
On their list.

Grandparents coming to wish you a Merry
Christmas.
Sarah Magyar, Grade 5
Durban Avenue Elementary School

Yusup
Cool, fast, funny
Wishes to run like a cheetah.
Dreams of money to buy lots of games.
Wants to have a good life.
Who wonders what else is in the world.
Who fears all kinds of spiders.
Who lives to play games.
Who believes in hard work.
Who loves family
Who when grows up wants to invent
And who is number one.
Yusup Badiev, Grade 5
Bartle Elementary School

Ice Cream
I cy
C old
E xciting

C reamy
R apture
E xcellent
A mazing
M agical
Mariela Perez, Grade 5
Roosevelt Elementary School

Ballet Dancers

Fall is a play, specifically a ballet
The leaves are the dancers, performers, and prancers.
The wind is the director and the performance protector
The trees, old and new, are surely the crew.

The leaves change costumes from red to green to brown
Then the wind pushes the leaves off the stage crew
Towards the distant ground
And then, they begin to dance.

The onlookers beam at this wonderful scene
As the vivid leaves sway and sashay
Like fire silhouetted against the sapphire sky.
Joy granted to the bystanders' eye
They flow gracefully with the wandering wind
Doing their dance, they turn and prance.

With the whispering wonderful wind
And then they slowly, dramatically drift to the ground,
Satisfied that they have done their part.

Charlie McMahon, Grade 5
Hopewell Elementary School

The Sparrow's Song

"The summer is gone," sang the little sparrow
Clinging to the bare branches so narrow.
Broken branches beneath the trees,
Lie in the rustling, dusty leaves.
Sienna and cinnamon colored leaves all around
Dance gracefully in the wind as they fall to the ground.

"The summer is gone," sang the little sparrow
Clinging to the bare branches so narrow.
Autumn is here, and nights have grown cold,
Crimson berries on trees are a sight to behold.
Mother Nature whispers on the gentle breeze,
"Prepare yourself for the winter freeze."

"The summer is gone," sang the little sparrow
Clinging to the bare branches so narrow.
As I sit and watch that little sparrow,
Clinging to that tree branch so narrow.
Quietly away that little sparrow flies,
Into the gray of the winter skies.

Helena Green, Grade 5
Hopewell Elementary School

Autumn

I feel the cool breeze on my face.
I see the colorful leaves on the ground.
I hear the crunch of the leaves under my feet.
I taste the warm apple cider on my tongue.
I smell the fresh scent of pine in the air.
It is autumn.

Clare Cahill, Grade 6
St Dominic School

The Moon

One night I was in my backyard
Playing at night
I tripped over a huge stump
and fell on my green grass
and above me there it is
the huge glow of the moon.

The crisp white glow
and its smooth, round surface.
There is a little glow around the moon.
It is all the stars in the black night sky.
But the glorious glow of the moon is brighter.

As I get up I see
a monstrous cloud pass above the moon,
It disappears into thin air

Matthew Zeveney, Grade 6
Christa McAuliffe Middle School

An Icy Win

I was racing along the cone-marked track
Then, I soon noticed I had to go back.
I left my stuff, straw, pots, and fish,
Then I found out I had left the food dish.

I was back on the road without a doubt,
Then my nice dogs had begun to pout.
They had gotten cut with huge shards of ice,
Soon after, I had to stitch their wounds…TWICE!

A dogsled with eight dogs dashed right past me,
Then I got past 'em and I shouted with glee!
We soon came out in the place of first,
Then I felt like a raging volcano, I was ready to burst!
My family came over and tried to hug me,
And soon afterwards, we drank some tasty hot tea.

Joshua Huertas, Grade 5
Roosevelt Elementary School

Life

For everyone life is different
Different love
Different friends
And different dreams
But no matter what
Life is precious
So take it like a gift
You never know when it's over
Always try your best
Make every moment right
The first time
Live your life well
Maybe you will find what you are looking for
Whatever it is

Serena Velazquez, Grade 6
Robert Morris Public School

My Presents

When I open my present,
what will it be?
A movie, a game, a flat screen TV!
It's almost Christmas,
this is agitating,
all I'm doing is waiting and waiting.

It's Christmas time,
what will I get?
A flat screen TV or maybe a pet,
I open it up,
I say holy cow,
I can't believe what I just got right now.

It's an iPod Touch!
I say thank you to my mom and dad,
because this Christmas wasn't at all that bad.

Nicholas Alvarez, Grade 5
Hawthorne Christian Academy

Shedding

Leaves aren't the only thing falling down
Creatures are getting their new winter's gown.

A rabbit's suit is quite a sight
In the bright winter light.

Even though the weasel's fur is white
It can still fit somewhere tight.

Foxes are getting a new blouse
So they can catch a small field mouse.

Predators can't catch their prize
While all the prey is in disguise.

Leaves aren't the only things falling down
Creatures are getting their new winter's gown.

Jeffrey Pennington, Grade 5
Central School

Beautiful Sky

This is ode to the moon, ode to the sky
The beautiful moon is a sight for sore eyes

High above sits the moon so bright
Lighting my way through the cold dark night

The moon is gleaming
With its brilliant shine
Oh how I wish it were all mine

It glows down on me, it shows its beautiful light
The moon and the stars look so bright

Bailey Kinsman, Grade 6
Christa McAuliffe Middle School

Clouds vs Moon

The moon.
The moon is massive.
The moon is powerful.
It gives me quite a fright.
The moon is not so mighty after all,
once the evil clouds come out to play.
The moon seems not so bold,
but what the moon does know,
is how to get those cruel, old clouds away.
The moon puffs up his cheeks,
as he booms with fury.
The moon gleams with glory.
The clouds seem afraid,
as they float away into the night,
like foam in the sea.
The moon grins with victory in his sight
as he sits in the sky like a giant blossomed flower.

Ashley Eckett, Grade 6
Christa McAuliffe Middle School

The Moon Is Our Night Sky

The moon is here
No, the moon is there
The moon shows its face any and everywhere

With its silky white surface
And its warm smile and stare
Up from the heavens and down to the stars
The moon shines above us brighter than all stars

The moon guides my way
through the darkest of nights
The moon guides my way
with its glorious lights

But if you don't see the moon in the sky
Just yell at the clouds for they are the reason why
The moon doesn't show in our night sky

Warren Johnson, Grade 6
Christa McAuliffe Middle School

Thanksgiving

T hanksgiving
H appy time of the year
A ll of your family gets together
N ow we cook the food
K inda hoping the turkey gets done soon!
S till waiting for the turkey!
G ames to play while we're waiting
I n the oven the turkey cooked to perfection
V ery good pumpkin pie for desert
I 'm excited to eat now because it's done
N ow we eat the good food and give thanks on Thanks-
G iving day!

Steven Shaw, Grade 5
Ocean Academy

Imagine

Aaah! She screamed,
Right into the night.
She toppled down the tunnel,
But still laughed in delight.

She found herself a rabbit,
With an attitude she could not bare.
Imagine being stuck,
With a time-conscious hare.

Then a man with a funny hat,
Whose house was all chocolate candy.
With 100 Oompa-Loompas,
All acting fine and dandy.

Then a boy running down,
With a chicken and a golden egg.
Thank God he climbed down the beanstalk,
Before he lost his head!

After all of these adventures,
To be able to do all day
She could do just a little bit more but…
She woke up.

Maiya Blaney, Grade 5
Hillside Elementary School

Can You Imagine?

Can you imagine
A book without words?
A sky without birds?
A school without nerds?

Can you imagine
Halloween without a scare?
A forest without a bear?
A baby-sitter that just doesn't care?

Can you imagine
A horse that doesn't neigh?
Santa Claus without his sleigh?
A year without May?

Can you imagine
The world without food?
Not being in a good mood?
My best friend being rude?

Can you imagine
A book without words?
A sky without birds?
A school without nerds?

Georgia Bandler, Grade 5
Hillside Elementary School

Who Are You?

Who am I?
Am I the girl in the corner?
Am I the one that stands out?
Am I the one that gets picked on?
Am I me?

Who am I?
Did I pick to be me?
Am I a cheerleading captain?
Am I a softball star?
Do I sit in the bleachers?
Can I play a guitar?

Is this me?
Do I shine?
Can I sparkle?
Will I succeed?
Is this what I wanted?
Is me who I want to be?

Brianna Incorvaia, Grade 6
Garfield Middle School

Who I Am

I am the wind
I will fly all day and night
Upon the sun's ray and the moon's light

I am the earth
I hide in the depths of a wonderless fright
I dig, I push my way through the ground
I am the reason the earth sends off sound

I am the fire
Burning bright
I am the reason there will be light
When I am angry I burn and glow
The fire in my eyes will always show

I am the water
I ride on the crashing waves
All the sea animals are my loyal slaves
I am the elements of life

Ben Merrick, Grade 5
Travell Elementary School

On That Horrible Day

On that horrible day lives were lost.
On that horrible day there were tears.
On that horrible day there were heroes, too.
On that horrible day there was sadness.
Since that horrible day,
We will never forget
The lives that we lost
And the ones that were saved.

Samantha Scherr, Grade 6
Township of Ocean Intermediate School

Fall

Fall, fall, fall
It is here, here, here
So we can cheer, cheer, cheer.

I love fall,
Fall is a time to rake and break leaves.
Jump in them, jump out of them,
Play about them, how about them?

Leaves are in the air,
Leaves are in your hair,
Leaves are everywhere.

Fall, fall, fall,
Is here to have a ball.

Delaney Crawford, Grade 4
St Joseph's Regional School

Chrissie

She is my best friend
And we'll be together till the end
We always have something to do
Her mother's name is Sue
She lives in a different state
But we'll always be mates
We have the same traits
And we stay up late
We say funny jokes
Our parents are folks
We love to shop
But afterwards we drop
We have the same hair
We play with pens
But we'll always be friends

Caitlyn Ghirardi, Grade 5
St Mary's School

Soccer

I love soccer, it's so much fun
when I score a goal
I get the job done.

Being a goalie is really great
sometimes the games
are really late.

Practice sessions are every week
To keep our skills
awesome and unique.

We always have two seasons
We never give up
But playing for fun is our main reason.

Ramon Ruiz, Grade 5
St Mary's School

Birds
Most birds roam the air.
Some birds cannot fly but walk.
They are flightless birds.
Sean McHugh, Grade 4
Catherine A Dwyer Elementary School

Hitler
Hitler was crazy.
A maniac with a 'stache.
Hitler was stupid.
Gabe Slon, Grade 5
Hillside Elementary School

The King of the Jungle
Lions are the king
they are brave, strong and love meat
don't hurt the lions
Jessica Heitmann, Grade 4
Catherine A Dwyer Elementary School

My Dog
My dog is smelly
and annoying and crazy
and she never sleeps
Fabio Sgarro, Grade 5
Hillside Elementary School

Water
The ocean is cool.
The sea can be beautiful.
The waves can be high.
Corey Miller, Grade 4
Catherine A Dwyer Elementary School

Blue Ocean
Shrimp in the water
A fisherman makes his catch
On a blue ocean
Andrew Moore, Grade 5
Bartle Elementary School

The Mets
The Mets rule so much.
They're better than the Yankees.
The Mets are awesome.
Elana Sklar, Grade 5
Hillside Elementary School

Falling Snow
Gently the snow falls
How fragile it seems to be
It is so peaceful
Cassie Soto, Grade 5
Catherine A Dwyer Elementary School

Eating on Thanksgiving
T hankful relatives are getting ready to stuff their stomachs.
H appy people gather around the table for a feast.
A hungry person is waiting behind me urging for more food.
N o one left behind the turkey, gravy, or corn.
K ind people stuffing their faces wanting seconds.
S mells of a fresh pumpkin pie is baking in the oven. I'm
G oing to get some leftovers, if I'm lucky.
I nteresting new flavors are in the food this year. A
V ery good smelling turkey is sitting on my plate.
" **I** love to eat at our tasty feast this Thanksgiving Day," my brother says.
N ever come to the festive table and choose not to eat.
G iving thanks, loving, and eating is what it is all about this Thanksgiving Day.
Michaela Weaver, Grade 6
Riverside Middle School

Thanksgiving Has Been Ruined
T hanksgiving has been ruined by commercials, store sales, and TV marathons.
H ave we no thanks for everything we have?
A lot of families still do celebrate thanks with feasts.
N ot all families do that, though.
K in is one thing we should be thankful for.
S ome kids even think Thanksgiving is an excuse to be off from school.
G ratitude should be the feeling of Thanksgiving.
I do not want this holiday to be an excuse to sell stores' inventories.
V alue what you have and be thankful for it.
I do realize many people already do.
N ot another year should go by with Thanksgiving as a commercial retail scam.
G ive thanks before Thanksgiving is completely ruined. "Help Thanksgiving," I always plead.
Max Farley, Grade 6
Riverside Middle School

My Outstanding Kiwi
On the outside, you look like a coconut that fell out of a tree.
You feel like a stem that brushes against my hand.
When I peel you, you sound like a saw cutting a board.
When I slice you, you sound like my mom cutting fish on a rainy day.
Inside you look like a wheel on an SUV.
You feel like a slimy snail in the sun on a beach.
You smell like an apple that had just been picked.
You taste like yogurt on a cold day.
Tell me, Mr. Kiwi, are you part of the banana family?
Jada Peterson, Grade 5
Roosevelt Elementary School

A Feeling
An instant feeling, a special feeling,
Of autumn coming soon, the crackling leaves,
The waving of trees, to greet you on that fine morning.
The piled leaves, the singing bees to start leaving for the winter.
Next is Halloween and trick-or-treating and lots of candy it's true.
Now October is over and the new month of November is coming,
And now it's Thanksgiving! Finally comes December, when the snow days come,
And the snowballs are thrown, and fireplaces are turned on, then the New Year arrives
And this cycle keeps going and going.
Rachael Ann Mrocka, Grade 6
St Mary's School

Snowy Owl

Her feathers are like rays of black and white
And her feet are like winter boots

She soars in the Arctic tundra
Looking for prey with her solid golden eyes

As she lands in the snow
She quietly yet swiftly catches her meal

She flies back to her wailing owlets
To give them tender loving care

As the cold days go by
She freely flies through the nights

Her talons are sharp
But her wings glisten as snow
Julia Selwyn, Grade 5
Hawthorne Christian Academy

Winter

Winter is a snowy season,
With snow and ice.

We can make snowmen,
Snow angels and igloos.

When we get cold,
We go inside to relax,
And have hot chocolate.

We sit at the table,
And have a large feast,
With our family and friends.

We share secrets,
Have cake and pie.
After that we go beddy by. (zzzzz)
Jayne Hessler, Grade 5
Hillside Elementary School

Can You Imagine?

Can you imagine
Drums without sticks
Or cake batter you can't mix?

Can you imagine
Numbers without the number six
Or a computer you can't fix?

Can you imagine
Candy stores without pixie sticks?
I can't imagine any of these things
How about you?
Cordell Spivey, Grade 5
Hillside Elementary School

Harold Taylor

H appy
A nxious
R eckless
O ut of order
L oud
D angerous

T hrilling
A thletic
Y oungster
L ovable
O bservant
R ascally
Harold Taylor, Grade 5
Mckinley Community School

Twin Towers

One early morning,
When everyone was at work,
Two planes crashed
Into the Twin Towers,
And it was not a blast.
Everyone asked for help,
So rescue came,
This event was no game.
People tried to survive,
But some died.
This event is known
Throughout the world
As 9/11.
Bailey Kappmeier, Grade 6
Township of Ocean Intermediate School

Kiarra Baskin

K ind
I ndependent
A thletic
R espectful
R esponsible
A nnoying

B eautiful
A wesome
S ensitive
K illing personality
I ntelligent
N utty loco
Kiarra Baskin, Grade 5
Mckinley Community School

Autumn

Pumpkins, mums, cool air
Frosty grass in the morning
Leaves falling from trees
Meghan McCarty, Grade 5
Bartle Elementary School

A Magical Horse

I have a horse inside my heart
With a gleaming coat
And a wavy mane.

I have a horse inside my heart
That wants to leap over
The fence
Of playfulness.

I have a horse inside my heart
That wants to gallop over
The hills
Of freedom.

I have a horse inside my heart
Who wishes she could run through
The fields
Of friendship.

I have a horse inside my heart
Who lives with me
Forever.
Emiko Kobayashi, Grade 4
Village School

Scarecrows

Sitting in a field
Lonely
No one in sight
Crows
Dancing around me
Scare them
I say to myself
Try try try
Ahhh
One bit me
That's the final straw
Cracking my straw fingers
Crack crack crack
Go
I cackled in my mind
Down like a mighty oak
I fell
Scaring myself, the crows, and ground
Jumping up
Feeling brave
I'm a scarecrow!
Kayli Alexis Yeisley, Grade 6
Great Meadows Regional Middle School

Black Holes

So many wonders
They're waiting to swallow up
The next best victim
Ray Dolan, Grade 5
Frances DeMasi Elementary School

Magical Night

When Jamie went to sleep,
Her teddy bear woke up from his nap
He stretched and yawned
And yawned and stretched

Berry, her teddy, jumped off the bed
And woke Jamie's brother's dolls
They danced and pranced
And pranced and danced
When it was 4 o'clock,
They stopped the party and
Put presents under Jamie's and her brother's pillow
Next, they went back to napping

When Jamie and her brother woke up,
They danced and pranced
And screamed and laughed
And the dolls smiled

Dana Ahn, Grade 4
Edward H Bryan Elementary School

Oh the Beautiful Night

Oh the mahogany leaves, they look like parachutes.
Oh the mahogany leaves, they crunch under my boots.

Oh the crisp air, it's relaxing and light.
Oh the crisp air, it's nowhere in sight.

Oh the somber sky, it's blacker than coal.
Oh the somber sky, tries to block the moon that full.

Oh the radiant moon, the darkness it duels.
Oh the radiant moon, looks like a big jewel.

Oh the dingy clouds, they're wispy and uncolorful.
Oh the dingy clouds, they still look so wonderful.

Oh the beautiful night, to some it's boring and dim.
Oh the beautiful night, at least always makes me grin.

Cami Watanabe, Grade 6
Christa McAuliffe Middle School

Staying Up

Cookies were set by the fire,
Next to a window where snow is admired.

Christmas carols are being sung,
As holiday bells are being rung.

Stars were shining around a glistening moon,
Where reindeer will fly by oh so very soon.

They would land on my roof and leave my gifts,
Then get back on the sled up over the snow drifts.

Charlie Weiner, Grade 5
Hillside Elementary School

The Cranky Snowman

I'm a snowman.
I am made in the snow.
People dress me with gloves, hats, and jackets.
But that makes me melt.
I think people build me for no reason.
They build me and let me melt.
They have no feelings for me.
I get eaten by children
And it hurts very badly.
That's why it's not fun
Being a snowman.

Robert Norton, Grade 5
Zane North Elementary School

Autumn

I love to watch the leaves fall,
It makes me feel so peaceful,
I find it cool to watch them day by day,
They fall round and round to the ground,
The leaves fall and fall again,
The leaves fall day and night,
They just won't stop,
More and more fall to the ground making big piles,
For me to jump in,
No matter what they won't be gone,
How can I be wrong?

Matthew Mastando, Grade 5
St Rose of Lima Academy

S Is for Scooter

S is for scooter
That I ride every day,
Who does tricks and jumps
And excites me in every way.
If I have a lot of pep
I can jump a lot of steps.
On my scooter I can fly,
My mom waves to me, as I scoot by.
It is a great thrill,
When I ride down a big hill.
There is no doubt that this is a good work-out.

Daniel Jubb, Grade 4
Good Shepherd Regional Catholic School

The Wright Swing

My favorite player on the Mets is David Wright
He swings the bat with a lot of might
As the ball flies through the air
The fans stand up and stare

As it soars over players heads
The pitcher dreads the curve ball
As David Wright touches them all
The fans all wonder who caught the ball

Ryan Miller, Grade 5
Roosevelt Elementary School

Me, Myself, and I
I am a funny girl who loves writing
I wonder if there is a book with more than a thousand pages
I hear the sound of pages from a book blowing in the spring breeze
I see an author writing a book
I want to know if I can help
I am a funny girl who loves writing

I pretend I am an author writing my first book
I feel my hand ghosting across the pages
I touch the dry ink of my writing creation
I worry that I might mess up and have to start all over again
I cry when I lose my best thought
I am a funny girl who loves writing

I understand that writing a book takes time and patience
I say that if you keep going you'll reach your goal someday
I dream about the day when I become a famous author
I try to make my writing as best as I can
I hope one day that I do write a book
I am a funny girl who loves writing
Holly Fowler, Grade 6
Olson Middle School

I Am
I am a kid who plays baseball.
I wonder if I will get a home run.
I hear the crowd screaming when I make a play.
I see the ball coming to me.
I want to get a triple.
I am a kid who plays baseball.

I pretend that I smack a home run.
I feel the sting on my hands when I hit the ball.
I touch the ball when I make a throw.
I worry I will strikeout.
I cry when I am sitting on the bench.
I am a kid who plays baseball.

I understand the umps call.
I say I will get a home run.
I dream of getting a home run.
I try to make good plays.
I hope to play baseball for the rest of my life.
I am a kid who plays baseball.
Alec Sozio, Grade 6
Olson Middle School

Snow
It's snowing outside!
It's cold!
It's fun!
Dad makes me shovel!
Dad makes me hot coca!
COUGH I'm so sick!
SNIFF I'm so energetic!
It's wet!
It's white!
It's snowing outside!
My hands are numb!
My hands are warm!
I hate my hat!
I love my gloves!
Snowball fights!
They hurt!
It's just snow!
I guess it's okay!
See, I told you so!
I love snow!!!!
Nina Anstatt and Carrie Wylie, Grade 6
Great Meadows Regional Middle School

Santa Claus Is Comin' to Town
Christmas is here,
Same as every year!
A big tasty turkey;
All of us feeling rather perky!
On the tree an angel waits,
To see if Santa will be late!
Everyone's in bed —
There are cookies for Santa…
so he'll be well fed!
Twelve strikes the clock
Tick-Tock! Tick-Tock!
In the chimney a thump,
And out Santa jumps!
He tiptoes to the tree,
Imagining children shouting with glee
He rummages in his bag,
As he checks each tag
The presents are found;
Inside one is a hound!
"Happy Christmas to all, and to all a goodnight!"
Kirsten Jeansson, Grade 6
Olson Middle School

Happiness
Happiness looks like the sun shining brightly;
It sounds like heavy rain falling to the ground;
It smells like a baby wearing powder;
It feels like a soft, fluffy, pillow.
It tastes like red, chewy gumdrops
melting in your mouth
Matthew Albarran, Grade 5
Perth Amboy Catholic Upper Grades School

Snowflakes Falling
Snowflakes falling.
Kids catching them on their tongues.
Deer eating snowmen's noses.
Yelling kids as they fly down a hill on a sleigh.
Carolers singing,
collecting food for the poor.
Jean Somalwar, Grade 5
Bartle Elementary School

Spring

Forest makes me think of spring
Aqua looks like the beautiful, clear pool
Apples taste like a sweet lollipop
Fire sounds like popping popcorn
Lemon smells like sweet, cold lemonade
Eggplant feels like soft, gooey marshmallows
Spring is the season of sweets

Makena Smargiassi, Grade 6
St Dominic School

Winter

Lots of kids in front of their houses.
Large snowflakes falling down on houses, trees, and people.
Good looking snowmen.
Kids starting snowball fights.
All white trees with a clear blue sky.
Most of all everybody has fun!

Christopher Place, Grade 5
Bartle Elementary School

Cheerleading

BOOM! We go up in a stunt.
CLAP! We clap our hands together.
HIT! We hit ourselves.
POP! The flyer flies in the air for a basket toss.
RATTLE! The crowd goes crazy!

Carly Joseph, Grade 5
Frances DeMasi Elementary School

Fire

Fire is hot and a light
The color is usually orange or blue
Fire is useful, but yet still destructive
When you go in the dark it shows you a path
And it was never meant to be touched with your bare hands

Johanna Clidoro, Grade 6
St Mary's School

S Is for the Sun

S is for the Sun that lights up
The day for everyone wants to play
Everyone from near and
far see the sun up in the sky
makes everyone laugh and sometimes cry.

Selena Rose Neris, Grade 4
Good Shepherd Regional Catholic School

A New Kid

There was a new kid who liked bottle lids.
She had a little sister who had a big blister.
They had a fat pig who wears their mother's wig.
The pig was so fat he broke the bat.
When he went through the door he broke the floor.

Kristy Taveras, Grade 5
Mckinley Community School

Do Your Best

Always try your hardest and you will succeed.
Always try your hardest and always believe.
Never give up, not in rain, snow, or sleet.
If you keep up the good work, it will help both you and your team.

If you're making progress,
That is great for you.
Even if you're not,
You'll catch up soon.

Don't be sad if you make a mistake.
Just do your best and that is great.

Since you tried your hardest, you did succeed.
This poem is a motivation and that's all you need.

Rachel Mills, Grade 6
St Mary Prep School

All About Me

I am…
Cool
Calm, quiet, chilly
I felt that way when I came home from Philly.
Mature
ripe, serious, mellow
Whenever I look at him I see a fine fellow.
I am not very…
Childish
Annoying, babyish, spoiled
My toys and games my sister has foiled.
Bad
Lousy, rotten, unacceptable
Please don't break the dark brown table.
…and that's all me!

Chloe Jenkins, Grade 5
Hillside Elementary School

Snowball

I am a snowball
And I come out in the winter when it is freezing.
I like the cold weather a lot
Because it feels great to me.
It is fun to have a snowball fight
With other snowballs.
I also like when people keep me
In their freezer
And they take me out to shove me in a face
Then when they are done
I go to the snow
And relax until somebody picks me up
And throws me at someone.
After every year
I get scared when I melt.

Christian Kaiser, Grade 5
Zane North Elementary School

A Great Time of Year

T hanksgiving is a great time of the year to be with family and friends.
H aving pumpkin pie is delicious to eat.
A ll can play in fall leaves, which are as cold as ice cubes from the rain.
N ever will I forget this day, because
K ind families are outside with their children.
S oon it will be time for the most delicious Thanksgiving meal.
G iving thanks for such good food.
I love this night and don't want it to end. A
V ery good time we have; and it is such a good night.
I nside we are with family and friends having fun, and I say to my mom and dad, "Let's not go to bed."
N ot so sleepy and I never want to dream, so I say to Dad, "I don't want to go to bed."
G ot to go to bed anyway, good night.

Diane Levy, Grade 6
Riverside Middle School

How to Make a Popular Girl

Take nail polish, clothes, bracelets, earrings, a rich mom and dad, stilettos, eye shadow, mascara, flats, and a mean 17-year old girl.
Put all the ingredients in a brand new blender.
Stir them together with a large spoon
Until the popular girl says, "Mother," and then you will know it's ready.
Pour the ingredients into a pie pan.
Bake in a rusty oven at 350 degrees until you see long eyelashes.
You can tell it's done when the girl says "Eww! Why am I in a rusty oven?"
Let cool until 7:00 a.m.
Add ice cream sprinkles.
Chop the girl's long hair and serve with donuts.
Taste the ear and the nose for best results.

Shermine Saint-Elien, Grade 5
Roosevelt Elementary School

How to Make an Older Person Young Again!

Take an old person who wants to be young, a tube top, skinny jeans, lipstick, earrings, and a new cell phone.
Put all of the ingredients in an extra-extra-large bowl.
Mix with a diamond whisk until it turns a pinkish, purplish, and bluish color.
Pour the mix in an extra-extra-large pan.
Cook in the prettiest pinkest oven at 387 degrees until the mixture turns a bright green color.
You can tell it's done when it has been in there for seven hours.
Let stand for three minutes then sprinkle on the old person.
Smell the clothes when on the new person.
The clothes should smell like perfume.
Warning: Person will stay green for 5 minutes.

Gina Schroeder, Grade 5
Roosevelt Elementary School

Windsong

The smell of the breeze in your hair,
The damp moss under your feet,
The earthy smell that emanates from the verdant forest in the morning,
The blinding rain pounding against the window pane,
Flying down to the ground,
The dew drops shining brilliantly when the light gently shines its rays upon them,
Puppies taking their first tentative steps into the vast world, stepping into the quagmired ground,
examining their tiny footprints.
All these things and more are windsongs.

Gersandre Gonsalves-Domond, Grade 6
Hilltop Country Day School

Thanksgiving Dinner

" **T** omorrow is Thanksgiving!" screamed my sister.
 H elping my parents set up for dinner is really fun
 A nd once my family comes we all hang out downstairs.
 N anny brings her rice pudding and Poppop makes his stuffing.
 K inship is very important to us.
 S ometimes we watch football, and
 G ifts are given from person to person.
 I love getting to spend time with my relatives, on this joyous day.
 V egetables are served along with many other delicious treats.
 I always eat a lot!
 N utmeg goes in our pumpkin pies. Yet,
 G iblet gravy is the best!

Shannon Conrey, Grade 6
Riverside Middle School

America, America

America, America both vulnerable and strong.
Your beauty and pride has been celebrated in song.
Your Twin Towers stood brave and tall on a beautiful day.
Whoever would have thought 9/11 would be doomsday.
Two planes crashed and your towers crumbled.
Your people ran and screamed, shuttered and stumbled.
Many died and many of them were never found.
Many witnessed the unforgettable sight and sound.
Our heroes raced, without fear in their step.
Working day and night, they hardly ever slept.
Something called terrorism tried to make us fall,
But America, America is still standing tall.

Julianna Yost, Grade 6
Township of Ocean Intermediate School

Turkey Hunting

 T urkeys are gobbling in the woods.
" **H** ave you seen one?" I said.
 A lso, sometimes they get shot.
 N o, I don't shoot them, I just eat them.
 K ids are screaming after the shots, but I am not.
 S unny day is perfect for hunting.
 G uns loaded, "Ka pow!" fires one.
 I can go with my dad hunting.
 V iolence doesn't solve anything, we do it so we can eat
 I think turkeys taste good like chicken, but bigger.
 N ot good because I hit a tree and the branch tips over.
 G ood we got a turkey. "Hooray!" I shout.

Francisco Baptista, Grade 6
Riverside Middle School

Happiness

Happiness looks like the first snowflake in winter;
It sounds like a blue jay humming a sweet tune;
It smells like a fresh red rose just picked;
It feels like a soft, fluffy, golden puppy;
It tastes like hot cocoa with whipped
    cream and marshmallows on top.

Nina Acosta, Grade 5
Perth Amboy Catholic Upper Grades School

I Am

I am nice and funny
I wonder if I will do good in college
I hear students talking
I see students when I play
I want to become a teacher
I am nice and funny.
I pretend that I'm a teacher
I feel food when I play cook
I touch the phone in class
I worry about bridges
I cry when I get hurt
I am nice and funny.
I understand everything about police officers
I say that the Easter Bunny is real
I dream to live in Hawaii
I try to be good in soccer
I hope to go to Princeton for college
I am nice and funny.

Madison Robb, Grade 4
Ethel M Burke Elementary School

The Mother Bird

In a nest that sits high up in a tree,
There are three little eggs that will hatch and be free.

The mother is scared that they will freeze through the night,
Yet she still takes off for a cold winter flight.

She searches for food for her young ones to eat,
Then all of a sudden, one hatches and stands on its feet.

It squawks and shouts calling for its mother,
While another egg cracks and it's the bird's baby brother.

They stayed up most of the night feeling fright,
Then fell fast asleep, snuggling so tight.

Early in the morning when they rose out of bed,
They awoke in time to see the shadow of their mother fly overhead.
Then the third bird hatched and they were happily fed.

Marley Harris-Deans, Grade 5
Hillside Elementary School

Chipmunk

Furry and adorable
Tiny and loving

Scurrying from yard to yard
Nibbling away at nuts in the summer

Oh how I wish I was loved too,
Sleeping in a cozy den on a cold winter night
Rather than on the streets, cold and alone.
    I am a…Chipmunk

Antonia Holton-Raphael, Grade 5
Hillside Elementary School

December Rain

Of all my life, my short sweet life, I have loved the December rain.
The chorus of pops, the cool, wet drops, which will return to mother sky again.
The joy of splashing and dashing around, doing what I please. All of the joy, the wonderful joy, it will put my mind at ease.
When the patter stops,
As do the cool wet drops,
I will return to my home again.

Of all my life, my short sweet life, I have loved the December rain.
The chorus of pops, the cool, wet drops, which will return to mother sky again.
When my life is filled with sorrow, and I do not know what to do, I look to that old December rain, knowing that will see me through.
The old December rain, comes through maybe twice a year, but that is enough,
Though life can be tough,
Till December rain will come again.

Chris DeCarolis, Grade 6
Cedar Drive Middle School

Greed

Can you imagine not being able to afford to live in your house?
Can you imagine all of your possessions being sold to pay only some of the bills
your parents couldn't have otherwise?
Can you imagine being taken away from them because they could no longer provide for you?
Maybe now you won't complain about what you don't have.
Can you imagine living on the streets?
Can you imagine sleeping outside in the freezing temperatures the night brings?
Can you imagine only having one outfit that is dirty and too small?
Maybe now you will begin to realize just how lucky you are.
Can you imagine having to hunt animals and go fishing in order to provide food for you family?
Can you imagine not being able to continue going to school to get an education?
Can you imagine all of the things you have been taking for granted to just vanish?
Maybe now you will be thankful and share what you have.

Victoria Monroe, Grade 6
St Mary's School

How to Make an Older Brother into an Older Sister

Take 3 cups of real flowers, 5 cups of pure love and joy, eyeliner, lipgloss, a coin of fun, and an older brother.
Put lipgloss and eyeliner in a blender.
Blend the eyeliner and lipgloss until there are no lumps.
Throw in 3 cups of real flowers, 5 cups of pure love and joy, and an older brother.
Broil in a pot on high,
until a flowery smell comes out and turns red.
You can tell it's done when you hear laughter, and a sister comes out.
Let stand until you feel loved.
Add the blended lipgloss and eyeliner with the coin of fun.
Taste love, joy, fun, and makeup.
Serves only one person.

Andrea Barwick, Grade 5
Roosevelt Elementary School

How Lovely Is Christmas

When you see something white and fluffy falling you would know that winter is coming
You would get a lot presents in this holiday but Christmas will never last or be able to stay
The family always gathers together and on this day it will last forever
Everyone shares warm and compassion to each other and everyone will have something to give to one another

Sampson Abah, Grade 6
Cinnaminson Middle School

Me, My Dreams, and My Goal

I am an active and determined future Marine.
I hear the national anthem in the misty, early morning.
I wonder if I will ever be able to honor my country.
I touch the white glistening stars in my dreams.
I say that I will make it in to the marines.
I am an active determined future Marine.

I pretend to be in the military protecting and honoring our country like my dad.
I worry about my dad in Iraq but I know he is doing something that I will achieve one day.
I cry when he has to leave to Iraq but I am proud of him and what he is doing.
I know why the war is going on and why my dad has to leave.
I am an active determined future Marine.

I feel that I can serve and protect people in other countries as told.
I imagine one day I will have the honor of wearing that white uniform of the US Marine Core.
I hope Wait No! I know I will be in the US Marine Core!
I will achieve my goal as a Marine
I am Kevin Robinson a determined future Marine.

Kevin Robinson, Grade 6
Olson Middle School

I Don't Understand

I don't understand…
  Why people try so hard to impress you, even though they are just making themselves look dumb
  Why teachers give homework
  Why computers freeze
  Why boys have cooties

But most of all…
  Why people are prejudiced
  Why there can't be peace on Earth
  Why people abuse poor, innocent animals
  Why people do things they know are wrong

What I do understand is…
  How people are unique in their own, special ways
  How true friends are forever
  How everyone has feelings
  How my family loves me for who I am

Melissa Boniface, Grade 6
Lounsberry Hollow Middle School

A Recipe for Love

Take a hug from your best friend, a kiss from someone you love, candy hearts, chocolates, and sprinkles.
Put the hug and the kiss in a big bowl ready to go into the oven.
Blend the candy hearts, chocolates, and sprinkles until they are blended all the way.
Pour them in a bowl.
Cook in a pan
At 250 degrees Fahrenheit
Until it's fully cooked.
You can tell it's done when it becomes a big circle.
Let stand until it turns a bright red.
Cut the circle into a heart and serve with love.
Taste the best love recipe ever!!

Kara Tylutki, Grade 5
Roosevelt Elementary School

Marines
One of the proud forces that protect this wonderful country called United States. The forces that not only protect the United States but the people of the United States of America. The forces that fought and protected us to give us freedom. So we can have a peaceful, relaxing, wonderful, and enjoying life.

Kamil Pietras, Grade 6
Kawameeh Middle School

Autumn
A peaceful breeze whispered…
I sat there, letting autumn come to me.

The joy, the bliss, the feeling of freedom,
The colorful, bright, and swaying trees,
The high flying purposeful birds,
Come, come, one and all!

The jack-o'-lanterns, the scary stories, the tricksters,
The mischief, eerie but playful,
The gift of Halloween,
Come, come, one and all!

The cornucopias, the turkeys, the pumpkin pies,
The family, the elders, and the youngsters,
The spirit of Thanksgiving,
Come, come, one and all!

As I sat there,
I saw the wonderment of it all.

Autumn is alive,
Autumn is laughter,
Autumn is generous,
Autumn begins.

Maia Iyer, Grade 5
St Rose of Lima Academy

Midnight with the Moon
Moon, tonight you emit light so bright
A continuous, imperishable satellite
Your course is round the Earth
You echo the sun's blaze
Until we depart and go our separate ways

The sun reaches the heavens
But you don't go down
You stay for a while unobserved, unseen
Still around

You entrap shape and change shape a picture perfect landscape
A charmed place to escape when dreams say
Au Revoir!
And you awake

O, moon tonight
Tuck me in tonight

Because when I am beside you I grasp that I shall be all right
O, moon tonight you glisten so bright
An eternal satellite
You circle round the Earth and mirror the sun's blaze
Till we die
And go our separate ways

Sophia Dunzelman, Grade 6
Christa McAuliffe Middle School

My Imaginary Room
My special place is my room
It is like a mummy's tomb
There are ancient pictures on the wall
And ugly bugs that like to crawl
I have a mummy who likes to play
With my toys every day
My room is such an eerie sight
Since creatures come out in the night
My room has a princess from a far away land
Who owns a necklace that is so grand
The aquarium in my room has beautiful fish
And they all like to eat a potato knish
My magical mirror makes me look pretty and tall
But it makes my brothers look fat and small
In my room a nest is my bed
It's my favorite place to rest my head
I love my room that's what I say
You should come to visit me there someday

Samantha Amico, Grade 4
Little Falls School #3

A World
When you look up at the stars every night
Do you feel a feeling with all your might
A feeling that is oh so strong
That there is a world up there beyond
A world beyond what the eye can see
A world beyond what the hand can touch
A world beyond what the tongue can taste
A world that you can understand
A world where you know all the news
A world where your skill isn't taken for granted
I tell you my friend that there is such a world
You see this world in your dreams
Almost as clear as the river flows
Almost as if it is paved in gold
You love this world and nothing more
No one else believes in this world
But to you it is clear
That there is such a world and it is near

Tom Salama, Grade 6
School Number 14

Kai Michaud
K icking at karate
A wesome
I ntelligent

M odel
I ngenious
C ourageous
H elping
A mazing drummer
U ltimate
D rums of thunder
Kai Michaud, Grade 5
Hillside Elementary School

Acorn
An acorn fell from a tree
The stem is hanging by a thread
It hits the ground
It has lost its cap
Hard
Purple
Green
Striped
In the shape of a pumpkin
Stripes like a tiger
To the squirrels it is breakfast.
Isaiah White, Grade 5
Frances DeMasi Elementary School

My Teacher
M y awesome teacher Ms. Frankle!
S uch an organized teacher!

F amous to me and my classmates!
R eally big sports fan!
A wesome at every subject!
N ow good at social studies!
K ind, caring, and intelligent!
L oving and also beautiful!
E ndless teaching, it's so fun!
Micah Taylor, Grade 5
Hillside Elementary School

The Intercepted Pass
Standing as a linebacker
Waiting for the pass,
As they throw the ball,
I run.
Just before the other team catches,
I dive and catch the ball.
I start sprinting with the ball
After I run to the end zone
I realize
I have gone the wrong way.
Michael Wehr, Grade 4
Lincoln Park Elementary School

The Night Sky's Best Friend
Did you know the Night Sky
Had a best friend?
Well it does!
His name is Moon.
He grows and grows until
He is big, round, and a circle!
When he reaches that point,
People call him "Full Moon."
I call him big, bold, and beautiful
Because he glows like a diamond!
I love the Moon because he adds
A little "flair" to the Night Sky!
Now you know,
The Night Sky does have a best friend!
Krysta Sousa, Grade 6
Christa McAuliffe Middle School

Summer Day
I love a summer day,
but some can be gray.
The sky is dark,
and all I hear is the dogs bark.
I sit and stare,
but yet I bare
to go outside.
When the sun comes out,
I scream and shout.
I get so excited,
that the sky is actually lighted.
I go outside and play a game.
Without any shame.
Like I said, I love a summer day.
Lily Durning, Grade 5
Roosevelt Elementary School

Beach
It was a nice day.
The sun was out and shiny.
So we went to the beach.
It was wonderful!

I went to the blue, clean ocean.
I love the warm water.
The water was so clear,
I could see my feet.

I found a glorious seashell.
I could hear the sea in a pretty seashell.
I love the beach.
I wish I lived there all the time.
Jackie T. Landaverde, Grade 5
Roosevelt Elementary School

Holiday Snow
Snow falling upon the ground,
brings joy to all around.
Falling like angels dancing in the sky,
when the wind blows by.
Anxious children watch and listen,
while the snowflakes twinkle and glisten.
Hearing sleigh bells,
for it is Christmas!
Melissa Ryan, Grade 6
Harding Elementary School

The Magic Window
I look out the window
and notice the sun
dancing on the
snow. The snow as white
as my marshmallows floating
in my cocoa.
Kids are riding down that hill
as if they were penguins.
Benjamin Harley, Grade 5
Bartle Elementary School

Friends
Friends are buds
No matter what.
Through thick and thin
And everything rough.
We are friends,
And so are you,
We love each other
Through and through.
Molly Krawczyk, Grade 6
Harding Elementary School

Reading
Lots of books that you can read
Books about scary monsters,
Books about creepy bugs,
Books about dogs and cats,
Books about wild animals,
Books about fairy tales.
Books about history and most of all —
Books that can make you travel!
Samantha Dawson, Grade 4
Ocean Academy

Home Run
Standing in the batter's box,
Waiting for the pitch to reach the plate.
Hands gripping the bat tightly,
I swing and hit it hard.
There it goes…
Another home run!
Summer Ramundo, Grade 4
Lincoln Park Elementary School

Soccer

I am a good soccer player all the time
I hear the ball wiping like a fan over the grass
I worry we will lose the game
I want a 2-0 win for us
I touch my teammate's hands as they tell me "good job"
I understand winning's fun, losing's not
I am a good soccer player all the time

I hope we will win lots of games
I try to play my best every game
I honor my coaches and teammates
I say my team is great to myself and others
I am a good soccer player all the time

I want a win every game we play
I cry if one of my teammate hurts
I pretend this is my very last soccer game and play hard
I feel the excitement bubbling on the sidelines like boiling water
I am a good soccer player all the time.

Erica Clapps, Grade 6
Olson Middle School

Braces

Braces are colorful, braces are work
Braces are cool, braces are smart
Braces are crazy
You can get braces in black, red, and orange
Braces oh braces you are the best
I like you so much
You straighten and fix my teeth so well
They're gonna look great I can tell
I can trust you with my teeth
You better do the job right
Sometimes they feel tight
There's a lot you can't eat, like caramel and corn
Chewing gum, taffy, and popcorn are gone
I need to brush you day and night
But most of all to brush you right
They protect your teeth from harm
Braces will hurt when you first get them on
But I bet I'll miss you when you're gone
You will rule with braces on

Michael Pannone, Grade 4
Edward H Bryan Elementary School

A Is for Angel

A is for Angel
Who stands by my side,
Guides me and my friends
Wherever we go.
He protects us from danger
Wherever we will be,
I call him guardian Angel
Because he is the best.

Rachel Haigh, Grade 4
Good Shepherd Regional Catholic School

Peace on Earth

I once dreamt a dream
That the world would be free
Across all of the continents,
And across every sea,
All for freedom and peace.
Humans must live in harmony!
From Mount Rushmore, to the Great Wall of China,
With peace and freedom the world will be united!
We must love all and all must love us,
This is one topic not to fuss about!
So, listen! Listen to me!
Listen to these words and you shall be free!
It DOESN'T matter what skin color you have,
It DOES matter if you respect others and yourself!
Some people sadly, kill in the name of God
And that my friend, is extremely odd!
All I want is peace on Earth!
All I want is PEACE ON EARTH!
So, somebody, anybody, give me PEACE ON EARTH!

Marc E. Bennett, Grade 4
Marie Durand Elementary School

The Mirror

When you look in a mirror
What do you see?
You see a face looking back
That face identical to yours
That same face can change our dying world forever
For that face can make the difference
By being involved in what is called "going green"
You can save the penguins
The Polar Bears too
That same face looking in the mirror
You can save the planet
Or much, much more
So when you look in that mirror
It proves something special
That any person or anything
Can make a difference in this world
Remember that face
When you do something that can hurt us…
Forever

Anna Perazza, Grade 6
Olson Middle School

Autumn

In autumn, leaves change their dark green coat,
They also fall in very large moats.
Children also go back to school,
The temperature drops making it cool.
Birds fly south, that's called migration,
Bears sleep, that's called hibernation.
Last but not least, we have the holidays,
Halloween and Thanksgiving, all fun days.

John Chan, Grade 5
St Rose of Lima Academy

The Cupcake

As Farrah walked out the door,
A cupcake fell on the floor,
It made a big mess,
On her brand new dress,
She won't make cupcakes anymore.
Tyson Etienne, Grade 5
Hawthorne Christian Academy

Winter

Winter
Snowy, icy
Loving, caring, laughing
I love snowball fights in winter
Happy
Jesse Ibarra, Grade 5
Bartle Elementary School

Baseball

Baseball
Ablaze, teamwork
Challenging, fun, hard
Thunderous cracking of the bat
Baseball
Tiffany Tirado, Grade 5
Bartle Elementary School

Funny Man

I once knew a guy from Berlin
whose face had a double chin.
When he was mad
or when he was sad,
he always ended up with a grin.
Matthew Gido, Grade 5
Richard E Byrd Elementary School

Hot Summer Air

The hot summer air.
Just sitting around us.
Not even a breeze.
Just sizzling in the hot summer air.
Too hot to do anything.
Gabrielle Smith, Grade 5
Richard E Byrd Elementary School

The Call of the Wild

I hear a howl, in the forest.
It sounds like a mournful cry.
When I hear it, it sounds like
a desperate song. I know it is coming
from the wolves, it is the call of the wild.
Eunice Cho, Grade 5
Richard E Byrd Elementary School

The Journey of a Leaf

The last leaf on the withered oak tree seeing it is defeated,
Falls, barely touching to the smooth cut grass
Only to be swept up again by the lively wind,
The elegant leaf slowly drifts past a rushing rippling, radiant stream.
It circles the trees with great haste,
Then it dances back to its starting place
But before it makes its complete descent,
It gets swept up again by the swooping whirling wind.
It passes by many homes
And cats of all different hues chase it from window to window
Only to realize that the chase is over before it began.
So the leaf carries on past barking dogs, playful squirrels, and children romping about.
The leaf keeps moving, occasionally getting snagged on branches of tall trees
And skimming the water like a bird's wing. Then suddenly the wind comes to a stop
And gently sets the leaf floating in a small lake
With that, the leaf drifts toward an enormous waterfall.
Just when the leaf is about to sink into the aqua-black hole of the sea,
The wild wind picks it up once again
And carries it back past the barking dogs, the playful squirrels, and the romping children.
And then making its final descent, coming to rest,
Ending its journey at the same place it began.
Robert Donaldson, Grade 5
Hopewell Elementary School

Painted Birds

I am an artistic girl who loves birds
I wonder if there has ever been an artist like me
I hear the fluttering of wings and paintbrushes
I see the birds burst into the newly painted sky
I want to be free, flying with those brilliant, beautiful birds
I am an artistic girl who loves birds

I pretend I have wings and I'm flying with the birds
I feel the birds' hard beaks like the handles of paintbrushes under my fingers
I touch the soft, velvety feathers of the birds' wings
I worry that these birds will drop from the sky when the color drops from my paintings
I cry when I see the colorful birds flying towards me from along the horizon
I am an artistic girl who loves birds

I understand the birds won't always fly back to me
I say good bye before each bird leaves my window sill
I dream of the day all birds are free
I try to free the birds with my paintings
I hope I will become a famous artist with the help of my bird paintings
I am an artistic girl who loves birds
Erin Welling, Grade 6
Olson Middle School

Ode to the Moon

One of the things I love to see is the moon staring back at me.
A blank canvas just waiting for someone to come up and start painting.
Surrounding the moon are stars shining bright, I find myself coming out every night.
Yellow like lemonade round like a bowl sometimes a crescent almost never full.
Soon I will be forever condemned to have the moon always high over my head.
Gillian Vallaster, Grade 6
Christa McAuliffe Middle School

The Moon

As I gaze upon the sky I see nothing, just nothing…
Oh moon, oh moon
Don't you notice, how dark it is without you in the night sky?

Oh moon, oh moon
You get bigger and bigger every day, when will you realize it's time to play?

Oh moon, oh moon
You leave many trees and animals in the dark, cold and weary.
With nothing to do nothing to look forward to, other than the warmth of the sun in the morning.

Oh moon, oh moon
When will you realize it's okay to play. I hope you come out soon because you are missing out another day.

Matthew Ferullo, Grade 6
Christa McAuliffe Middle School

Thanksgiving Time

T hinking of the good turkey Mom makes every year is when I
H ead towards the back door to pick our herbs. I can't wait until Thanksgiving because I
A nxiously sit at the table, and watch our dinner cook. "It's almost done," Heather yells to her mom.
N ot listening to her, I yell again, "Our turkey is almost done!"
K nowingly, her mom ignores Heather because she talks too much.
S inging, on the way to the door, I step outside and look at our pumpkin decorations.
G iving all my friends a big hug for Thanksgiving makes me excited for this day.
I 've been waiting all year for Mom's good turkey and now it's time to eat it.
V ery happy am I, as I rush to the kitchen and the oven goes "Ding!"
I t's done…finally and I am so happy.
N ext, I go to the door and hug our guests as they arrive quickly for our feast.
" **G** ood turkey," everyone says to Mom and finally it is time for our pie.

Kristyna Hill, Grade 6
Riverside Middle School

So Long Summer

The summer is packing up ready to go and autumn is coming, creeping in slow.
Leaves start to tumble and cartwheel off trees the air makes them dance in the fall breeze.
The summer is packing up ready to go and autumn is coming, creeping in slow.
Soothing summer sunsets have become the past and the dark nights of fall are here at least.
The summer is packing up ready to go and autumn is coming, creeping in slow.
The swimsuits are away, the sandals we will pack and my winter coats are now hanging on the rack.
The summer is packing up ready to go and autumn is coming, creeping in slow.
Squirrels are busy as bees gathering nuts and seeds and now they will rest having met their winter needs.
The summer is packing up ready to go and autumn is coming, creeping in slow.
The fires are burning spreading warmth all around and everywhere frost-covered lawns can be found.
The summer is packing up ready to go and autumn is coming, creeping in slow.
So long to summer, see you next year and on to fall parties that bring lots of cheer.

Bryn Salmon, Grade 5
Hopewell Elementary School

Lazy

Your kitchen window is drying off from the endless rain that seemed to have stopped its crying. The birds squawk as cars honk, and the sun rises with a beautiful rainbow by its side, your mom tells you to go outside, but you're just too lazy. A nice book's fine with you, but once you're done you don't bother to find another so instead just watch as your baby sister makes a mess of her water. As time goes by just lying bored, finding a way out of every chore, heedless and negligent, indolent and ignored, eye lids falling over one eye, looks like you'll be falling asleep for awhile…

Madeleine Parrish, Grade 4
Tamaques Elementary School

The Hues of Fall
The foliage in Montclair
looks just like bright red hair
it is just so beautiful
looking at it's almost cruel
Whilst you see the nice fall flames
you pass by in Jersey trains
and you walk by staring gaily
wondering at the beauty
You marvel in the bright red hues
sometimes just like bright red juice
always pretty, always nice
it reminds you of some spice
And you stare at the leaves
loving the way the color weaves
now you're in the Jersey feeling
as the leaves have started peeling
But though some leaves are on the trees
many are taken by the breeze
now as they're scattered on the ground
they make, merely, the slightest sound
And that is the hues of fall
Noah Slon, Grade 5
Hillside Elementary School

Sports
In football I two hand touch,
In baseball I am clutch

In hockey I always fall,
In basketball I score with the ball

I always play,
I play all day

Even if I get beat,
I still will never cheat

Because sportsmanship rules,
And people that don't do it are fools

If you even dare,
To cheat it won't be fair

Don't ruin the game,
Or else you won't have any fame.
Jonah Ganchrow, Grade 6
Yeshivat Noam

Dragonfly
A golden dragonfly
swoops down over the
surface of a silver lake
its crystal wings beating
steadily over the shallow water.
Ana Wilson, Grade 5
Bartle Elementary School

The Real Heroes
Do you know who heroes are?
Some people might say
Men in red capes,
Or women in blue tights.
No, they are ordinary people,
Like you and me.
Men and women
Who decided to care for someone
Other then themselves
For a change.
Now they suffer
From diseases and poisoning
They developed
During their generosity.
So you see
The "heroes" you read about in comics
Who you thought weren't real
Have been there all along.
See we need more of these people
In case of something as serious
As 9/11 were to happen.
Augustus Thornton, Grade 6
Township of Ocean Intermediate School

He's Not Weird
They call him names,
They think it's a game,
He's not weird.
He may scream a lot,
He may not play a lot,
He's not weird.
They think he's three,
He's eleven you see?
He's not weird.
They stare at church,
They don't know that it hurts,
He's not weird.
He's my twin,
He makes me grin,
He's not weird.
He has special needs,
He's special indeed,
But he's not weird.
I love him so,
I want you to know,
He's not weird.
Jadyn Trayvick, Grade 5
Hillside Elementary School

Flowers
The sun shines
The flowers grow.
The world gives great smiles,
Here and below.
Lara Manookian, Grade 5
Hillside Elementary School

Basketball
I like playing basketball
With friends and family members.
Basketball is a good sport —
It helps you stay in shape.
It's a really good sport to play
And fun too!

I like playing basketball
It is a lot of fun
If you're good at it
You might get
A scholarship for college
and to play for the NBA!
Shawn Scott, Grade 5
Ocean Academy

The Big Race
I am a sled dog
a strong Siberian husky
the race is very, very difficult
but I still got it done.
It was challenging
and also hard
especially with moose
and huge boulders!
I am grateful
that I won
and the job is done.

Whoooooo!!!!
Connor Evans, Grade 5
Roosevelt Elementary School

Charlie
Charlie is my parrot,
he is not very quiet.
One day he was so loud there was a riot.
He is shy around strangers but
when they leave Charlie sings to me
and he never leaves me be!

Charlie is green, yellow, red, and blue
and he won't hurt you.
He usually does obey,
and we teach him a trick every day.
Would I give Charlie up? NEVER.
He is the best parrot ever.
Alexa Long, Grade 6
St Mary School

My Class
My class likes learning
A learning environment
It is exciting
Nathan Hughes, Grade 4
St Peter Elementary School

Bubbles
Bubbles, bubbles in the air
Bubbles everywhere
Round and soft
Floating up above
Bubbles, bubbles in the air
Fun to blow, fun to catch
But if you blow it high
They will glide up to the sky!
Fabricio J. Lobo, Grade 4
Marie Durand Elementary School

Writing
So easily flowing
From pencil to paper
From letters
To words
To poems
A way to let ideas flow
A way for people to tell stories
Something I love to do!
Naomi Uma Bell, Grade 5
Bartle Elementary School

Swimming
S ummer fun
W inning ribbons
I ncludes everyone
M eets
M eeting new people
I ntense laps
N ever give up
G row stronger
Julia Handy, Grade 4
Edward H Bryan Elementary School

Dreams
Dreams, dreams are all I need
All I need to be successful
Dreams, dreams are the gift of life
Dreams, dreams that I love so much
Never leave me or I will be nothing
Nothing at all and feel so empty inside
So dreams, dreams please
Never leave my precious sight!
Gisellyn Miranda, Grade 4
Marie Durand Elementary School

The Little Girl
There was once a little girl
Who had lots of tiny curls
And she had a big blue bow
That she liked to show
And she really liked to twirl
Like a big big girl
Leila Alidoost, Grade 5
Hillside Elementary School

Snowy Owl
Beauty shape
Crystal clear white
Stands really still
On silent flight
Preetha Benjamin, Grade 5
Hawthorne Christian Academy

Northern Lights
The Aurora's shining brightly,
Its colors faded oh so slightly.
It's like a sunrise, very nice.
Its brilliance reflected on the ice.
Ariella Libove-Goldfarb, Grade 5
Bartle Elementary School

Crayon
Smooth, slippery
Coloring, rolling, shrinking
Making a design on your paper
Full of color!
Anjali Patel, Grade 4
Ethel M Burke Elementary School

Snake
Slimy hand
Rattling, slithering, hissing
I am really scared
Reptiles are not nice.
Thomas Maloney, Grade 4
Ethel M Burke Elementary School

Jack-O'-Lanterns
If pumpkins get cut out
and get made into shapes
how come they don't pout
and try to get taped?
Sean Yi, Grade 5
Hillside Elementary School

American Flag
Colorful, beautiful
Flying, soaring, moving
In the sky so high
Freedom.
Darby Casey, Grade 4
Ethel M Burke Elementary School

Christmas
I wait I wait for Christmas to come
The snow, the presents and all the trees
Do you want Christmas to come?
I sure do!!!!!
Taylor Suto, Grade 4
Springfield Township School

Winter
Cold weather is here
Snowballs flying through the air
The snow is falling
Ashley Driemel, Grade 6
Lounsberry Hollow Middle School

Index

Author Autograph Page

Author Autograph Page

Author Autograph Page

Author Autograph Page

Author Autograph Page

Author Autograph Page

Author Autograph Page

Author Autograph Page